INSPIRE / PLAN / DISCOVER / EXPERIENCE

BRAZIL

The Amazon in the Anavilhanas archipelago

BRAZIL

CONTENTS

An azulejo-framed door in São Luís

DISCOVER 6

EXPERIENCE RIO DE JANEIRO 68

EXPERIENCE BRAZIL 128

NEED TO KNOW 358

DISCOVER

Dusk falling over Rio de Janeiro city

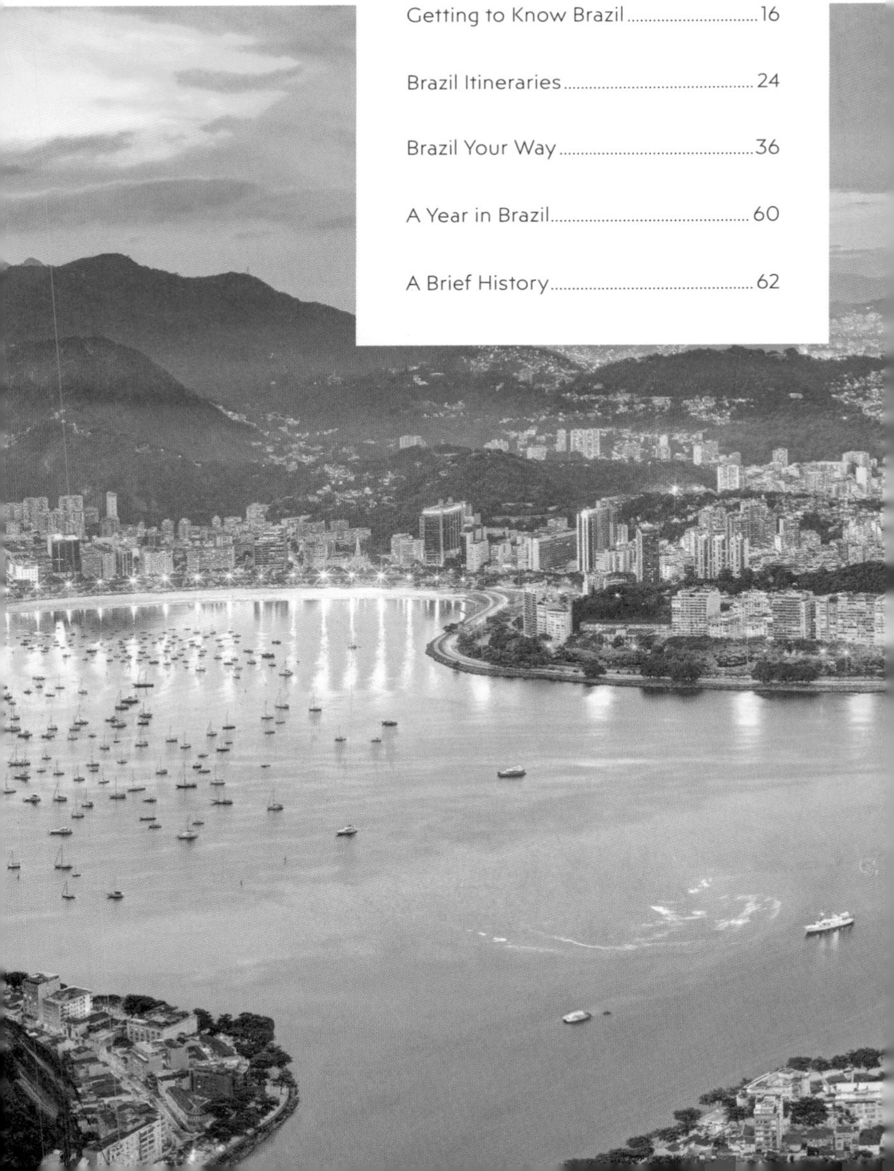

WELCOME TO
BRAZIL

Lush rainforests and sunny, white-sand beaches. Scintillating cities that pulsate to the beat of some of the world's best music. Blowout barbeques and Amazonian delicacies to tantalize your tastebuds. And let's not forget *futebol,* the beautiful game. Whatever your dream trip to Brazil entails, this DK Eyewitness travel guide is the perfect companion.

1 Enjoying a meal against the backdrop of Sugar Loaf Mountain.

2 Canoeing in the Amazon.

3 A delicious meal of Brazilian seafood.

4 Ipanema sea front, Rio de Janeiro.

The largest of the South American countries, Brazil's landmass occupies nearly half of the entire continent. Incredible landscapes cover everything from red-rock canyons in the south and the world's biggest freshwater wetland in the west to miles of pristine beaches in the east and the deep jungle of the Amazon in the north, home to more diverse plant and animal species than anywhere else on earth.

The cities, too, won't disappoint. Brazil's mammoth metropolises fizz with an infectious energy and zest for life, and no matter where you are there is always something to celebrate. Festivals abound throughout the year, including the colorful folklore celebrations of Bumba Meu Boi in São Luís, São Paulo's famous film festival, and, of course, the famous Carnaval that descends on Brazil's city streets every year.

Search for majestic jaguars in broad daylight on the Paraguay river in the Pantanal, party all day long with carefree Cariocas during Rio's Carnaval, visit some of the best restaurants in São Paulo, and drink world-renowned sparkling wine in the Vale dos Vinhedos. Whatever you choose to do, this stunning country will touch your heart and engage your soul.

Brazil's sheer size and diversity can make it hard to know where to start. We've broken the country down into easily navigable sections, with detailed itineraries, expert local knowledge, and colorful, comprehensive maps to help you plan the perfect visit. Whether you're staying for a weekend, a week, or longer, this DK Eyewitness travel guide will ensure that you see the very best this captivating country has to offer. Enjoy the book and enjoy Brazil.

REASONS TO LOVE
BRAZIL

Brazil's natural beauty and local charm are astounding. The beaches are divine, the nightlife insatiable, and its people so vibrant that you are sure to fall head over heels for their homeland. What's not to love?

1 THE AMAZON

Home to roughly half of the country's Indigenous peoples and to species still unrecorded by scientists, the world's largest rainforest *(p336)* is an absolutely incredible region to visit.

FOZ DO IGUAÇU 2

Let the cool spray soak your skin as you take in the towering heights and thunderous roar of Foz do Iguaçu *(p216)* – made up of hundreds of waterfalls and surrounded by lush rainforest.

3 CARNAVAL

Party for four days straight with millions of people in Rio de Janeiro *(p68)*, or head to Olinda *(p300)* to mingle with intense *frevo* dancers sporting colorful costumes and umbrellas.

4 SÃO PAULO NIGHTLIFE

São Paulo *(p150)* has easily South America's most diverse nightlife. Go bar hopping, listen to live *sertanejo* music, and dance to Brazilian funk in the continent's biggest city.

BAROQUE ARCHITECTURE 5

Brazil's Baroque architecture is built to impress. Head to former gold mining town Ouro Preto *(p186)* or the Portuguese settlement of Olinda for the country's best-kept European-style buildings.

AÇAÍ NA TIGELA 6

Treat your tastebuds to this blend of bananas and frozen, mashed açaí berries. Sweet, nutritious, and a powerhouse of energy, Brazil's cooling superdessert is best enjoyed on a hot afternoon.

SAMBA 7

Sultry and irresistible, samba is at the heart of Brazilian music. Visit some of Rio de Janeiro's samba schools to learn some moves – try Beija Flor, Grande Rio, or Manguiera.

BRAZILIAN HOSPITALITY 8

Brazilians are famously friendly and welcoming. Revel with Sao Paulo's Paulistanos, drink *tereré* with locals in Mato Grosso do Sul, or share an ice-cold beer with Rio's residents, Cariocas.

9 COLORFUL BAHIA

From Salvador's *(p258)* colorful architecture to the orange of *moqueca* fish stew, Bahia's colors are enticing. Visit Trancoso *(p290)* for turquoise sea, pastel buildings, and the prettiest green square in Brazil.

10 SEDUCTIVE BEACHES

Brazil's long beaches are central to the country's culture, and are perfect for partying, socializing, or simply chilling out. Some of the best stretches of sand are found in Santa Catarina *(p212)*.

INDIGENOUS CULTURE 11

Brazil is home to over 300 Indigenous groups, who have an unrivalled knowledge of and deep connection with nature, and make some of the country's best handicrafts.

AMAZING WILDLIFE 12

Brazil's wildlife includes elusive jaguars, colorful birds, howler monkeys, and humpback whales. Visit the Pantanal's vast wetlands *(p250)* to try to track down the area's big five.

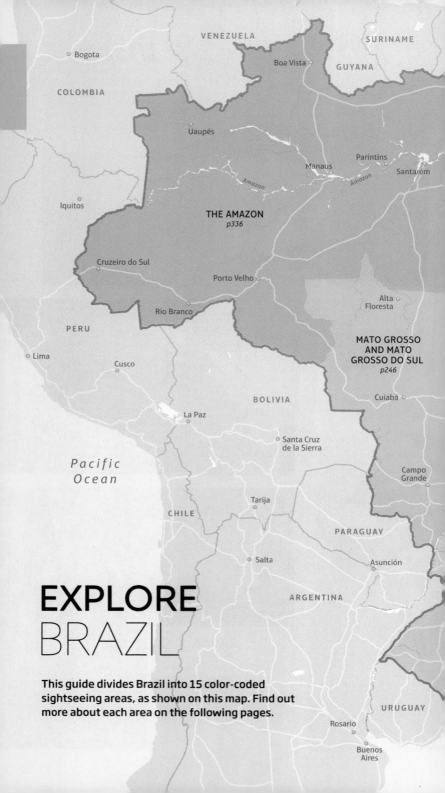

VENEZUELA

SURINAME

COLOMBIA

Bogota

Boa Vista

GUYANA

Uaupés

Parintins

Manaus

Santarém

Amazon

Amazon

Iquitos

THE AMAZON
p336

Cruzeiro do Sul

Porto Velho

Alta
Floresta

Rio Branco

**MATO GROSSO
AND MATO
GROSSO DO SUL**
p246

PERU

Cuiabá

Lima

Cusco

BOLIVIA

La Paz

Santa Cruz
de la Sierra

Campo
Grande

*Pacific
Ocean*

Tarija

CHILE

PARAGUAY

Salta

Asunción

ARGENTINA

EXPLORE
BRAZIL

This guide divides Brazil into 15 color-coded
sightseeing areas, as shown on this map. Find out
more about each area on the following pages.

URUGUAY

Rosario

Buenos
Aires

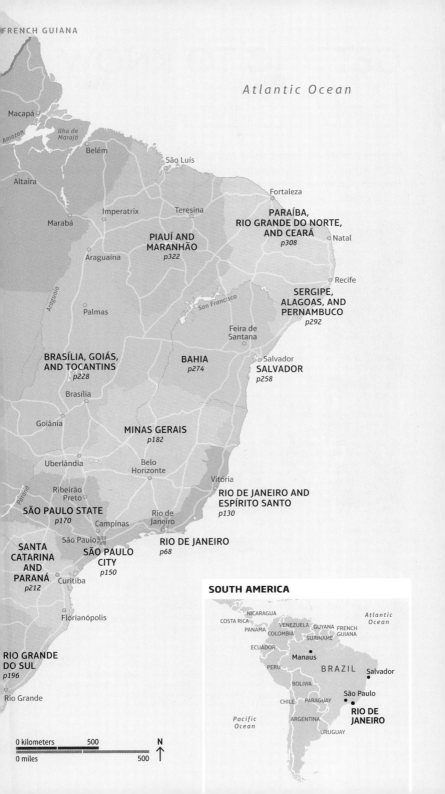

FRENCH GUIANA

Atlantic Ocean

Macapá

Amazon

Ilha de Marajó

Belém

São Luís

Altaira

Fortaleza

Marabá

Imperatrix

Teresina

PARAÍBA,
RIO GRANDE DO NORTE,
AND CEARÁ
p308

Natal

Araguaina

PIAUÍ AND
MARANHÃO
p322

Araguaia

Recife

San Francisco

SERGIPE,
ALAGOAS, AND
PERNAMBUCO
p292

Palmas

Feira de
Santana

BRASÍLIA, GOIÁS,
AND TOCANTINS
p228

BAHIA
p274

Salvador

SALVADOR
p258

Brasília

Goiânia

MINAS GERAIS
p182

Uberlândia

Belo
Horizonte

Vitória

Paraná

Ribeirão
Preto

RIO DE JANEIRO AND
ESPÍRITO SANTO
p130

SÃO PAULO STATE
p170

Campinas

Rio de
Janeiro

São Paulo

SANTA
CATARINA
AND
PARANÁ
p212

SÃO PAULO
CITY
p150

RIO DE JANEIRO
p68

Curitiba

Florianópolis

RIO GRANDE
DO SUL
p196

Rio Grande

0 kilometers   500

0 miles   500

N

SOUTH AMERICA

NICARAGUA

COSTA RICA

PANAMA

VENEZUELA

COLOMBIA

GUYANA

SURINAME

FRENCH
GUIANA

Atlantic
Ocean

ECUADOR

Manaus

PERU

BRAZIL

Salvador

BOLIVIA

São Paulo

Pacific
Ocean

CHILE

PARAGUAY

RIO DE
JANEIRO

ARGENTINA

URUGUAY

GETTING TO KNOW
BRAZIL

Beyond Brazil's exuberant cities and enticing urban beaches lie rainforests teeming with wildlife and watery oases of beautiful lagoons and deserted coastlines. Each of the country's varied states feature their own distinct cultures and unique, tropical landscapes just waiting to be discovered.

PAGE 68

RIO DE JANEIRO

A favorite among travelers, Rio de Janeiro City seduces visitors with lush mountain tops, fine sandy beaches, and an exuberant, rhythmic energy. The lively beaches in the south are a city hot spot; Copacabana and Ipanema are where Cariocas spend their weekends and afternoons sunbathing and socializing. Further north, alternative bars and hip restaurants are testament to Botafogo's increasing trendiness, and winding roads take you up to the artsy realms of Santa Teresa and down to the hip and notoriously alternative nightlife hub of Lapa.

Best for
Samba, city beach life, and vibrant nightlife

Home to
Morro do Corcovado and Cristo Redentor, Praia de Ipanema, Sugar Loaf Mountain, Museu Nacional de Belas Artes

Experience
Dance the night away at Lapa's samba clubs

PAGE 130

RIO DE JANEIRO AND ESPÍRITO SANTO

Gorgeous islands and splendid surf: the southeast of Brazil offers the finer things in life. Rio state's coastline is dotted with forest-clad islands and attractive towns nestled in the mountains – be sure not to miss Petrópolis, once home to the Portuguese royal family, and historic Paraty. Further north, Espírito Santos is full of little known but exciting destinations: tiny Itaúnas is backed with massive sand dunes and Vitória claims the world's biggest urban mangrove forest.

Best for
Surfing, island hopping, and sailing

Home to
Paraty, Ilha Grande, Parque Nacional do Itatiaia, Petrópolis

Experience
Wandering around Paraty's cobblestoned streets admiring the well-preserved Baroque architecture in the old center

PAGE 150

SÃO PAULO CITY

A gigantic metropolis, São Paulo is famous for its fine dining and superb nightlife. The heart of the city is centered around Avenida Paulista, a busy avenue lined with swanky skyscrapers, world-class museums, and shopping malls. Cutting through the city's main boulevard, Rua Augusta offers something completely different. With an alternative vibe and full of bars and arthouse cinemas, it buzzes with life after hours. Further northwest, cafés, designer shops, and the city's best street art sit cheek by jowl on Vila Madalena.

Best for
Fine dining, street art, and alternative nightlife

Home to
Pinacoteca de São Paulo, Parque do Ibirapuera

Experience
The colorful graffiti of Beco do Batman

→

SÃO PAULO STATE

PAGE 170

The state of São Paulo offers spectacular natural scenery: sumptuous beaches line the coast and dream-like mountains rise further inland. The eastern shore-line is dotted with beach resorts where Paulistanos party all night long in the summer; just off the coast, the island retreat of Ilhabela is perfect for hiking to hidden waterfalls. On land, Mata Atlântica's myriad trees and Serra da Mantiqueira's rolling hills offer a tranquil setting, perfect for a weekend away from the hustle and bustle of the city.

Best for
Island beaches, bird-watching, and city escapes

Home to
Ilhabela

Experience
Sunbathing on deserted beaches on Ilhabela

MINAS GERAIS

PAGE 182

Try traditional cuisine and Brazil's best cachaça (a spirit made from sugarcane juice) in Minas Gerais is a must for foodies, or mouthwatering *feijão tropeiro* (beans mixed with toasted cassava flour) in Belo Horizonte. Charming Baroque towns are sprinkled across Minas, while, further south, Ouro Preto and Tiradentes, surrounded by rolling hills, headline Brazil's prettiest Portuguese settlements. Don't miss the magnificent Inhotim Museum, southwest of Belo Horizonte, with outdoor art installations.

Best for
Cachaça, Baroque architecture, and tasty regional cuisine

Home to
Ouro Preto, Diamantina

Experience
Admiring grand cathedrals, beautiful fountains, and quaint museums in Ouro Preto

PAGE 196

RIO GRANDE DO SUL

Rio Grande do Sul is the southern-most state in Brazil, best known for its *gaúcho* cowboy culture, excellent meat dishes, and European heritage. This beautiful region rewards foodies with award-winning wine and mouth-watering barbecues. Blessed with beautiful *fazendas* (ranches), it's also the perfect spot to go horse-riding. To the west of the regions, don't miss the 17th-century Spanish Jesuit ruins of São Miguel das Missões.

Best for
Gaúcho culture, wine, and Jesuit ruins

Home to
Porto Alegre

Experience
A tour through the spectacular Vale dos Vinhedos, tasting award-winning sparkling wines as you go

PAGE 212

SANTA CATARINA AND PARANÁ

Featuring Brazil's biggest waterfall – the astonishing Foz do Iguaçu – as well as mile-long stretches of sand, Santa Catarina and Parana are musts for many inter-national tourists. The country's jet set flock to the island of Florianópolis in the summer for sun-drenched shores and endless parties, while keen surfers and travelers seeking a more laid-back atmosphere head east to Praia Joaquina and south to Ribeirão da Ilha.

Best for
Remarkable waterfalls, oyster dishes, and sandy shores

Home to
Foz do Iguaçu, Serra da Graciosa, Florianópolis and Ilha de Santa Catarina

Experience
A helicopter ride over the impressive Foz do Iguaçu falls

→

PAGE 228

BRASÍLIA, GOIÁS, AND TOCANTINS

Modern architecture, Baroque buildings, and striking natural beauty can be found in these three central states. Unique Brasília showcases renowned modern architecture, while Tocantins is home to the beautiful Jalapão State Park, little visited by international travellers. Goiás offers fine food, the lush Chapada dos Veadeiros National Park, and pretty Pirenópolis – a hippie haven near buzzing Brasília.

Best for
Quirky towns and lesser-known national parks

Home to
Brasília, Pirenópolis, Parque Nacional Chapada dos Veadeiros

Experience
Oscar Niemeyer's iconic architecture in Brasília, including the national museum and avant-garde Catedral Metropolitana

PAGE 246

MATO GROSSO AND MATO GROSSO DO SUL

Featuring the world's biggest freshwater wetland and Texas-like cowboy culture, central-west Brazil is a brilliant mix of wildlife, first-class fishing, and deep-rooted country traditions. Mato Grosso do Sul is home to anacondas, giant anteaters, and vast cattle *fazendas*, as well as the ecotourism hot spot Bonito, with its crystal-clear rivers and incredible caves. The capital city of neighboring Mato Grosso is a foodie hot spot. The region is also the best place to spot fierce felines.

Best for
Spotting wildlife, fishing, and stunning sunsets

Home to
Pantanal

Experience
A night on a houseboat in the middle of the world's biggest freshwater wetland, the Pantanal

SALVADOR

PAGE 258

Once the capital of Brazil, fun-loving Salvador offers ostentatious Baroque churches, a huge variety of live music, and an incredibly rich and well-preserved Afro-Brazilian heritage. Add excellent restaurants, a stellar nightlife, and gorgeous urban beaches, and Bahia's capital becomes an unmissable spot. Stroll around the cobblestoned streets of the Pelourinho – the city's historic center, home to colorful buildings from the 17th and 18th centuries and various capoeira schools – sip fresh coconut juice on Ponta da Barra Beach, and get your groove on at weekly samba parties.

Best for
Carnaval, Baroque architecture, and live music

Home to
Igreja e Convento de São Francisco

Experience
Partying until dawn in the hip neighborhood of Rio Vermelho

BAHIA

PAGE 274

Colorful, culturally rich, and with a cuisine that will tantalize your taste-buds, Bahia is a must for everyone visiting Brazil. With a relaxed vibe, gorgeous white beaches, and swaying coconut palms, the region encapsulates Brazil's notorious joie de vivre. Kick back and relax in the sun along the beautiful Linha Verde or in the charming village of Trancoso, or head inland to plunge into an active adventure in the enormous Parque Nacional de Chapada Diamantina.

Best for
Fabulous food and joie de vivre

Home to
Parque Nacional de Chapada Diamantina, Linha Verde

Experience
An exciting, fast-paced capoeira performance

$\rightarrow$

SERGIPE, ALAGOAS, AND PERNAMBUCO

Beautiful architecture, expansive museums, and booming beach resorts are scattered around these three small – by Brazilian measures – states in the northeast. Off Pernambuco's shore lies the spectacular Ilha de Fernando de Noronha with superb marine life while Recife is home to excellent museums, lively bars, and historic sites. Just a few miles north, Olinda keeps it old school with cobblestoned streets and Baroque buildings.

Best for
Beach resorts, fresh seafood, and forró music and dance

Home to
Recife, Olinda, Ilha de Fernando de Noronha

Experience
Diving with sea turtles and sharks in the waters off remote Ilha de Fernando de Noronha

PARAÍBA, RIO GRANDE DO NORTE, AND CEARÁ

Beach dwellers and kitesurfers are drawn to these northeastern states by their high cliffs, perfect winds, and stunning stretches of sunny sand creased with palm trees. The coast is home to two fun-loving cities, Natal and Fortaleza, as well as small fishing villages where life feels miles away from any city hubbub. Here you can snorkel in warm waters, drive across massive sand dunes, and watch kitesurfers racing across sunny waters.

Best for
Sand dunes and kitesurfing

Home to
Fortaleza

Experience
Adrenaline-filled kitesurfing just offshore from Natal's high sand dunes

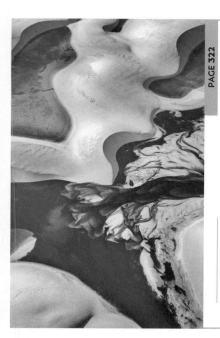

PAGE 322

PIAUÍ AND MARANHÃO

The adventure-filled northern states of Maranhão and Piauí are home to two spectacular national parks: Lençóis Maranhenses, an otherwordly landscape of turquoise lagoons and great stretches of rolling white sand dunes, and Serra da Capivara, an exciting trove of prehistoric paintings. Visitors to the region are also drawn to the charming historic center of São Luís, which features a range of excellent *pousadas* and a particularly lively reggae scene.

Best for
Adventure, Baroque architecture, and reggae

Home to
Parque Nacional de Serra da Capivara, Parque Nacional dos Lençóis Maranhenses, São Luís

Experience
A trip to Parque Nacional dos Lençóis Maranhenses to admire its striking lagoons

PAGE 336

THE AMAZON

Mystical and magical, the Amazon makes up a stunning 40 percent of Brazil's landscape. The lungs of the earth, the jungle is home to the majority of Brazil's Indigenous peoples and supports an incredible variety of plants and animals. Humid Manaus, in the heart of the region, is home to the stunning Teatro Amazonas, while the Mamirauá Reserve in the northwest, near the Colombian border, is the best spot for incredible wildlife.

Best for
Rainforests, river cruises, and Indigenous culture

Home to
Belém, Manaus

Experience
Cruising down the rivers of Mamirauá Reserve searching for the endemic Uakari and black-headed squirrel monkeys

$\rightarrow$

1 São Paulo's cityscape, from the top of the Terraço Italia Tower.

2 Interior of the Mercado Municipal.

3 Reading in Ibirapuera Park.

4 Bright graffiti on Beco do Batman.

Vast and varied, Brazil brims with travel possibilities. These suggested itineraries pick out all the highlights to help you plan your time in this beautiful country.

2 DAYS
in São Paulo

Day 1

Morning For a great introduction to the city's excellent coffee culture, start your day with a frothy cappuccino at Coffee Lab in Vila Madalena *(Rua Fradique Coutinho 1340)*. And just a ten-minute walk from the café you'll find a taste of São Paulo's renowned street art; Beco do Batman *(p161)* is a graffiti-filled alleyway that makes for cool and colorful photo opportunities.

Afternoon Lunch on distinctly Brazilian flavors at Becoartes *(Rua Gonçalo Afonso 99)* just around the corner from the Beco do Batman. Afterwards, spend the early afternoon strolling around the independent shops and galleries in this famously artsy area, taking time to marvel at the crafts found at Projeto Terra *(Rua Harmonia 150 – loja 4)* and the psychedelic artwork at Galeria Alma da Rua 1 *(Rua Gonçalo Afonso 96)*. Once you've had your fill of artisanal wonders, take a taxi to entrance 5 of the lush Parque do Ibirapuera *(p156)*. From here you can hire a Sampa Bike and cycle around the lakes. Streamline the process by registering online beforehand *(www.bikeitau.com.br)* or downloading the Bike Itaú app.

Evening Make dinner reservations at Vista *(www.vistasaopaulo.com.br)*, the gourmet restaurant on the eighth floor of the Museum of Contemporary Art (MAC). Sample some of their delicious seafood options, before finishing your night with superb drinks, great live music, and a stunning view across São Paulo's skyline on the rooftop of the affiliated Bar Obelisco.

Day 2

Morning Take the metro to Luz station, where the wonderful visual art museum of Pinacoteca de São Paulo *(p154)* is first on the agenda. From here, it's a leisurely 20-minute stroll to the Mercado Municipal *(p164)*, a blur of vibrant hues and mouthwatering produce – feast your eyes on the mounds of sumptuous strawberries and dragon fruit. Grab a quick bite at Tigrão, just by the escalators; their *pastel carne do sol* is delicious, especially accompanied by a freshly squeezed sugarcane juice.

Afternoon Head out for a walk through the lively downtown area to get to the Catedral da Sé *(p158)*, with its magnificent crypt. Next up it's a short walk to Liberdade, São Paulo's Japanese neighborhood. On Sundays there is a great market showcasing all manner of Brazilian-Japanese fusion street food – look out for red-bean-filled pancakes made to order. End your afternoon with some Japanese tapas and beer at the tiny Bar Kintaro *(p160)*.

Evening Take the metro to Avenida Paulista *(p166)* and enjoy a refreshing *açaí na tigela* at Açaí Verão on the bottom floor of Shopping Center 3. Right beside the center is the eclectic Rua Augusta, the city's LGBTQ+ neighborhood. Allow yourself some time to wander and soak in the vibrant atmosphere, before catching a movie at the sophisticated Espaço Itaú Augusta. Then treat yourself to a late dinner at Alexander Ataca's Michelin-starred restaurant D.O.M. *(www.domrestaurante. com.br)*, just a short taxi ride away.

←

1 Aerial view of the Amazon rainforest around Manaus.

2 Manaus's Teatro Amazonas.

3 A giant Samauma tree.

4 A boat ride in the Mamirauá Reserve with a local guide.

5 DAYS
in the Amazon

Day 1

Fly into urban Manaus in the very heart of the tropical Amazon rainforest. Start at the impressive Renaissance-styled Teatro Amazonas *(p344)* before taking a taxi to the Museu do Índio to learn about the Tukano people; call in at the museum shop for great crafts. Lunch at Canto da Peixada *(www.cantodapeixada.com)*, which is perfect for trying local river fish that can't be found anywhere else in the world. In the evening, continue your sampling of Amazonian food with dinner reservations at Banzeiro restaurant *(www. restaurantebanzeiro.com.br)*.

Day 2

Take a one-hour flight from Manaus to Tefé, then a boat ride up the river to the community-run Uakari Lodge, deep in the Mamirauá Sustainable Development Reserve *(p348)*. Bring binoculars, sunscreen, insect repellent, and small bills, as you'll be visiting Indigenous communities where you can buy handmade goods. Book into a floating jungle lodge with a hammock-strung patio, and spend an evening watching the tranquil water and listening to howler monkeys roar nearby.

Day 3

The sounds of the jungle waking up will serve as your morning alarm. Enjoy a generous breakfast and be ready to head out for your first excursion at day break. During the dry season (August to April), you can hike the jungle with experienced guides, while in the wet season (May to July) you'll be able to paddle through the rainforest instead. Return to the lodge for lunch, and then spend the afternoon aboard a boat on the Mamirauá Lake, looking for the region's Amazon river dolphins. The boat will set course for home as the sun begins to set, so you should be treated to spectacular views on the way back.

Day 4

Start your day with a visit to a nearby community, where a local host will show you around the village – don't forget your stash of small bills in case you want to buy any of the goods on sale. Get back to the lodge for lunch, and perhaps a little siesta, and then it's back on the water in the afternoon – this time for a canoe trip on the river. When you're all paddled out, return to the lodge for some downtime in your hammock and a delicious buffet dinner. Get a good night's sleep in preparation for a long day's travel tomorrow.

Day 5

Rise early and after breakfast return to Tefé by motorboat – if you're lucky you might spot some more dolphins on the way. Fly back to Manaus and check into the Tropical Manaus Ecoresort *(Av. Coronel Teixeira 1320; (92) 3305 7999)* for secluded riverside views and some well-deserved pampering after your days in the jungle.

7 DAYS
in South Brazil

Day 1

Get an early flight to Porto Alegre *(p200)* and pick up a car at the airport. Drive into the city center and spend the morning exploring Mercado Público, which offers a perfect opportunity to familiarize yourself with the regional food. Have a meat-filled lunch at traditional *churrascaria* NB Steak *(www.nbsteak.com.br)*, then drive north-ward to Brazil's best-known mountain resort, Gramado *(p202)*. Stroll around the flower-filled Parque Knorr and admire the Alpine styled chalets; in the evening, go all in on the Swiss theme and treat yourself to cheese fondue at Belle du Valais *(Ave das Hortências 1432)*. Bunk down for the night at the luxurious Saint Andrews boutique hotel *(www.saint andrews.com.br/pt)*, which has gorgeous mountain views and impeccable service.

Day 2

Swap your mountain setting for Italian vibes at Bento Gonçavales *(p206)*. Ride the charming steam train to Garibaldi and back, passing through vineyards. Head on to Vale dos Vinhedos *(p210)* and check into

Casa Valduga *(www.casavalduga.com.br)*. Spend the afternoon tasting the bodega's sparkling wines, then stroll through the picturesque surroundings. Come nightfall, indulge in a wine-paired dinner at the hotel restaurant, allowing a few hours to work your way through Italian chef Franco Gioelli's delectable creations.

Day 3

Rise early for the six-hour drive through the interior to Rio Grande do Sul's best-kept Jesuit ruins: São Miguel das Missões *(p202)*. Stroll around this UNESCO World Heritage Site, marveling at the intricate Guaraní-Baroque architecture. Stay until sunset, when the ruins bask in the warm golden light, and then spend the night at the simple, well-located Pousada Missões *(www.pousadadasmissoes.com.br)*.

Day 4

It's another sunrise start, this time to set off for Foz do Iguaçu *(p216)*. Splurge on your accommodations here and stay right by the thunderous cascades, at the

① The magnificent Foz do Iguaçu falls.
② Mercado Público, Porto Alegre.
③ A vineyard at Vale dos Vinhedos.
④ Florianópolis, Santa Catarina.
⑤ Praia do Campeche, Santa Catarina.

pastel-pink Hotel das Cataratas Belmond (www.belmond.com). It's the only hotel in the national park, so leave plenty of time to enjoy the surroundings while the park is off-limits to everyone else. Dine at the hotel before getting a good night's sleep.

Day 5

Wake up at dawn to see the falls and the rainforest bathed in magical morning light; this is a great opportunity to take striking photographs. For unbeatable views, treat yourself to a helicopter ride across the cascades. In the afternoon, drop your car off at the airport and fly to Florianópolis (p222) and its splendid beaches. Pick up another hire car and drive to the lovely fishing village of Ribeirão da Ilha, with its excellent sea-food restaurants. It's a busy place in January and February but off-season you have the place pretty much to yourself. Spend the evening strolling around the colorful Portuguese houses and photo-graphing the moored fishing boats, before a dinner of oysters at the popular Ostradamus (www.ostradamus.com.br).

Day 6

Wake yourself up with an early swim before driving to Praia do Campeche (p224), one of the island's finest beaches. Have a healthy, Thai-inspired lunch at Mercado Sehat (www.mercadosehat.com.br), then drive on to the charming village of Santo Antônio de Lisboa, a well-preserved Azorean settlement, before returning to Florianópolis. Stroll the fruit, vegetable, and seafood stalls at the city's Mercado Público, then head to the exclusive Ponta dos Ganchos resort (www.pontados ganchos.com.br). It's set on a private peninsula lined with deluxe bungalows; be sure to book well in advance.

Day 7

Spend your morning enjoying the resort's amenities and the tranquil setting of the private beach, with its brain-stilling soundtrack of crickets and chirping birds, and picturesque backdrop of passing local fishing boats. Rouse yourself in the early afternoon to go for a leisurely hike in the surrounding area, before heading back to Florianópolis for a flight home.

7 DAYS

in Salvador and North Brazil

Day 1

Fly into Salvador (p258) for the best introduction to Afro-Brazilian culture. Buy an *acarajé* (a deep-fried bean snack) from traditionally dressed Bahian locals, and set off to explore the historic crown jewel of Brazil: the Pelourinho (p272). Don't miss the ostentatious São Francisco church (p262), covered in over 882 lb (400 kg) of gold. Nearby, the Mercado Modelo is a great place to buy souvenirs like intricately carved wooden masks. Stay at the elegant Pestana Convento do Carmo (Rua do Carmo 1), set in a convent building dating from the 1500s.

Day 2

Rise early and fly south to Ilhéus (p289), the setting for most novels by renowned Brazilian author Jorge Amado. Visit Bar Vesúvio (Rua Dom Eduardo 190) and Bataclan Cabaret (www.grupovesuvio.com. br/bataclan), which feature in Amado's novel *Gabriela, Clove and Cinnamon*. Continue south to hippie-chic Trancoso (p290), which offers colorful houses, miles of beaches, and a trendy vibe. Check into

UXUA Casa Hotel and Spa (p290) and book one of their capoeira (p287) classes to try your hand at this Afro-Brazilian martial art form. After working up an appetite, enjoy dinner at the lovely hotel restaurant.

Day 3

Have a cappuccino at the Santo Café Trancoso (Rua do Telégrafo) and then stroll around the pretty town center. Pop into the tiny Igreja de São Joao Batista on the square, then stop for some *moqueca* (fish stew) at Silvana & Cia (www.silvanae cia.com.br). Wander down to the beach to relax for the rest of the afternoon, perhaps taking a horseback ride along the sea. Refresh yourself with a drink at UXUA Praia Bar (p290), before making your way back up to the village.

Day 4

You'll spend most of today traveling to Praia do Carneiros, but it'll be worth it to reach this white-sand paradise. First, take a bus to Porto Seguro, then catch a flight to lively Maceió (p306). Pick up a hire car

① Traditional Bahian attire.
② A selection of Bahian food.
③ Catedral São Sebastião, Ilhéus.
④ Praça do Marco Zero, Recife.
⑤ Praia do Carneiros.
⑥ Carnaval parade in Olinda.

at the airport and drive north, breaking for lunch in the sleepy fishing village of Tamandaré. When you arrive at Praia dos Carneiros, treat yourself to a leisurely dinner under the palm trees at Restaurante Beijupirá *(www.beijupira.com/br)*. Then check into a luxurious bungalow at Hotel Pontal dos Carneiros *(www.pontaldos carneiros.com.br)* and spend the night stargazing from your private patio.

Day 5

Continue north to Recife *(p296)*, the sun-drenched capital of Pernambuco. Explore this beautiful old city, starting at the colorful Praça do Marco Zero. Next, check out the Parque das Esculturas, then move on to the interactive Museu Cais do Sertão. Have lunch at the adjacent Cais Rooftop Lounge Bar *(Ave Alfredo Lisboa)*, then walk around the corner to the Paço do Frevó cultural center to experience Recife's unique music and dance style. Your last stop is the gorgeous Capela Dourada, before catching a bus north to artsy Olinda *(p300)* to stay at the charming Pousada do Amparo *(Rua do Amparo, 199)* in the historic center.

Day 6

Start your day with a walk around this quaint little town, soaking in the laid-back atmosphere. Most museums close for lunch, so this is the time to check out Museu do Mamulengo's massive puppet collection. Lunch at Oficina do Sabor *(www.oficinadosabor.com)*, then make like the locals and head to your hotel for a siesta and pool break. Later, stroll around the pretty Convento de São Francisco and the Igreja e Mosteiro São Bento with its vast gold altar.

Day 7

Head to Recife airport and fly to Ilha de Fernando de Noronha *(p302)*, a Brazilian paradise. Check into Pousada Maravilha *(www.pousadamaravilha.com.br)*, which has luxurious rooms and bungalows with stunning sea views. Wear your most comfortable shoes and hike to the wild and isolated Baia do Sancho, accessed via steep, rock-hewn stairs. This is one of the world's most beautiful beaches, and you can spend the day here snorkeling amid glassy, fish-filled waters.

1 The vast Parque do Ibirapuera.

2 A downtown São Paolo restaurant.

3 A diver exploring the waters around Ilhabela.

4 A black-tufted marmoset, one of Brazil's common monkey species.

10 DAYS
in Rio and the Costa Verde

Day 1

Start your trip in São Paulo *(p150)*, with a morning cycling around the Parque do Ibirapuera *(p156)* on a Sampa Bike. Then take the metro up to the Pinacoteca de São Paulo *(p154)*, and devote a couple of hours to exploring this wonderful visual art museum. When you've seen enough, stroll on to Liberdade *(p166)*, São Paulo's Japanese neighborhood; there is a great market here on Sundays, packed with all manner of Brazilian-Japanese street food. Treat yourself to a tasty snack-style dinner, and then take the metro to Avenida Paulista for an evening in the vibrant Rua Augusta neighborhood.

Day 2

Pick up a rental car and drive south to the coast via São Bernardo do Campo (aim to leave mid-morning to avoid rush hour). Wind your way through hills to Guarujá *(p176)*, where you can take a leisurely lunch of fresh, Italian-inspired seafood at Il Faro restaurant *(Avenida Miguel Estéfano 4659)*, paired with attractive views of the sea. Continue to São Sebastião *(p176)*, winding your way along the coast past the city of Santos *(p180)*, where Pelé played for years in the eponymous football club. Upon arrival in São Sebastião, take a ferry to Brazil's largest tropical island, Ilhabela *(p174)*, which is adored by Paulistanos for its waterfall, sailing, gorgeous beaches, and lush natural scenery. Check into the trendy DPNY Beach Hotel *(www.dpny.com.br)* for a fashionable overnight stay.

Day 3

Spend the day exploring Ilhabela. There are only two roads on the island; one paved and the other only suitable for 4WD vehicles, so leave the car and walk when needed. Visit Parque Estadual Ilhabela, inhabited by ocelots and monkeys, and watch the surfers take on the waves at the island's longest beach, Bonete. The enticing Cachoeira da Água Branca waterfall is an hour's hike in the state park – a trip that's amply rewarded with refreshing natural swimming pools. If you're a diver, schedule some time in the water; there are plenty of shipwrecks waiting to be explored around the island's waters. Afterwards, freshen up for dinner at Viana *(Praia do Viana)* – try the jumbo shrimp, for which Ilhabela is famous.

Day 4

Return to the mainland and drive through the lush Mata Atlântica *(p140)* to the art hub of Paraty *(p134)*. If you're here in August, visit the annual Festa Literária Internacional de Paraty, which draws Brazilian and international writers, and the Pinga Festival, when samples of local cachaça (Brazilian rum), regional food, and live music are on offer. Check into Pousada Literaria *(Rua do Comércio 362)* and spend the day wandering the cobblestoned streets and Baroque buildings. Stop by the Galeria Aecio Sarti to take in some local art, and visit Forte Defensor Perpétuo at the hilltop for stunning views of Paraty. End your evening with dinner at Banana da Terra *(Rua Dr. Samuel Costa 198)*.

Day 5

Jump aboard a yacht in Paraty and cruise around the area's pristine beaches and isolated islands. Return to shore in the afternoon and head southeast to Paraty-Mirim, a half-hour drive away. The end of the drive is along a bumpy dirt road, so check conditions before leaving. Stay in the middle of the Atlantic jungle at Remo Hostel (Estrada de Paraty-Mirim 7000), where you can enjoy a digital detox (no Wi-Fi) in a stunning treehouse. The lush surroundings, homemade food, and views of the sea are gloriously restorative; spend a low-key evening reading and chatting to your fellow guests.

Day 6

Drive toward Angra dos Reis, which is the jumping-off point for romantic Ilha Grande (p136). Leave the car and take the passenger ferry across to the pedestrianized island, mainly inhabited by fishers. There are no banks or ATMs on the island, so do make sure you have a good cash stash. Check in to the lovely Japanese-Brazilian guesthouse Pousada

do Preto (www.pousadadopreto.com.br), tucked away on a small beach. Test your balance with an afternoon of stand-up paddling, and then relax on the pousada deck to watch the sun sink into the ocean.

Day 7

Spend the morning beach-hopping – make sure not to miss the beautiful Praia de Lopes Mendes. Then take the ferry back to the mainland and drive east to Rio (p68). Check into Mango Tree Hostel (Rua Prudente de Morais 594), and take a tour of the art on offer in the city: walk to Praça Mauá to marvel at street artist Kobra's massive colorful murals, then taxi to the beautiful Museu Nacional de Belas Artes (p80) for its wealth of antique art. Finish your day with innovative dishes at Lasai (Largo dos Leões 35).

Day 8

Enjoy a sumptuous Brazilian hostel breakfast while watching the sun rise over Ipanema Beach (p106). Follow this with a refreshing morning stroll on the sand,

1 Lush greenery of the Mata Atlântica.
2 A boatful of revelers near Ilha Grande.
3 Stand-up paddlers off Ilha Grande.
4 Aerial views from Cristo Redentor.
5 Copacabana Beach, Rio de Janeiro.

then pick up a Sampa Bike and pedal off to Copacabana (p104), one of the world's most famous beaches. After a couple of hours on the sands, taxi to Parque Lage for lunch amid gorgeous mountaintops and tropical forest at the PLage Café (www.plagecafe.com.br). Then take some time to explore the surrounding rainforest before catching a ride to Estaçao da Estrada do Ferro Corcovado. Take the cog train up to Cristo Redentor (p118), passing through dense Mata Atlântica in the world's largest urban forest, Parque Nacional da Tijuca (p126). Drink in the stunning views over the city, then enjoy a dinner of traditional Brazilian food at nearby Nova Capela (Ave Mem de Sá 98). End your night as Brazilians do best – on the dance floor at Bar da Ladeira (Rua Evaristo da Veiga 149).

Day 9

Splash out on some Brazilian beachwear at Blue Man (www.blueman.com.br) in Ipanema and put it straight to the test with a leisurely morning at the beach. After lunch, leave the city behind and drive to Brigitte Bardot-devoted Búzios (p146) – still a swanky holiday hub 60 years after the French actress first "hid" here. Stay at the chic Insolito Boutique Hotel & Spa (www.insolitohotel.com), which stands on the edge of one of the area's most beautiful beaches. Allow yourself a lazy afternoon wandering the resort town; take the mandatory photo with Brigitte's statue on Orla Bardot and shop for gifts at Rua das Pedras. Dine on fine Brazilian surf and turf at Mistico (Rua Morro do Humaitá 13).

Day 10

For a truly Brazilian final day, hire a beach buggy and explore Búzios's surrounding beaches, but make sure to avoid Praia da Tartaruga around turtle nesting season (Oct–Mar). The peninsula is well signposted, so you don't really need a map. For good surf, visit Praia Brava on the eastern shore, while Ferradurinha on the southern tip offers natural swimming pools. Drive back to Búzios and indulge in a French meal at its prettiest restaurant, Cigalon (Rua das Pedras 199).

Welcome to the Jungle

The Amazon rainforest is as mystical, huge, and fragile as it is full of life. Experience the marvels of this threatened ecosystem at Mamiráua Sustainable Development Reserve *(p348)*, visit one of the region's beautiful eco-lodges, or test your limits on a survival tour outside Manaus *(p342)* led by local guides.

↑ Trees in the Amazon rainforest forming a lush green canopy

BRAZIL FOR
NATURAL WONDERS

Venture deep into the Amazon forest, feel the spray of thunderous waterfalls on your face, or relax on glorious sun-soaked beaches. Whatever you're looking for, this dazzling country will not disappoint.

Dramatic Waterfalls

Brazilians love their waterfalls, and it's no wonder. Refreshing cascades come in all shapes and sizes, from sweetly subtle like Cascatinha do Taunay in Parque Nacional da Tijuca *(p126)*, to bold and thunderous like the biggest of them all: Foz do Iguaçu *(p216)*. Experience their sheer power during a thrilling boat ride through churning waters. Get up close at the walkway to the enormous cascade Garganto do Diabo, roaring over the edge and down to the steaming chasm more than 262 ft (80 m) below.

The breathtaking Iguaçu falls, made up of 275 separate waterfalls

Seductive Sunsets

The fiery sky of a Brazilian sunset is a spectacular sight. Admire the endless dunes of Lençóis Maranhenses (p328) as they change color with the dimming light, or take a sunset scramble to the top of the Chapadão plateau, from where you can watch the sun as it plunges into the Atlantic.

→

Sunset across the dunes of Lençóis Maranhenses National Park

Wondrous Waterways

So big it is visible from space, the mighty Amazon river flows across South America from the Andes to the Atlantic. Plenty of local operators offer the chance to cruise down this epic channel on a riverboat trip. The southwestern corner of Mato Grosso do Sul is a veritable aquatic playground; head to the Rio da Prata in Bonito (p256) to snorkel in glassy, turquoise water while curious fish swim alongside.

←

An underwater photographer exploring the tropical waters in Bonito, Mato Grosso do Sul

TOP 4 ECO-FRIENDLY TRAVEL TIPS

Keep to the Path
Stay on designated trails to protect delicate ecological environments.

Protect Local Species
Refrain from picking flowers or taking rocks and sand home.

Leave No Trace
Avoid polluting the local environment by disposing of your rubbish properly.

Respect Wildlife
Always observe the local wildlife from a distance.

↑ Craggy granite peaks in the Parque Nacional da Serra dos Órgãos

Majestic Mountains

There's no shortage of magnificent mountain ranges in Brazil. Intrepid visitors can hike through winding valleys and past plunging cliffs in the Parque Nacional da Serra dos Órgãos (p146). For great views, the iconic Sugar Loaf Mountain (p116) can't be topped, with fun-loving Rio de Janeiro laid out below.

Markets Galore

Discover the boundless variety of fresh produce at the country's many markets. São Paulo's Mercado Municipal *(p164)* is one of the best, famous for mortadella sandwiches, spices, and an incredible fruit selection, as well as places serving national delights. For a taste of the Amazon, head north to Belém *(p340)*, where the Ver-o-Peso market sells local cuisines inspired and influenced by the nearby rainforest. Exploring the adjacent fish market, stocked fresh from the Amazon river, makes for a truly traditional experience.

→
A worker carting fresh produce to the market in Belém

BRAZIL FOR
FOODIES

Blessed with an abundance of sun, soil, and tropical rainforest, Brazil is an inspiring playground for those seeking to try new flavors. Sample fine dining in São Paulo, unique tropical fruits in the Amazon, delicious crab and fresh fish on the coast, and coconut-charged cuisine in Bahia.

City Dining at its Finest

For those in search of fine dining, Brazil offers 14 restaurants - divided between Rio and São Paulo - that have been awarded those sought-after Michelin stars. The most prestigious of these is São Paulo's D.O.M. *(p25)*, where chef Alex Atala combines European avant-garde recipes with Amazonian ingredients to deliver a truly mind-blowing food experience. In Rio, book in a visit to Felipe Bronze and Cecilia Aldaz's ORO *(www.oro restaurante.com.br),* which attracts haute-cuisine-loving foodies with its impressive wine list and gourmet take on the city's beloved street food.

→
The dining room at D.O.M., a Michelin-starred restaurant in São Paulo

Tim-Tim!

The caipirinha is of course king of the cocktails in Brazil, but did you know Cariocas also love a G&T? Brazilian gin and sparkling wine are one of the country's better-kept secrets, but both are rapidly gaining an international reputation. National gin treasures include Amázzoni and Virga – get your hands on a bottle if you can, whether to treat yourself or as a souvenir that's guaranteed to be well-recieved. To sample some award-winning fizz, head to Vale dos Vinhedos *(p210),* a first-class wine region in Rio Grande do Sul.

← A flourishing vineyard in Vale dos Vinhedos

TOP 5 **MUST-TRY BRAZILIAN FOODS**

Açai na tigela
Purple guarana and açai-flavored sorbet, usually topped with bananas and granola.

Brigadeiro
Popular sweets made from condensed milk, cocoa powder, sugar, and butter.

Feijoada
Brazil's national dish, black bean casserole with pork, served regularly at restaurants.

Moqueca
A slow-cooked, brightly colored fish stew.

Acarajé
Street-food fritters from the northeast made of peeled beans and dried prawns.

↑ A bowl of *moqueca,* flavored with coriander and coconut milk

Brazilian Fusion

The product of Indigenous culinary traditions and international influences, Brazilian food is a delightful smorgasbord. Munch on *bolinho de bacalhau,* a Portuguese cod fritter snack; savor the African-influenced seafood stew *moqueca;* slurp on the Japanese noodle dish *yakisoba* in São Paulo; grab slices of Italian-style pizza; try spicy Bahian flavors, or sample dishes that draw from a range of Indigenous recipes from the Amazon.

FLAVORS OF BRAZIL

Food across Brazil showcases the variety of the country's rich local produce, landscape, and climate. In the south of the country visitors will find an abundance of meat and wine, while the north offers unique river fish, plenty of fruits and root vegetables. In between are two states that stand out: Minas Gerais and Bahia, each offering a very distinct local cuisine.

NORTHERN FLAVORS

The rich flora and fauna of the Amazon dominates the Brazilian food on offer in the north, where the açaí berry and unique freshwater fish such as tambaqui, aruanã, and tucanaré are all common ingredients. Typical dishes include *caldo do piranha* (piranha soup), *peixe na folha de patioba* (grilled fish cooked with onions, tomatoes, and coriander wrapped in a *patioba* leaf), and *tacacá* (shrimp soup with manioc broth), a common street food in Pará. In the Amazon, the native açaí berry - primarily used as an ingredient in desserts and smoothies throughout the rest of the country - is in fact eaten raw as a savory component.

↑ Preparing a range of mouthwatering traditional Bahian dishes

BAHIA AND BEYOND

Coconut, seafood, and *dendê* oil (an orange palm oil) are frequent ingredients in Bahia's delectable and flavorsome African-inspired cuisine. Coconut milk is the base of the region's popular *moqueca baiana* (fish stew), while creamy *vatapá* (breadcrumbs with tomatoes, onions, and chili) is often served

with prawns. Delicious *acarajé* (bean-based fritters), meanwhile, are deep-fried in *dendê* oil. Further northeast, in Brazil's arid interior, the cuisine varies significantly, and salty *carne do sol* (dried meat) and corn are both key staple foods. Crepes made of manioc (cassava-root flour) filled with different toppings, which can be both sweet and savory, are also a ubiquitous part of northeastern Brazil's traditional diet.

MINAS GERAIS

Famous for its rustic food, Minas Gerais's specialties include mouthwatering *pão do queijo* (cheese bread), tummy-lining *feijão tropeiro* (a hearty stew of beans, dried meat, and bacon), and the daunting but delicious *mocotó* (cow's feet soup). The region also produces Brazil's best cachaça (a fresh-tasting sugarcane alcohol with herbal notes that is the country's national spirit) and a variety of cheese, with the award-winning artisanal *queijo canastra* – a hard white cheese of local cow's milk – being made in the Serra da Canastra mountains.

SOUTHERN INSPIRATIONS

Meat and wine rule in the south of Brazil, which is home to vast, sweeping pastures

↑ Bottles of cachaça, Brazil's national spirit, lined up on a shelf

and enjoys a cool climate that is ideal for growing grapes. In Rio Grande do Sul, belly-popping *churrascarias rodizio* (all-you-can-eat steakhouses) are hugely popular, while lush vineyards found in the enchanting Vale dos Vinhedos produce Brazil's renowned sparkling wine. *Chimarrão*, a bitter herbal hot drink consumed daily by *gaúchos* and locals, is also common. The region's south European heritage is evident in its food throughout – expect to see jars of tangy sauerkraut, plates of sausage, and bowls of mouthwatering fondue.

↑ A counter laden with cheese at the lively Mercado Central in Belo Horizonte

DRINK

Casa da Cachaça
This tiny bar has over 100 varieties of tongue-tingling cachaça, including the rare Havana from Minas Gerais, considered one of the best in Brazil. Guests can often be found squeezing out onto the pavement of Rio's Lapa neighborhood to get a chance to sample this diminutive bar's variety of different flavored spirits.

🗺 D6 🏠 Ave Mem de Sá, 110 🌐 casadacachaca delapa.com.br

$$$

Lively Samba

The rhythms of samba flow through Brazil during Carnaval. Join the fun months beforehand at the country's samba schools – social clubs found throughout Brazil, with the biggest and most famous found in Rio's favelas. Or to do something truly Carioaca, dance a night away in one of Lapa's atmospheric samba clubs.

→

A brightly costumed samba dancer during Rio's Carnaval

BRAZIL FOR
RHYTHM

A wonderful medley of styles, Brazil's music is testament to the vibrant mix of cultures and influences that make up the country's population. Move your body to the infectious beats of *forró* in the northeast, funk in Rio, acoustic *sertanejo* in rural areas, and samba across the country.

Favela Funk

Pronounced "foonkee" and nothing like the 1960s American variety, Carioca funk has its roots deep in the heart of Rio's favelas during the 1980s. It has since captured the country's club culture, becoming a mainstream phenomenon. Inspired by hip-hop brought back from the US, its explicit lyrics reference topics such as poverty, racial inequality, violence, and social injustice, all set to a mix of Miami bass, gangsta rap, and Afrobeats tempo.

MUSICAL ROYALTY

Numerous Brazilian musicians have gained international fame, including Polar Prize winner Gilberto Gil, soft-singing Vanessa da Mata, and funk-inspired pop queen Anitta *(above)*. Almir Sater is a big name among *sertanejo* and blues lovers, and Bahian-born Astrud Gilberto became a star in the 1960s with "The Girl from Ipanema."

A Little Bit Country

Perhaps surprisingly, country music *(sertanejo)* is the most popular sound in Brazil. Usually associated with the rural interior, it has now been brought to São Paulo's trendiest clubs by city hipsters. To experience the real thing, however, head to Mato Grosso do Sul – Brazil's answer to Texas – where country tunes are blasted from cars and in clubs, and are very much ingrained in the local cowboy culture.

$\rightarrow$

Country artist Luciano performing an arena show in downtown Rio

Fabulous Festivals

There's no shortage of music festivals in Brazil. Ranging from electronic dance frenzies to heavy rock 'n' roll festivities, the biggest events are hosted in São Paulo and Rio. Rock fans should check out Rock in Rio; one of the country's most famous festivals, it's headlined by big international artists and is held, as the name suggests, in Rio de Janeiro, usually every second year. For something more off the beaten track, head to the Bananada festival in Goiâna to enjoy a predominantly Brazilian lineup.

$\leftarrow$

A packed crowd enjoying a performance during the Festival Bananada

Northeast's Number One

A northeastern two-step dance and music style, *forró* is a way of life for the people in this corner of Brazil. In mid-July, make for the beach town of Itaúanas *(p149)* for FENFIT, an eight-day festival devoted entirely to the genre, with live music and late-night parties. Caruaru *(p307)* – Brazil's self proclaimed *forró* capital – takes things even further, hosting the São João de Caruaru festival that offers lively *forró* festivities for the whole month of June.

$\rightarrow$

A couple dancing to the infectious music of a *forró* band

$\uparrow$ A singer performing onstage at a funk party in Rio

Films and Filmmakers

Brazilian filmmakers don't shy away from the issues affecting the country, with films such as *Cidade de Deus* and *Capitães da Areia*. São Paulo's film festival - Brazil's biggest- showcases independent movies. It's the perfect chance to discover emerging Brazilian directors and actors, and get acquainted with the city's splendid arthouse cinemas, such as Cinema Itaú or Cinemateca Brasileira.

Alexandre Rodrigues in the 2002 film *Cidade de Deus*

BRAZIL FOR
STORYTELLING

Given Brazil's diverse culture and history, the country's creatives have plenty of unique stories to share. These are told through a profound variety of art forms, from curated world cinema to the words of globally famous writers. Here are some of the best ways to discover them.

Brazilian Literature

The life of Jorge Amado, one of Brazil's most famous modern authors, is celebrated at the Fundação Casa do Jorge Amado *(p264)* museum. Fans of Rachel de Queiroz's *O Quinze*, meanwhile, should head to the author's birthplace in Fortaleza *(p312)* and visit the small tribute to her on Praça General Tiburcio. Guided tours of Casa do Sul, the former home of radical writer Hilda Hilst, are also on offer to biliophiles.

INSIDER TIP
FLIP Lit

The Festa Literária
Internacional de Paraty
(FLIP) is one of Brazil's
preeminent literary fes-
tivals, with programs
held in Rio each July
(www.flip.org.br).

Marvelous Museums

São Paulo has the most
museums of any city in South
America, many of which house
famous Brazilian artworks.
Visit both MASP (p162), the
country's first modern art
museum, and the Pinacoteca
de São Paulo (p154), a visual
art museum set in elegant
brick surroundings.

→
The striking interior of the
Pinacoteca de São Paulo

Favela Writing

The diary of Carolina Maria de Jesus, *Child of
the Dark*, was published in the 1960s, and
was at that time the only Brazilian author
from a favela that had been translated into
English. Tour Rio's favelas with local guides
from Brazilidade or Favela Tours (p111) for
a deeper understanding of favela life and
to learn about the community from an
insider's perspective. Revenue from such
tours is invested back into the community.

←
The colorful main square of the
Santa Marta favela in Rio de Janeiro

Colorful Streets

Famed for its larger-than-life
murals, São Paulo is home to
some of the world's best graffiti. Eduardo Kobra is the city's
most famous street artist -
look out for *A Doce Bailarina*
on the steps of Pinheiros, or
We Are One in Rio. São Paulo's
Beco do Batman is also a
draw, adorned by colorful
imaginings by local artists.

→
A Karen woman from
Myanmar, part of Eduardo
Kobra's Rio mural, *We Are One*

↑ The turquoise facade
of the Fundação Casa
de Jorge Amado

Game Day

Attending a soccer game in Brazil is an unforgettable day out - listening to thousands of people chant, jump, and cheer in ecstasy is euphorically contagious. To blend in with fiercely loyal fans at Arena Corinthians in São Paulo (p150), grab one of the team's soccer jerseys at the official stadium shop; then post-match, indulge in a sandwich filled with barbecued meat and onion. In Rio? Head to the Estádio do Maracanã (p91), the largest stadium in Brazil, to watch local teams battle it out.

$\rightarrow$
A hard-fought match between Brazil's Corinthians and Chapecoense teams

BRAZIL FOR
SOCCER FANS

Brazilians are fervent *futebol* fans, and going to a soccer game here is an invigorating experience, characterized by unanimous chanting and passionate displays of emotion. Whether you're keen to watch, learn, or play, Brazil offers plenty of ways to enjoy the beautiful game.

Footvolley

Founded in the mid-1960s, *futevôlei* (footvolley) is a combination of volleyball and soccer. It began on Copacabana beach (p104) but is now played all over Brazil; head to Posto 11 and Riba in Leblon (p108) to practice or just to watch the locals - sometimes including professional tennis player Natalia Guitler - play.

THE MARACANAÇO TRAGEDY

"O Maracanaço" refers to the Brazilian soccer "tragedy" of the 1950 World Cup, when Brazil unexpectedly lost to Uruguay. The phrase has passed into common parlance in Brazil, and is used for other footballing defeats - such as their 1-7 loss to Germany in 2014 - and even political debacles.

Silky Skills

With a distinctive style, Brazilian soccer players are famous for their fast foot-work and excellent dribbling techiques. To see beautifully honed soccer skills first-hand, head to a game at the massive Maracanã Stadium *(p91)*, where matches are among the world's most exciting. Alternatively, those seeking a more budget-friendly showcase can watch locals refine their technique at Ipanema *(p106)*. And in São Paulo, learn about the history behind Brazil's number one passion at the interactive soccer museum *(p167)*.

← Cariocas playing football on Ipanema beach, Rio

TOP 5 BRAZILIAN SOCCER PLAYERS

Pelé
Won his first World Cup at only 17 years old.

Marta
Holds the record (17) of the most goals scored at a FIFA World Cup.

Ronaldo
This world-famous player has two World Cup winner's medals to his name.

Garrincha
Considered the finest dribbler of all time.

Romário
The star of Brazil's 1994 World Cup victory.

Soccer megastar Pelé in action for his long-time Brazilian team, Santos ↑

↑ *Futevôlei* match between Brazil and China

The World's Greatest

Some – if not *the* – best and most famous soccer players in the world are from Brazil (only the Argentinians would disagree). Unsurpassed in history, Pelé, the country's national pride, has been voted the greatest of all time by FIFA. Head to Santos by the coast, where Pelé played for 18 years, to soak in the sea air that shaped the number one in the world.

Expect the Unexpected

Beaches and Baroque architecture? Definitely a thing. Head to Praia dos Carneiros for the picture-perfect postcard shot of a tiny 16th-century church with a backdrop of swaying palm trees and white sand. Another unusual sight can be seen at Praia do Rio Vermelho in Salvador *(p258)* each February, when flowers and gifts are floated out onto the sea by men and women dressed in white paying tribute to Yemanjá, the Candomblé Goddess of the Sea.

BRAZIL FOR
BEAUTIFUL BEACHES

With over 4,600 miles (7,400 km) of coastline, Brazil has a plethora of beaches, from vast dunescapes and watersport wonderlands to child-friendly bays and party hot spots. Prepare to be spoiled for choice.

Secluded Bays

Head to the Baía do Sancho, hidden in a tranquil cove on paradise archipelago Ilha de Fernando do Noronha *(p302)*, to relax amid untouched nature. Further inland, Alter do Chao has beautiful white sand and warm waters lapping at a peaceful shore. Take a canoe out on the water, or climb the low forested hills for a breath-taking view over the thick surrounding jungle.

An isolated curve of golden sands at the Baía do Sancho

INSIDER TIP
Birthday-Suit Bathing

While skimpy bikinis are everywhere, baring all is a big no-no in Brazil, unless you're heading to a specifically nudist beach. If you want to go skinny dipping, head for the naturist section at Praia Tambaba; or for clothing-optional sunbathing spots, check out Floripa's Praia do Galheta.

←
The tiny church at Praia dos Carneiros, built right at the water's edge

Best of Both Worlds

Urban beaches are the perfect playground for Brazil's city dwellers. Mingle with Cariocas at Ipanema (p106) or at nearby Copacabana (p104), the undisputed king of city beaches. For a true city vacation vibe, take in gorgeous views at Natal's lovely Ponta Negra beach.

→
Colorful parasols dotting one of Brazil's bustling urban beaches

Surf's Up

Praia do Mocambique on Ilha de Santa Catarina (p222) offers stunning natural beauty, and is a surfing hot spot thanks to its strong waves and isolated location. Chilled Jericoacoara (p320) attracts kitesurfers with its strong, steady winds, while Praia de Maracaípe is known for its towering waves.

→
A local kitesurfer taking advantage of the steady winds in Jericoacoara

Ocean Dwellers

Brazil's huge coastline allows splendid opportunities for spotting marine life. Watch dolphins in Baía dos Golfinhos in Praia da Pipa, or right whales off the coast of Ilha de Santa Catarina *(p222)*. In the waters surrounding the remote islands of Abrolhos *(p291)*, dives with rays and turtles can also be arranged.

Spinner dolphins in the Baia dos Golfinhos

BRAZIL FOR
WILDLIFE
ENCOUNTERS

Thanks to its vast rainforest and natural wetlands, Brazil offers an incredibly varied array of plant and animal life. Here are some of our favorite ways to experience one of the world's finest wildlife destinations.

Creatures of the Savanna

The Brazilian *cerrado*, or savanna, is home to amazing animals. Take a guided safari with ecotourism group Onçafari *(www.oncafari.org)*, track maned wolves at Pousada Trijunção *(www.pousadatrijuncao. com.br)*, or plunge into the rainforests and swamps of Mosaico Juréia-Itatins in search of tapirs, which have mostly disappeared from coastal Brazil but live here in healthy numbers.

Feline Favorites

Elusive, majestic, and believed by some Brazilian Indigenous peoples to hold divine power, the jaguar is the king of the Amazon rainforest, the swamps of Pantanal, and the lush Mata Atlântica. For your best chance to spot these fierce felines in a rural environment head to Caiman Ecological Lodge, where Onçafari runs a successful jaguar conservation project, or check out Porto Jofre in Pantanal *(p250)*, where the animals venture along the river banks from June to October. Pantanal Jaguar Safaris *(www. pantanaljaguarsafaris.com)* offer knowledgeable guides.

→
A young male jaguar prowling through the grass

High Fliers

A twitcher's paradise, Brazil has the world's richest diversity of avifauna. Head to Reentrâncias Maranhenses *(p334)*, where you'll find an array of shorebirds, or Cristalino Lodge *(p254)* in the south corner of the Amazon. The lodge has knowledgeable guides and two observation towers looking out over the treetops, where you may spot some of the region's colorful macaws.

←
A group of tourists observing scarlet ibis on one of Brazil's bird-rich rivers

In the Treetops

Brazil's impressive rainforest canopy makes the perfect home for slow-moving sloths, endemic monkeys, and troublesome toucans. Spend a night at Uakari Lodge *(p348)* in Mamirauá and linger on the rivers of the reserve, scouting for the endearing white uakari monkey and black-headed squirrel monkey.

↑
A giant anteater snuffling its way across the *cerrado*

→
A three-toed sloth clinging to a tree trunk in the Amazon rainforest

Indigenous Traditions

Today Brazil is home to more than 300 Indigenous groups, together speaking over 270 languages and dialects, and each carrying their own traditions, culture, and history. Learn more about these communities at Rio's excellent Museu do Índio *(p120)* – don't miss the garden longhouse. Admire São Paulo's Oca do Ibirapuera, Oscar Niemeyer's fascinating homage to Brazilian Indigenous architecture, or spend a day with an Indigenous community in the Amazon when you visit the Mamirauá Sustainable Development Reserve *(p348)*.

→

The domed white roof of the Oca do Ibirapuera

BRAZIL FOR
WORLD
CULTURE

Infused with African, European, Asian, and indigenous history and religion, Brazil is a veritable melting pot of global cultures. From food to festivals and museums to architecture, there's a whole world of things to celebrate.

Eastern Influence

Brazil has the world's largest Japanese diaspora, and São Paulo is home to the majority of Brazil's Japanese community. Visit the distinctly Japanese area of Liberdade *(p167)* to sample tasty street food, or to enjoy the gorgeous Hanamatsuri flower festival, hosted there every April. In Parque do Ibirapuera *(p156),* the serene Pavilhão Japonês offers a welcome break from the bustle of the city.

←

Pleasingly simple buildings at the Pavilhão Japonês in São Paulo

LANGUAGES OF BRAZIL

The official language of Brazil is Portuguese, but it is different in style, pronounciation, and vocabulary from the version spoken in Portugal. Brazil's Indigenous communities also have over 270 distinct languages and dialects, some of which have influenced Brazilian Portuguese. This is particularly true of the Tupí language, from which countless words and expressions, including place names, have been added to the nation's vocabulary.

African Roots

West African heritage is alive and kicking in Bahia. Sample deliciously spiced street food in Salvador (p258), or visit the Museu Afro-Brasileiro to learn more about Candomblé, a religious mix of African Spiritualism and Portuguese Catholicism. Time your visit to take in the religion's Festa da Boa Morte, held in Cachoeira (p283) in August.

←

A Baiana (traditionally dressed Bahian woman) selling tasty local street food in Salvador

Catholic Culture

Catholicism is Brazil's official religion, and Catholic churches are consequently found all over the country. Many of the ornate buildings are worth a visit; head to Oscar Niemeyer's Catedral Metropolitana Nossa Senhora Aparecida (p234) in the capital, or check out Recife's flashy and gorgeously ornamental Capela Dourada (p298).

↑ The soaring ceiling of Catedral Metropolitana Nossa Senhora Aparecida

A New Year's Eve Like No Other

Visitors to Brazil over New Year's Eve are in for a treat. It's a big affair - especially in Rio city, which throws its second-biggest party after Carnaval on Copacabana beach. The festivities attract over two million tourists and Cariocas dressed in white (for good luck), with live music performances and a spectacular midnight firework show (p61). Vai Tapajós music festival also provides an incredible end-of-year party, while locals in the know flock to Trancoso (p290) to celebrate at exclusive beach parties on Praia do Coqueiros.

→

Colorful fireworks exploding above Copacabana

BRAZIL FOR
NIGHTLIFE

Brazilians are world-famous party professionals. Samba nights in Rio, street parties in Salvador, clubbing in São Paulo, moon parties along the coast, or simply sharing a few bottles of ice-cold Skols: whatever the occasion, there's no shortage of fun to be had in Brazil.

A crowded bar in Leblon, ↑
bustling with locals
enjoying an evening out

Joie de Vivre, Brazilian-Style

Famously carefree and sociable, Brazilians epitomize the French expression for the exuberant enjoyment of life. This is especially evident in their love of dancing, with a huge range of clubs found in all major cities. Shimmy to traditional rhythms at the annual Festa de Reis festival in Laranjeiras (Sergipe), dance to forró at Natal's Rastapé (www.rastapecasade forro.com.br), try pagode music at São Paulo's Galleria Bar (https://galleriabar. com.br), or sway to samba at Rio's Leviano (www.leviano.com.br). There's also been a - literal - rise in rooftop bars across the country. Try Bar Obelisco (MAC, Ave Pedro Álvares Cabral 1301, São Paulo) for spectacular views and superb cocktails. Or relax at Rio's Bar dos Descasados (www.santateresahotel rio.com) with the city laid out below.

LGBTQ+ Friendly

In June São Paulo hosts the world's biggest Pride. The city's Rua Augusta has a great gay scene, with clubs such as Eagle *(Rua Augusta 620)* packed until late. In Rio, dance the night away at the Galeria Café *(galeriacafe. com.br)*, and in Porto Alegre, pop into intimate Porto Carioca *(www.porto cariocabar.com.br)*.

A performer on stage at the world's biggest Pride parade in São Paulo city

---

💬 INSIDER TIP
Party Like a Local

There a few things to bear in mind if you want to party with Brazilians. First and foremost, be fashionably late. House parties never start on time, so arrive at least an hour or two later than agreed. Secondly, dress up. There's no such thing as too fancy. And finally, dance! The locals pour their heart and soul into partying, so leave all inhibitions behind and do the same.

↑ Participants walking under a rainbow flag São Paulo's Pride parade

Amazing Art

In addition to big-hitters such as São Paulo's Pinacoteca and Museu da Arte, and Rio's Museu de Arte Moderna Fine Art and Museu Nacional de Belas Artes, Brazil's smaller towns also have thriving creative communities. Head to art hub Paraty *(p134)* for works by local artists at the Galeria Aecio Sarti, or exhibitions at Casa da Cultura. Rua do Amparo in Olinda *(p300)* is lined with galleries filled with colorful art by local painter Sérgio Vilanova. For folk art – the straw basketry is particularly good – stroll around Feira de Artesanato in Caldos do Jorro. Alternative Pirenópolis *(p238)* is filled with quirky artists' workshops, and Bahia is also a creative hub.

BRAZIL FOR
ARTS AND CRAFTS

Whether you want to get your hands on a handmade hammock, some state-of-the-art gold embellished jewellery, or intricate hand-carved wooden boxes, Brazil is the perfect place for high-quality handicrafts.

Shop the Fairs

São Paulo's art fairs are an excellent way to familiarize yourself with some of the country's premium designers. Museu Casa de Brasileira hosts a high-quality annual Christmas fair in collaboration with Mercado das Madalenas, while Feira Jardim Secreto prides itself on its small-scale sellers. In Rio's Ipanema, Feira Hippie is the place to be every Sunday to source handmade jewellery and beautiful local art.

Customers browsing the stalls at Feira Hippie in Rio

 INSIDER TIP
Shop Direct

There's no certification system in place when it comes to Indigenous arts and crafts, so for authentic products it is always best to buy your items directly from the maker, or via reliable sellers like Leo Rocha Arte Indígena. Another excellent retailer is the small shop in Pataxó village, 4 miles (6 km) from Caraíva (p288).

←
Brazilian artist Iza do Amparo working at her studio in Olinda

Independent Designers

Brazil's innovative fashion scene is bristling with cool designers. Floral fans should check out Patricia Bonaldi's label PatBO (www.patbo. com), which features colorful, romantic clothing; she has stores in Rio, São Paulo, and Belo Horizonte. Rio-based Frescobol Carioca (www. frescobolcarioca.com) makes casual cotton and linen loungewear perfect for hot and humid Carioca weather, and Adriana Degreas offers exclusive dresses and swimwear at her flagship São Paulo store (www.adrianadegreas.com). For beautiful jewellery, try Casa Mo, whose work can be found at pop-up markets in São Paulo.

→
Walking the catwalk in a floaty creation by Adriana Degreas

Indigenous Handicrafts

Brazil's Indigenous communities have passed on their skills from generation to generation. Shop for intricate wooden masks in Parintins or Kadiwéu ceramics in Bonito. One of Brazil's best fair trade shops is in Chapada Guimaraes: Leo Rocha Arte Indígena, where every handmade item, from hammocks to necklaces, is marked with the name of its maker and tribe.

←
Traditional Indigenous woven reed-and-grass baskets, delicately patterned

Gloriously costumed
dancers performing ↑
before a packed crowd

BRAZIL FOR
CARNAVAL

The colorful Brazilian Carnaval is a stunning spectacle, attracting millions
of visitors each year with its glittering costumes, rhythmic samba, and
all-night street parties. For those lucky enough to be in Brazil during
this time, here are the best ways to join the fun.

Off the Beaten Track

Glamorous Rio is undoubtedly the star
of the show, but Corumbá, Olinda, and
Salvador also offer astonishingly lively
Carnavals. Hit Olinda's cobblestoned
streets for the week-long festivities; watch
the *blocos* parade their huge puppets or
marvel at young *frevó* dancers. At the
Museu do Mamulengo *(p301),* strike a
pose with its wonderful giant dolls.

A street in Olinda, filled ↑
with festivalgoers
ready to celebrate

The Main Event

Carnaval in Rio is a once-in-a-lifetime experience: the biggest, most bombastic street party in the world. It draws an astonishing two million participants per day, with a televised parade from the Sambódromo (p98). Other festivities include cachaça- and beer-filled street parties that last for 24 hours straight, including the huge Cordão da Bola Preta parade in downtown Rio and the charmingly eccentric Bloco Céu Na Terra in Santa Teresa. Some start very early – many revellers have a beer in hand at 7am. For an extravagant take on Rio's Carnaval, there's a costume ball at the Belmond Copacabana Palace (p109) with an elegant dress code. Even when it's not Carnaval, the city still offers visitors a taste of it; take a tour of Cidade de Samba (p98) for dance shows and other revelry-related fun.

← Samba school dancers inside Rio's Sambódromo

TOP 4 KEY CARNAVAL TERMS

Batería
The percussion band – made up of only drummers – are the ones in charge of the beat of the parade.

Bloco
This refers to the neighborhood groups or bands that parade on the streets and get the crowds going.

Rainha de Bateria
An expert dancer, often a woman, performs the role of band leader. They dance samba in front of the drummers to motivate them.

Foliões
The partygoers who take part in Carnaval festivities – an excellent job for visitors!

💬 INSIDER TIP
Take Your Seat

Sambódromo seating is all unassigned except for Section 9, also called the "tourist section". If you want to sit among the locals, make sure you arrive early enough to grab a good seat.

Practice Makes Perfect

Preparations start months before the main event, with the country's samba schools beginning rehearsals in November. To learn some of the well-synchronized choreography, visit one of Rio's excellent schools, such as Portela and Mocidade. Have fun but don't joke around – the rehearsals are a joyful yet serious affair. Olinda's historic core hosts pre-Carnaval events, but with a more relaxed focus on the street parties.

↑ A twirling dancer practicing for the Carnaval in Rio

A YEAR IN
BRAZIL

JANUARY

Procissão dos Navegantes *(Jan 1)*. Decorated boats sail across the Baia de Ilha Grande.

△ **Lavagem do Bonfim** *(Jan)*. Salvador's second most popular festival (after Carnaval), blending Catholicism and Candomblé.

FEBRUARY

△ **Carnaval** *(early Feb)*. The country's biggest party, celebrated with parades and dancing.

Yemanjá *(Feb 2)*. In Salvador decorated boats carry gifts to the Candomblé Goddess of the Sea.

Festa Nacional da Uva *(Feb/Mar in even-numbered years)*. Grape festival, including a celebration of wine produced by Brazil's Italian immigrants.

MAY

△ **Festival Bananada** *(mid-May)*. A week-long festival that showcases rising musical talent.

Festa do Bembé do Mercado *(mid-May)*. A festival of traditional Bahian music and dance set up to mark the abolition of slavery in 1888.

Festa do Divino Espírito Santo *(May/Jun, 50 days after Easter Sunday)*. Based on the Pentecostal Advent of the Holy Spirit.

JUNE

△ **São Paulo Pride** *(early Jun)*. Running since 1997, this is one of the biggest such events in the world.

Festa Junina *(weekends throughout Jun)*. A Catholic festival commemorating the birth of saints Anthony (13 Jun), John (24 Jun), and Peter (29 Jun).

Bumba Meu Boi *(late Jun)*. A hugely popular festival based on a northern Brazilian legend about a bull.

SEPTEMBER

São Paulo Biennial *(early Sep in odd-numbered years)*. This art festival features works by leading artists from across Brazil and abroad.

XXXPERIENCE *(late Sep)*. A huge São Paulo electronica and house music dance festival.

△ **Rock in Rio** *(late Sep/early Oct)*. A massive rock festival, held in the Sambódromo.

OCTOBER

Oktoberfest *(mid-Oct)*. The world-famous celebration of German beer, music, and way of life.

São Paulo International Film Festival *(mid-Oct)*. View more than 300 films hosted across the city.

△ **Cirio de Nazaré** *(2nd Sun)*. One of the world's largest festivities honoring the Virgin Mary.

MARCH

△ **The Brazilian Grand Prix** (*late Mar/early Apr*). The Formula 1 car race held at São Paulo's Interlagos circuit attracts a mix of Paulistano celebs and petrolheads.

Lollapalooza Brazil (*3 days in late Mar*). Pop festival featuring major artists from around the globe; held at Interlagos, São Paulo race circuit.

Semana Santa (*Mar/Apr*). Religious celebration in Nova Jerusalém and Minas Gerais.

APRIL

Dia Índio (*Apr 19*). A nationwide day in honor of Brazil's Indigenous peoples, with educational events, music, dance, and art workshops.

△ **Hot-Air Balloon Festival** (*Easter week*). A spectacular annual hot-air balloon event that has been held in Torres since 1989.

Festa Nacional da Maçã (*Apr/May*). São Joaquim's national apple festival offers exhibitions of farm produce and livestock, as well as folk dancing, pop concerts, and parades on horseback.

JULY

Festival de Inverno (*Jul 1–30*). Held in Campos do Jordão, this is Latin America's most prestigious festival of classical music and jazz.

△ **Festival Literaria Internacional de Paraty** (*mid-Jul*). A major international literary festival, held in the historic port town of Paraty.

Festival Internacional da Dança (*2nd fortnight*). Huge dance festival in Joinville, Santa Catarina.

AUGUST

Festa da Nossa Senhora das Neves (*Aug 5*). Ten days of street celebrations in João Pessoa, marking the feast day of the city's patron saint.

△ **Festa do Peão de Boiadeiro** (*3rd Thu*). The world's largest rodeo event, receiving almost a million visitors over ten days.

Festival Gastronômico (*late Aug*). A ten-day food festival in Tiradentes, inspired by the rich and meaty cuisine of Minas Gerais.

NOVEMBER

△ **Padre Cícero Pilgrimage** (*Nov 2*). Every year, up to two million pilgrims flock to the statue of patron saint Padre Cícero in Paraíba, considered one of the most important religious sites in Latin America.

Feira Nacional de Artesanato (*late Nov/early Dec*). A major crafts fair with products from all across Brazil, held in Belo Horizonte.

Natal Luz (*late Oct–early Jan*). Christmas starts early in Gramado at this 60-day, family-focused festival.

DECEMBER

△ **Reveillon** (*Dec 31*). Live music by global popstars and an incredible firework display as Copacabana hosts the world's wildest beach party.

Yemanjá (*Dec 31*). Hundreds of devotees dressed in white take to the sea in Rio, symbolically jumping over seven waves to get closer to the Candomblé Goddess of the Sea and present offerings.

A BRIEF HISTORY

Home to the earliest peoples in South America, Brazil grew during its colonial era to become the center of the Portuguese empire. Although there is a persisting tendency towards political and social turbulence, today this vibrant country is one of the world's leading economies.

Pre-Columbian Brazil

The first inhabitants of Brazil migrated from North America and across the Pacific Ocean in several successive waves some 30,000 years ago. Some settled in the Amazon Basin, but many ventured up the Amazon river as far as the Andes, living off fish, plants, and animals. The middle Amazon region, around Santarém, was an important center for ceramic art and trading, home to thousands of seminomadic Indigenous people. Little archaeological evidence has survived of the earliest inhabitants of the area, but ceramic remains suggest the existence of complex Indigenous societies that lived in communal longhouses.

1 Map of South America from a Spanish atlas, 1582.

2 Thousands of years old rock painting made by Pre-Columbian peoples.

3 A European woodcut showing a group of feasting Tupinambás.

4 Engraving illustrating the Tupinambá.

Timeline of events

22000–9500 BCE
Migrations of the earliest humans take place in successive waves to the mid-Amazon region.

13000 BCE
Early hunting communities flourish near Pedra Furada, in Piauí state.

3000 BCE
Shell-mound sediment in Rio de Janeiro dated to this era is evidence of human activity, related to the Goitacá and Tamoio peoples.

c. 10000 BCE
Cave paintings in the Serra da Capivara National Park are dated to this period.

Initial Settlement

By the end of the 15th century BCE, more than five million Indigenous people had settled all around Brazil, traveling by dugout canoes down rivers and along the coast. Settlements contained thousands of inhabitants living in well-structured social groups. Despite sharing similar languages and customs, different communities often fought each other. Slash-and-burn farming was favored in the dense forests, where the heavy rainfall leached nutrients from the soil. Maize and manioc were the main crops cultivated, as these grew abundantly on the vast grasslands that were widespread in this late Ice Age era.

Community Life

As the migrants moved south across the country, some formed large groups, notably the Tupí-Guaraní and the Tupinambá. While the seminomadic Tupí-Guaraní lived off slash-and-burn farming, the Tupinambá settled on the northeast coast and cultivated crops. These communities also set up trade routes – up river or by sea – and traded items such as fruits, nuts, and feathers from the rainforest in exchange for gold jewelry, precious stones, and prized Spondylus oyster shells.

ANCIENT CAVE PAINTINGS

Established in 1979, the Parque Nacional de Serra da Capivara (p326) contains more than 300 archaeological sites. Several of these contain incredible rock paintings, tens of thousands of years old, made by the Pre-Columbian peoples. Evidence at one site, Pedra Furada, may even suggest that some Indigenous communities inhabited this area over 50,000 years ago.

300–500 CE
Slash-and-burn agriculture is widely practiced across the Amazon Basin.

1000 BCE
Prehistoric cultural developments in Marajó and Santarém are dated to this period.

500–1300
This is a period of major growth and expansion of Marajoara culture.

1000
Hierarchical societies of Indigenous peoples settle along the Amazon river.

The Arrival of the Europeans

Brazil's coastline was widely inhabited by the Tupinambá and other Indigenous communities when Spanish explorer Vicente Yáñez Pinzón landed on the northeastern shore on January 26, 1500. Limited by the Treaty of Tordesillas, he could not claim the "newfound" land for Spain. Signed in 1494 between Portugal and Spain, the treaty stated that all lands colonized west of a meridian near the Cape Verde Islands would belong to Spain, and all those east of this line would belong to Portugal. On April 23, 1500, Pedro Álvares Cabral landed in southern Bahia, marking the Portuguese arrival in Brazil and bolstering Portugal's position as a mercantile power rivaled only by Spain.

Colonization and Expansion

Colonial *donatários* – aristocrats and minor gentry – were expected to develop and govern the *capitanias*, or captaincies, on behalf of the Portuguese monarch, but they were met with adverse climatic conditions and strong opposition from the Indigenous peoples. In 1549, Portugal sent Tomé de Sousa as Brazil's first governor to protect the captaincies that survived these conflicts. The Tupinambá put up a particularly fierce

WHAT'S IN A NAME?

Officially, Brazil was named after *pau-brasil*, or brazilwood, a highly prized local tree. But this name, meaning "blessed land" in Gaelic, also appeared in the Irish legend about St. Brendan. It became part of European maritime folklore, designating an imagined land in the Atlantic. When Cabral found a new land in that general area, it is possible that he identified it with this Gaelic Brazil.

Timeline of events

1500
Portuguese explorer Pedro Álvares Cabral lands in Bahia, northeast Brazil.

1532
Sugarcane is first introduced to Brazil; it goes on to become a top cash crop.

1534
King João III divides the land into 15 *capitanias*, or captaincies.

c. 1538
The first enslaved Africans are shipped to Brazil to work on sugar plantations.

1549
Salvador is founded by Tomé de Sousa and becomes the first capital of Brazil.

resistance, but they and other Indigenous peoples were soon all but wiped out – either by the Portuguese, who employed divide-and-conquer tactics, or by the diseases they brought with them. Jesuit influence also accompanied this early period of colonization. The first Jesuits had arrived in 1549 and acquired power in Brazil through their influence at the Portuguese court. A zealous missionary movement began, aimed at converting the Indigenous groups.

Sugar and the Slave Trade

Portugal needed to fund its costly imperial wars with Spain, and sugar, introduced into Brazil in 1532, was quickly established as a lucrative product. Setting up his capital in Salvador, Tomé de Sousa enlisted the support of the Jesuits. The Indigenous people who did not convert to Christianity were enslaved and made to work in *engenhos* (sugar plantations) or in the wood trade. Many refused the forced labor, and many more died from introduced diseases. From the 1550s, plantation owners began importing enslaved people from Africa, with up to 15 million transported over the course of 300 years. Sugar soon became the base of the booming Brazilian economy.

1 Artwork showing Pedro Álvares Cabral.

2 Illustration depicting Tomé de Sousa, the first governor of Brazil.

3 A sketch depicting enslaved plantation workers carrying sugar into a mill.

Did You Know?

An estimated 1,500 languages were spoken across Brazil before the arrival of the Portuguese.

1554
Jesuits found São Paulo on 25 January, the Catholic feast day of the Conversion of Saint Paul.

1555
French forces establish a colony, France Antarctique, on Guanabara Bay.

1565
France Antarctique is destroyed and Rio de Janeiro is founded.

1595
The first Tupí language grammar is published by Jesuit missionary José de Anchieta.

Colonial Wars, Independence, and Empire

For the next 200 years, the Portuguese struggled to fend off Dutch and French forces. Boosted by the discovery of gold in the south and west, however, Portugal regained control of the whole country, and made Rio de Janeiro the new capital in 1763. The gold boom was followed by a rising clamor for independence initially led by Tiradentes, a leader of the Brazilian revolutionary movement known as Inconfidência Mineira. Brazil's independence was finally proclaimed on September 7, 1822, by Dom Pedro I, ruler of the new Brazilian empire.

From Dictatorship to Democracy

The introduction of coffee in the early 1800s triggered another economic boom, which in turn led to an upsurge in the slave trade. By the late 1800s, increasing political pressure called for this traffic to be stopped and on May 13, 1888, the government passed the Lei Aurea law, abolishing slavery. However, Afro-Brazilians still had no property or education, and struggled to find work after European immigrants replaced their labor, a detrimental legacy that is still felt to this day. Soon after slavery was abolished, the monarchy was overthrown by a military

1 Portrait of Dom Pedro I.

2 Brazilian President Juscelino Kubitschek touring the recently completed city of Brasília in 1961.

3 President Dilma Rousseff giving a speech following her re-election victory in 2014.

Did You Know?

Favelas are thought to have gained their name from the *favela* tree.

Timeline of events

1661
The Dutch formally withdraw from Portuguese territories.

1789
The Inconfidência Mineira uprising is quelled, and rebel leader Tiradentes is hanged.

1888
The Lei Aurea (Golden Law) is passed, abolishing slavery in Brazil.

1960
Brasília is inaugurated as the new capital of Brazil.

1985
Civilian Tancredo Neves is elected president, heralding the return of civilian rule.

coup supported by Brazil's coffee barons, paving the way for a long period of dictatorial rule, armed conflict, and political instability. In 1956, Juscelino Kubitschek was elected president and ushered Brazil into modernity, with his most notable legacy being the creation of the city Brasília. Mild structural reforms took place under president João Goulart (1961–64), but corporate elites sponsored another military coup in 1964, leading the country into an era of right-wing military rule. It was only in 1989 that democracy returned to Brazil and it emerged as a vibrant modern nation.

Brazil Today

As an economic superpower rich in mineral resources and with a large, well-educated workforce, Brazil has much to celebrate. And yet, political corruption is rife and drug-gang violence in its inner-city favelas reflects a considerable wealth gap. Outgoing president Jair Bolsonaro vowed to clean up Brazilian politics, but opponents criticized his hinted threats to repeal or relax laws protecting both the environment and Indigenous peoples. In response, in 2022, the electorate voted in the left-wing Luis Inácio "Lula" da Silva, who had previously served from 2003 to 2010.

THE AMAZON RAINFOREST FIRES

Thousands of wildfires swept across the southern Amazon in August 2022 with more than 31,000 alerts, the highest August outbreak since 2010. Most of these fires were caused by increased deforestation led by farmers trying to gain more farmland. Environmental groups such as the Rainforest Alliance are working to provide support to local communities fighting the fires.

2011

Dilma Rousseff becomes Brazil's first female president; she was impeached in 2016.

2014

Brazil hosts the FIFA World Cup.

2018

Jair Bolsonaro, a member of the extreme-right Partido Social Liberal (Social Liberal Party), is elected president.

2016

Rio de Janeiro city hosts the Olympics.

2022

The proliferation of forest wildfires in the Amazon Basin draws international attention.

EXPERIENCE
RIO DE JANEIRO

Sunbathing at Copacabana Beach

EXPLORE
RIO DE
JANEIRO

This guide divides Rio de Janeiro into four
color-coded sightseeing areas, as shown
on this map, plus an area containing sights
beyond the city center. Find out more
about each area on the following pages.

VASCO DA GAMA

BENFICA

SÃO CRISTÓVÃO

RUA FIGUEIRA DE M

Rio de Janeiro Zoological Garden

Maracanã

MARACANÃ

R. DR. SATAMINI

GRAJAÚ

ANDARAÍ

AV. ÉDISON PASSOS

Parque Nacional
da Tijuca

TIJUCA

USINA

Pedra do Sapo
1,150 ft (351 m)

AV. ÉDISON PASSOS

ALTO DA BOA VISTA

RUA JARDIM BOTÂNICO

AVENIDA BORGES DE MEDEIROS

LEBLON

AVEN

AV DELFIM MOREIRA

Praia do
Leblon

BRAZIL

NICARAGUA

COSTA RICA

PANAMA

VENEZUELA

COLOMBIA

GUYANA

SURINAME

FRENCH
GUIANA

Atlantic
Ocean

ECUADOR

PERU

Manaus

BRAZIL

Salvador

BOLIVIA

CHILE

PARAGUAY

São Paulo

RIO DE
JANEIRO

Pacific
Ocean

ARGENTINA

URUGUAY

Baía de
Guanabara

AVENIDA RODRIGUES ALVES

Morro
da Saúde

SANTO CRISTO

Museu do
Amanhã

Morro da
Conceição

Mosterio de
São Bento

AV FRANCISCO BICALHO

AVENIDA   PRESIDENTE   VARGAS

AVENIDA ENGENHEIRO FREYSSINET

Campo de
Santana

Sambódromo

CENTRO
p76

AV RIO BRANCO

CENTRO

Museu
Histórico
Nacional

Airport RJ
Santos Dumont

RIO
COMPRIDO

SANTA
TERESA

Catedral
Metropolitana

LAPA

Chácara do Céu

Parque do
Flamengo

RUA ITAPIRU

TÚNEL SANTA BÁRBARA

SANTA TERESA
AND LAPA
p92

Parque
Guinle

Baía de
Guanabara

LARANJEIRAS

RUA   DAS   LARANJEIRAS

RUA   PAISSANDU

AVENIDA INFANTE DOM HENRIQUE

FLAMENGO

Museu Carmen
Miranda

Morro Cara
de Cão

TÚNEL ANTÔNIO REBOUÇAS

FLAMENGO AND
BOTAFOGO
p112

Museu Casa de
Rui Barbosa

Enseada de
Botafogo

Praia de Urca

URCA

Praia
de
Fora

Morro do
Corcovado

RUA SÃO CLEMENTE

Museu do
Índio

TÚNEL DO PASMADO

Sugar Loaf
Mountain

△
Pão de Açúcar
1,299 ft (398 m)

Cristo
Redentor

RUA VOLUNTÁRIOS DA PÁTRIA

BOTAFOGO

Praia
Vermelha

AGOA

Morro de Saudade

Morro de São João

Morro de Babilônia

LEME

RUA SANTA CLARA

Praia do
Leme

IPANEMA AND
COPACABANA
p100

AVENIDA ATLÂNTICA

COPACABANA

agoa Rodrigo
de Freitas

PESSOA

Praia do
Copacabana

Atlantic Ocean

PITÁCIO

Morro do
Cantagalo

IPANEMA

VISCONDE DE PIRAJÁ

VIEIRA

SOUTO

aia do
anema

Praia do
Arpoador

Parque
Garota
de Ipanema

Praia do
Diablo

0 kilometers   1

0 miles   1

N
↑

GETTING TO KNOW
RIO DE JANEIRO

Sugar Loaf Mountain, Copacabana, Ipanema: iconic names that instantly conjure up Rio, the world's favorite party city with an infectious spirit. When your town is blessed with year-round sunshine, endless beaches, and steaming tropical forests, why wouldn't you be full of joie de vivre?

CENTRO

PAGE 78

Striking historical monuments and soaring office blocks line the wide boulevards of this former capital city, but duck down the atmospheric backstreets and you'll find traditional *boteco* bars, packed with office staff unwinding after work. One of Centro's most exciting features is its formerly rundown dockside, now redeveloped as the biggest urban regeneration project in Brazilian history. The rebranded Porto Maravilha has been transformed into a dazzling pedestrian-friendly waterfront district, with museums, galleries, open-air restaurants, palm-lined promenades, and leafy parks.

Best for
Historic and futuristic modern architecture, and city-center buzz.

Home to
Museu Nacional de Belas Artes, Praca XV de Novembro

Experience
Listening to Benedictine monks sing a mesmerizing Gregorian chant at the Mosteiro de São Bento

PAGE 92

SANTA TERESA AND LAPA

Straddling downtown Rio, these well-preserved old neighborhoods are linked by the Escadaria Selarón, a colorfully tiled stairway climbing from dockside Lapa up to hillside Santa Teresa. With its quietly aging mansions, Santa Teresa is an arty residential district, with an abundance of galleries, craft shops, boutique hotels, and gourmet restaurants. Lapa is one of Rio's hippest entertainment spots, with superb live-music venues, samba clubs, and *gafieiras* (local dance halls).

Best for
Charming local atmosphere, buzzing Lapa nightlife, and great hilltop views from Santa Teresa

Home to
Circo Voador, Rio Scenarium, Clube dos Democráticos, Chácara do Ceu, Parque das Ruínas

Experience
Riding a rattling bonde *tram up to Santa Teresa from downtown Rio, over the iconic white Arcos da Lapa*

PAGE 100

IPANEMA AND COPACABANA

Rio's most famous neighborhoods flank their – equally renowned – eponymous beaches. The gloriously wide sandy arc of Copacabana merges into Leme, and further west the contiguous Ipanema and Leblon beaches are topped by another landmark: the twin peaks of Dois Irmãos. Together, they form the main part of the beachside Zona Sul area, which has most of Rio's hotels, restaurants, shops, and entertainment venues. Ipanema and Leblon are more upscale and chic, while Copacabana is returning to its former glory.

Best for
People-watching and shopping in Ipanema

Home to
Praia de Copacabana, Praia de Ipanema

Experience
Applauding the sunset over Dois Irmãos alongside the locals

→

PAGE 112

FLAMENGO AND BOTAFOGO

These adjacent areas on Guanabara Bay are home to the iconic Sugar Loaf Mountain and the magnificent Cristo Redentor atop Morro do Corcovado. Aside from these main monuments, Flamengo and Botafogo offer travelers a more off-beat experience of the city. At the foot of Sugar Loaf is the sheltered Praia Vermelha, a popular local family beach. Good-value hotels and hostels pepper leafy Flamengo, whereas Botafogo features historic mansions, quirky bars, and museums.

Best for
Off-beat attractions, down-to-earth local vibe, and spacious bayside parks

Home to
Sugar Loaf Mountain, Morro do Corcovado, Cristo Redentor

Experience
Panoramic views across Rio's cityscape from Cristo Redentor on Morro do Corcovado

BEYOND THE CENTER

Rio has plenty of enticing attractions for visitors looking to explore further afield: surf-pounded beaches out west, a vast forest park wrapped around its steep mountainsides, and a beautiful islet-sprinkled bay. The western suburbs of Barra de Tijuca and São Conrado feel distinctly Westernized, with plush gated condos, giant shopping malls, and an Olympic-standard golf course. Across the water is Niterói, a proudly independent city, famous for its fish market and stunning modern art gallery designed like a UFO hovering over the sea.

Best for
Uncrowded beaches and peaceful forest trails

Home to
Prainha and Grumari beaches, Museu de Arte Contemporânea, Museu Casa do Pontal, Parque Natural Chico Mendes

Experience
Wandering around cool Niterói, pausing at the Museu de Arte Contemporânea to take in the enchanting view of Rio

CENTRO

Centro (downtown Rio), at the mouth of Guanabara Bay, is where the city was formally born in 1565. The area was once the realm of the Tupí peoples (notably the Temininós and Tupinambás), but most were killed within decades of the arrival of the Europeans by the newly introduced diseases that came with them.

The French landed first, in 1555, and established the colony of France Antarctique. Two years later, the Portuguese destroyed this settlement, laying the foundations of Rio city. Rio flourished as a port in the 17th century. The sugar trade was booming, and relied heavily on forced labor. With thousands of enslaved Africans shipped to Rio to be taken to plantations inland, the city became the largest slave port in the Americas. Gold and diamonds that were pouring out of Minas Gerais were also exported from Rio. The city received a further boost in 1763 when it superseded Salvador as the country's capital. Rio's significance was confirmed in 1808 when the Portuguese Royal Court moved to Brazil. Paço Imperial was built on Praça XV de Novembro as the residence of emperors Pedro I and Pedro II. Building continued on a grand scale, culminating with the Teatro Municipal in 1909.

In 1960 the national capital moved to Brasília, and in 1975 Rio city became the capital of Rio de Janeiro state. Despite the loss in status, Centro remains the city's historic core and financial district, headquarters to some of Brazil's largest firms, including the Brazilian Development Bank, Petrobras, and Vale.

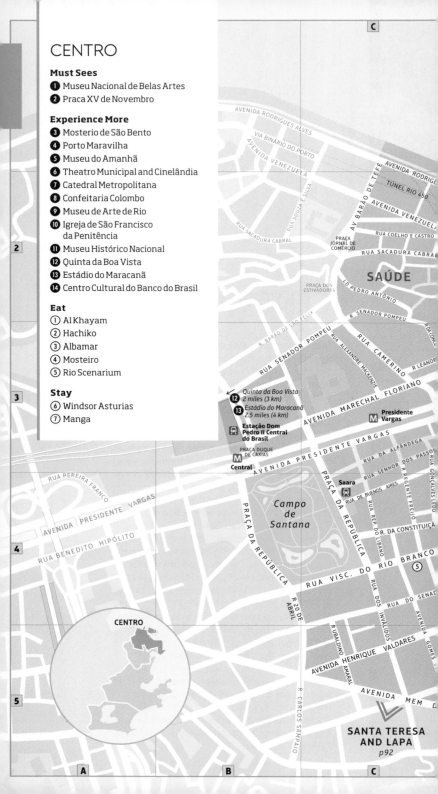

CENTRO

Must Sees

1. Museu Nacional de Belas Artes
2. Praca XV de Novembro

Experience More

3. Mosterio de São Bento
4. Porto Maravilha
5. Museu do Amanhã
6. Theatro Municipal and Cinelândia
7. Catedral Metropolitana
8. Confeitaria Colombo
9. Museu de Arte de Rio
10. Igreja de São Francisco da Penitência
11. Museu Histórico Nacional
12. Quinta da Boa Vista
13. Estádio do Maracanã
14. Centro Cultural do Banco do Brasil

Eat

1. Al Khayam
2. Hachiko
3. Albamar
4. Mosteiro
5. Rio Scenarium

Stay

6. Windsor Asturias
7. Manga

*Quinta da Boa Vista
2 miles (3 km)*

*Estádio do Maracanã
2.5 miles (4 km)*

Estação Dom
Pedro II Central
do Brasil

PRAÇA DUQUE
DE CAXIAS

Central

Presidente
Vargas

Saara

Campo
de
Santana

CENTRO

SANTA TERESA
AND LAPA
p92

❶ ⬆️ ⬆️

MUSEU NACIONAL DE BELAS ARTES

📍E4 🏠Av Rio Branco 199, Centro Ⓜ️Cinelândia 🕐10am-6pm Tue-Fri, 1-6pm Sat, Sun, & public hols (some rooms closed until late 2025) 🌐mnba.gov.br

Housing the most comprehensive collection of Brazilian art in the country, the National Museum of Fine Arts was established in 1937 in the former Brazilian Academy of Fine Arts building. The collection comprises close to 20,000 pieces, including fine, decorative, and popular art.

The National Museum of Fine Arts is one of Latin America's most important permanent art collections, featuring Brazilian artists from the colonial period and the 19th and 20th centuries. Artists include Frans Post, known for painting Brazilian landscapes in classical Dutch style; Jean Baptiste Debret, who painted the immortal *Battle of Guararapes* (1879); Vitor Meireles; and Pedro Américo, whose *A Batalha do Avaí* (1877) is one of the world's largest easel paintings. There is also an extensive collection of non-Brazilian works and a fine selection of 17th- and 18th-century Baroque Italian art. The museum was created from a prized art collection brought here from Europe by Portugal's King Dom João VI and his court when they fled Napoleon in 1808.

↑ The Renaissance-inspired facade of the Museu Nacional de Belas Artes

① The Museu Nacional de Belas Artes is housed in an ornate building that dates from 1908.

② The museum's galleries display thousands of pieces of art, including many sculptures.

③ Visitors admire artworks displayed in a gallery lit by skylights at the Museu Nacional de Belas Artes.

TOP 5 COLLECTION HIGHLIGHTS

The Sculpture Gallery
This striking corridor is lined with statues, including some by Rodin.

Pernambuco Landscapes
Some of the earliest Brazilian landscapes painted by 17th-century ex-pat artists, Frans Post among them.

Almeida's Arrufos
This 1887 painting by Belmiro de Almeida is considered his masterpiece.

European Engravings
An important archive of sketches and engravings, including some by Goya and Picasso.

Café by Portinari
An example of Social Realism by Cândido Portinari, one of Brazil's most influential Modernist painters.

2

PRAÇA XV DE NOVEMBRO

 E3 **M** Uruguaiana **⊟** 4 Estação de Barcas

Originally called the Largo do Paço, Praça XV de Novembro is the historic heart of Rio, and was once the center of Brazil's political and commercial power. Today, the square and the surrounding area are packed with historic buildings and streets. Restoration of Paço Imperial in the 1980s and renovation of Praça XV in 2016 have helped bring culture back to the city center.

①

Paço Imperial and Exhibition Galleries

 Praça XV de Novembro 48 **⊙** Noon–5pm Tue–Sat **W** amigosdopacoimperial. org.br

The Imperial Palace has been the backdrop for many key events in Brazilian history, including the signing of the Lei Aurea, or Golden Law, in 1888. This bill brought in the abolition of slavery in Brazil, and was greeted by widespread public celebrations.

The palace was built in 1743 as the seat of government and the governor's residence. Following the arrival of the Portuguese royal family in 1808, it became first the Paço Real (Royal Palace) and then the Paço Imperial in 1822, after the formation of the Brazilian Empire. Since 1985, the Paço Imperial has become a leading cultural center, with concerts, exhibitions, and workshops, as well as housing rare books in its Biblioteca Paulo Santos.

---

②

Casa França-Brasil

 Rua Visconde de Itaborai 78, Centro **⊙** 10am–5pm Tue–Sun **W** casafranca brasil.rj.gov.br

The Franco-Brazil Center was opened in 1990. This cultural center located in an 1820 customs house hosts exhibitions and events. Designed by the prominent French architect Grandjean de Montigny, it features an eclectic mix of Neo-Classical and Brazilian Baroque styles. Having played a range of roles, from bank archive to courthouse, today the center maintains the long-standing cultural links between France and Brazil.

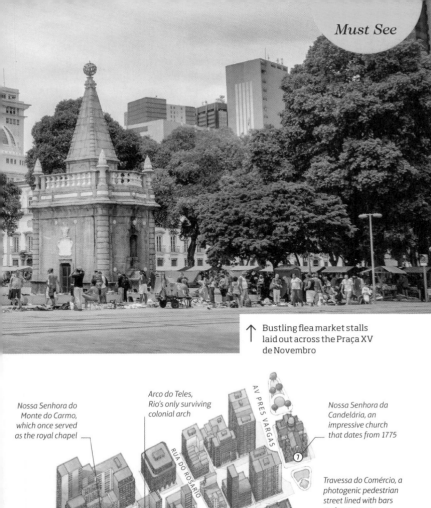

↑ Bustling flea market stalls laid out across the Praça XV de Novembro

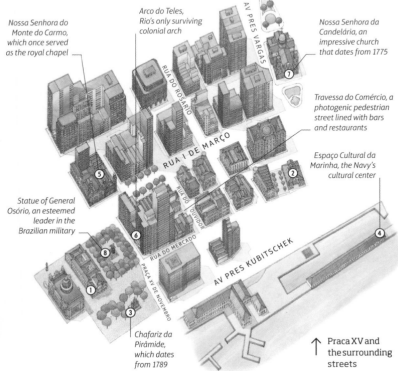

Nossa Senhora do Monte do Carmo, which once served as the royal chapel

Arco do Teles, Rio's only surviving colonial arch

AV PRES VARGAS

Nossa Senhora da Candelária, an impressive church that dates from 1775

⑦

RUA DO ROSÁRIO

Travessa do Comércio, a photogenic pedestrian street lined with bars and restaurants

RUA I DE MARÇO

Espaço Cultural da Marinha, the Navy's cultural center

⑤

②

Statue of General Osório, an esteemed leader in the Brazilian military

RUA DO OUVIDOR

④

⑥

⑧

RUA DO MERCADO

AV PRES KUBITSCHEK

①

PRAÇA XV DE NOVEMBRO

③

Chafariz da Pirâmide, which dates from 1789

↑ Praca XV and the surrounding streets

③ Chafariz da Pirâmide

The Chafariz da Pirâmide (Pyramid Fountain) was built in 1789 to distribute fresh water to the city and to visiting ships. It was designed by Mestre Valentim, one of the city's most important Baroque architects. The squat stone building is topped by a pyramid and stands in the center of Praca XV, in defiance of the soaring modern buildings that loom above it today. The water that used to flow from Rio Carioca into the shells at the fountain's base has long since dried up, but the monument remains one of the city's most respected landmarks.

Did You Know?

The submarine *Riachuelo* was built in the English town of Barrow, a major center for ship building.

The Espaço Cultural da Marinha, the Navy's cultural center, was inaugurated in 1996. Located in the old docks, the center is the starting point for tours of Baía de Guanabara.

④ Espaço Cultural da Marinha

📍 Avenida Alfredo Agache 20, Centro 📞 (21) 2532 5992 🕐 For renovation

The Espaço Cultural da Marinha, the Navy's cultural center, was inaugurated in 1996. Located in the old docks, the center is the starting point for boat tours of Baía de Guanabara. With its pastel blue-and-pink facade and delicate spires, the building stands out in the bay like a fairy-tale palace. It was built in 1889 by French architect Viollet-le-Duc, and originally inaugurated with a ball hosted by Emperor Dom Pedro II. Following major reconstruction work to downtown Rio for the 2016 Olympic Games, the site now also features the Museu Marítimo do Brasil.

⑤ Nossa Senhora do Monte do Carmo da Antiga Sé

📍 Rua Sete de Setembro 14 🕐 8:30am–3:30pm Mon–Fri, 9:30am–noon Sat & Sun 🌐 antigase.org

Once serving as the royal chapel, this was Rio's cathedral from 1808 until 1976, and is still sometimes called the Antiga Sé (Old Cathedral). The church was built in 1761 but renovated in Neo-Classical style in the early 19th century. It has witnessed many historic events, including the coronations of King Dom Joao VI in 1816, Dom Pedro I in 1822 and Dom Pedro II in 1841.

↓ The gilded interior of Nossa Senhora do Monte do Carmo da Antiga Sé

The wide Arco do Teles, which leads to a lively, cobblestoned area of the city

EAT

Al Khayam
This lively Middle Eastern restaurant offers a mouthwatering menu - try the delicious *kussa mehchie* (zucchini stuffed with rice and meat). There are also occasional belly-dancing shows.

◊ Rua do Ouvidor 16
◊ Sun ◊ alkhayam.com.br

$$$

Hachiko
Tucked away behind the Palácio Tiradentes, this Japanese restaurant serves superb fusion cuisine, including sashimis, sushis, and ceviches. Its tasting menu includes vegan options, and dishes for those with specific dietary requirements.

◊ Travessa do Paço 10
◊ Sun ◊ hachiko.com.br

$$$

 ⑥
Arco do Teles
Today a pedestrian walkway, the Arco do Teles dates from 1757 and is all that remains of the old Senate House that was destroyed by a fire in 1790. It is Rio's only surviving colonial arch. It now serves as the entrance to a network of old cobblestoned backstreets that are lined with bars and open-air cafés. Locals and visitors alike dive through the archway to escape the din of downtown and enjoy a cozy lunch or cool sundowner. Travessa do Comércio, just beyond the Arco, is a photogenic pedestrian street where Carmen Miranda lived as a small girl. The area is liveliest in the evening when the bars fill up.

⑦
Nossa Senhora da Candelária
◊ Praça Pio X, Centro
◊ (21) 2233 2324 ◊ 7:30am-4pm Mon-Fri, 8am-noon Sat, 9am-1pm Sun

Building of this church began in 1775 and was not completed until 1877. The impressive structure is modeled on Lisbon's Basilica da Estrela. A grand Italianate temple with a marbled interior shipped from Verona, Candelária has long been considered the church of choice for Rio's high society. Its name is thought to have derived from a chapel built in 1610 in homage to Our Lady of Candles, which stood on the same site.

⑧
Statue of General Osório
General Manuel Luís Osório defended the Brazilian Empire in the War of the Triple Alliance between 1864 and 1870. This large equestrian statue was erected in Praça XV in 1894 to honor Osório's military achievements, highlights of which are shown in relief on the stone plinth beneath. It was cast in France, of bronze smelted from enemy cannons used during the war. Osório (1808–1879) was born and brought up in Rio Grande do Sul, southern Brazil. His remains were once held within the plinth, but were returned to his birthplace in 1993.

The bronze statue of General Manuel Luís Osório

↑ The lavish gilded Baroque interior of the Mosteiro de São Bento

EXPERIENCE MORE

3

Mosteiro de São Bento

📍E2 🏠Rua Dom Gerardo 68 (entrance by elevator at No 40) Ⓜ Uruguaiana 🕐8am-6pm daily 🌐mosteirode saobentorio.org.br

Benedictine monks from Bahia founded São Bento in 1590. Named after the hills on which it is located, the monastery was built between 1617 and 1641; much of this historic edifice has remained structurally untouched since that time. The exterior of the main building reflects the simplicity of the time of its construction and gives no hint of the opulence of the Baroque interior.

A number of the works on display were carved by one of the monks, Frei Domingos da Conceição (1643–1718). They include the main altar of the monastery's church. The painting displayed on it, which was created around 1676, is dedicated to Nossa Senhora de Montserrat (the Black Virgin).

São Bento is still very much a working monastery. The Benedictine monks are protective of the complex and their work and have tried hard to prevent the church from becoming little more than a tourist attraction. As a result, many areas, such as the beautiful cloisters, remain out-of-bounds except on special occasions. Mass for the public is held daily at 5:15pm, with a full Gregorian chant at 8am on Saturdays, and at 10am on Sundays. Visitors should dress appropriately, with their knees and shoulders well covered, if they wish to view the interior of the monastery.

4

Porto Maravilha

📍D2 🏠Praça Mauá Ⓜ Carioca, Uruguaiana

As part of the preparations for the 2016 Olympics, Rio revamped its docks, now called Porto Maravilha (Port of Wonder), into a 2.1-mile (3.5-km) pedestrian boulevard named Orla Conde. This area used to be a slave-trading port during Brazil's period of colonial rule. Its regeneration unveiled numerous artifacts and ruins related to African heritage, now exhibited at Instituto Pretos Novos, which also offers tours covering the area's history. Also at the docks is AquaRio, South America's largest aquarium, with underwater tunnels offering views of over 350 marine species.

Instituto Pretos Novos
 🏠Rua Pedro Ernesto 32/34 🕐1-7pm Tue-Fri, 11am-2pm Sat 🌐pretos novos.com.br

Did You Know?

Porto Maravilha gained 10 miles (17 km) of cycle paths and 15,000 trees in 2016.

BOTECOS

The restaurants and bars that dot the city are called *botecos* or *botequins*. All are busy with waiters rushing around carrying light snacks and glasses of ice-cold beer. Rio's most famous are Bar Luíz (*www.barluiz.com.br*) and Garota de Ipanema (*https://bargarotade ipanema.com.br*).

AquaRio

 **Praça Muhammad Ali** **9am-6:30pm daily** **aquario marinhodorio.com.br**

5

Museu do Amanhã

D1 **Praça Mauá 1** **Uruguaiana** **10am-6pm Tue-Sun** **museu doamanha.org.br**

The Museum of Tomorrow is dedicated to science and technological advancements in building sustainable cities. Its interactive displays explore the impact of human beings on the fragile environment and on what the future holds.

The eco-efficient building, designed by Neo-Futurist Spanish architect Santiago Calatrava, is an impressive attraction in its own right. It's particularly worth seeing at night, when it is beautifully lit up. For the best views of this striking modern building, head just across the bay.

The museum is extremely popular and there are particularly long lines on weekends. Tickets must be booked online in advance (there is no ticket counter at the museum).

6

Theatro Municipal and Cinelândia

E4 **Av Rio Branco** **Cinelândia** **daily; tours: 4pm Wed-Fri (English-speaking guide available on Fri)** **theatro municipal.rj.gov.br**

Rio's Municipal Theater, built between 1905 and 1909 and inspired by the Opéra Garnier in Paris, is the city's main venue for ballet, opera, and orchestra (it includes the Municipal Symphony Orchestra of São Paulo), and attracts talent from both Brazil and abroad. It was renovated in the early 2010s; tours now include its picturesque inner stairway, a restaurant with Persian-style decor, and a snippet of ongoing rehearsals.

Farther south is the heart of Cinelândia or "cinema land," the area around which the city's movie houses sprang up in the 1920s. Many are still in operation, most notably the Cine Odeon BR which opened in 1926 and closed in 1999 to be renovated. It reopened a year later as the headquarters of the Rio Film Festival.

The opulent Theatro Municipal, inspired by Paris's Opéra Garnier ↓

❼
Catedral Metropolitana

📍D5 🚇Av República do Chile 245 Ⓜ Cinelândia
🕐7am-5pm daily
🌐catedral.com.br

Rio's striking Metropolitan Cathedral, with its truncated conical shape, was conceptualized by Ivo Calliari (1918–2005), a Catholic priest.

The cathedral's first stone was laid on January 20, 1964, and the inauguration of the still unfinished building was held 12 years later, in 1976, marking the 300th anniversary of the Diocese of Rio.

Standing 248 ft (75 m) high, with no interior columns, this huge cathedral has a seating capacity of 5,000 and can accommodate up to 20,000 people standing. The interior is dominated by four magnificent stained-glass windows that stretch 197 ft (60 m) to the ceiling. They represent the apostolic (yellow), Catholic (blue), ecclesiastical (green), and saintly (red) traditions.

The **Museu Arquidiocesano de Arte Sacra** (Sacred Art Museum) in the basement includes several historical items in its collection, such as the baptismal fonts used for christening the Brazilian royal family, the golden rose gifted to Princess Isabel

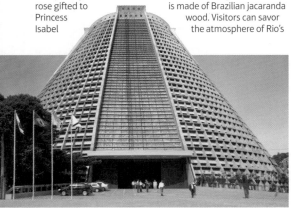

↑ The pyramidal Modernist exterior of the Catedral Metropolitana, designed by Edgar Fonseca

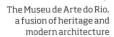

→ The Museu de Arte do Rio, a fusion of heritage and modern architecture

by Pope Leo XIII to celebrate her signing the Lei Aurea, the law that abolished slavery, and the throne of Dom Pedro II.

Museu Arquidiocesano de Arte Sacra
🕐9am-noon & 1-4pm Wed, 9am-noon Sat & Sun

❽
Confeitaria Colombo

📍D4 🏠Rua Gonçalves Dias 32 Ⓜ Carioca 🕐11am-6pm Mon- Fri, 10am-6pm Sat
🌐confeitariacolombo.com.br

A Rio institution, the famous Colombo Tearoom dates from 1894 and remains a wonderful mix of Art Nouveau and belle époque. Located in what was then the very heart of Rio, it was a meeting point for intellectuals, artists, and politicians. Regulars included politician Ruy Barbosa, former president Getúlio Vargas, and composer Heitor Villa-Lobos.

The tearoom's mirrors were shipped in from Belgium and its marble from Italy, while much of its original furniture is made of Brazilian jacaranda wood. Visitors can savor the atmosphere of Rio's past by eating a snack in the serene Bar Jardim, or enjoying a meal at the restaurant.

❾
Museu de Arte do Rio

📍D2 Ⓜ Uruguaiana
🏠Praça Mauá 5
🕐10:30am-5pm Thu-Sun
🌐museudeartedorio.org.br

The Rio Museum of Art displays works illustrating the history, life, landscape and social fabric of the city of Rio de Janeiro.

The museum is strikingly housed in a heritage-listed palace, formerly known as Dom João VI, which has been creatively fused with the more modern exterior of the city's former bus station

The exhibits are arranged by theme over four floors, and feature art ranging from the Baroque period through to 20th-century Modernists. The museum also hosts regular temporary exhibitions.

Visitors should head up to the sixth floor to enjoy wonderful views over the bay.

Igreja de São Francisco da Penitência

📍 D2 🏠 Largo de Carioca 5 Ⓜ Carioca ⏰ 9am-4pm Mon-Fri, 9am-noon Sat; museum: 9am-3pm Tue-Fri 🌐 saofranciscodapenitencia.org.br

The church of São Francisco da Penitência is considered one of the richest and most beautiful examples of Baroque art in Brazil. Built between 1657 and 1772, the church exhibits various works of the Portuguese artist Francisco Xavier de Brito. His art heavily influenced the Brazilian artist Aleijadinho (p192).

One of the highlights of the church is the 1738 painting of the glorification of St. Francis by Caetano da Costa Coelho, which was the first Brazilian painting to be done in perspective.

Museu Histórico Nacional

📍 F4 🏠 Praça Marechal Âncora Ⓜ Cinelândia ⏰ 10am-5pm Wed-Fri, 1-5pm Sat, Sun & public hols 🌐 mhn.museus.gov.br

Founded in 1922, Brazil's leading history museum recounts the country's story up to 1889, including its colonial past. Its collection is a real mix of items: see paintings and period furniture, admire coins and carriages, and gaze at 19th-century firearms, locomotives and rarities such as the pen used by Princess Isabel to sign the Lei Aurea decree that abolished slavery in Brazil in 1888. The museum building itself is one of the oldest in Rio.

EAT

Albamar

Set in the last surviving tower of the old Municipal Market, this seafood restaurant offers a fine view of Guanabara Bay.

📍 F3 🏠 Praca Marechal Ancora 184 🌐 novoalbamar.com.br

$$$

Mosteiro

Named after the São Bento monastery, this restaurant specializes in *bacalhau* (salt cod).

📍 D2 🏠 Rua São Bento 13 📞 (21) 2233 6478

$$$

Rio Scenarium

This vast restaurant and live music venue is housed in a quirky vintage furniture depot.

📍 C4 🏠 Rua do Lavradio 20 🕐 Sun-Tue 🌐 rioscenarium.com.br

$$$

> **The church of São Francisco da Penitência is considered one of the richest and most beautiful examples of Baroque art in Brazil.**

STAY

Windsor Asturias

Housed in a 1930s building, this good business hotel offers unfussy rooms and a rooftop terrace with lovely views.

E5 Rua Senador Dantas 14 windsorhoteis.com

$$$

Manga

This hostel is well located for sightseeing and close to the metro for Ipanema and Copacabana beaches.

D5 Rua do Lavradio 186 (21) 2509 5201

$$$

12

Quinta da Boa Vista

B3 Av Pedro II (between Rua Almirante Baltazar & Rua Dom Meinrdo, São Cristóvão) São Cristóvão 6am-5pm daily

The Quinta da Boa Vista, the landscaped grounds of a former royal estate, includes the **Museu Nacional** and the **BioParque do Rio** (Rio Zoo). Founded by Dom João VI in 1818, the Museu Nacional is the country's oldest scientific institution. Its permanent exhibits covered a variety of fields from archaeology, biodiversity, and botany to ethnology, geology, and palaeontology. It suffered a terrible fire in September 2018 in which much of the collection was tragically lost. The museum's gardens and the former royal palace are an attraction in their own right, and their lakes and grottos are very popular with Cariocas on the weekends.

The BioParque do Rio is considered one of the best in the world and is Brazil's oldest zoo, having been founded in 1888. It is home to approximately 140 species and more than 1,000 animals, including one of the most complete collections of Brazilian mammals and butterflies. Particular highlights include the Brazilian monkeys and birds. It reopened in 2020 after a major renovation, with fewer animals and a "cage-free" design.

Museu Nacional

Until 2027 museunacional.ufrj.br

BioParque do Rio

9am-5pm daily riozoo.com.br

Did You Know?

The zoo's decorative main gates were a gift from the second Duke of Northumberland.

Brazil playing Peru at the Estádio do Maracanã in the Copa América final in 2019 ↑

→ The beautiful dome of Rio's Centro Cultural do Banco do Brasil

Estádio do Maracanã

 B3 Rua Prof Eurico Rabelo (gate 18), Maracanã Maracanã Daily tourmaracana.com.br

Rio's Maracanã Stadium is one of the world's most famous soccer grounds. It is also the largest in Brazil, hosting over 78,000 spectators. The stadium, which was refurbished for the 2007 Pan-American Games, was built for the 1950 World Cup and inaugurated with a game between Rio and São Paulo.The first game played by the Brazilian team took place on June 24, 1950, with Brazil beating Mexico 4–0. A month later, Brazil played Uruguay in the final and lost 2–1, thus starting its eternal soccer rivalry with Uruguay. The stadium fell into disrepair after the 2016 Olympic Games.

It has now reopened and can be visited on a tour. On match days the last tour finishes three hours before kick-off.

Centro Cultural do Banco do Brasil

E2 Rua Primeiro de Março 66 Carioca 9am-9pm Mon & Wed-Sat, 9am-8pm Sun bb.com.br/cultura

Located in an impressive building dating from 1880 in what used to be Rio's financial quarter, the Centro Cultural do Banco do Brasil (CCBB) was originally the headquarters for the Trade Association and the Bank of Brazil. In 1989 it was converted into a major cultural center with three theaters, four exhibition rooms, a cinema, a large public library, and a bookstore. Many of the center's events are free to attend.

The building itself is worth a visit, with its imposing columns, rotunda (the old trading floor), marbled lobby, and grand staircases.

SANTA TERESA AND LAPA

In the 18th century, the boundaries of downtown Rio began to expand south into Lapa, which was marshland at the time, and west into the hills, and the growing city saw a great spurt of construction: the church of Our Lady of Gloria was built in 1739 close to the bay; the Arcos da Lapa aqueduct was finished in 1750; the Santa Teresa Convent, which gave its name to the hills on which it stood, was built in the 1750s; and the Passeio Público, Rio's first public park, opened in 1783.

In the 19th century, Santa Teresa flourished as a refined neighborhood favored by Rio's colonial upper classes. Escaping downtown's pestilential heat, they built elegant mansions on its hillsides, cooled by the fresh forest air. In 1877 the Santa Teresa *bonde* (tram) made its debut, incorporating the old aqueduct and linking the district to Centro; the tram is still running today.

In its early days, harborside Lapa was notorious for its gambling houses and red-light district. Latterly, it was also the haunt of writers, artists, and politicians, who added an intellectual flair to the bawdy scene. By the mid-20th century, though, both neighborhoods had fallen on hard times. A makeover in the 1990s transformed Lapa into an alternative playground and Rio's hippest nightlife zone, with its rundown warehouses repurposed as samba clubs, dance halls, and bistros. In contrast, Santa Teresa has preserved much of its original 19th-century architecture and is now home to galleries and art studios. Linking the two neighborhoods is artist Jorge Selarón's famous staircase, the vibrantly tiled Escadaria Selarón.

SANTA TERESA AND LAPA

Experience
1. Bondinho de Santa Teresa
2. Chácara do Céu
3. Largo dos Guimarães
4. Escadaria Selarón
5. Museu de Arte Moderna (MAM)
6. Sambódromo
7. Ingreja Nossa Senhora da Glória do Outeiro

Eat
1. Espirito Santa

Drink
2. Armazem Sao Thiago

D

RUA URUGUAIANA

AVENIDA PASSOS

RUA DA CARIOCA

Igreja da São
Francisco da Penitência

Igreja Santo
Antônio

AVENIDA REP. DO CHILE

AV REPÚBLICA DO PARAGUAI

Catedral
Metropolitana
de São Sebastião

R DOS ARCOS

NDE

Arcos da Lapa

R SILVIO ROMERO

Convento
de Santa
Teresa

Escadaria
Selarón ❹

rque
s Ruínas

ARROS

R CASSIANO

R HER
DE

MENEGILDO
DE BARROS

SANTA
TERESA

R BENJAMIN
CONSTANT

R DO FIALHO

SANTA CRISTINA

RUA SANTO AMARO

E

LARGO DA
CARIOCA

Carioca Ⓜ Ⓡ

RUA SENADOR DANTAS

AV EVARISTO DA VEGA

❶ Bondinho
de Santa
Teresa

Ⓡ Ⓜ
Cinelândia

Teatro
Mesbla

R DO PASSEIO

PRAÇA
DO
MONROE

PRAÇA
CARD.
CÂMARA

Passeio
Público

R TEIXEIRA
DE FREITA

PRAÇA
DEODORO

RUA JOAQUIM SILVA

RUA T.
REGADAS

ESCADARIA
SELARÓN

R PINTO
MARTINS

R GONÇ
FONTES

LADEIRA
TAYLOR

LD. DE STA. TERESA

LAPA

RUA DE LAPA

R CONDE LAGES

RUA HERMENEGILDO DE BARROS

RUA CÂNDIDO MENDES

AVENIDA AUGUSTO SEVERO

PRAÇA
PARIS

RUA DA GLÓRIA

Glória Ⓜ   LARGO
PAULA
CÂNDIDO

GLÓRIA

RUA DO CATETE

RUA ANTÔNIO MENDES CAMPOS

LD. DA GLÓRIA

❼
Ingreja Nossa
Senhora da
Gloria do
Outeiro

PRAÇA LUÍS
DE CAMÕES

Memorial
Getúlio Vargas

RUA RUSSEL

RUA SILVEIRA MARTINS

Museu da
Republica

Catete Ⓜ

**FLAMENGO AND
BOTAFOGO**
p112

F

SANTA TERESA
AND LAPA

TREVO DOS
ESTUDANTES

RUA JARDEL JERCOLIS

❺

Museu de Arte
Moderna (MAM)

AVENIDA INFANTE DOM HENRIQUE

*Enseada
da Glória*

Monumento Nacional
aos Mortos da II
Guerra Mundial

*Parque do
Flamengo*

AV INFANTE DOM HENRIQUE

*Marina
da Glória*

PRAIA DO FLAMENGO

AVENIDA INFANTE DOM HENRIQUE

PRAIA DO FLAMENGO

0 meters   500
0 yards   500

N
↑

6

7

8

9

10

EXPERIENCE

EXPERIENCE Santa Teresa and Lapa

1

Bondinho de Santa Teresa

📍D7 🚏Estação Carioca, Av Rio Branco 156 Ⓜ Carioca 🕐8am-5pm Mon-Fri, 9am-5pm Sat, 9am-4pm Sun 🌐bondesdesantateresa.rj.gov.br

Restored to their original yellow painted livery, these historic wooden trams wind and wobble their way through the twisting streets of Santa Teresa. Known as *bondes*, they date back to 1859, when they were the first trams to serve Rio.

Today, powered by electric cables overhead, the open-sided *bondes* travel from downtown Carioca, across the iconic Arcos viaduct. The tiny **Museu do Bonde** in Santa Teresa has model trams and other related memorabilia.

Museu do Bonde

🏛Centro Cultural Laurinda Santos Lobo, Rua Monte Alegre 306, Santa Teresa 🕐Until further notice

 GREAT VIEW
Parque das Ruínas

The Parque das Ruínas is one of Santa Teresa's highest points; from here a stunning view stretches across the city center to Sugar Loaf Mountain, Guanabara Bay, and Corcovado.

2

Chácara do Céu

📍C8 🏛Rua Murtinho Nobre 93, Santa Teresa 🕐Noon-5pm Wed-Mon 🌐museuscastromaya.com.br

Perched on a quiet hilltop, this Modernist mansion was the home of industrialist and art collector Raimondo Ottoni de Castro Maya (1894–1968). Today, it houses one of the finest private collections of modern art in Rio. Period furniture, sculptures, and paintings by leading Brazilian

artists, such as Cândido Portinari and Eliseu Visconti, are displayed alongside works by famous international names. The gardens, designed by landscape architect Roberto Burle Marx, offer fantastic views over the rooftops.

3

Largo dos Guimarães

📍C9 🚏Estação Largo dos Guimarães, junction of Rua Paschoal Carlos Magno & Rua Almirante Alexandrino Ⓜ Glória

This little square in the heart of Santa Teresa is the social hub of the neighborhood and the main stop for the *bonde* tram from downtown Carioca. The elegantly fading colonial buildings flanking the square house art galleries, craft shops, and a tiny art house cinema. The whole area comes alive during Carnaval, with its own street parties and parade; even the *bondes* are decorated and rock to the samba rhythm.

↑ Beautifully restored tram making its way through Santa Teresa

4
Escadaria Selarón

 D8 🏠 Rua Manuel Carneiro Ⓜ Cinelândia

These steps leading up to Santa Teresa from Lapa were transformed into a colorful artwork by Chilean-born artist Jorge Selarón (1947–2013). From his tiny workshop halfway up, Selarón laid some 2,000 ceramic tiles and mirrors, illustrated with an eccentric mix of designs. The iconic steps, which are a popular photo spot for visitors, provide a shortcut to the Santa Teresa Convent.

↑ The colored steps of Jorge Selarón's Escadaria Selarón

5
Museu de Arte Moderna (MAM)

 F7 🏠 Av Infante Dom Henrique 85 Ⓜ Cinelândia 🕙 10am–6pm Thu–Sat, 11am–6pm Sun 🖥 mam.rio

Rio's Modern Art Museum (MAM) has one of the best collections of 20th-century art in Brazil, surpassed only by MASP in São Paulo (p162). It also houses one of the largest archives of Brazilian films.

The museum was far ahead of its time in its design and architecture when it was built in 1958, with a striking Postmodern glass-fronted and concrete exterior. In 1978, a fire destroyed many of its unique exhibits, including the works of Miró, Picasso, Salvador Dalí, Max Ernst, and René Magritte. It has taken time and the generosity of collectors in Brazil and abroad to rebuild the collection. Today, the MAM is once more a highly regarded institution, not only for its own archive but also for its globally-acclaimed, visiting exhibitions.

Located close to its gardens is a monument to the victims of World War II. In 1980, it was here that Pope John Paul II said mass to a crowd of more than two million people.

EAT

Espirito Santa
A local favorite, this restaurant specializes in Amazonian cuisine. Its menu features fusions of rainforest fruits, vegetables, and fish.

 C8 🏠 Rua Almirante Alexandrino 264, Santa Teresa

$$$

DRINK

Armazem Sao Thiago
Also known as Bar do Gomes in honor of its previous owner, this long standing drinking hole, located in a converted warehouse, is one of the best *botecos* in town, serving up great-value *feijoada* and an extensive array of nibbles and tipples since 1919.

 B9 🏠 Rua Áurea 26, Santa Teresa 🕙 Mon 🖥 armazemsaothiago. com.br

$$$

CARNAVAL IN RIO

One of the world's most spectacular festivals, Carnaval is celebrated all over Brazil, but the festivities in Rio are justly famous, unmatched for their sheer scale and splendor. Falling in February or early March, Carnaval is full of parties, upscale balls, and the famed samba parade.

SAMBA SCHOOLS

These large social clubs are found in Rio's poorer neighborhoods, often linked to the local favelas. Mangueira, one of the most prominent schools, was founded in 1928, and Portela, which began in 1923, has won the most Carnaval titles. Many top schools date from the 1940s and 1950s, while Grande Rio formed as late as 1988.

GIANT PUPPETS

Spectacular, enormous puppets are put together to decorate the floats and fascinating costumes are created for the parade participants. Carnaval is a non-stop industry so its talented craftspeople work all year round. Their elaborate designs can be seen at close quarters in the Cidade de Samba in downtown Rio.

PARTY-LOVING CARIOCAS

Carnaval is linked to the calendar of the Catholic Church. Traditionally, it is the last celebration of excess and joy before the austerity and fasting of the Lenten period. Today, Carnaval is considered more important than any other event, including Christmas and New Year. This week-long holiday for partying around the clock symbolizes the end of summer.

THE SAMBA PARADE

Rio's main samba schools showcase their talents at the famous parade, each with around 2,500 *passistas* (dancers) and at least 200 in the *bateria* (percussion section). Schools choose a theme and perform a complex series of dance steps as they move along the parade route, flaunting their elaborately designed float, puppets, and costumes.

↑ Unidos da Tijuca samba school *passistas* performing in the Carnaval parade

↑ Carnaval dancers from the Caprichosos samba school parade at the Sambódromo

⑥ Sambódromo

 A7 📍 Av Marquês de Sapucaí Ⓜ Praça XI ⏰ 9am-4pm Mon-Fri 🗓 Partially Dec-Carnaval 🌐 sambadrome.com

The Sambódromo, also known as the Passarela do Samba, is where Rio's famous samba schools parade each February during the city's Carnaval.

Before Carnaval was as popular as it is today, samba schools simply paraded through the streets and spectators stood on the sidewalk, and later, on specially built stands, to admire the spectacle. As the crowds continued to grow exponentially, the disruption caused by the building of the stands each year meant another solution was needed.

The renowned Brazilian architect, Oscar Niemeyer, came up with the idea for the Sambódromo, an area which accommodates 60,000 people and was inaugurated in time for the 1984 Carnaval.

In order to complement the city's Sambódromo, a large complex, known as the **Cidade do Samba** (City of Samba), was established in 2005. This space is used by the city's main samba schools to build their floats and make their vibrant costumes. Throughout the year, visitors are allowed to enter the building to watch samba schools prepare for Carnaval and see how a samba school puts on its parade. Bear in mind that the schedules vary depending on the time of year.

Cidade do Samba
📍 Rua Rivadávia Correa 60, Gamboa 🌐 cidadedosambarj.globo.com

> INSIDER TIP
> **Plan Ahead**
>
> Make the most of your Carnaval experience by planning ahead. Each *bloco* (neighborhood group) has its own vibe, from booming and boisterous to low-key and chilled. Do your research and find which one suits you. Hotels and hostels offer shuttles to party locations across the city.

⑦ Igreja Nossa Senhora da Glória do Outeiro

 E9 📍 Praça Nossa Senhora da Glória 135, Glória Ⓜ Glória ⏰ 9am-noon & 1-4pm Mon-Fri, 9am-noon Sat & Sun 🌐 outeirodagloria.org.br

The beautiful octagonal church of Our Lady of Gloria sits majestically on top of a hill beside the freeways that cut through Flamengo Park. The spot where the church was built, in 1714, was first used as a place of worship in 1608, when the image of Our Lady was placed in a grotto.

The church, which was completed in 1739, became the favorite place of worship for Dom Pedro VI and his family after their arrival from Portugal in 1808. It is known for its hand-painted tiles dating from the 1730s.

The church can be reached by car, by foot up the steps known as Ladeira de Nossa Senhora, or by cable car from Rua do Russel 312. There are bay views, as well as a small sacred art museum (same hours but closed Monday).

IPANEMA AND COPACABANA

Once the realm of the Indigenous Tupinambá people (Tamoios), the mesmerizing beaches of Ipanema and Copacabana were initially ignored by the first European residents of Rio. In the years after the arrival of the Europeans, most of the Tupinambás died from exposure to introduced diseases or moved inland, and the beaches slowly started to be inhabited by a handful of Portuguese fishers and sugarcane farmers. In the 17th century, a chapel dedicated to Our Lady of Copacabana – the patron saint of Bolivia – was built on Copacabana beach, lending its name to the whole district. Ipanema beach was named for the area's main landowner, José Antonio Moreira Filho, Baron of Ipanema, which was then part of São Paulo state.

The development of Copacabana began in earnest after the completion of the Túnel Alaor Prata (better known today as Tunel Velho, meaning "Old Tunnel") in 1892. The tunnel made the beaches easily accessible from downtown Rio, and the first tram line reached Ipanema in 1902. Sea bathing became fashionable during World War I, with the seaside promenade of Avenida Atlântica being inaugurated in 1919 and the lavish Copacabana Palace hotel following four years later. In 1922 the area was rocked by the Eighteen of the Copacabana Fort military revolt, but this was quickly suppressed by the authorities. By the time the "The Girl from Ipanema" achieved global superstardom four decades later, the area had already become one of Rio's trendiest, synonymous with sea, sun, and sand.

IPANEMA AND COPACABANA

Must Sees
1. Praia de Copacabana
2. Praia de Ipanema

Experience More
3. Jardim Botânico
4. Jockey Club Brasileiro
5. Praia de Leblon
6. Forte de Copacabana
7. Feira Hippie de Ipanema
8. Museu da Imagem e do Som
9. Museu da Favela
10. Praia de Arpoador
11. Lagoa Rodrigo de Freitas

Eat
1. Sud, O Pássaro Verde Café
2. Alvaro's

Drink
3. Espetto Carioca
4. Cabanna
5. Gavea Beach Club

Stay
6. Belmond Copacabana Palace

FLAMENGO AND BOTAFOGO
p112

BOTAFOGO

AVENIDA PASTEUR

Morro da Babilônia

LEME

RUA 19 DE FEVEREIRO
RUA GENERAL POLIDORO
R ARNALDO QUINTELA
RUA ALVARO RAMOS
AV. LAURO SODRÉ
IN VENCESLAU BRÁS

RUA PINHEIRO GUIMARÃES
RUA GENERAL POLIDORO
R. DR. SAMPAIO CORREIA

Morro da
Saudade

Morro de São João

Parque da
Chacrinha

Túnel Novo

RUA GUSTAVO SAMPAIO
AVENIDA ATLÂNTICA
*Praia
do Leme*

R EUCLIDES DA ROCHA
Túnel Velho

**Cardeal
Arcoverde** Ⓜ

PRAÇA
CARDEAL
ARCOVERDE

LADEIRA DO LEME
RUA BARATA REBEIRO
AV. PRINCESA ISABEL

RUA SIQUEIRA CAMPOS
RUA FIGUEIREDO DE MAGALHÃES

**Siqueira
Campos** Ⓜ

RUA TONELERO
RUA PAULA FREITAS
RUA R MIN. VIVEIROS DE CASTRO
RUA R RODOLFO DANTAS

Ⓘ ⑤

RUA SANTA CLARA

s Cabritos

Túnel Major Vaz

COPACABANA

AVENIDA ATLÂNTICA

⑥

④

③

COPACABANA

RUA POMPEU LOUREIRO
R CONSTANTE RAMOS
RUA BARATA RIBEIRO
RUA LEOPOLDO MIGUEL
NOSSA SENHORA DE
AVENIDA ATLÂNTICA

**① Praia de
Copacabana**

antagalo Ⓜ

ENRIQUE
OSWORTH

ntagalo

Túnel Pref. Sá
Fr. Alvim

RUA SÁ FERREIRA

**General
Osório** Ⓜ

RUA FRANCISCO SÁ
RUA RAUL POMPÉIA

⑧ **Museu da
Imagem e da Som**

ÊS CARNEIRO
R BULHÕES CARVALHO
AINHA ELIZABETH
R JOAQUIM NABUCO
AV FRANCISCO BHERING
R FRANCISCO OTAVIANO

**Forte de
Copacabana**

⑥

*Ponta de
Copacabana*

*Atlantic
Ocean*

*Parque
Garota de
Ipanema*

*Praia
do Diabo*

⑩
**Praia de
Arpoador**

0 meters   800
0 yards   800

N
↑

**IPANEMA AND
COPACABANA**

16

17

18

19

❶ 🍴 🍽 🛍

PRAIA DE COPACABANA

📍E17 Ⓜ Siqueira Campos ℹ Av Princesa Isabel 183; (21) 2298 7890

One of the world's most celebrated beaches, Copacabana stretches from Morro do Leme in the northeast to Arpoador in the southwest. Popular all year round, it is especially famed for its New Year's Eve celebrations.

The iconic Copacabana is at the center of Rio life for both locals and visitors. Along with more tranquil Leme, the beach makes up a magnificent 3-mile (5-km) stretch of sand from the Hilton Copacabana in the north to the Forte de Copacabana in the south. Once remote, it became easily accessible in 1892, when a tunnel was cut through from Botafogo, but its popularity skyrocketed when the Neo-Classical Copacabana Palace was opened in 1923; this grand hotel continues to draw the rich and famous even today. Pause for a snack at the popular beachfront kiosks, admire the catch of the day at the *posto de pescadores* (fishers' post), or – when you tire of the beach – visit the Forte de Copacabana.

WHAT'S IN A NAME?

The name Copacabana is believed by scholars to derive from the Andean fertility god, Kotakawana, whose temple stood on the shores of Lake Titicaca. When Christianity came to the area in the 16th century, a basilica in honor of Our Lady of Copacabana was built on the site of the temple. In the 17th century, sailors who credited her with saving them from shipwreck built a chapel dedicated to her in Rio, near Arpoador Rock. This chapel gave the area and beach their name. The Forte de Copacabana has since been built at this site, and offers sweeping views of the bay.

Did You Know?

In 2013, Pope Francis said a mass at Praia de Copacabana, attracting three million worshipers.

1 Copacabana's wavy mosaic promenade was designed by Roberto Burle Marx, one of the most famous landscape architects in Brazil.

2 Beach volleyball is popular at Copacabana, with many nets lining the sands.

3 On New Year's Eve the area becomes Rio's spiritual and festive heart, with millions of people flocking to the beach to party, watch the fireworks, and honor Yemanjá, Goddess of the Sea.

↑ Copacabana beach, still dotted with beachgoers as the sun dips low in the sky

DRINK

Rio's beach kiosks are popular with locals, who take the bare minimum onto the sand. Most kiosks are open late every day, serving ice-cold drinks at parasol-shaded tables.

Espetto Carioca
📍E17 🏠Avenida Atlântica, Praia de Leme
📞(21) 3228 6748

Cabanna
📍E17 🏠Avenida Atlântica, Praia de Copacabana
📞(21) 99339 8851

Gavea Beach Club
📍F17 🏠Avenida Pref. Mendes de Moraes KS4A & B 📞(21) 9437 5275

Did You Know?

Every evening here, as the sun goes down behind Dois Irmãos, residents toast "the best sunset in Rio."

2 🍴 🖥 🛍

PRAIA DE IPANEMA

📍 **C18** Ⓜ **General Osório, Nossa Senhora da Paz**

A long stretch of sun-soaked white sand, framed by the twin peaks of Dois Irmãos, Ipanema is one of Rio's most beautiful and chic beaches. Set behind the beach is a glamorous, boutique-lined neighborhood that is a popular base for visitors to the city.

Almost as well known as Copacabana *(p104)*, Ipanema shot into the limelight in the 1960s with the globally famous song by Antônio Jobim and Vinícius de Moraes, "The Girl from Ipanema". The name of this fashionable area is credited to the Indigenous Tupí-Guaraní people, who called it Y-panema or "rough water." The area started becoming a residential hub around 1884, and today it is considered one of the most desirable places to live in Rio.

←

Crowds of locals gathered at Arpoador to watch the spectacular sinking sun

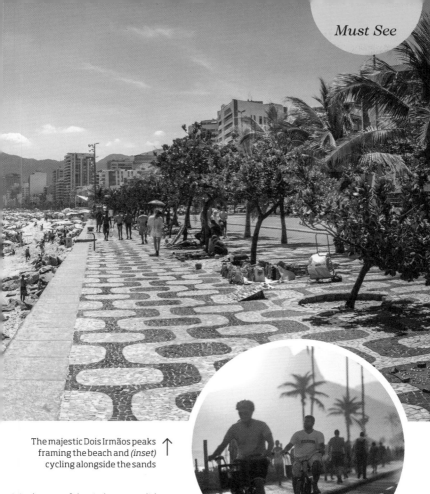

The majestic Dois Irmãos peaks framing the beach and *(inset)* cycling alongside the sands

It is also one of the city's most stylish neighborhoods, with its back streets featuring chic boutiques, bars, restaurants, and nightclubs. Avenida Vieira Souto is the most prestigious address in Rio, while running parallel, two streets back, is Rua Visconde de Pirajá, Ipanema's main shopping area. At the Copacabana end of the street is Praça General Osório, the public square that plays host every Sunday to the city's popular Feira Hippie de Ipanema, or Hippie Fair *(p109)*, a part of local life since it began in 1968.

The mile-long stretch of Ipanema beach runs from Leblon in the west to Arpoador in the east. Arpoador extends the beach by another half-mile (1 km), and is popular with the surf set, while the rock next to it is a great spot to watch the sunset.

THE GIRL FROM IPANEMA

One of the most played in popular music history, the bossa nova song "The Girl from Ipanema" was written in 1962 by Antônio Carlos Jobim and Vinícius de Moraes. In 1964, Stan Getz, Jobim, and the Gilbertos took bossa nova to a global audience with the release of *Getz/Gilberto*. With "The Girl from Ipanema" as the opening track, the album ultimately won four Grammys.

The name of this fashionable area is credited to the Indigenous Tupí-Guaraní people, who called it Y-panema, or "rough water."

←
A fountain in the
lush grounds of Rio's
Jardim Botânico

spectacular settings of any racecourse in the world. Races are held all year round, so it is easy to catch the action. The biggest race of the year – and one of South America's most important – is the Grande Prêmio Brasil do Turfe, first run in 1933. It traditionally takes place every June.

5

Praia de Leblon

Q A18 **M** Jardim de Alah, Antero de Quental **🚌** Av Atlantica/Rua Hilario Gouvea; (21) 2547 4421; open 8am-6pm

For many years, Praia de Leblon sat in the shadow of Praia de Ipanema, but today it is considered just as fashionable and desirable as its neighbor, with perhaps an even greater density and mix of bars, clubs, and restaurants. Rua Dias Ferreira, at the most westerly point, has a particularly eclectic mix. Like Ipanema, there are only a few hotels along the beachfront, Avenida Delfim Moreira.

While the beaches of Copacabana and Leme flow seamlessly into each other, Leblon and Ipanema are separated by Jardim de Alah and the canal that links the Lagoa Rodrigo de Freitas with the sea.

EXPERIENCE MORE

3

Jardim Botânico

Q A17 **🏠** Rua Jardim Botânico 920 & 1008, Gávea **🕐** 8am-5pm daily **🚪** Jan 1 & Dec 25 **🌐** jbrj.eleven tickets.com

Rio's Jardim Botânico was founded in 1808 by the Prince Regent, Dom João VI. Originally meant to acclimatize plants and spices coming from Asia, it later became the Royal Garden and opened to the public in 1822. Among its many illustrious visitors were Charles Darwin in 1832 and Albert Einstein in 1925.

Today, Jardim Botânico includes an area of natural rainforest, and is home to many species of plants, as well as innumerable types of birds and animals. The garden's signature is the 200 imperial palms that line its main avenues.

4

Jockey Club Brasileiro

Q A17 **🏠** Rua Jardim Botânico 1003, Gávea **M** Botafogo **🚌** **🕐** 5-11pm Mon & Tue, 2-8pm Sun; races: 5pm Mon & Tue, 2pm Sun **🌐** jcb.com.br

With a great view of the Lagoa Rodrigo de Freitas and the Corcovado mountain, the Brazilian Jockey Club undoubtedly has one of the most

6

Forte de Copacabana

Q D19 **🏠** Av Atlântica Posto 6 **🕐** 10am-6pm Tue-Sun (entry free on Tue) **🌐** fortedecopacabana. com.br

The name Copacabana, believed to have its origins in Quechua, an ancient

> Today, Jardim Botânico includes an area of natural rainforest, and is home to many species of plants, as well as innumerable types of birds and animals.

language still spoken in Peru, was given by the Incas to a site by Lake Titicaca, where they built a temple. In the 17th century, the captain of a Spanish galleon erected a chapel in honor of Our Lady of Copacabana, who he claimed came to his aid during a shipwreck. Built in 1914, on the promontory of the chapel as Rio's defense against attack, the Forte de Copacabana offers scenic views of the entire sweep of Copacabana.

7

Feira Hippie de Ipanema

C18 **Praça General Osório** **M General Osório, Nossa Senhora da Paz** **9am–6pm Sun**

At the Copacabana end of Rua Visconde de Pirajá is Praça General Osório, the public square that plays host to Rio's popular **Feira Hippie de Ipanema** (Hippie Fair), every Sunday. The fair has been a part of life in Ipanema and Rio since opening in 1968.

There is certainly plenty of overpriced bric-a-brac on sale here, but it is possible to find the occasional gem. In particular, look for models of Rocinha houses made of wood or papier mâché, and for rope sculptures made by a favela artist. In addition to crafts, other stalls at this central Ipanema market sell an array of household items and clothes.

8

Museu da Imagem e do Som

D19 **Av Atlântica 3432** **Hours vary, check website** **mis.rj.gov.br**

The Museum of Image and Sound places an emphasis on the history of Brazilian music and film. The modern, eight-story building is due to open at the end of 2023 and will feature a state-of-the-art collection of films, sound recordings, and photographs of leading figures in Brazilian culture.

EAT

Sud, O Pássaro Verde Café

Superb restaurant with one of Brazil's top chefs, Roberta Sudbrack.

B16 **Rua Visconde de Carandaí 35** **21 3114 0464**

$\$$$$$$$\$$

Alvaro's

This traditional restaurant serves the best *feijoada* in Rio.

A18 **500 Av Ataulfo de Paiva, Leblon** **alvaros.com.br**

$\$$$$$$$\$$

STAY

Belmond Copacabana Palace

This luxury Art Deco hotel offers grand suites and ocean views – great for a special treat.

E17 **Av Atlantica 1702** **belmond.com**

$\$$$$$$$\$$

← Shoppers browsing artistic offerings at the Feira Hippie de Ipanema

Museu da Favela

C18 Rua Nossa Senhora de Fátima 7, Cantagalo General Osório Tours: Mon & Thu (times vary, check website) museudefavela.org

Based in the Cantagalo and Pavão-Pavãozinho favelas, overlooking Ipanema, the Museu da Favela (MUF) is a living museum run by and about its residents. A range of guided tours are offered, allowing visitors to explore the favelas' narrow, winding streets, look at graffiti art, and learn about the daily lives of some of Rio's citizens. Nearby the MUF, forested areas can be visited, as well as workshops and a store selling favela-made handicrafts.

Praia de Arpoador

D18 Ipanema General Osório

This beach around the rocky headland at the southern end of Copacabana features cafés, coconut stalls, and juice bars. Arpoador extends the Ipanema beach by half a mile, and strong waves make it particularly popular with surfers. The large rock next to the beach is a great spot from which to watch the sunset.

Lagoa Rodrigo de Freitas

B17 Lagoa Jardim de Alah

The picturesque Lagoa Rodrigo de Freitas, or Lagoa (lagoon) as it is often called, sits at the foot of Corcovado peak and separates the Serra da Carioca from Ipanema and Leblon. A full circuit of the lagoon is about 5 miles (8 km) and is popular with joggers and cyclists. There are plenty of places to stop en route, with kiosks selling everything from coconut water to full meals. Some even offer live music in the evenings. The lagoon is also bordered by more conventional restaurants and bars, especially along the Ipanema stretch.

Several sports clubs are located here. Among the most famous are the Jóquei Clube Brasileiro (p108), the **Sociedade Hípica Brasileira**, the city's main equestrian center, and the headquarters of the Clube de Regatas do Flamengo. Flamengo, along

Did You Know?

Every year, the world's largest artificial Christmas tree is set up on a pontoon on Lagoa Rodrigo de Freitas.

with Botafogo, Vasco da Gama, and Fluminense, is one of Brazil's top soccer teams and has won the National and South American titles on many occasions. All these clubs also have rowing divisions as the lagoon is Brazil's main rowing center. Several international regattas have been held here. Visitors can explore the area by boat, as *pedallos* and other craft are available for rent. It is also possible to hire bicycles.

The nearby **Fundação Eva Klabin** is one of Rio's prolific cultural centers and museums. Its exhibits are part of the private collection of Eva Klabin, whose family made a fortune in paper in the 20th century.

Also around the lagoon, the scenic **Parque da Catacumba** is interspersed with sculptures by artists Roberto Moriconi, Bruno Giorgi, and Caribé. Views over Ipanema and the lagoon can be glimpsed, as well as a roaming monkey or two.

Sociedade Hípica Brasileira

Av Borges de Medeiros 2448 (21) 2156 0156 Only for events shb.com.br

Fundação Eva Klabin

Av Epitácio Pessoa 2480 Tours: 2 & 4pm Tue-Sun evaklabin.org.br

Parque da Catacumba

Av Epitácio Pessoa 3000 (21) 2247 9949 8am-5pm Tue-Sun (summer: to 6pm)

Dawn at Praia de Arpoador, an extension of Praia de Ipanema

↑ Colorful buildings in the hillside favela of Pavao Pavaozinho in Copacabana

RIO'S FAVELAS

Rio has about 1,000 favelas - areas of informal, often precarious urbanization, most of which lack basic services. What started as a handful of shacks on a hillside has quickly grown into a series of cities in their own right, each as much a part of the landscape as Corcovado and Sugar Loaf.

SPRAWLING CITIES

Estimates suggest that about 20 per cent of the city's population may now live in favelas. The inhabitants of these colorful urban areas mostly have low-wage jobs in wealthier areas, while some make a living from small local businesses. Some of the favelas have grown into giant communities, such as Rocinha in São Conrado, with about 200,000 residents. Others, such as Pavão, Cantagalo, Vidigal, and Chapéu Mangueira, occupy hilly Zona Sul areas offering breathtaking views.

↑ Children sitting on the steps at the entrance to the Santa Marta favela

TOURING FAVELAS

Favelas are complex and vibrant communities. Many have drug lords who run *bocas de fumo*, where narcotics are sold. This practice has been reduced since the mid-2000s, but not completely. It is still advisable to visit these areas as part of a guided tour. Favela Tour *(www.favelatour. com.br)* is run by Marcelo Armstrong, who was brought up in an apartment block adjoining the Vila Canoas favela. He has been guiding visitors around Vila Canoas and Rocinha since 1992. Brazilidade *(call (21) 98871 1228)* in Santa Marta is run by local resident Sheila Souza. Revenue from her tours is reinvested in the community.

↑ Young Brazilians looking at an art installation depicting a favela

FLAMENGO AND BOTAFOGO

As Rio expanded south in the early 19th century, merchants and bankers started to build mansions in the largely uninhabited areas of Flamengo and nearby Botafogo – the Indigenous peoples whose homelands these were had long since been displaced. In 1838 horse-drawn buses began running between Centro and these two new districts, bringing further growth and development. Flamengo's Palácio do Catete was completed in 1867, serving as Brazil's presidential palace between 1897 and 1960; it is now the Museu da República. Posh rowing clubs were established in Botafogo in 1894 and in Flamengo a year later – these would turn into two of Brazil's most successful football clubs in 1904 and 1912 respectively. The area's tourist potential was realized early on: a rack railway to Corcovado's summit was opened in 1884, a cable car was built on Sugar Loaf Mountain in 1912, and the now iconic Cristo Redentor statue was constructed between 1922 and 1931.

By the mid-20th century, many Cariocas had moved from older parts of the city to Flamengo and Botafogo, with the pleasant new neighborhoods soon filling up. In response, the Aterro was built in Flamengo in 1965, a broad strip of land around the peninsula that was the first of several landfill schemes designed to give the expanding city much-needed gardens and recreational space. Today, both districts remain relatively wealthy residential areas, with mansions and apartments lining tree-shaded avenues.

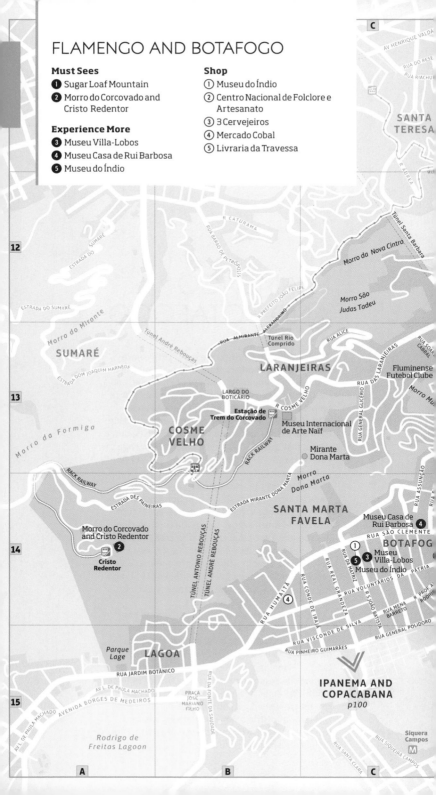

FLAMENGO AND BOTAFOGO

Must Sees
1. Sugar Loaf Mountain
2. Morro do Corcovado and Cristo Redentor

Experience More
3. Museu Villa-Lobos
4. Museu Casa de Rui Barbosa
5. Museu do Índio

Shop
1. Museu do Índio
2. Centro Nacional de Folclore e Artesanato
3. 3 Cervejeiros
4. Mercado Cobal
5. Livraria da Travessa

C
AV HENRIQUE VALDA
RUA DO RESE
RUA RIACHU

SANTA TERESA

R CATURAMA
Túnel Santa Barbara
Morro da Nova Cintra

12
ESTRADA DO SUMARÉ
R BARÃO DE PETRÓPOLIS
R PREFEITO JOÃO FELIPE
Morro São Judas Tadeu

ESTRADA DO SUMARÉ
Túnel André Rebouças
RUA ALMIRANTE ALEXANDRINO
Túnel Rio Comprido
RUA ALICE
RUA SOAN CABRAL

Morro do Mirante
SUMARÉ
ESTRADA DOM JOAQUIM MARNEDE
LARANJEIRAS
RUA DAS LARANJEIRAS
Fluminense Futebol Clube
Morro Mu

13
Morro da Formiga
LARGO DO BOTICÁRIO
Estação de Trem do Corcovado
R COSME VELHO
Museu Internacional de Arte Naïf
RUA GENERAL GLICÉRIO

COSME VELHO
RACK RAILWAY
Mirante Dona Marta

RACK RAILWAY
ESTRADA DES PAINEIRAS
ESTRADA MIRANTE DONA MARTA
Morro Dona Marta
RUA ASSUNÇÃO
RIB

SANTA MARTA FAVELA
Museu Casa de Rui Barbosa 4

14
Morro do Corcovado and Cristo Redentor 2
Cristo Redentor
TÚNEL ANTONIO REBOUÇAS
TÚNEL ANDRÉ REBOUÇAS
RUA SÃO CLEMENTE
BOTAFOG
1 Museu Villa-Lobos
5 3
Museu do Índio
RUA VOLUNTÁRIOS DA PÁTRIA
R PROF A RODRIG

RUA DA MATRIZ
RUA REAL GRANDEZA
RUA MENA BARRETO

RUA HUMAITÁ
RUA CONDE DE IRAJÁ
RUA S JOÃO BATISTA
4

Parque Lage
LAGOA
RUA VISCONDE DE SILVA
RUA GENERAL POLIDORO

RUA JARDIM BOTÂNICO
RUA PINHEIRO GUIMARÃES

AV L DE PAULA MACHADO
PRAÇA JOSÉ MARIANO FILHO
RUA DA FONTE DA SAUDADE

15
AV L DE PAULA MACHADO
AVENIDA BORGES DE MEDEIROS
IPANEMA AND COPACABANA
p100

Rodrigo de Freitas Lagoon
Siquera Campos
RUA SQUEIRA CAMPOS
RUA SANTA CLARA

A
B
C

D
LAPA
RUA JOAQUIM
RUA MIURTINHO
RUA DE LAPA
AVENIDA AUGUSTO SEVERO
Glória Ⓜ
R BENJAMIN CONSTANT

SANTA TERESA
AND LAPA
p92

RUA BENTO LISBOA
CATETE
RUA SILVEIRA MARTINS
Ⓜ ②
Catete
Oi Futuro
Flamengo
Largo do Ⓜ
Machado
Castelinho do
Flamengo
RUA DAS LARANJEIRAS
RUA CONDE DE BAEPENDI
arque
Guinle
RUA IPIRANGA
R BARÃO DO FLAMENGO
③
RUA PAISSANDU
PINHEIRO MACHADO
Flamengo Ⓜ
RUA PAULO VI
RUA MARQUÊS DE ABRANTES
RUA SEN. VERGUEIRO
Casa de Arte e Cultura
Julieta de Serpa
FLAMENGO
AV OSVALDO CRUZ
AVENIDA RUI BARBOSA
Museu Carmen
Miranda

D

Ⓜ🚇
Cinelândia
AVENIDA PRES. WILSON

E
PRAÇA
SENADOR
SALGADO
FILHO

*Enseada
da Glória*

AVENIDA INFANTE DOM HENRIQUE

*Parque do
Flamengo*

Museu de
Folclore
Edison Carneiro

*Baía de
Guanabara*

AVENIDA INFANTE DOM HENRIQUE

*Praia do
Flamengo*

E

F

FLAMENGO AND
BOTAFOGO

| 0 meters | 800 |
| 0 yards | 800 |
N ↑

11

12

13

*Morro Cara
de Cão*

Fortaleza de
São João

AVENIDA JOÃO LUIS ALVES

URCA

*Praia de
Fora*

AV SÃO SEBASTIÃO

*Praia de
Urca*

Sugar Loaf
Mountain
❶

*Pão de Açúcar
1,299 ft (398 m)*

14

*Praia de
Botafogo*

*Enseada de
Botafogo*

AVENIDA DAS NAÇÕES UNIDAS
PRAIA DO BOTAFOGO
PRAÇA
PIMENTEL
DUARTE
otafogo

Tunel do
Pasamedo
AVENIDA PASTEUR
AV VENCESLAU BRAS
AVENIDA LAURO SODRE
RUA LAURO MULLER

AVENIDA PORTUGAL
R RAMON FRANCO

Morro da Urca

🔎
🔎
ℹ️
🔎

*Praia
Vermelha*

ALVARO RAMOS
rro de São João

Túnel
Novo
Morro da Babilônia

Cardeal
Arcoverde Ⓜ
RUA BARATA REBEIRO
LADEIRA DO LEME
AV PRINCESA ISABEL
LEME
RUA GUSTAVO SAMPAIO
AVENIDA ATLÂNTICA
COPACABANA
ℹ️ *Praia
do Leme*

Forte Duque
de Caxias
*Ponta do
Leme*

Morro do Leme

15

D

E

F

❶ 🗺 🍴 🛍

SUGAR LOAF MOUNTAIN

📍F14 📍Av Pasteur 520, Praia Vermelha, Urca 🚌107, 513, Circular 1, Circular 2 🚠From Praia Vermelha 🕐9am–7pm (last cable car at 6:30pm) 🌐bondinho.com.br

None of Rio's magnificent views are more breathtaking than those from the top of the 1,312-ft (400-m) granite and quartz Pão de Açúcar (Sugar Loaf), which looms at the mouth of Guanabara Bay.

From the summit of the monolithic Sugar Loaf, it is easy to see how early explorers mistakenly believed that they had sailed into the mouth of a great river, which they named "January River", or Rio de Janeiro. The Sugar Loaf experience takes in two mountains, Morro do Urca and Pão de Açúcar (Sugar Loaf). It is possible to scale both mountains via organized rock climbs on most weekends. Demanding less effort, the cable car, originally opened in 1912, stops at the 705-ft- (224-m-) high Morro da Urca before ascending to the summit. At the top, winding trails meander through shady forests to a number of lookout points – visit early in the day or after rain for the best views.

↑ A rock climber tackling one of the sheer routes up the side of Sugar Loaf

Did You Know?

British nanny Henrietta Carstairs made the first recorded solo ascent of Sugar Loaf in 1817.

JAMES BOND'S MOONRAKER

In 1979, Sugar Loaf and its cable car formed the backdrop for a main action sequence in the James Bond film *Moonraker*, starring Roger Moore. During filming, the Great Train Robber, Ronald Biggs, was kidnapped by a group of British mercenaries in 1981 near the mountain's cable car station. The kidnappers had posed as members of the film's production crew, luring Biggs in by offering him a cameo in the movie.

The smooth Sugar Loaf has become a popular rock-climbing spot, with over 60 known routes to the top.

The summit offers unforgettable views out over Copacabana, Ipanema, and the scenic Corcovado and Tijuca.

The cable car carries as many as 1,360 passengers every hour.

↑ A cable car ascending steadily to the towering summit of Sugar Loaf mountain

→
The city of Rio, laid out beneath Corcovado mountain and its statue

2

MORRO DO CORCOVADO AND CRISTO REDENTOR

📍 A14 🚠 Morro do Corcovado 🚉 Cosme Velho station: open 8am–5pm Mon–Fri, 8am–6pm Sat & Sun (trains depart every 20 min) 🚌 117, 422, 583 & 584, then official Paineiras Corcovado shuttle van 🚐 ℹ️ Corcovado: corcovado.com.br, paineirascorcovado.com.br

The iconic Cristo Redentor (Christ the Redeemer) watches over Rio de Janeiro from the hulking Corcovado mountain. The journey to Christ's feet, through the streets of Cosme Velho and the Parque Nacional da Tijuca *(p126)*, is as rewarding as the panorama from the summit.

The 2,316-ft (706-m) Corcovado mountain derives its name from *corcova* (hunchback), which describes the physical appearance of the mountain itself. On the summit, the iconic Cristo Redentor statue towers over Rio. It is Brazil's most recognizable landmark, and was the winning design in a competition for a monument that would represent the spirit of the city. Officially inaugurated in 1931 to mark the centenary of Brazil's independence, the enormous statue sits in the center of the tropical jungle of Parque Nacional da Tijuca (which contains the world's largest urban forest).

↑ Passengers boarding the cog train that takes visitors up the mountainside

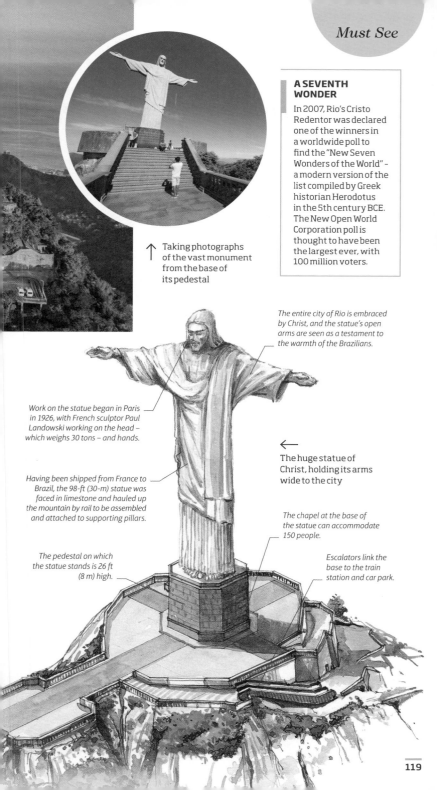

↑ Taking photographs of the vast monument from the base of its pedestal

A SEVENTH WONDER

In 2007, Rio's Cristo Redentor was declared one of the winners in a worldwide poll to find the "New Seven Wonders of the World" – a modern version of the list compiled by Greek historian Herodotus in the 5th century BCE. The New Open World Corporation poll is thought to have been the largest ever, with 100 million voters.

The entire city of Rio is embraced by Christ, and the statue's open arms are seen as a testament to the warmth of the Brazilians.

Work on the statue began in Paris in 1926, with French sculptor Paul Landowski working on the head – which weighs 30 tons – and hands.

← The huge statue of Christ, holding its arms wide to the city

Having been shipped from France to Brazil, the 98-ft (30-m) statue was faced in limestone and hauled up the mountain by rail to be assembled and attached to supporting pillars.

The chapel at the base of the statue can accommodate 150 people.

The pedestal on which the statue stands is 26 ft (8 m) high.

Escalators link the base to the train station and car park.

EXPERIENCE MORE

3

Museu Villa-Lobos

C14 Rua Sorocaba 200, Botafogo Botafogo
10am-5pm Mon-Fri
museuvillalobos.museus.gov.br

Famed for his extensive and varied repertoire, Heitor Villa-Lobos (1897–1959) is considered one of the greatest composers in Latin America. Some think that it was through his work that Brazilian music first became popular abroad, eventually gaining universal appeal with the advent of bossa nova (p125).

Villa-Lobos's best-known work is his cycle of the nine *Bachianas Brasileiras*, which pays homage to both Bach and Brazilian folk music. Such was his versatility that he wrote a variety of music, from *choros* (an upbeat waltz or polka), concertos, symphonies, and orchestral works to chamber music, operas, and ballets, as well as a number of

> ## 1,000
> The number of compositions credited to Villa-Lobos.

guitar and solo piano pieces. The Villa-Lobos Museum, which moved to a stately 19th-century mansion in Botafogo in 1986, houses an extensive collection of musical instruments. It also has 2,300 pieces of sheet music that range from Villa-Lobos's original compositions to arrangements of his pieces by other composers. The museum is also home to an extensive audiovisual archive, thousands of personal photographs and items of correspondence, and household items such as games and utensils that give a glimpse of the composer's day-to-day life.

The museum helps organize the Villa-Lobos Festival that begins on the anniversary of his death, November 17, each year. His second wife, Arminda Neves d'Almeida, set up the museum in 1960, one year after his death. Its aim is to preserve the composer's personal collection of artifacts and keep his work alive.

> **Some think that it was through Villa-Lobos's work that Brazilian music first became popular abroad.**

4

Museu Casa de Rui Barbosa

C14 Rua São Clemente 134, Botafogo Botafogo
10am-4pm Tue-Fri; garden: 9am-5:30pm daily
casaruibarbosa.gov.br

A renowned politician, jurist, and diplomat, Rui Barbosa de Oliveira (1849–1923) helped shape many important Brazilian policies, including those pertaining to direct elections and the abolition of slavery. He made his mark internationally during the 1907 Peace Conference at the Hague, where he argued that all countries should be treated equally. Barbosa contested twice for the Brazilian presidency – in 1910 and 1919 – but lost on both occasions. Barbosa was also a great essayist and was one of the founders (and presidents) of the Brazilian Academy of Letters. The 1850 building

HEITOR VILLA-LOBOS

Latin America's most famous composer of all time, Heitor Villa-Lobos (1887-1959) was born and brought up in the middle-class suburb of Laranjeiras. A child prodigy, he learned to play the cello at six years old. It was his travels around Brazil in his youth, however, listening to local folk songs, and discovering the music of Bach, that inspired his greatest masterpiece, *Bachianas Brasileiras*.

housing the Rui Barbosa Museum was the statesman's home from 1895 until his death in 1923. When it opened to the public in 1930, it was the first private residence in Brazil to be turned into a museum. The museum showcases a collection of Barbosa's personal possessions, such as furniture and art, and a library containing 200 of his own works.

↑ Museu Casa de Rui Barbosa's ornate pink facade

5
Museu do Índio

🔵 C14 🔵 Rua das Palmeiras 55, Botafogo Ⓜ Botafogo 🕐 9am-5:30pm Mon-Fri, 1-5pm Sat, Sun & public hols 🌐 museudoindio. gov.br

Founded in 1953, the Museum of the Indian is run by the Fundação Nacional dos Povos Indígenas (Funai) with the aim of giving an insight into the lives of Brazil's Indigenous groups. Housed in a 19th-century mansion, this dynamic institution has nearly 18,000 Indigenous artifacts, more than 163,000 photographs, and over 600 films. With over 830,000 books and magazines, it also has one of the most complete libraries covering topics related to Indigenous peoples.

The museum has been undergoing a major seven-year restoration program and is expected to open in late 2023.

↑ Examining objects on display at the engaging Museu do Índio

SHOP

Museu do Índio
Find Indigenous Amazonian crafts, including ceramics, weavings, and jewelry, in this store at the Museu do Índio.

🔵 C14 🔵 Rua das Palmeiras 55, Botafogo 🌐 museudoindio.gov.br

Centro Nacional de Folclore e Artesanato
One of the best places to buy high-quality crafts and art.

🔵 D12 🔵 Rua do Catete 179-181, Flamengo 🕐 10am-6pm Tue-Fri, 3-6pm Sat & Sun 🌐 cnfcp.gov.br

3 Cervejeiros
Serves various artisan beers from all over Brazil. This shop also has a bar with occasional live music and karaoke.

🔵 D13 🔵 Rua Senador Vergueiro 2, Loja A, Flamengo 📞 (21) 2147 6787

Mercado Cobal
This huge market is off the tourist trail and has a very local buzz. Find fresh produce, wine, flowers, as well as a range of restaurants.

🔵 B14 🔵 Rua Voluntários da Patria, Botafogo 🕐 24hr

Livraria da Travessa
Large bookshop with a wide range of books, including English-language titles, DVDs, and CDs.

🔵 C14 🔵 Rua Voluntários da Pátria 97 📞 (21) 3195 0200 🌐 travessa.com.br

BEYOND THE CENTER

Rio city has grown dramatically since the 1960s, absorbing several towns and villages that surrounded it. Across Guanabara Bay, Niterói is the only Brazilian town founded by an Indigenous leader. The Temininós helped the Portuguese to eject the French from Rio, and, as a mark of gratitude, their chief Araribóia was encouraged to establish a village on this site in 1573. Like almost all the coastal Indigenous peoples, the Temininós were wiped out by European diseases in subsequent years, but Niterói grew to become one of the wealthiest cities in Brazil. The similarly affluent Barra da Tijuca to the west, developed in 1969, is now Rio's fastest-growing suburb, supercharged by construction for the 1992 UN Earth Summit, the 2012 UN Rio+20 summit, and the 2016 Olympics. Rio is still expanding, with poorer migrants moving into favelas on the city's northern, western, and southern outskirts. These hillside shantytowns first appeared in the late 19th century, and today are home to about 20 per cent of Rio's population.

Experience

1. Barra da Tijuca
2. Praia Prainha and Grumari
3. Niterói
4. Parque Nacional da Tijuca
5. Baía de Guanabara

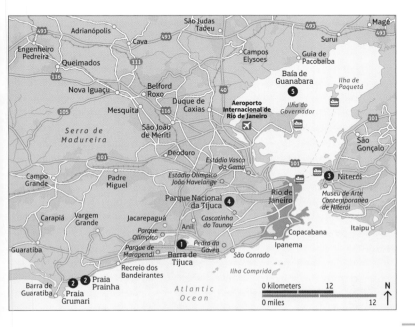

EXPERIENCE

❶ Barra de Tijuca

🅰E6 🚗Rio de Janeiro
Ⓜ Jardim Oceânico 🚌Praça
Pio X 119 🌐visit.rio

The fastest growing suburb of Rio, Barra da Tijuca is home to the **Sítio Roberto Burle Marx**, a superb collection of tropical plants from around the world. Burle Marx *(p169)* was one of the most important landscape architects of the 20th century. The beautiful gardens and open-air nurseries house around 3,500 plant species.

Barra is bordered by the long **Praia da Barra da Tijuca**, which stretches for over 11 miles (18 km). Crowds from all over Rio are drawn to this beach at weekends, but farther along it becomes less crowded and unspoiled.

Inland, the **Cidade das Artes**, suspended 33 ft (10 m) above the ground, houses one of the largest concert halls in Latin America. It is home to the Brazilian Symphony Orchestra and a cultural center, which has several movie theaters.

Close by, the interactive **Museu Seleção Brasileira** is

> **Crowds from all over Rio are drawn to this beach at weekends, but farther along it becomes less crowded and unspoiled.**

a shrine to the national soccer team, with trophies, photos, and memorabilia on display. The sport arrived in Brazil in 1894 and the national squad played its first match and won its first trophy, the Copa Roca, 20 years later. From then on, the club dominated the international scene *(p90)*.

Almost the entirety of the collection in the charming **Casa do Pontal** is based on the Frenchman Jacques Van de Beuques' private collection. It consists of more than 8,000 works of Brazilian folk art including sculptures, models, and mechanized sets.

Sítio Roberto Burle Marx

🏛 🚗Estrada Burle Marx 2019 🕐9:30am & 1:30pm Tue–Sat, by appt only 🌐sitio burlemarx.blogspot.com

Praia da Barra da Tijuca

🚗 Av Sernambetiba

Cidade das Artes

🏛 🚗Avenida das Américas 5300 🕐9am–6:30pm daily 🌐cidadedasartes.rio.rj.gov.br

Museu Seleção Brasileira

🏛 🚗Av Luís Carlos Prestes 130 🕐10am–6pm daily 🌐museuselecaobrasileira. cbf.com.br

Casa do Pontal

🏛 🚗Estrada do Pontal 3295 🕐9:30am–5pm Tue–Sun 🌐museucasadopontal.com.br

❷ Praia Prainha and Grumari

🅰E6 🚗Av Estado da Guanabara

Prainha and Grumari are the city's most unspoiled beaches, and are deserted during the week. Prainha, just 164 yards (150 m) long, is particularly

←
A couple walk along the white sands of Praia do Pontal in Barra

↑ The stunning Museu de Arte Contemporânea designed by Oscar Niemeyer

popular with the surf crowd, while Grumari is larger and attracts families.

Niterói

E6 🚇 Ipanema, Copacabana: 740D; Lapa: 775D, 565D; Botafogo, Flamengo: 110 from Cinelandia Metro, 760D, 775D 🚌

Cariocas like to joke that the best thing about Niterói is its view across the bay to Rio de Janeiro. The view is indeed stunning, but Niteroi also possesses its own charm.

Praia de São Francisco in Guanabara Bay is best known for its soft, white sand and calm waters. Niterói's other beaches – Camboinhas, Itaipu, and Itacoatiara – lie on the Atlantic coast.

The imposing **Fortaleza de Santa Cruz** (Santa Cruz Fort) sits on a rocky outcrop just outside the city and guards the entrance to huge Guanabara Bay. Parts of the fort date from the 16th century, when the French built an improvized fortification to protect the city. The structure continued to grow until it became Brazil's most important fortress.

The more modern **Museu de Arte Contemporârnea** (MAC-Niterói) appears to hover above the neighborhood of Boa Viagem. Inaugurated in 1996, it was the brainchild of the acclaimed Brazilian architect Oscar Niemeyer (p237). Its exhibits consist of 1,000 pieces of Brazilian art donated by the eminent art collector, João Sattamini.

The view from inside the museum at dusk, when Rio's lights twinkle from across the bay, is enchanting.

Fortaleza de Santa Cruz
🕐 ⊘ 📍 Estrada Gaspar Dutra, Jurujuba ⏰ 10am–4pm Tue–Sun

Museu de Arte Contemporânea
🕐 ⊘ 📍 Mirante da Boa Viagem, Niterói ⏰ 10am–6pm Tue–Sun 🌐 cultura niteroi.com.br/macniteroi

BOSSA NOVA

The sultry rhythms of bossa nova blend traditional Brazilian music and US jazz, spiced up with romantic lyrics. Led by talented musicians, such as Tom Jobim (right), Sérgio Mendes, and João Gilberto, bossa nova gained a cult following in Rio's beach suburbs Barra, Prainha, Grumari, and Niterói in the late 1950s. It became a worldwide sensation in the mid-1960s, thanks to its unofficial anthem, "The Girl from Ipanema", by Jobim and de Moraes.

Parque Nacional da Tijuca

⬛E6 🚌345 from Uruguai ⓂUruguai ⏰8am-5pm daily 🌐parquenacional datijuca.rio

Covering around 15 sq miles (39 sq km), the Tijuca National Park encompasses the last remaining tracts of Atlantic rainforest that once surrounded Rio de Janeiro. It includes the Floresta da Tijuca (Tijuca Forest), Serra da Carioca (Carioca Mountains), and the monoliths of Pedra da Gávea and Pedra Bonita. Other well-known points of interest within the park include the Dona Marta, the Vista Chinesa (with a Chinese-style pavilion), and the Mesa do Imperador, all of which offer spectacular city views.

Sights within the Floresta da Tijuca include Cascatinha do Taunay, a stunning waterfall near the main gate named after the French painter Nicolau Taunay (1755–1830); the 19th-century Mayrink Chapel, featuring the work of Cândido Portinari (1903–62), one of the most important Brazilian painters; the lovely Os Esquilos restaurant; and the hundreds of species of plants, birds, and mammals that live here, many threatened by extinction.

Many of the park's 150-odd trails were originally made by Brazil's Indigenous people and enslaved people from Africa. One of them, dating from the 19th century, takes walkers up from Largo do Bom Retiro, a picnic spot in the Floresta da Tijuca, to the 3,940-ft- (1,201-m-) high Tijuca Peak. It is easy to get lost in the dense foliage, so stick to the main trails and do not go without a guide if planning on trekking. Book in advance if you need a guide.

Another attraction near the Floresta da Tijuca is the **Museu do Açude**, a museum housed in the Neo-Colonial building that once served as the residence of the successful businessman, Raymundo Ottoni de Castro Maya (1894–1968). The only museum within the park, it is known for its French, Dutch, Spanish, and Portuguese tiles from the 17th and 18th centuries, and for Castro Maya's personal collection of Asian art.

Museu do Açude

🚶🏻‍♂️ ♿ ⬛Estrada do Açude 764, Alto da Boa Vista 📞(21) 3433 4990 ⏰11am-5pm Wed-Mon 🌐museuscastromaya.com.br

Baía de Guanabara

⬛E6

Without Baía de Guanabara, Rio de Janeiro would probably have been known by a different name. On January 1, 1502, the navigators Andre Gonçalves and Amerigo Vespucci became

Did You Know?

Tijuca National Park, which forms a vast green blanket around Rio, is the largest urban park in the world.

the first Europeans ever to sail into the bay. Assuming it was the mouth of a great river, they called it Rio de Janeiro or "River of January." Guanabara, meaning "Lagoon of the Sea," was the name given to the dominant bay by Indigenous Brazilians and is more accurate.

The bay, encompassing countless islands, is flanked by downtown Rio to its southwest and Niterói to its southeast. As well as the ferry services that begin in Centro at the public square, Praça XV, boats can be hired from the **Marina da Glória** in Flamengo Park, set between downtown Rio and Copacabana, the city's center of all nautical activities.

One of the more pleasant ways to enjoy the bay is by taking the special cruise that starts from the **Espaço Cultural da Marinha** (Navy Cultural Center) in Centro. The cultural center is an important site of the Brazilian Navy collection. The cruise is offered on the historic tugboat, *Laurindo Pitta*, built in England in 1910. The boat, which took part in World War I, passes interesting sights along its route, including

fine nautical exhibits such as an Imperial Barge built in Salvador in 1808.

The Tom Jobim International Airport is located on the largest of the islands in the bay, Ilha do Governador.

The tiny **Ilha Fiscal** houses a palace built in 1889 by Emperor Dom Pedro II in the ornate style of a 14th-century French castle. The castle's highlights include its exceptional carved stonework and cast-iron work, and the turret's mosaic floor, which is made from different species of hardwood. Also of note are the wall paintings by 19th-century Dutch artist Frederico Steckel, and the tower clock and stained-glass windows, which were imported to Brazil from England.

Ilha Paquetá, north of the bay, is an oasis of calm where no cars are allowed. Ferries and hydrofoils cruise up the bay to the island from the Estação das Barcas in front of the historic Praça XV. Crossing the bay is the Rio-Niterói Bridge (officially the Presidente Costa e Silva Bridge), which is one of the longest in the world at 8 miles (13 km). The project was financed by

Britain, and construction began in 1968 in the presence of Queen Elizabeth II.

Marina da Glória
⬜ Av Infante Dom Henrique, Glória ☎ (21) 2555 2200
🌐 marinadagloria.com.br

Espaço Cultural da Marinha
◈◈⬜ ⬜ Av Alfred Agache 215, Centro ☎ (21) 2532 5992
↻ For renovation

Ilha Fiscal
◈◈ ⬜ Baía de Guanabara ☎ (21) 2233 9165 ↻ For tours only Thu–Sun

---

💬 INSIDER TIP
Get Away From the Crowds

Explore further afield to escape the Copacabana and Ipanema crowds. Western beaches, such as Barra da Tijuca and Guaratiba, are relatively empty, or climb Pico da Tijuca in Tijuca National Park for stunning 360-degree views of Rio.

← The sun rising over Guanabara Bay and the towering Sugar Loaf Mountain

EXPERIENCE
BRAZIL

RIO DE JANEIRO AND ESPÍRITO SANTO

In 1565 the Portuguese established Rio de Janeiro city; as a result, the various Tupí peoples that lived along the coast were soon displaced. Paraty was founded in 1597 in the territory of the Tupiniquim; they too were soon decimated by introduced diseases. Sugar production boomed in the region in the 17th century, fueling the slave trade – thousands of enslaved Africans were shipped in to work on the plantations. By the 18th century, both Paraty and Rio city were flourishing as ports for exporting gold and diamonds from neighboring Minas Gerais. In 1843, Petrópolis was built in Rio state as the summer capital of the Brazilian emperors, and its Palácio Rio Negro remains an official residence of the president of Brazil.

The Portuguese had established an outpost at Vila Velha in Espírito Santo in 1535, which functioned as the new captaincy's capital until Vitória was founded in 1551. Despite their fierce resistance, the Indigenous inhabitants of the region, the Goitacá, were eventually annihilated by the colonizers. Espírito Santo was annexed to Bahia in 1715, but had recovered its autonomy and become a province by 1821. By the mid-19th century, encouraged by the Brazilian government, German and Italian immigrant farmers colonized the state's largely undeveloped interior, creating the agricultural and coffee economy that exists today. In contrast, Rio state is an industrial giant, with Brazil's second-largest economy fueled by extensive offshore oil deposits.

RIO DE JANEIRO AND ESPÍRITO SANTO

Must Sees

1. Paraty
2. Ilha Grande
3. Parque Nacional do Itatiaia
4. Petrópolis

Experience More

5. Teresópolis
6. Parque Nacional da Serra dos Órgãos
7. Búzios
8. Vitória
9. Pedra Azul
10. Itaúnas
11. Guarapari

Guanhães

Governador Valadares

Virginópolis

Ipatinga

Caratinga

MINAS GERAIS

Ouro Preto

Manhuaçu

Mariana

Pico de Bandeiras 9,500 ft (2,890 m)

Oliveira

Congonhas

MINAS GERAIS
p182

São João del Rei

Lavras

Barbacena

Muriaé

Bom Jesus d Itabapoan

Tiradentes

Itaperuna

Miracema

Sã Fidé

Bom Jardim de Minas

Juiz de Fora

Além Paraíba

Paraíba do Sul

Itaocara

Caxambu

RIO DE JANEIR

Preto

Três Rios

Cordeiro

Concei de Mac

PARQUE NACIONAL DO ITATIAIA

Marquês de Valença

Nova Friburgo

Trajano de Morais

Serra do

Agulhas Negras 9,100 ft (2,787 m)

3 Resende

PARQUE NACIONAL DA SERRA DOS ÓRGÃOS 6 5 TERESÓPOLIS

Má

Mac

Volta Redonda

PETRÓPOLIS 4

SÃO PAULO STATE
p170

Barra Mansa

Mage

Itaboraí

Silva Jardim

Barra de São João

Rio Claro

Itaguaí

RIO DE JANEIRO

São Gonçalo

Araruama

São Ped da Aldei

Angra Dos Reis

p68

Rio de Janeiro

Saquarema

7

Baía da Ilha Grande

2

BÚZIOS

PARATY 1

ILHA GRANDE

Trindade

Punta de Juatinga

Ubatuba

BAHIA
p274

Teófilo
Otôni

Mucurici
Serra dos Aimorés
Montanha

Ecoporanga
Agua Doce
do Norte
Pinheiros
⑩ ITAÚNAS

Nova Venécia
São
Mateus
Conceição
da Barra

137
381

São Gabriel
da Palha
101

Conselheiro
Pena
Pancas
Rio
Bananal
*Lagoa
Juparanã*

Aimorés
Linhares

259
Doce
Jacupemba
Colatina
Povoação
Regência
259

Itaguaçu
Itarana
Ibiraçu
Aracruz

Afonso
Cláudio
**ESPÍRITO
SANTO**
Santa Cruz
Nova Almeida

Iúna
Serra
PEDRA
AZUL **⑨**
⑧ VITÓRIA
Vila Velha

Venda
Nova
262
Alfredo
Chaves
60

Vargem Alta
Iconha
⑪ GUARAPARI

choeiro de
tapemirim
Anchieta

uquí
Itapemirim

Mimoso do Sul

101
Itabapoana

Morro do Coco

58
Travessão
São João da Barra
Atlantic

Campos dos Goitacazes
Ocean

*Lagoa
Feia*
Santo Amaro
de Campos

Quissamã

0 kilometers   60
0 miles   60

N
↑

RIO DE JANEIRO AND
ESPÍRITO SANTO

↑ The lively streets of Paraty's Old Town, brimming with shops and restaurants

1

PARATY

🄰E6 🄰Rio de Janeiro �🚌Rua Jango Pádua
🄸Av Roberto Silveira 36; www.paraty.com.br

One of the most photographed towns on the Brazilian coast, Paraty has been a UNESCO World Heritage Site since 1958. The area of Paraty (meaning "river of fish" in the Tupí language) developed as an important port from where gold was shipped to Europe, and today is an ideal base for exploring Brazil's dazzling coastline.

Casa de Cadeia

🄰Rua Travessa Santa Rita
🄲(24) 3371 1056 🄲For restoration

The 18th-century Casa de Cadeia served as the town's prison until 1890. Retaining its original iron prison bars, it now hosts exhibitions and also houses the Casa do Artesão (Artisan's House).

Matriz Nossa Senhora dos Remédios

🄰Praça Monsenhor Helio Pires

Originally meant for the white elite, this stately church took 100 years to build. When it was near completion in 1873, architects discovered that the soil was too muddy to support it. It was left in its current incomplete state, without bell towers and slowly subsiding to the left. Today, it serves as a parish church.

3

Santa Rita dos Pardos Libertos

🄰Largo da Santa Rita 🄲(24) 3371 8751 🄲9am-noon & 2-5pm Tue-Thu, Sat & Sun

The facade of Paraty's oldest church now graces travel brochures of the city. It was built in 1722 by – and for – all those who were refused entry to the church of the ruling elite because of the color of their skin. These would have included the illegitimate offspring of the aristocracy, their children, Indigenous people, and freed enslaved people. In design the church is typically Jesuit, with three windows in the upper chancel and a curvilinear door. Except for the beautiful altarpiece in the sanctuary and fine wood-work on the doorways, its interior is plain. It was decon-secrated in the 20th century and now serves as the sparse Museu de Arte Sacra (Museum of Sacred Art). Displayed religious artifacts include gold monstrances.

> **TOP 3 PARATY BEACHES**
>
> **Praia do Jabaquara**
> Shallow and spacious, this beach is a short walk north from the center of Paraty town.
>
> **Paraty-Mirim**
> This spot, lying 17 miles (27 km) east of town, can be reached via boat or an unpaved road.
>
> **Saco de Mamangúa**
> A scenic drive from Paraty, this channel is lined with old villages and secluded beaches set within lush forest.

EXPLORING AROUND PARATY

The bays and islands off Paraty are a favorite playground for Brazil's rich elite, who moor their expensive yachts in the Paraty Marina or fly into the adjacent airport for a weekend cruise. Paraty's city beach is Praia do Pontal and it lies across the Rio Perequê-Açu. The water is not very clean, but the *barracas* (restaurants) are pleasant. Ilha dos Meros, 9 miles (14 km) northeast of Paraty, is a great snorkeling spot, while the small town of Trindade to the south is popular with surfers from São Paulo.

⑦ Quilombo do Campinho da Independência

🏠 BR 101, km 584
📞 (24) 999 316 875;
(24) 998 88 943

Founded at the end of the 19th century by three enslaved women who escaped captivity, Quilombo do Campinho da Independência is a remnant of a rebel slave community. Today, the site consists of about 120 families who have retained much of their cultural heritage. Visitors can book a tour of the area and learn about the local traditions, handicrafts, and cuisine, and enjoy an unforgettable lunch in the restaurant.

④ Nossa Senhora do Rosário e São Benedito

🏠 Rua Tenente Francisco Antônio 📞 (24) 3371 1467

Enslaved people worshipped at Nossa Senhora do Rosário e São Benedito, which was built in 1725. The interior of this church is almost entirely free of embellishment, except for heavy gilt on the altarpiece. Its design resembles the Minas Gerais chapels of the same period. Every November, locals celebrate A Festa dos Santos (Feast of All Saints) here, where they remember some of the building's historical past. Mass is followed by a procession where church-goers carry figures of a king and queen, and icons of saints.

⑥ Nossa Senhora das Dores

🏠 Rua Fresca

The colonial aristocracy attended this graceful chapel. Built in 1800, it was renovated in 1901. There are some fine carvings on the balustrades in the building's upper chancel. A catacomb-like cemetery adjoins the chapel.

⑤ Forte Defensor Perpétuo

🏠 Morro do Forte 📞 (24) 3373 1038 🕐 8:30am-noon & 2-5:30pm Mon & Wed-Fri, 9am-noon & 2-5pm Sat & Sun

Located on the northern headland, just out of town, this 19th-century fort looks more like a squat townhouse. Rusted cannons and remnants of a wall sit in front of it. The Centro de Artes e Tradições Populares (Center for Popular Art) occupies its main room, displaying local handicrafts and items related to the local people's traditional way of life.

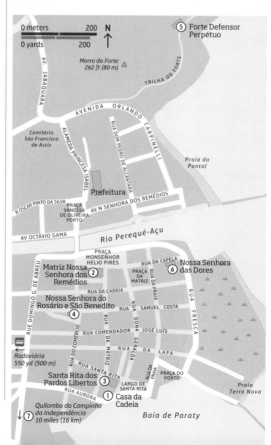

②

ILHA GRANDE

📍 E6 🏠 Rio de Janeiro 🚢 From Angra dos Reis, Mangaratiba or Conceição do Jacareí 🏛 Parque Estadual da Ilha Grande (PEIG), Av Nacib Monteiro de Queiroz s/n; www.ilhagrande.com.br

Alluring Ilha Grande is an offshore tropical island that lies between Rio de Janeiro and Paraty to the south. The island is a haven for Rio's jet-set, but the endless sandy beaches, miles of lush jungle trails, and peaceful blue lagoons ensure that every visitor is able to find their own personal patch of paradise.

💬 INSIDER TIP
Sun, Sea, and Snorkeling

One of Ilha Grande's best snorkeling sites is at Lagoa Azul, a clear pool brimming with shoals of fish on the far north end of the island. Another excellent spot to swim with the fish can be found at Saco do Céu, which is easily reached via a popular boat trip from Abraão.

The prettiest of southeastern Brazil's many islands, Ilha Grande remains unspoiled by development and heavy tourism, due in great part to its long isolation. Once a notorious pirate lair, it later became a landing port for Rio-bound enslaved people, and in the late 20th century was the site of an infamous prison for political prisoners. Nowadays, Ilha Grande is populated mostly by fishers and small tourist businesses.

Some 60 per cent of the 75-sq-mile- (193-sq-km-) island is protected and forms part of the Parque Estadual da Ilha Grande, with mangrove swamps, virgin Atlantic rainforest, and coastal vegetation, all home to abundant wildlife. The village of Vila do Abraão is the main settlement, from which wooden fishing boats offer tours of the island. The most popular trip is to the sheltered cove at Palmas, from where a trail leads to the long beach of Lopes Mendes. Also in this region is the port of Angra dos Reis. Once a colonial town, it is today mainly a jumping-off point for the islands of Ilha Grande and Ilha da Gipóia.

↑ The island settlement of Abraão, fringed by lush greenery against a backdrop of rocky mountains

THE COSTA VERDE

The Costa Verde (Green Coast) stretching south of Rio, past Paraty *(p134)* and Trindade, truly embodies its name. Rainforests swathe the coastal mountains, which reach almost 9,143 ft (2,787 m) in the alpine meadows and the forests of Parque Nacional do Itatiaia. From here, they plunge into steep ridges to meet an emerald ocean, tinged with turquoise at numerous long sandy beaches. Beyond are a scattering of breathtaking islands in the deep, bottle-green Atlantic. Ilha Grande is the largest, and is particularly lush, while the white sand beaches of Ilha da Gipóla, the second largest, are bustling with animated bars floating offshore.

1 Fishing boats offer tours around Ilha Grande, setting sail from the main settlement of Abraão.

2 The island's Parque Estadual da Ilha Grande is home to a proliferation of wildlife, including brown howler monkeys.

3 After hours catching waves, local surfers leave their boards outside one of Vila do Abraão's beach cafés.

PARQUE NACIONAL DO ITATIAIA

△ E5 🏠 Estrada do Parque Nacional, Km 8,5 Rio de Janeiro 🚌 From Itatiaia
🌐 parquedoitatiaia.tur.br

Under three hours' drive from downtown Rio, this superb national park offers visitors the chance to explore some of Brazil's most inspirational and crowd-free landscapes. Itatiaia is wildlife rich and well served with walking trails, either self-guided or with local tour guides.

Brazil's oldest national park, Parque Nacional do Itatiaia (Itatiaia National Park) was established in 1937 to protect the high alpine meadows and the gradations of thick Mata Atlântica, or Atlantic rainforest (p140), that cover the park's steep mountain ridges. The scenery here is magnificent. The park's highest regions are capped by giant boulders, eroded into organic shapes by millions of years of rain and wind. They sit on expansive grassland coursed by babbling brooks, which become fast-flowing rivers once they reach the warmer forested areas below. Here they tumble, roar, and fall over waterfalls and rapids. The trees around them are busy with primates. Curious brown capuchin monkeys are a common sight along the numerous trails. Scarcer are the shy muriqui monkeys, a threatened species. Birdlife, too, is prolific in the park, home to 350 species, many of which are endangered; the park plays a crucial role in their conservation. Dusky-legged guans wander along the few paved roads, brilliant seven-colored and black and gold cotingas flit about with toucans, and the early morning air buzzes with the sound of hummingbirds.

The park can be crowded on weekends, but during the week the trails are quiet. The ranger station provides simple walking maps with routes clearly marked.

STAY

Pousada Esmeralda
Comfortable chalets with a spring-fed outdoor pool.

△ E5 🏠 Estrada do Parque Nacional, Km 4.5
🌐 pousadaesmeralda.com.br

⑤⑤⑤

Hotel Donati
Nestled in the center of the park, this historic hotel has an indoor natural spring water pool and walking trails through the forest.

△ E5 🏠 Estrada do Parque Nacional, Km 9.5
🌐 hoteldonati.com/br

⑤⑤⑤

↑ The park's boulder-strewn peaks reaching into the clouds

→ A colorful toucan, many of which can be spotted throughout the park

Did You Know?

This is the only part of Rio de Janeiro State to ever see snow, albeit rarely.

↑ Hiker following a path through the rugged landscape of Parque Nacional do Itatiaia

MATA ATLÂNTICA

Stretching from northern Brazil south to Uruguay, the Mata Atlântica (Atlantic rainforest) is a green belt of tropical biodiversity, covering some 38,610 sq miles (100,000 sq km). Around 40 per cent of its 20,000 plant species and 30 per cent of its 2,315 animal species are endemic. Closer to the equator, tall trees drip with epiphytes, orchids, and entangled creepers. Further south, forests house the distinctive araucaria, monkey-puzzle pines. Besides its abundant wildlife, it shares its habitat with around 60 per cent of Brazil's population.

ENDANGERED ECOSYSTEM

Squeezed out by ever-expanding coastal cities, particularly Rio de Janeiro and Sao Paulo, most of the Mata Atlântica has disappeared. Of the original forest that once carpeted the coastline, less than 7 per cent remains. The rainforest has a high proportion of endemic plants and animal species, so once the forest habitat has gone, species extinction will inevitably follow. Besides making way for cities, ports, and their associated infrastructure, much of the Mata Atlântica has fallen victim to deforestation, replaced by cattle pastures, logging, and crops, most notably soya. Soya plantations have spread far and wide across South America, including this rainforest. Nearly all the soymeal produced becomes animal feed. With the world's insatiable appetite for meat and soya products, demand is expected to double over the next 50 years.

↑ The endangered golden lion tamarin, Brazil's tiny, long-tailed primate

↑ Exposed roots of a dense mangrove forest near Romana Island in the Amazon region

SUSTAINABLE HOPE

Despite losing much of the Mata Atlântica, some residents are trying to protect what is left. One of the forest's pin-up animals is the golden lion tamarin, a tiny, long-tailed primate. Fewer than 3,500 of these endangered animals remain in the wild, some inhabiting the Reserva Biológica Poço das Antas, a 12,500-acre (5,000-ha) forest reserve near Rio de Janeiro. Villagers offer ecotourism tours, guiding visitors around the forests in hope of a glimpse of the tamarins. Similar ecotourism projects have been established for the forest flora and fauna.

Thick riverine vegetation and evergreen rainforests of the Mata Atlântica

TOP 4 MATA ATLÂNTICA ECOTOURS

Asociação Mico-Leão-Dourado
⬛E6 🚗BR-101, Km 219, Silva Jardim, Rio de Janeiro (state), 28820-000 🕐8:30am-4pm Thu-Sat (adv booking only) 🌐micoleao.org.br
This association offers unforgettable visits to the heart of the golden lion tamarin's habitat.

Legado das Aguas
⬛E6 🚗BR-116 Rodovia Regis Bittencourt, Km 394, Miracatu, São Paulo (state), 11850-000 🕐Mon 🌐legadodasaguas.com.br
Navigate the forest's incredible scenery on a land or water tour.

Reserva Ecológica de Guapiaçu (REGUA)
⬛E6 🚗Estrada de Guapiaçu, s/no, Guapiaçu, Cachoeiras de Macacu, Rio de Janeiro (state), 28680-000 🕐Adv booking only 🌐regua.org
One of South America's most biodiverse and endemic-rich biomes, this wildlife- and bird-watching site has lush wetlands, trails, and a visitor lodge.

Eco Lodge Itororó
⬛F5 🚗Estrada do Curuzu, Nova Friburgo, Rio de Janeiro (state), 28616-330 🕐Adv booking only 🌐ecolodge-itororo.com
This secluded eco-lodge offers trekking expeditions over the Organ Mountain Range and bird-watching tours.

Petrópolis's Catedral de São Pedro de Alcântara, rising from a forest of lush greenery ↑

4

PETRÓPOLIS

 E5 🚌 **Rua Porciúcula** 🅻 **Centro de Informação Turística de Petrópolis, Estrada Ayrton Senna; www.petropolis.rj. gov.br/turispetro/index**

Located in the mountains near Rio, Petrópolis owes its creation to the Brazilian royal family, who built a summer residence here in the 1800s. The city rose in importance accordingly, and today, Petrópolis is popular for its royal attractions, mountain scenery, and the national park of Serra dos Órgãos (p146).

①

Palácio Rio Negro

🏠 **Av Koeller 255, Centro** 🅲 **(24) 2246 2423** 🔒 **For renovation**

Built in 1889 at the behest of Barão do Rio Negro, a wealthy coffee baron, the palace acted as the seat of the state government between 1894 and 1902, when the city was the capital of Rio de Janeiro state. It then became the summer residence of the presidents of Brazil; President Vargas converted the wine cellar into a Roman-style bathhouse. The palace is still an official presidential residence but is rarely used and now open to the public.

②

Catedral de São Pedro de Alcântara

🏠 **Rua São Pedro de Alcântara 60, Centro** 🅲 **(24) 2242 4300** 🕘 **9am-5pm Tue-Sat**

Though this cathedral's first stone was laid in 1884 by Dom Pedro II, much of its current structure dates from 1925. Built in French-Gothic style with a beautiful rose window, it has a striking interior decorated in Carrara marble. The walls here depict detailed scenes from the Crucifixion.

The Imperial Chapel, to the right of the main entrance, contains the mortal remains of King Dom Pedro II, Princess Regent Dona Teresa Cristina, their daughter Isabel, her husband Count d'Eu, and several other members of the royal family. Statues of the royal family are also featured inside the chapel. The 1848 baptismal font is the original.

③

Casa de Santos Dumont

🏠 **Rua do Encanto 22, Centro** 🅲 **(24) 2247 5222** 🕘 **10am-5pm Tue-Sun**

In 1918, the great Brazilian aviator Alberto Santos Dumont (1873–1932) designed and built his summerhouse in the style of a French chalet and named it "A Encantada," or "enchanted". The three floors

Did You Know?

In 1906 Alberto Santos Dumont became the third person in history to fly a powered aircraft.

contain a lounge-cum-dining room, a bedroom, a work room and an office. The bathroom's alcohol-heated shower was the first of its kind in Brazil. There is no kitchen because Dumont had all his meals sent in by the then Palace Hotel.

The fascinating personal collection of this inventor includes everyday objects, such as furniture, photographs, and various artifacts, including beautiful vases and lamps.

Quitandinha

🏠 Av Joaquim Rolla 2 📞 (24) 2245 2020 🕐 9am–5pm Tue–Sun & public hols

An imposing palace built in Norman style, Quitandinha is located southwest of the town center. Entrepreneur Joaquim Rolla built it in 1944 to be the largest casino complex in South America. For the exterior, Rolla copied the large casinos that were popular at the time along the Normandy coast, while the interior was by Dorothy Drape, a famous Hollywood set designer.

Quitandinha's glory ended in 1946, when President Dutra banned gambling. Remarkably well preserved, today it is a luxury hotel and convention center, with private condominiums. The guided tour takes visitors back in time to the 1940s, when Quitandinha's guests were global celebrities.

⑤
Palácio de Cristal

🏠 Rua Alfredo Pachá, Centro 📞 (24) 2247 3721 🔧 For renovation

The metal structure and glass enclosure of the Palácio de Cristal (Crystal Palace) were made in France in 1879 and shipped to Brazil. Inaugurated on February 2, 1884, the palace is a fine example of the architectural style that emerged during the French industrial revolution.

Although it was originally planned as a greenhouse for growing orchids, and later an exhibition hall, the Palácio de Cristal ended up as the imperial ballroom, and has been the sight of many spectacular parties. Most momentous were the extravagant balls hosted by Princess Isabel and Count d'Eu. It was during one such event in 1888 that Isabel signed an order liberating 103 enslaved people. On May 13 of the same year, Isabel went on to sign the Lei Aurea (Golden Law), the decree that abolished slavery in Brazil.

Although most of its former glory is lost, the palace today serves as an exhibition hall. It occasionally hosts art shows and cultural events.

EAT

Imperatriz Leopoldina
Treat yourself to an afternoon tea in the elegant setting of the Solar do Imperio hotel.

🏠 Avenida Koeler 376 🌐 solardoimperio.com.br

$$$

Casa do Alemão
Ideal for snacks on the go, this little German café offers everything from strudel to Brazilian standard *misto quente* (toasted sandwiches).

🏠 Rua 16 de Março 138 🕐 Sun 🌐 casa doalemao.com.br

$$$

Casadinho Tradição Mineira
Head for this well-stocked buffet to gorge upon meaty Minas cuisine and excellent sushi.

🏠 Rua do Imperador 148 🌐 tradicaomineira. com.br

$$$

⑥ 🎨 🍴 ☕

PALÁCIO IMPERIAL

📍 Rua da Imperatriz 220, Petrópolis 🕐 Museum: 10am-6pm Tue-Sun; sound and light show: 8pm Thu, Fri, & Sat 🌐 museuimperial.gov.br

With its delicate pink facade and classical columns, this grand Imperial Palace looks over Petrópolis from its wooded hillside. The interior is sumptuously furnished with personal possessions belonging to the Portuguese Royal Family, and the formal gardens in front are magnificently laid out, with plants from all over South America and around the world.

Built at the behest of Dom Pedro II between 1845 and 1864, the Neo-Classical Imperial Palace was used by the emperor as his summer residence every year from 1848 until Brazil's declaration of a republic in 1889. In that year, the palace was leased out as a college, and continued to function as such until President Vargas passed a decree in 1943 creating the Imperial Museum. Among the highlights of the museum, which faithfully reflect the daily life of the Brazilian royal family, are artifacts, paintings, and furniture that belonged to the emperor and his family,

plus the Imperial Crown Jewels. The most valuable piece in this collection is the Imperial Crown of Dom Pedro II. This stunning headdress was made for his 1841 coronation, which took place when he was just 15 years old.

> **Among the highlights of the museum are artifacts, paintings, and furniture that belonged to the emperor and his family, plus the Imperial Crown Jewels.**

Did You Know?

The study houses Brazil's first telephone, given to Dom Pedro II in 1876 by Alexander Graham Bell.

① The palace interiors are richly decorated, with items on show including rare musical instruments and portraits of the royal family.

② The Palacio de Cristal, the palace's impressive greenhouse, with blue-tinted glass and a decorated roof.

③ A statue of Dom Pedro II stands in the courtyard of the Palácio Imperial, amid landscaped gardens.

MUSEUM GUIDE

The ground floor displays a series of royal exhibits, with prominence given to the Crown Jewels. These regal artifacts include the Imperial Scepter, which was made for Dom Pedro I's coronation in 1822, and is topped by an open-mouthed dragon. The first floor houses the State Room; the throne on show here came from the palace in São Cristovão. This floor also houses the royal bedrooms, along with a study. The museum itself is set in a wonderfully picturesque garden designed by Jean Baptiste Binot, a French landscape artist.

←
The striking facade of the Palácio Imperial, painted a pretty pale pink

↑ Dedo de Deus (God's Finger) in the Parque Nacional da Serra dos Órgãos

EXPERIENCE MORE

⑤ Teresópolis

🅐E5 🄰Rio de Janeiro
🚌From Rio de Janeiro City
𝙞Av Feliciano Sodré 675;
(21) 2742 3352 (ext 240)

Set amid pretty countryside in the mountainous region of Região Serrana, Teresópolis has one of the mildest climates in Brazil. It is known for its artisan fair in Praça Higino da Silveira, lined with hundreds of stalls selling furniture, jewelry, food, and clothing.

Just 3 miles (5 km) south is **AraBotânica**, one of Brazil's largest orchidarium. The 20th-century landscaper Roberto Agnes created a floral paradise in these gardens, with some 50,000 plants. One of the area's highlights is the Passeio das Flores, a walkway through the Atlantic Rainforest, made from recycled timber and sustainable materials.

AraBotânica

⊛⊚ 🄰Estrada Francisco Smolka 601, Teresópolis
🕘9am–4:30pm Wed–Sun
🅦arabotanica.com.br

⑥ Parque Nacional da Serra dos Órgãos

🅐E5 🄰Rio de Janeiro
🚌From Rio de Janeiro & São Paulo 𝙞Avenida Rotariana, Teresópolis; (21) 2642 0579 🕘7am–4pm daily

Created in 1939, this national park covers an area of approximately 100 sq miles (200 sq km) stretching from Teresópolis across to Petrópolis. The park offers good climbing and hikes, including a spectacular 20-mile- (32-km-) long trek between both cities. Among the park's most notable peaks are the 7,475-ft (2,263-m) Pedra do Sino, the highest in the mountain range, and the more famous Dedo de Deus (God's Finger), which stands 5,512 ft (1,680 m) high.

Of the many entrance points to the park, the most popular and best equipped is 3 miles (5 km) south of Teresópolis. Early and late entry is permitted with advance ticket purchases.

⑦ Búzios

🅐F6 🄰Rio de Janeiro
🚌From Cabo Frio
𝙞Travessa dos Pescadores 111; (22) 2623 4254; https://turismo.buzios.rj.gov.br

Since French film actress Brigitte Bardot visited Búzios in 1964, with her then boyfriend Brazilian actor Bob Zagury, this peninsula has developed from a quiet string of isolated fishing villages lost in semitropical *maquis* (vegetation) into one of the country's most stylish low-key resorts. Large private homes, chic designer boutiques, and little *pousadas* cling to its hills and overlook the numerous beaches. Beach buggies driven by vacationers buzz along the scruffy roads. Yachts bob in the bay in front of Búzios town, which is little more than a cluster of cobble-stoned streets lined with smart boutiques and lively restaurants. During high season, the resort buzzes with cruise-ship passengers and Brazilian tourists who shop by

Did You Know?

Officially Armação dos Búzios, this town was named after "armação," wooden shelters once used for whale hunting.

day on Rua das Pedras, the town's main thoroughfare, sip cocktails in the evening at one of the oceanfront *pousadas*, and then dance the night away in the Ibiza-style clubs and beachside bars.

Búzios's *raison d'être* is its beaches, which range from half-moon bays to long stretches of fine white sand. The best way to see them is to rent a beach buggy and explore, armed with one of the ubiquitous free maps of the peninsula. It is difficult to get lost here: the peninsula is

extremely well signposted, and only 4 miles (6 km) long and 2 miles (4 km) wide.

Many of the beaches, including the two sets of twin sheltered coves – at Praia João Fernandes, Praia João Fernandinho, Praia Azeda, and Praia Azedinha – are within half an hour's walk of town. Others are a beach buggy ride away. Praia da Ferradura, on the opposite side from Búzios, is one of the most beautiful beaches near town, and one of the least spoiled by hotel development. Fishers still work from here at dawn and dusk. Praia Brava, at the peninsula's eastern extreme, is washed by some of the region's fiercest waves and is a popular surf beach. Olho de Boi, which can be reached only via a rocky trail that runs from Brava's southern end, is surrounded by rugged hills

↑ Bronze statue of Brigitte Bardot on the Búzios promenade

on all sides, and is an unofficial nudist beach. Ferradurinha, at the peninsula's southern extreme, has clear, calm waters and natural swimming pools, which are perfect for a dip.

BEACHES OF COSTA DO SOL

The region of Costa Do Sol is a stretch of coast extending between Niterói *(p125)* and Búzios, best known for its landscape, outstanding beaches, and upmarket resorts. The area's attractive beaches and sparkling waters make it ideal for a dip or for relaxing on the sand. Its crashing waves and steady breeze also make it popular for windsurfing. Below are five of the best beaches to visit in this picturesque area.

CABO FRIO
A busy resort area, Cabo Frio's beautiful shoreline overflows with visitors and locals. The area is also popular with surfers.

MARICÁ
Quiet Maricá sits at the foot of forest-covered hills and looks over its own lagoon.

SAQUAREMA
Saquarema is best known for surfing; all of the beaches have powerful waves.

ARRAIAL DO CABO
The town itself is uninspiring but its clear waters are home to the best diving in southeastern Brazil.

ARARUAMA
Ringed by myriad long, white-sand beaches, this lake is good for windsurfing.

↑ Sunset at Praia Grande, in Arraial do Cabo

8 Vitória

🗺F5 🏛Espírito Santo ✈
🚗🚌 From Rio 🛈Secretaria
Municipal de Turismo, Av
Marechal Mascarenhas
de Morais 1927, Bento
Ferreira; (27) 3382 6000

The capital city of Espírito Santo is dominated by a lovely bay with sheltered crescent coves, and surrounded by open ocean. Vitória was originally made up of 36 distinct islands, but landfills have reduced these to just a handful, connected by a series of bridges. **Praia do Camburí**, the main beach south of the city, is a 4-mile (6-km) stretch, dotted with a range of restaurants and hotels.

Across the Baía de Vitória lies Vila Velha (Old Town), reached by the Terceira Ponte. Only a few colonial buildings remain here, among them the architectural symbol of the city, the peaceful **Convento da Nossa Senhora da Penha**. Sitting high up on a palm-covered hill overlooking Vitória Bay, the monastery's thick fortified walls reflect both the sunrise and sunset.

Founded in 1558, it features 16th-century wood carvings and one of Brazil's first paintings, *Nossa Senhora das Alegrias*, by an unknown early 16th-century Iberian artist. At the base of the hill is the 1551 Igreja Nossa Senhora do Rosário, the oldest church in the state.

South of Vilha Velha, **Praia da Costa** is not as busy a beach as Camburí and is a good place to go bodysurfing.

Manguezal de Vitória, northwest of Vitória, is the largest stretch of urban mangroves in South America, occupying 8.9 sq km (3.4 sq miles). These dense clusters of vegetation fringe the city's rugged, riverine islands and are an important nursery for marine life. Boat trips allow visitors to spot the shy animals hidden within them.

Convento da Nossa Senhora da Penha

🏛Rua Vasco Coutinho, Prainha, Vila Velha,Vitória
📞(27) 3329 0420 ⏰6am-5pm Mon-Sat, 4am-4:30pm Sun

Manguezal de Vitória

♿ 🏛Santuário de Santo Antônio 📞(27) 3222 3810
🚤Boat tours by Cores do Mar

9 Pedra Azul

🗺F5 🏛Espírito Santo
🚌 From Vitória 🛈Rota do
Lagarto (Rodovia Angelo
Girardi), Km 2, Pedra Azul
⏰8am-5pm Tue-Sun
🌐pedraazuldoarace.com.br

Sitting in a tiny island of remnant Mata Atlântica forest is the Parque Estadual da Pedra Azul. In the middle of

Fishing boats taking part in a maritime procession in Vitória

parties (December to March), and its exciting *forró* dance festival in July.

 11
Guarapari

△ F5 △ Espírito Santo ▭ From Vitória 🛈 Av Munir Abud, 234, Praia do Morro; (27) 3362 3005, (27) 3261 5203

Espírito Santo's busiest beach resort is fringed by dozens of long, white beaches, said to be mildly radioactive due to natural deposits of monazite found in the sand. The best beach, Praia do Morro, lies to the north of the city and has a nature reserve. Praia do Meio, also to the north, has rock pools filled with clear water, and is good for snorkeling.

Guarapari offers light adventure activities, such as rappeling and rafting, and some of the best diving in the southeast. The town also has a lively nightlife scene.

Located about 6 miles (10 km) north of Guarapari is the coastal nature reserve, **Parque Estadual Paulo César Vinha**, with its mangroves, dunes, and unique reddish lagoon, the Lagoa de Caraís.

Parque Estadual Paulo César Vinha

△ Rodovia do Sol, Km 38 ☎ (27) 3636 2522

the park stands the 1,640-ft- (500-m-) high Pedra Azul (Blue Stone). Forming a stunning centerpiece, this natural wonder is an almost polished blue-grey, but seems to shift in hue and shade depending on the light.

The forest surrounding Pedra Azul is small but it is the nesting ground for a diverse variety of wildlife. Hummingbirds, tanagers, and tiny tufted-eared marmosets are a common sight. The park is also home to many species of wild flora, including cedar as well as colorful orchids, cassias, and bromeliads.

The visitors' center at the foot of the stone is a good place to collect a map of the park. The easiest trekking circuit, around the stone's base, is 0.8 miles (1.3 km). The trail leading through the natural pools of the park is 1 mile (1.6 km) long, and tougher, so it is advisable to hire a guide. Equipment and booking are required for climbing the stone. Camping is forbidden.

10
Itaúnas

△ F5 △ Espírito Santo ▭ From Vitória 🛈 (27) 3243 6650/7241

This little fishing town with long strands of beaches stretching to its north and south lies tucked away in the far north of Espírito Santo. The beaches have drifted into dunes so large that the first settlement here lies submerged, the remains of the original church tower occasionally appearing after a strong wind. The town lies next to the Rio Itaúnas, where caimans and capybaras live, along with a variety of rare birds and small mammals.

The smattering of hotels in town offer dune buggy tours, crossing dozens of towering dunes and empty turtle-nesting beaches, eventually reaching the sandy cliffs on the state border with Bahia. Avoid dune buggy tours during nesting season (September to March), when marine turtles come onshore to lay their eggs on the beach.

Itaúnas itself is a lively town and quite famous, particularly among students, for its exuberant *samba* and *axé* (Afro-Brazilian pop music)

An aerial view of the imposing Pedra Azul (Blue Stone)

> ### Did You Know?
> The capybara, native to South America, is the largest living rodent in the world.

Street artist Eduardo Kobra's mural of architect Oscar Niemeyer

SÃO PAULO CITY

South America's biggest and richest city began life as a humble village, built around the Jesuit college co-founded by Portuguese scholar and writer Father José de Anchieta in 1554. Anchieta became a passionate defender of the various Tupí peoples who inhabited the area at the time, but most had died out by 1700.

São Paulo remained a poor and isolated village well into the 18th century, when it began attracting gold miners and *bandeirantes* (fortune hunters), viewed today not only as intrepid explorers but also vicious enslavers of Indigenous peoples. While profits from gold mining and the slave trade were substantial, coffee is what really made São Paulo rich. In the 19th century the city became the hub for Brazil's coffee plantations, and with a railway to Santos port built in 1869, its export trade boomed. After slavery was abolished in Brazil in 1888, immigrants from the Middle East, Italy, Japan, and Portugal poured into the region, creating the cosmopolitan blend that exists today.

The city played an influential role in Brazilian politics well into the 20th century, with the powerful elite here and in Minas Gerais taking turns to choose Brazilian presidents – this corrupt arrangement was dubbed Café com Leite or "coffee with milk," as coffee drove São Paulo's economy and Minas ran on dairy farming. Industrialization boosted the city's fortunes still further, but in 1932 Paulistanos – residents of São Paulo – rose against dictator Getúlio Vargas; the failure of this revolt eroded the autonomy that the states had enjoyed so far. The city's 1977 labor strikes, led by future president Lula, and the 1983–84 campaign for direct elections helped end Brazil's military dictatorship. Today, São Paulo is the country's financial capital, with a GDP that dwarfs most South American countries.

SÃO PAULO CITY

Must Sees

1. Pinacoteca de São Paulo
2. Parque do Ibirapuera

Experience More

3. Catedral Metropolitana
4. Igreja de São Francisco de Assis
5. Pátio do Colégio
6. Theatro Municipal
7. Centro Cultural Banco do Brasil
8. Farol Santander
9. Museu Arte Sacra
10. Estação da Luz
11. Estação Pinacoteca
12. Sala São Paulo
13. Museu de Arte de São Paulo (MASP)
14. Avenida Paulista
15. Museu do Futebol
16. Liberdade
17. Parque da Independência
18. Jardim Botânico
19. Museu de Arte Contemporânea
20. Instituto Butantã
21. Parque Burle Marx

Eat

1. Prêt no MAM Restaurant
2. Santiago Bakery
3. Benedita Balaio Restaurante
4. Balaio Restaurante

Drink

5. Guarita Bar
6. Bar Kintaro

Stay

7. Tivoli Moffarej
8. We Hostel
9. Guest Urban

Shop

10. Mercado do Municipal de Pinheiros
11. Projeto Terra
12. PatBO

Beyond the Center

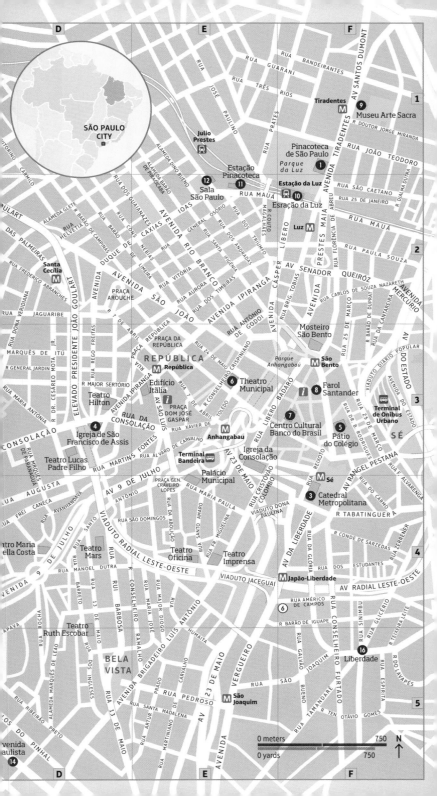

PINACOTECA DE SÃO PAULO

**♀F1 ⌂Praça da Luz 2, Jardim da Luz Ⓜ Luz 🚌
🕐10am-6pm Wed-Mon Ⓦpinacoteca.org.br**

The Pinacoteca De São Paulo is one of Brazil's most important art museums. Its collection is housed within a spacious building in the Parque da Luz, which bathes the artworks in light. In addition to its major Modernist Brazilian art, the gallery also has many fine European paintings and sculptures.

The Pinacoteca is a significant repository of Brazilian art, with an archive of over 10,000 paintings and sculptures representing all major artists and artistic movements. The galleries trace the evolution of Brazilian styles from the 19th-century colonial period to Modern and contemporary art, including the 1960s Avant Garde. In the mid-1990s, the Pinacoteca was renovated by the noted architect Paulo Mendes de Rocha, who filled the original Neo-Classical building with carefully positioned partitions and capped it with a translucent roof, creating a magical sense of space and light. The Pinacoteca also has a separate annex, the Estação Pinacoteca *(p160)*, which houses many of Brazil's finest Modernist paintings.

↑ Visitors exploring the museum's modern, airy galleries

↑ The building's original brick walls, topped by an impressive translucent roof

GALLERY GUIDE

The Pinacoteca's permanent collection, located on the second floor, features long-term displays, which change periodically. This floor also houses temporary exhibitions and Modern Brazilian art, where Anita Malfatti's bold painting *Tropical* (1917) is a fine example of the latter. The third-floor galleries cover the history of Brazilian art since the colonial period, including unexpected formal portraits of colonial dignitaries. The first floor features an educational area, activities for families, and a café.

↑ *OSGEMEOS: Segredos*, a panoramic art exhibition at the Pinacoteca de São Paolo

Locals relaxing in the Parque do Ibirapuera, with views of the São Paulo skyline ↑

PARQUE DO IBIRAPUERA

📍B4 🏛Av Pedro Álvares Cabral ⏰5am-midnight daily
🌐ibirapuera.org

Parque do Ibirapuera is the largest green space in central São Paulo, and its native Brazilian woodlands and lakes are a welcome respite from the city's urban sprawl. Opened in 1954, it houses several museums and exhibition spaces, where major displays have included China's Terracotta Warriors and the Rodin retrospective.

Museu Afro Brasil

🏛Gate 10 ⏰10am-5pm Tue-Sun (to 9pm last Tue of month) 🌐museuafro brasil.org.br

The Afro Brazil Museum is devoted to celebrating Afro-Brazilian culture. It hosts films, dance, exhibitions, music, and theater events. Opened in 2004, the museum is based on the private collection of its founder, Brazilian artist Emanoel Araujo, who was originally from northeastern Brazil. Its permanent exhibition has more than 6,000 artworks from the 18th century to the present day, from Brazil, Haiti, Cuba, the USA, and Africa. Considered to be the largest collection of its kind in the Americas, the paintings, sculpture, ceramics, jewelry, photographs, and textiles are displayed in an airy gallery designed by Oscar Niemeyer.

Bosque da Leitura

🏛Gate 7, Av República do Líbano 1151 ⏰10am-4pm Sat & Sun

The Bosque da Leitura, or "reading wood," is the place to head for at the weekends. Visitors can borrow a book and read in the shade of the trees. Cultural events and entertainment are also on offer throughout the year, from open-air cinema, to lecture, to "Slow Parenting" family days. These tranquil woods provide a peaceful breathing space in the heart of frenetic São Paulo.

Museu de Arte Moderna (MAM)

🏛Gate 3, Ave Pedro Álvares Cabral ⏰10am-6pm Tue-Sun 🌐mam.org.br

The best of Brazilian modern and contemporary art is showcased in this building designed by Lino Bo Bardi and Oscar Niemeyer. The mural on

---

 INSIDER TIP
Bike Sampa

This is São Paulo's increasingly popular bike-sharing scheme. Over 2,600 bikes are available to hire from 260 stations around the city, several in and around Parque do Ibirapuera. Rates start at around US$4 a day.

↑ The park's Museu de Arte Moderna, its walls brightened by colorful murals

EAT

Prêt no MAM Restaurant

This bright, airy restaurant overlooking MAM's sculpture garden is the perfect place to stop for lunch or grab a quick bite between art exhibits.

⌂ Gate 3 ⏰ Mon
🌐 mam.org.br

$$$

part of its facade is by graffiti artists OSGEMEOS. MAM's modern art collection comprises some 4,000 artworks, principally Brazilian, but also international artists. Every two (odd-numbered) years, the museum holds a Panorama of Brazilian Art exhibition, focussing on contemporary art from different regions around the country. Outside the museum is a sculpture garden, with about 30 pieces, created by Roberto Burle Marx, Brazil's most famous landscape designer.

④

Planetário Aristóteles Orsini

⌂ Gate 3, Av Pedro Álvares Cabral ☎ (11) 5575 5206
⏰ 10am, noon, 3pm, 5pm Sat & Sun; events vary, call ahead

Located in the middle of the park, this restored, state-of-the-art planetarium is one of the most impressive in Latin America and is particularly popular with children. All shows are in Portuguese, although the visual display can still be enjoyed by non-speakers. Sessions last around 30 minutes, and are held in the 9-m- (30-ft-) high dome

building with a seating capacity of 300. The planetarium was founded in 1959, at which time it was the only one of its kind in Latin America. It was reopened to the public in late 2021, following restoration works, including the upgrading of its Starmaster projector, which now displays the constellations fully across its 59 ft (18 m) diameter dome.

EXPERIENCE MORE

3
Catedral Metropolitana

📍 F4 📌 Praça da Sé, Centro
📞 (11) 3107 6832 Ⓜ Sé
🕐 8am-7pm Mon-Fri (to 5pm Sat and 1pm Sun)

At the heart of old downtown São Paulo, the striking Catedral Metropolitana (also known as Catedral da Sé) watches over the large pebbled Praça da Sé, shaded by tropical fig and palm trees. Gradually built between 1912 and 1954, it finally gained its full complement of 14 turrets in 2002.

Built by German engineer Maximilian Hehl, its exterior is a fusion of Renaissance and Neo-Gothic, with an overly narrow nave squeezed between two enormous 318-ft- (97-m-) high spires and a bulbous copper cupola. The cavernous interior, said to seat up to 8,000 people, looks starkly European. The only obvious local influences are visible in the delicately carved capitals. The stained-glass windows were designed in Germany and Brazil.

The building's facade has watched over the country's largest public protests. In the late 1980s, crowds famously gathered in the adjoining square to demand the end of military rule.

4
Igreja de São Francisco de Assis

📍 D3 📌 Largo de São Francisco 133 📞 (11) 3291 2400 Ⓜ Sé
🕐 7am-6:30pm daily

Immediately to the west of Catedral Metropolitana is the smaller Igreja de São Francisco de Assis, one of the city's oldest churches. Parts of the Portuguese Baroque interior, featuring a carved altar and gilded ornaments, date from the mid-1600s.

The well-preserved church is sometimes referred to as O Convento São Francisco, after the exquisite Baroque convent that stood here until the 1930s, when it was demolished along with other parts of the old colonial center.

5
Pátio do Colégio

📍 F3 📌 Praça Pátio do Colégio 2 📞 (11) 3105 6899 Ⓜ Sé
🕐 9am-4:45pm Tue-Sun
🌐 pateodocollegio.com.br

The Pátio do Colégio has an interesting history behind it.

In 1554, the Colégio de São Paulo de Piratinga was inaugurated by the Jesuits on a small bluff. This eventually became a school, then a church; and around this arose the buildings that formed the core of the original city of São Paulo.

In 1760, the Jesuits were all expelled from the city, but the college and chapel remained and became known as the Pátio do Colégio. However, the buildings were later demolished in 1886. Upon their return in 1954, the Jesuits immediately built an exact replica of their original church and college, which is what stands here today. Most of the buildings are occupied by the **Museu Padre Anchieta**, named after Joseph of Anchieta, the Jesuit captain who led the first mission. Its collection features a Modernist portrait of the priest and a collection of Guaraní artifacts from the colonial era.

Capoeira (Afro-Brazilian martial art) performers, outside the Catedral Metropolitana

Did You Know?

In 1922, Theatro Municipal held an arts festival marking the start of Brazilian Modernism.

6
Theatro Municipal

📍E3 🏛 Praça Ramos de Azevedo Ⓜ Anhangabaú 🕐 Ticket office: 10am-7pm Mon-Fri (to 5pm Sat & Sun) 🌐 theatromunicipal.org.br

The Municipal Theater is considered one of the country's most important venues, seating up to 2,200 people. It was modeled on the Paris Opera and the city waited in fevered anticipation for its inaugural night. The theater opened on September 12, 1911, with a production of *Hamlet*, starring the Italian baritone Titta Ruffo. Visits are limited, so book ahead.

7
Centro Cultural Banco do Brasil

📍F3 🏛 Rua Álvares Penteado 112 Ⓜ São Bento/Sé 🕐 9am-8pm Wed-Mon 🌐 culturabancodobrasil.com.br

This early 20th-century building, with a lovely Art Deco glass ceiling, was once the Bank of Brazil. It now houses the Centro Cultural Banco do Brasil. Inside the cultural center, there are a series of spaces devoted to showing contemporary arts, including photography, fine art, cinema, and theater.

←

8
Farol Santander

📍F3 🏛 Rua João Bricola 24 Ⓜ São Bento

Reopened in 2018 after major refurbishment work, this 161-m- (527-ft-) high edifice was built in 1939, and looks like a miniature version of the Empire State Building in New York. It was the tallest skyscraper in Latin America until 1968. The 35-floor skyscraper is now occupied by Santander bank, but has a public observation deck on the 26th floor providing spectacular city views. It also has the Accademia Gastronomica restaurant on the 31st floor.

EAT

Santiago Artisan Bakery
Head here for delicious crusty bread with rosemary and sea salt.

📍B4 🏛 Rua Tavares Bastos 750, Perdizes 🕐 8am-7pm Tue-Sat (to 2pm Sun)

⑤⑤⑤

Benedita
This bistro is away from the hustle and bustle and serves Brazilian home-cooked food.

📍B4 🏛 Rua Havai 258, Sumaré ☎ (11) 3875 4764 🕐 Noon-3pm Mon-Fri (to 4pm Sat & Sun)

⑤⑤⑤

Balaio Restaurante
Food honoring national flavors at cultural center Instituto Morales Salles.

📍C5 🏛 Paulista Ave, 2424 🌐 balaioims.com.br

⑤⑤⑤

Passengers on the platform at the Estação da Luz, which dates back to 1901

9

Museu Arte Sacra

F1 Av Tiradentes 676 Tiradentes Circular Turista 9am-5pm Tue-Sun museuartesacra.org.br

Often overlooked by visitors, this small museum has one of the finest collections of religious artifacts in the Americas. The exhibits are housed in a large wing of a distinguished colonial building, the early 19th-century Mosteiro da Luz. Restful and serene, the entire complex is a peaceful haven from the frenetic chaos of São Paulo.

The museum's priceless objects and artifacts include lavish monstrances (ceremonial vessels), ecclesiastical jewelry, and church altarpieces. Of particular note is the statuary, with pieces by many of the most important Brazilian Baroque masters; one of the gems is the 18th-century *Mary Magdalene* by artist Francisco Xavier de Brito, which displays an effortless unity of motion, and a sense of melancholy contemplation. Among the sculptures, mostly by anonymous Brazilian Indigenous artists, two pieces stand out – an African-Brazilian São Bento (with blue eyes), and an exquisitely detailed 18th-century Neapolitan nativity crib comprising around 2,000 pieces, which is the most important of its kind outside Naples.

10

Estação da Luz

F2 Praça da Luz 1 Luz (11) 3371 7274

One of modern Brazil's key symbols of industrial progress, São Paulo's railway station was built in 1901. Designed by a prominent British railway station architect, Charles Henry Driver, its design imitates the Victorian eclectic style.

Just like the rest of São Paulo's railways, Estação da Luz was the creation of Brazil's first industrialist, Visconde de Mauá. In 1854, Mauá opened his first railway, which was designed and run by the British. Romanesque red-brick arches and stately cast-iron pillars support a single vault that covers four tracks and platforms. Today, the Estação da Luz serves only the São Paulo city area. The station also houses the Museum of Portuguese Language.

11

Estação Pinacoteca

E2 Largo General Osório 66 Luz 10am-5:30pm Wed-Mon pinacoteca.org.br

Located in an attractive Neo-Classical building, this annex of the Pinacoteca de São Paulo *(p154)* is one of the city's best contemporary exhibition spaces. Some of Brazil's finest Modernist paintings, taken from the archive of São Paulo's Fundação José e Paulina Nemirovsky museum, are displayed here.

There are also key pieces by Cândido Portinari, Anita Malfatti, and Lasar Segall. International art is represented by Marc Chagall and Pablo Picasso, among others.

DRINK

Guarita Bar

A trendy, small bar serving top-notch cocktail creations. Try the Gaelito with bourbon, Campari, and cardamom.

B4 Rua Simão Álvares 952, Pinheiros (11) 99880 6892

$$$

Bar Kintaro

Tiny hidden gem in Liberdade inspired by a typical Japanese pub – very popular with the locals.

F4 Rua Thomaz Gonzaga 57, Liberdade (11) 3277 9124

$$$

STREET ART IN SAO PAULO

The graffiti capital of Brazil and South America, São Paulo is home to some of the continent's finest street murals. It is also the birthplace of one of the country's best street artists: Eduardo Kobra. Street art can be found citywide but is most common in and around Vila Madalena.

BECO DO BATMAN

São Paulo's most famous and popular street art collection can be found on Beco do Batman – an inspiring alleyway in the neighborhood of Vila Madalena. Also known as Batman Alley, the famed spot started in the 1980s with a mural of the iconic comic book superhero. Today, the area is covered with colorful designs by national and international artists.

AROUND TOWN

Graffiti can be found all over São Paulo. A jaw-dropping, 134-ft- (41-m-) tall mural pays homage to Formula 1 driver Ayrton Senna on the corner of Avenida Paulista and Consolação. Another impressive artwork at Escadão da Alves Guimarães portrays colorful ballet dancers on a large staircase. Both pieces are by Brazil's best muralist, Eduardo Kobra.

CONTROVERSY

However popular among visitors and street artists, São Paulo's graffiti has not come without controversy. In 2017, the city's largest open-air street art gallery on Avenida 23 de Maio was painted over on order from the city's mayor João Doria, as part of his "Pretty City" campaign.

↑ Spectacular street art on the famous Beco do Batman

↑ A large, colorful mural from Brazil's best graffiti artist, Eduardo Kobra

↑ A street artist on Rua Belmiro Braga in the Vila Madalena neighborhood

↑ View over Avenida Paulista and the Museu de Arte de São Paulo (MASP)

> ### LINA BO BARDI
>
> Italian-born Lina Bo Bardi was a Modernist architect who pushed boundaries with her unconventional work. In 1939, she graduated from the Rome College of Architecture, then in 1942, at the age of 28, she opened her own architectural studio in Milan. In 1946 she moved to Brazil where she designed social housing projects and furniture. Her most famous legacy is the iconic MASP building, where she applied a daring vision to its interior space. Exuding a raw, Brutalist energy, the museum is a striking addition to Avenida Paulista.

⑫   Sala São Paulo

📍 E2 🏛 Praça Júlio Prestes 16 Ⓜ Luz 🚇 🎫 Ticket office: noon–6pm Mon–Fri 🌐 salasaopaulo.art.br

Known for the finest acoustics in Latin America, this concert hall was inaugurated in 1997. It is the city's premier classical music venue for symphonic and chamber music, and the home of Brazil's top orchestra, the Orquestra Sinfônica do Estado de São Paulo (OSESP). The orchestra's artistic director, Arthur Nestrovski, is a composer and classical guitarist specializing in Brazilian music.

The grand railway building, the Estação Júlio Prestes, in which the hall is housed, was designed in 1938 by Brazilian architect Cristiano Stockler. Guided tours should be booked a day in advance.

⑬   Museu de Arte de São Paulo (MASP)

📍 C5 🏛 Av Paulista 1578 Ⓜ Trianon-Masp 🕐 10am–8pm Tue, 10am–6pm Wed–Sun 🌐 masp.art.br

Brazilian entrepreneur Assis Chateaubriand founded the Museu de Arte de São Paulo (MASP), the country's first modern museum, in 1947. He invited renowned Italian critic and collector Pietro Maria Bardi – husband of Italian-Brazilian architect Lina Bo Bardi – to manage it. The museum has a number of important pieces by northern European and Spanish artists such as Bosch, El Greco, Rembrandt, Velázquez, and Goya. Bardi's first acquisitions also include the now priceless works by Degas, Turner, Van Gogh, and Titian. Italian artists in the collections include a range of Renaissance names, such as Mantegna, Raphael, and Tintoretto. Modern French art is represented by works by Millet, Seurat, Manet, Cezanne, Toulouse-Lautrec, Chagall, and Picasso. There are also works by prominent Brazilian Modernist artists such as Brecheret, Cândido Portinari, and Tomie Ohtake.

These artworks comprise the southern hemisphere's most significant collection of European art, which also features works from Africa, Asia, and the Americas. There are more than 10,000 artworks in the collections, including paintings, sculptures, photographs, and installations. The oldest item is the statue of the goddess Hygieia, dating to 400 BCE. Among more modern artworks is Paulistano Marcelo Cidade's *Tempo Suspenso de um Estado Provisório* (2011). The extensive collection is constantly rotating, as artworks are taken in and out of the archive.

Inaugurated in 1968, Lina Bo Bardi's striking modern building focuses on the use of glass and concrete in the creation of a Brutalist structure with a light interior. The covered plaza below the museum, popularly known as Vão Livre ("free span"), is intended as a public square. This space is often full of street artists and market stalls selling crafts and antiques.

Instead of being hung on walls in the traditional manner, the artworks in the permanent collection are mounted on panels of clear glass fixed into concrete plinths. These were designed by Lina Bo Bardi, and are scattered around the second floor of the museum. There are no divisions of rooms or rigid timelines. The art seems to float in the air, providing visitors with a unique experience of walking among many artistic ages and cultures, freed from the weight of chronology. Captions are displayed on the backs of the works.

The museum includes a cultural center that hosts courses, seminars, and talks. There are also three floors that host a variety of temporary exhibitions. Entry to the museum is free on Tuesdays.

↑ Visitors examining paintings on display at the Museu de Arte de São Paulo

MARKETS IN SÃO PAULO

Brazil's biggest city, São Paulo, attracts people from all over the country, and one of its many drawcards is its great selection of markets. They are the perfect places to enjoy the hustle and bustle of the city and familiarize yourself with Brazil's rich variety of fruit and vegetables, and thriving food scene. São Paulo is also home to Brazil's biggest flower market, a stunning display of the country's colorful flora.

CEAGESP FLOWER MARKET

One of the most colorful places in São Paulo, this off-the-beaten-tourist-track flower market is the biggest in Brazil and takes place on Mondays and Fridays. It features more than one million flowers, plants, and products relating to floral care. It opened in 1969 and is at its busiest just before Mother's Day when about 2,000 tonnes of roses are bought.

MERCADO MUNICIPAL

Situated right in the heart of Sampa's city center, this municipal market is famous for its enormous *mortadella* sandwiches and vibrant fruit displays of fluorescent pitayas, green watermelons, deep red

INSIDER TIP
Beat the Rush

Head to Ceagesp Flower Market early, at 9am when it opens, to avoid the crowds and get some great snaps of the colorful flowers with few people around. Early risers will benefit from good deals and the freshest products.

← Bars and restaurants overlooking the market stalls in Mercado Municipal

↑ Marketgoers explore the wares at the Feira da Liberdade

strawberries, and dark purple jaboticaba. Designed by architect Francisco Ramos de Azevedo and opened in 1933, the 135,625-sq-ft- (12,600-sq-m-) market specializes in meats, fruits, vegetables, and spices. It has become one of São Paulo's most popular tourist destinations.

FEIRA DA LIBERDADE

In the middle of São Paulo's Japanese neighborhood, this lively and very popular food and handicraft fair takes place every Saturday and Sunday. It began in 1975 to showcase the work and skills of Brazil's Asian population and share a part of Japanese culture with the Brazilian society. Today, sellers of different nationalities trade plants, candles, and paintings, although many of the 200 stalls still represent the city's Japanese heritage, some serving *imagawayakis* (pancakes stuffed with red beans) and *yakisoba* (stir-fried buckwheat noodles).

MERCADO MUNICIPAL DE PINHEIROS

Opened in 1910, Mercado Municipal Engenheiro João Pedro de Carvalho Neto, colloquially called Mercado Municipal de Pinheiros, has long been a meeting point for Paulistanos (locals). Since 2014 it has had a revival and is now one of the city's best markets to source high-quality produce and rare ingredients from all over Brazil. It is made up of 39 "boxes" or shops selling spices, cheese, cold cuts, fruit, and vegetables. Today, it reflects São Paulo's status as Brazil's gastronomic hub with shops selling craft beer, restaurants serving Napoli-style pizza and ceviche, and a shop sourcing uncommon ingredients from the Mata Atlântica, the *cerrado*, and the Amazon. It is open from 8am to 6pm Monday to Saturday.

↑ Shoppers browsing the many aisles of local produce in the bustling Mercado Municipal

The lush Parque Trianon and *(inset)* the exterior of the Casa das Rosas, both located on Avenida Paulista

⑭
Avenida Paulista

📍D5 Ⓜ Brigadeiro, Trianon-Masp, Consolação

Modern São Paulo's first symbol of prosperity, Avenida Paulista and its crowded skyscrapers continue to attest to Brazil's status as the major economic power of South America. Though often compared to New York's Fifth Avenue, it is a corporate valley, business-like and functional.

By the turn of the 19th century, Avenida Paulista had become São Paulo's most desirable address, and was lined with expansive and opulent mansions owned by extremely wealthy Brazilian moguls, many prospering from the coffee trade. Having suffered large-scale demolition

after World War II, the avenue lost its character by the 1960s. Today, only one mansion remains, the French-style **Casa das Rosas**, which is now one of the area's many cultural centers. Art shows are often held in the 1935 mansion, which also has a rose garden and Art Nouveau stained-glass windows. Visiting hours have been reduced due to ongoing renovation.

A stroll along Avenida Paulista is an attraction in its own right, especially on Sundays, when it becomes a pedestrian park. Together

with the Praça da Sé *(p266)*, Paulista is one of the city's most important venues for protests and celebrations. There's also a range of museums, bookshops, and other cultural centers. The **Instituto Itaú Cultural**, near Brigadeiro metro station, hosts a variety of free concerts and exhibitions, and houses the largest currency museum in Brazil. The **Centro Cultural FIESP**, located at Trianon-Masp, is a business headquarters with a small cultural center that hosts free live music, theater, and art shows.

Immediately to its north is the wonderfully lush **Parque Trianon**, the only green respite from the concrete. In the quiet of the early morning, small mammals, including agouti and marmosets, can be seen foraging here.

SÃO PAULO FASHION WEEK

Established in 1996, São Paulo's fashion week is Latin America's most important fashion event. All of the top Brazilian names are showcased here, including designer Amir Slama and fashion brands with flagship stores on the famed Avenida Paulista. The show takes place twice a year – in January and March or April – in Oscar Niemeyer's Bienal building in Parque Estadual Cândido Portinari, Senac Lapa Faustolo, Sao Paulo's College of Technology, and Komplexo TEMPO nightclub in the Moóca district.

Casa das Rosas

Av Paulista 37 (11) 3285
6986 Noon-4pm Wed-Sat;
gardens: 7am-10pm daily

Instituto Itaú Cultural

Av Paulista 149 (11)
2168 1777 11am-8pm
Tue-Fri, 11am-7pm Sat & Sun

Centro Cultural FIESP

Av Paulista 1313 (11)
3322 0050 10am-8pm
Wed-Sun

Parque Trianon

Rua Peixoto Gomide 949
6am-5:30pm daily

 15

Museu do Futebol

B3 Estádio do
Pacaembu, Praça Charles
Miller s/n Clínicas
177C-10, 208M-10, 6232-
10 9am-5pm Tue-Sun
museudofutebol.org.br

The Museum of Football
is not to be missed by any
fan of "the beautiful game."
Explore the history of soccer in
Brazil and its impact on both
local society and the global
community. The focus here is
as much on Brazilian people
as it is on the sport itself,
allowing visitors to get a sense
of how habits and behaviors
have changed in this country
throughout the 21st century.

 16

Liberdade

F5 Praça da Sé, via Av
da Liberdade Praça de
Sé, Liberdade Liberdade
Rodoviária

São Paulo is home to a large
Japanese population (p52).
Liberdade, located just south of
the city center, is the hub of this
community, as well as many
people of Korean and Chinese
heritage. The area is small and
is easily explored on foot. On
Sundays, there is a market in
the **Praça de Liberdade**, where
stalls serve steaming lacquer
bowls of miso soup and
yakisoba noodles. Liberdade's
main thoroughfare, Rua Galvão
Bueno, runs south from this
square, lined with the bulk of
the shops and decorated with
red Japanese arches, or *torii*.
Many of the neighborhood's
most traditional Japanese
restaurants are located on, and
around, Rua Tomaz Gonzaga.

At the corner of Galvão
Bueno and Rua São Joaquim,
an unassuming block houses
the compelling **Museu da
Imigração Japonesa** (Japanese
Immigration Museum). It has
two floors of artifacts and
displays devoted to telling
the story of the Japanese
immigrant community, their
origins, and their lives in early
20th-century Brazil. On the
same street is one of São

STAY

Tivoli Mofarrej

Stylish hotel with
impeccable rooms and a
rooftop bar, hosting live
jazz weekday nights.

C5 Alameda Santos
1437, Jardins
tivolihotels.com

We Hostel

Beautifully decorated
hostel offering
good-value rooms.

B4 Rua Morgado de
Mateus, Vila Mariana
567 (11) 2615 2262

Guest Urban

Trendy design hotel
close to Pinheiro's many
bars and restaurants.

B4 Rua Lisboa 493,
Pinheiros guest
urbansp.com.br

Paulo's many Buddhist
temples, the **Templo Busshinji**.
Visitors are welcome to attend
the various ceremonies, the
most impressive of which is the
Cerimônia de Kannon, which
takes place each month.

Museu da Imigração Japonesa

Rua São Joaquim 381
(11) 3209 5465 10am-
5pm Tue-Sun

Templo Busshinji

Rua São Joaquim
285 8am-5pm Mon-Sat
sotozen.org.br

 ←

Children playing table
football at the fascinating
Museu do Futebol

⓱ Parque da Independência

📍C4 🏠Av Nazareth, Ipiranga 🚌5108-10 🕐5am–8pm daily (Museum: 11am–5pm Tue–Sun; entry only by advance booking online) 🌐museudo ipiranga.org.br

In 1822, Dom Pedro I declared the famous "Grito de Ipiranga," or call for independence from Portugal, on the banks of the Rio Ipiranga. This day is also known as Independência ou Morte, or Independence or Death. The formal park that now occupies this site includes a 1890 palace, one of the earliest monuments of independent Brazil.

The mock French Renaissance gardens in front of the palace include an enormous bronze sculpture to the nation's independence, *Monumento a Independência*, made by the Italian sculptor Ettore Ximenes in 1921. In the chapel at the base of the monument a tomb contains the remains of Dom Pedro I and Empress Leopoldina.

The Museu Paulista is housed in the palace at the top of these formal gardens. It reopened in late 2022, following a major 10-year restoration, with the interior totally modernized. Devoted to the nation's history, its exhibits include old maps, traditional colonial furniture, and rare documents. Pedro Américo's monumental canvas *Independência ou Morte* (1888), depicting the young prince shouting his *grito* (cry), sits in the handsome Salão Nobre.

⓲ Jardim Botânico

📍B5 🏠Av Miguel Stéfano 3031 📞(11) 3031 2961 🚌 🕐9am–5pm Tue–Sun 🌐jardimbotanico.com.br

The Jardim Botânico is the largest area of green in São Paulo's metropolitan area. It combines formal gardens, laid out around a series of lakes, with areas of forest large enough to support several resident troops of red howler monkeys. Their guttural calls can be heard at dawn and dusk and sometimes the monkeys can be seen in the trees. There is plenty of other wildlife too, including agoutis, pacas, and tufted-eared marmosets.

The entrance to the park is through an avenue of magnificent royal palms, surrounded by tropical and subtropical trees. Most are labeled with their common and scientific names (the former in Portuguese only). Glass houses in one of the park's gardens, the Jardim de Lineu, contain a number of Atlantic rainforest plants. There is also a botanical museum that preserves a bank of Brazilian seeds.

Beyond the Jardim de Lineu are lovely areas of ponds and lawns popular with picnickers on the weekends.

INSIDER TIP
Avoid the Jam

Avoid traveling by car in the city during rush hour (7–10am and 5–8pm). Instead, cycle, walk or take the metro. An hour can easily be added to your journey at these times, especially just before Christmas.

⓳ Museu de Arte Contemporânea

📍B4 🏠Av Pedro Alvares Cabral 1301, Ibirapuera 🚌 🕐11am–9pm Tue–Sun 🌐mac.usp.br

A treasure trove of modern and Postmodern European and

Brazilian art lies tucked away in the campus of São Paulo's most distinguished university. The collection at the Museu de Arte Contemporânea (MAC) is an amalgamation of donations given by wealthy individuals since the early 20th century and prizes from São Paulo's Art Biennials. The collection comprises some 10,000 works of art, from important, little-seen works by Pablo Picasso, Max Ernst, and Henri Matisse, to the cream of Brazil's artists, including Modernists such as Anita Malfatti and Victor Brecheret. MAC also holds three of the most celebrated works by one of the most significant Latin American Modernists, Tarsila do Amaral – *A Negra, Estrada de Ferro Central do Brasil*, and *Floresta*.

Instituto Butantã

📍 A4 🏠 Av Vital Brazil 1500, Cidade Universitária 🚇 🕐 7am–5pm daily 🌐 butantan.gov.br

The Instituto Butantã is a biomedical research center affiliated to the University of São Paulo. Founded in 1901 by Brazilian physician, Vital Brasil,

to conduct research into venomous animals, the institute is now one of the leading producers of anti-venoms and sera in the world. It is also one of the city's principal tourist attractions, as it is located in a pretty forested garden full of hummingbirds.

Special enclosures alongside the center and an adjacent museum house many of South America's rare snakes and arachnids. Smaller but even deadlier creatures can be seen through microscopes in the institute's **Museu de Microbiologia**. This modern space also includes interactive displays that are particularly popular with children.

21

Parque Burle Marx

📍 A5 🏠 Av Dona Helena Pereira de Morais 200 🚌 6291-10, 637A-10, 677A-10, 807P-10 🕐 7am–7pm daily 🌐 parqueburlemarx. com.br

Roberto Burle Marx (1909–94) was South America's greatest landscape architect and one of the three core designers of the city of Brasília (*p236*). He was one of the first architects to combine sculptural and painting techniques with landscape design. His gardens in the Parque Burle Marx have been compared to abstract paintings, utilizing shapes, and some curvilinear and rectilinear patterns to create blocks of color and texture, broken by paths and areas of woodland.

Marx was a keen ecologist and promoted the use of Brazilian native species, and the park is surrounded by a small area of forest that comprises plant and bird species from the Mata Atlântica.

←

Looking toward the grand Museu Paulista in the Parque da Independência

SHOP

Mercado do Municipal de Pinheiros
Superb food market with an excellent assortment of artisanal cheese, cold cuts, fruit, wine, and nuts.

📍 B4 🏠 Rua Pedro Cristi 89, Pinheiros 🌐 mercadomunicipal depinheiros.com

---

Projeto Terra
Shop selling a unique selection of original, high-quality jewelry, woven baskets, and intricately carved wooden boxes.

📍 B4 🏠 Rua Harmonia 150, Vila Madalena

PatBO
Flagship store of the exclusive Brazilian fashion label. Expect flowing dresses, colorful beachwear, and fine accessories.

📍 B5 🏠 Rua Bela Cintra 1950, Jardins 🌐 patbo.com.br

Although Marx contributed to the landscape design of Parque do Ibirapuera (*p156*), this park is the only exclusive example of his work in his home city. The gardens were originally private, commissioned for the millionaire industrialist "Baby" Pignatari in the 1940s.

As well as landscaping, Burle Marx was allowed to experiment and place abstract structures in the gardens. These include mirrors of water and rectangular blocks remi-niscent of the low Mixtec buildings seen in the archaeo-logical site of Mitla, Mexico. The constructions near the avenue of palms at the park's entrance are by Oscar Niemeyer.

SÃO PAULO STATE

São Paulo was once inhabited by numerous Tupí peoples, primarily the Tupinambá/Tamoio and Tupiniquim communities. Despite fierce resistance put up by the Indigenous Tamoio Confederation, the Tupí failed to stop Portuguese colonization along the coast – they were gradually wiped out by disease or enslaved by the colonizers. Portuguese explorer Martim Afonso de Sousa established São Vicente on the coast in 1532, the first permanent Portuguese settlement in Brazil – the captaincy of São Vicente was the precursor of the modern state of São Paulo. Portuguese development of the interior remained limited until sugar production ramped up in 18th century; the inland city of Campinas was founded only in 1774.

By the late 19th century coffee dominated the state, especially in the Paraíba valley, helping to make the region one of the richest in South America. Sugar and coffee were exported through Santos, founded in 1546 and today Latin America's biggest port. Immigration from Japan and Europe, especially Italy, had transformed the state by the 1890s, with the new arrivals filling new factories and working the coffee plantations as paid laborers.

Today, not only is São Paulo the most populous and wealthy state in Brazil, accounting for an astonishing third of the nation's GDP, but it is also rich in natural wonders, with the full majesty of the Mata Atlântica – the Atlantic coastal forest – unfolding around Mosaico Juréia-Itatins and Cananéia in the Litoral Sul.

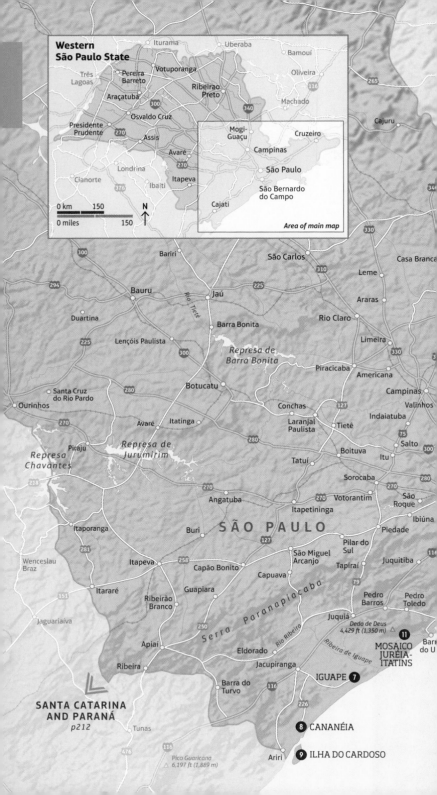

Iturama
Uberaba
Bamouí
Oliveira
Três Lagoas
Pereira Barreto
Votuporanga
Ribeirão Preto
Machado
265
Araçatuba
300
340
Cajuru
Presidente Prudente
Osvaldo Cruz
270
Mogi-Guaçu
Cruzeiro
Assis
Campinas
116
Avaré
270
São Paulo
Cianorte
Londrina
São Bernardo do Campo
376
Ibaiti
Itapeva
Cajati
34

0 km 150
0 miles 150
N

Area of main map

330
Bariri
São Carlos
Casa Branca
310
Leme
294
Bauru
Jaú
225
Araras
Duartina
Rio Claro
Barra Bonita
Limeira
225
Lençóis Paulista
300
Represa de Barra Bonita
330
Piracicaba
3
Santa Cruz do Rio Pardo
280
Botucatu
Conchas
Americana
Campinas
Ourinhos
127
Valinhos
270
Avaré
Itatinga
Laranjal Paulista
Indaiatuba
Tietê
75
Represa de Jurumirim
280
Boituva
Salto
Piraju
Itu
300
Represa Chavantes
Tatuí
Sorocaba
280
218
270
Votorantim
São Roque
Angatuba
Itapetininga
270
Ibiúna
Itaporanga
SÃO PAULO
Piedade
Buri
127
Pilar do Sul
116
Wenceslau Braz
Itapeva
256
São Miguel Arcanjo
Juquitiba
151
Itararé
Capão Bonito
Capuava
Tapiraí
79
Guapiara
Pedro Barros
Pedro Toledo
Jaguariaíva
Ribeirão Branco
Serra Paranapiacaba
Juquiá
Dedo de Deus 4,429 ft (1,350 m) △
11
Apiaí
250
Eldorado
Rio Ribeira
Ribeira de Iguape
MOSAICO JURÉIA-ITATINS
Barra do U
Ribeira
Jacupiranga
IGUAPE 7
SANTA CATARINA AND PARANÁ
p212
Barra do Turvo
116
Tunas
226
8 CANANÉIA
116
Pico Guaricana 6,197 ft (1,889 m) △
Ariri
9 ILHA DO CARDOSO

SÃO PAULO STATE

Must See
1. Ilhabela

Experience More
2. Ubatuba
3. São Sebastião
4. Maresias
5. Guarujá
6. São Vicente
7. Iguape
8. Cananéia
9. Ilha do Cardoso
10. Santos
11. Mosaico Juréia-Itatins

Passos

265

146

Tapiratiba

Poços de Caldas

Campanha

MINAS GERAIS

Cazambu

Bom Jardim de Minas

459

Cristina

Pouso Alegre

Agulhas Negras
9,143 ft (2,787 m)

MINAS GERAIS
p182

459

Itajubá

RIO DE JANEIRO
AND
ESPÍRITO SANTO
p130

Lindoia

Amparo

381

360

Bragança
Paulista

381

Piracaia

Itatiba

Atibaia

65

undiaí

Franco da
Rocha

48

São
Paulo

Sao Paulo Airport

SÃO PAULO
CITY
p150

21

São José dos
Campos

Jacareí

Itaquaquecetuba

Moji
das Cruzes

Salesópolis

Cubatão

SÃO VICENTE 6 10 SANTOS

Praia
Grande

55

5

GUARUJÁ

Itanhaém

Campos
do Jordão

Lorena

Pindamonhangaba

50

Cacapava

116

Taubaté

Lagoinha

São Luís do
Paraitinga

Paraitinga

Cunha

Piquete

Areias

Bananal

Bairro dos
Macacos

Serão da
Bocaina

Mambucaba

101

Paraty

Ilha Grande

125

55

2 UBATUBA

Paraibuna

50

88

Caraguatatuba

MARESIAS
4

3

SÃO SEBASTIÃO

ILHABELA
1

Ilha do São Sebastião

Ponta do Boi

Ilha de
Alcatrazes

Atlantic
Ocean

SÃO PAULO
STATE

0 kilometers   50

0 miles   50

N
↑

❶

ILHABELA

🅰 E6 🚢 From São Sebastião to Barra Velha ℹ Rua Prefeito Mariano Procópio de Araújo Carvalho, 86; www.ilhabela.sp.gov.br

The well named "Beautiful Island" is a forested playground for its many visitors. Fringed with lovely beaches, its interior parkland is home to an abundance of flora and fauna. Offshore shipwrecks are a haven for marine life, while its west coast is lined with relaxing *pousadas*.

One of Brazil's largest islands, Ilhabela rises steeply out of the Atlantic, a short distance offshore from São Sebastião. With a coastline sculpted by dozens of bays and beaches, it is covered in rainforest, much of it bisected by fast-flowing mountain streams. Visitors from São Paulo throng here during weekends, but during the week (outside of holiday season) the island is all but deserted. Much of the forest is protected as part of the Parque Estadual de Ilhabela and there is plenty of wildlife, including ocelots and several species of primates. The presence of biting flies, or *borrachudos*, on the island make insect repellent essential.

Ilhabela has just two roads. One is paved and runs the entire length of the western, leeward coast. Most of the numerous *pousadas* and guesthouses lie here, as do the villages of Perequê (where the ferry arrives), Borrifos, São Pedro, and Vila Ilhabela. The latter has a few colonial remains. Rusting 18th-century cannons adorn its waterfront and there is a little avenue of Portuguese buildings, including a 16th-century church, the Matriz de Nossa Senhora d'Ajuda.

The island's other road is a dirt track, usable only by 4WDs, which cuts across the interior from Perequê into the park and to the windward beaches. The most spectacular of these

The palm-fringed coastline of Ilhabela, which is dotted with *(inset)* picturesque churches →

ILHABELA'S WATERFALLS

Ilhabela's forests are full of waterfalls, but many are either completely inaccessible or reachable only by trail. A short distance inland from Perequê beach, Cachoeira da Toca waterfalls plunge in a series of little cascades into swimming pools, replete with natural waterslides. Água Branca is larger, with more pools. It is an hour's walk along a trail that begins at the entrance to the state park, just beyond the turnoff to Cachoeira da Toca.

is the Baía de Castelhanos, a perfect half-moon of sand backed by rainforest-covered slopes. The island's longest beach, and the best for surfing, is Bonete, which is 9 miles (15 km) south from Borrifos village, along a rough forest trail.

Numerous shipwrecks off Ilhabela also make the island a popular scubadiving destination, despite the murky water.

EXPERIENCE MORE

❷
Ubatuba

🅰E6 🚫🚍 ℹ️ Av Iperoig 214;
www.turismo.ubatuba.sp.
gov.br

Lying at the northern extreme of São Paulo state and sitting at the feet of the Serra do Mar mountain range, Ubatuba is a little beach resort with a small colonial center lined with terraced houses. Glorious beaches surround the resort.

The most popular beaches, especially Praia Grande, have excellent infrastructure, including play areas for children. Even in high season it is easy to find a quiet stretch of sand or lonely cove tucked away along the coast to the south of Ubatuba.

The **Aquário de Ubatuba** in the town center contains some of the largest tanks and most diverse range of tropical marine life in all of Brazil. The office of the **Projeto Tamar**, a Brazil-wide organization that monitors and preserves turtle nesting beaches, is also located in town. Visitors are permitted to witness supervised turtle hatchings.

The Serra do Mar rises in a vertiginous green wall a short distance north of Ubatuba and an easy drive away from the town. Carpeted in thick primary forest, it is home to many endangered endemic species and prolific birdlife.

The twin beaches of Domingas Dias and Lázaro, whose white sands curve gently on either side of a forest-clad promontory, are located 11 miles (18 km) south of Ubatuba.

Aquário de Ubatuba
♻️ 🏠 Rua Guaraní 859
📞 (12) 3834 1382
🕙 10am–10pm daily
🌐 aquariodeubatuba.com.br

Projeto Tamar
🏠 Rua A Atanázio 273 📞 (12)
3832 6202 🕙 10am–5pm
Thu–Tue 🌐 tamar.org.br

---

❸
São Sebastião

🅰E6 ℹ️ Rua
Expedicionário Brasileiro
181; www.turismosao
sebastiao.com.br/home

São Sebastião is the oldest town on the northern coast of São Paulo state. It was first occupied by the Tupinambá people in the north and the Tupiniquins in the south, separated by the Serra de Boiçucanga mountain range, located 18.6 miles (30 km) south of the city center.

This region became the northernmost Portuguese

EAT

Dine on delicious
seafood dishes at these
charming restaurants.

Manacá
🅰E6 🏠 Rua Manacá
102, São Sebastião
🌐 restaurante
manaca.com.br

$$$

O Rei do Peixe
🅰E6 🏠 Rua Guarani 480
🌐 oreidopeixe.com.br

$$$

↑ Summer crowds enjoying the beach at Ubatuba

outpost for the Indigenous slave trade. As it grew, it became one of the country's first sugar-growing centers and was among the first cities to receive enslaved African people.

The region was founded in the early 17th century, when Brazil's coastline was cloaked in a forest larger than the Amazon. The city's colonial streets lie in the few blocks between the shoreline and central Praça Major João Fernandes, easily recognizable by the 17th-century church, **Igreja Matriz**. This is largely a 19th-century reconstruction devoid of much of its original church art. However, the refurbished **Museu de Arte Sacra**, housed in the nearby 17th-century chapel of São Gonçalo, preserves a number of beautiful, delicate images of Christ. Dating from the 16th century, they were found within wall cavities of the Igreja Matriz during its restoration in 2003.

There are also a few streets lined with houses and civic buildings, the most impressive of which is the **Casa Esperança** on the waterfront; now home to a textiles store. Built from stone, wattle and daub, and congealed with whale oil, the exterior is whitewashed with lime made from crushed shells.

Igreja Matriz

⌂ Praça Major João Fernandes 📞 (12) 3892 1110 🕐 2–4pm Mon, 8am–6pm Tue, Thu & Fri, 9am–noon Sat

Museu de Arte Sacra

⌂ Rua Sebastião Silvestre Neves 90 📞 (12) 3892 4286 🕐 8am–5pm Mon–Fri, 9am–2pm Sat

Casa Esperança

⌂ Av Altino Arantes 144 🕐 9am–5pm Mon–Fri, 8:30am–noon Sat

---

④ Maresias

🅰 E6 🛈 Rua Sebastião Silvestre Neves, 214, São Sebastião, 17 miles (27 km); (12) 3892 2620; www.maresias.com.br

South of São Sebastião lie a number of beautiful beach resorts. Maresias, the liveliest of the lot, is busy with young, hip Paulistanos at weekends and holidays. Praia de Maresias is famous for its powerful surf, which has been the site of many international surfing competitions. Toque Toque Grande and Toque Toque Pequeno, 6 miles (9 km) southeast, are smaller, quieter beaches, sheltered by rainforest-covered spurs. They are separated by the pretty Praia das Calhetas, known for its marvelous snorkeling.

---

⑤ Guarujá

🅰 E6 🛈 Av Marechal Deodoro da Fonseca 723; 9am–5pm Mon–Fri; (13) 3344 4600; www.guaruja.sp.gov.br

Situated close to São Paulo, and on the way to Santos (*p180*), this beach town is a popular weekend and day-trip destination for São Paulo residents. It is known as the "Pearl of the Atlantic" and has about 14 miles (23 km) of white beaches that stretch along the coastline. The longest of these, Enseada Beach, is popular with surfers, and its shores are lined with hotels and kiosks. The town center is a pleasant place to stroll, but the water's edge is Guarujá's biggest drawcard, especially for fishing, swimming, and sunbathing.

↑ One of Guarujá's many pretty beaches, beautifully illuminated at night

São Vicente

E6 Rua Frei Gaspar, 384, São Vicente; open 9am-5pm Mon-Fri; www.sao vicente.sp.gov.br/publico

The laid-back port town of São Vicente is known more for its historical significance than the usual tourist attractions.

In 1532, Portuguese explorer Martim Afonso de Sousa established a small settlement on the eastern shores of South America, eventually leading to the colonization of Brazil. Only a handful of relics belonging to that time in history can be found in São Vicente today.

The 18th-century Baroque parish church, the **Igreja Matriz de São Vicente Mártir**, is one of the few historical buildings in the city to have survived the ravages of time. The current building is named in honor of the Spanish saint who is patron of the city. Also in the city center are the remains of Martim Afonso's former home, and the first fortress built in Brazil. These are housed inside the impressive late 19th-century **Casa Martim Afonso**, which is being renovated.

Igreja Matriz de São Vicente Mártir

Praça João Pessoa s/n, Centro (13) 3468 2658
8am-7pm Mon-Sat, 8am-noon & 5-7pm Sun

Casa Martim Afonso

Praça 22 de Janeiro 469, Centro (13) 3568 8948
For renovation

Iguape

E6 Av Adhemar de Barros 1070; open 8-11:30am & 1-5:30pm Mon-Fri; www.iguape.sp. gov.br

This pretty little colonial town sits in a pocket of the Brazilian coastal rainforest, the Complexo Estuarino Lagunar de Iguape-Cananéia biosphere reserve, a UNESCO World Heritage Site. The verdant Serra do Mar mountains rise up behind the town, which is surrounded by pristine mangrove wetlands and lowland subtropical forest on all sides. The Mirante do Morro do Espio has a lovely view of the port and surrounding area.

Iguape was founded in 1538 by the Portuguese. No buildings remain from that time but the city center preserves the largest and oldest heritage-listed collection of post-17th-century colonial architecture in the state. Most are civic buildings and townhouses painted in primary colors and clustered around Praça São Benedito.

The **Museu Histórico e Arqueológico** is housed in a 17th-century building that was once the first gold foundry in Brazil. It showcases various historical material. The **Museu de Arte Sacra** in the Basílica do Bom Jesus houses some 150 ecclesiastical objects dating from the 17th to 19th centuries.

Just across the Rio Ribeira do Iguape estuary, east of the town center, are stretches of fine white-sand beaches that make up Ilha Comprida. They are accessible by road, or a 5-mile (8-km) walk.

Museu Histórico e Arqueológico

Rua das Neves 45 (13) 3841 3358 10am-noon & 2-6pm Fri-Mon

Museu de Arte Sacra

Basílica do Bom Jesus de Iguape, Praça da Basílica 10am-noon & 2-6pm Fri-Mon

↑ Groups of surfers and *jangadas* (traditional fishing boats) on the Iguape coastline

8

Cananéia

AE6 🚌 *i* Av Independência 374, Cananéia; www.cananeia. sp.gov.br

Cananéia is the farthest south of São Paulo's colonial seaside towns, and like the others lies nestled at the feet of the Serra do Mar mountains. Outside of the high season few visitors make it here and the town's crumbling colonial streets and central square often have a tranquil atmosphere.

The most compelling reason to come to Cananéia is to take a boat trip out to the beaches and islands that are heritage-listed by UNESCO as part of the Lagamar estuary. Fishing boats and launches can be chartered from the docks to Ilha do Cardoso, while car and passenger rafts ferry across the estuary in front of the town to the southern reaches of the Ilha Comprida. The beaches here lie a short distance beyond the island's ferry port.

While in Cananéia, it is worth visiting the tiny town museum, **Museu Municipal**,

↑ An array of colorful local fishing boats bobbing in Cananéia's calm bay

which preserves bits of nautical miscellany. Pride of place goes to what is reputed to be the second-largest great white shark ever, weighing a hefty 7,716 lb (3,500 kg), now stuffed and hanging safely from the museum ceiling.

Museu Municipal
 🏠 Rua Tristão Lobo 78 📞 (13) 3851 1753 🕐 1:30-5:30pm Tue-Sun

9

Ilha do Cardoso

AE6 🚌 From Cananéia *i* Núcleo Perequê, Cananéia; www.cana neia.net

Just a 30-minute boat ride south of Cananéia, Ilha do Cardoso, a rugged 58 sq-mile-(150 sq-km-) island, rises dramatically out of the Atlantic Ocean. The island is primarily an ecological reserve, which also has beautiful deserted beaches and walking trails.

Several species of turtle nest on the island, caimans live in the rivers and estuaries, and jaguars and pumas still hunt in the forests that cover the upper reaches. The island is also rich in birdlife. Seven

traditional *caiçara* fishing communities live on Ilha do Cardoso, preserving a semi-Indigenous way of life. Today, many of these local *caiçaras* also act as tour guides and boaters.

TOP 3 LOCAL FESTIVALS

Festa do Mar
Annual food festival in June, attracting more than 35,000 visitors with live bands, dance performances, and plenty of regional seafood dishes.

Festas de Agosto
Taking place in mid-August, this week-long festival consists of canoe racing, religious processions, live music, beach volleyball tournaments, and more.

Festa da Tainha
Annual mullet festival held in July on Ilha do Cardoso, a short boat ride from Cananéia, honoring the ray-finned fish. Regional mullet dishes are the main focus.

←
The exterior of the Museo do Café in Santos, formerly the Coffee Stock Exchange Building, and *(inset)* its elegant interior

10

Santos

E6 Praça Mauá, Centro Histórico; open 11am-5pm Tue-Sun; www.prefeituradesantos.org

When Santos was founded in 1535, it was one of Portugal's first settlements in the Americas. As a port, it first dealt with sugar, then grew rich on coffee, which was brought out of the mountains on Brazil's first trains, built by the British in the late 19th century.

Unlike São Vicente, Santos has preserved vestiges of its historical legacy, and, under recent enlightened municipal governance, is reinventing and refurbishing itself. Once very run down, the city center is undergoing a spruce-up. Scottish trams in British racing green run through its streets, taking visitors on a whistle-stop tour of the various attractions.

The jewel in the city's crown is the Art Nouveau **Museu do Café**. Its modest Victorian exterior hides an opulent marble-floored turn-of-the-19th-century stock exchange, now a museum, together with a café serving excellent coffee. When it was built, coffee was the most important and coveted commodity in Brazil. The museum's auction room is crowned by a magnificent stained-glass skylight, which has an arresting representation of Brazil, the *Mãe Douro*. This and the beautiful Neo-Renaissance painting of Santos that adorns the walls of the stock exchange are by Brazil's most celebrated mid-19th-century artist, Benedito Calixto.

A number of Calixto's paintings are also displayed in the **Pinacoteca Benedito Calixto**, which is housed in one of the few remaining coffee-baron mansions. The landscapes shown here give an idea of the city's once breathtaking natural beauty.

Santos has a handful of interesting churches, but the only one open to the public is the **Santuário Santo Antônio do Valongo**, which has a mock-Baroque interior that dates from the 1930s. The fine original 17th-century altarpiece remains preserved in the Franciscan chapel to the left of the main entrance; the statue of Christ is particularly striking.

The beaches here were once very dirty, but they are now much cleaner and lively with bustling bazaars, and people playing volleyball and soccer.

FOOTBALL LEGEND

Pelé, one the world's most famous sportspersons, was born in Tres Corações, Minas Gerais, in 1940. He started his soccer career in Santos in 1956 and later joined the Brazilian national team; he went on to play in three of Brazil's five World Cup-winning teams. He died in December 2022.

Santos also houses the small but very popular **Aquário de Santos**, which displays, in addition to a stunning range of tropical marine life, three of the five species of sea turtles found in Brazil.

For all its history, it is for soccer that Santos is most famous outside Brazil. Pelé (Edson Arantes do Nascimento) played here for almost all his professional life. The Santos Football Club has an excellent museum, the **Memorial das Conquistas**, devoted to the club's illustrious history (advance booking is required).

Museu do Café

🏛️☕ 🚪Rua 15 de Novembro 95 🕐9am-6pm Tue-Sat (from 10am Sun) 🌐museu docafe.org.br

Pinacoteca Benedito Calixto

🚪Av Bartolomeu de Gusmão 15 🕐9am-6pm Tue-Sun 🌐pinacotecadesantos.org.br

Santuário Santo Antônio do Valongo

🚪Largo Marquês de Monte Alegre 13 📞(13) 3219 1481 🕐9am-5:30pm Tue-Fri (to 4pm Sat, to 6pm Sun)

Aquário de Santos

🏛️ 🚪Av Bartolomeu de Gusmão, Ponta da Praia 📞(13) 3278 7830 🕐9am-6pm Thu-Tue

Memorial das Conquistas

🏛️🏛️ 🚪Rua Princesa Isabel 77, Vila Belmiro 🕐9am-6pm daily (except on match days; check website to book in advance) 🌐memorial dasconquistas.com.br

---

Mosaico Juréia-Itatins

🗺️E6 🚌To Iguape or Peruíbe, then taxi 🛈Peruíbe: Estrada do Guaraú 4, 164 Bairro Guaraú; (13) 3457 9243

Brazil's coastal rainforest stretches along the coast of São Paulo State in a series of rippling mountains and low-land forests divided by broad rivers, mangrove wetlands, and pristine beaches, as well as by traditional fishing and farming communities. The Mosaico Juréia-Itatins encompasses six protected rainforest areas, four of which are open to visitors. Peruíbe is a good base for information. This region protects Atlantic rainforest and its associated ecosystems. It is one of the most important breeding grounds for marine species in the southern Atlantic and the myriad forest types growing here protect one of the world's greatest diversities of vascular plant, vertebrate, and invertebrate species. There is a unique range of butterflies, birds, and mammals. Larger animals, such as jaguars and tapirs, which have all but disappeared from coastal Brazil, live in healthy numbers here.

Juréia itself protects many habitats; as a result the scenery is magnificent. The extensive forest swathes the high slopes of the Serra do Itatins in the eastern part of the park and continues to the lowland coastal areas, mixing with mangrove wetlands and perfuming the park's beaches. These beautiful stretches of fine sand, many cut by clear rivers or washed by waterfalls, are so deserted that caimans can occasionally be seen basking in the sun at dawn.

Did You Know?

The jaguar is the largest of all the big cats found in the Americas.

↑ Mosaico Juréia-Itatins's lush green rainforest, blanketing the coast of São Paulo State

View of Ouro Preto old town and its colonial, hillside homes

MINAS GERAIS

Indigenous peoples lived in this region for millennia before the Europeans arrived – the skeleton of the "Luzia Woman," discovered here in 1974, is 11,500 years old. By the 17th century, the Xakriabá, Maxakali, Crenaques, Pataxós, and many other Indigenous peoples had made this area their home. When São Paulo *bandeirantes* (fortune hunters) arrived in the 1600s, these Indigenous communities were killed, enslaved, or decimated by disease.

The Brazilian gold rush began here in 1693, and, almost overnight, miners' camps at Ouro Preto and Sabará mushroomed into cities. Indeed, the region owes its very name – Minas Gerais means "general mines" – to the gold. Gold profits in the 18th century fueled the construction of opulent palaces and churches and paid for fabulous Baroque religious artwork by the likes of Brazilian sculptor Aleijadinho. Ouro Preto became the state capital, famous as the birthplace of the 1789 Inconfidência Mineira (the Minas Conspiracy), the first attempt to free Brazil from the Portuguese. It was an utter failure – the plotters were betrayed before any uprising was organized.

By the mid-19th century, with the gold rush long over, Ouro Preto had become a backwater, with its rugged topography limiting new development. A site for a new capital was chosen in the center of Minas, and Belo Horizonte was inaugurated in 1897 as the first of Brazil's major planned state capitals. Alongside São Paulo, Minas Gerais influenced national politics well into the 20th century, with wealthy oligarchs from both places selecting Brazilian presidents in turn, a corrupt deal known as Café com Leite or "coffee with milk," named after the major products of each state.

MINAS GERAIS

Must Sees
1 Ouro Preto
2 Diamantina
3 Basílica do Senhor Bom Jesus de Matosinhos

Experience More
4 Mariana
5 Parque Nacional Serra do Cipó
6 Belo Horizonte
7 Tiradentes
8 São João del Rei
9 Parque Nacional Serra da Canastra

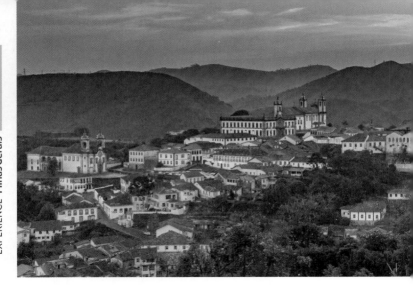

❶

OURO PRETO

🅐E5 🚌From Belo Horizonte 🛈Rua Cláudio Manoel, 61; open 11am–5pm daily; www.ouropreto.org.br

Ouro Preto, or "Black Gold," earned its name from the tarnished gold nuggets mined in the area. By the mid-18th century the gold rush had turned Ouro Preto into a wealthy town and it nurtured some of the continent's finest artists. The town was also the base of the Inconfidência Mineira, an unsuccessful separatist movement led by Tiradentes against Portuguese colonists.

①

Igreja de São Francisco de Assis

🅐Largo de Coimbra 🅒(31) 3551 3282 🕙8:30am–noon, 1:30–5pm Tue–Sun

This understated, elegant little church was constructed between 1766 and 1802 and seems modest next to many of Latin America's grand Baroque churches. It is characterized by gentle curves, from the elegant S-shaped balustrades of its facade to the exquisitely unified, undulating lines of its interior. The quality of the church's beauty lies in the mastery of its art, created by two of Brazil's greatest artists, Aleijadinho and his long-term partner Manuel da Costa Athayde (1762–1830). The tablet on the church's facade showing St. Francis receiving the stigmata is believed to have been Aleijadinho's first great carving. It was followed by others, including the ornately carved door-case and the front of the sacristy at the rear of the church.

---

②

Matriz de Nossa Senhora do Pilar

🅐Praça Mons Castilho Barbosa 🅒(31) 3551 4736 🕙Museum: 9–10:45am & noon–4:45pm Tue–Sun

Commissioned by two of the wealthiest ecclesiastical orders in Ouro Preto, this church was intended as a

---

CHICO REI

Chico Rei, enslaved in Ouro Preto's 18th-century gold mines, is thought to have been a former king from the present-day Democratic Republic of Congo. The king, his family, and his people were captured by Portuguese traders, shipped to Brazil and sold into slavery. Having eventually gained his freedom, Chico Rei became the owner of a mine in turn, and earned legendary status for his tireless efforts to free other enslaved people.

↑ Sunset over the whitewashed houses of Ouro Preto

showpiece of their influence. Its inauguration in 1731 witnessed grand processions of clergy in opulent vestments and horses in velvet mantles mounted by knights in diamond-studded robes.

Today, the greatest display of wealth is inside the church, with the crypt housing some 400 pieces in the Museu de Arte Sacra. Nearly half a ton of both gold and silver were used to gild its spectacular interior, which is largely the work of 18th-century sculptor Francisco Xavier de Brito, an expatriate Portuguese. The gilt carving of Christ on the Cross on the door-case and the Resurrection scene on the tabernacle are regarded as de Brito's finest work.

③
Matriz de Nossa Senhora da Conceição

◨ Praça Antônio Dias ☎ (31) 3551 3282 🕓 8:30am-noon & 1:30-5pm Tue-Sun

Built by Manuel Francisco Lisboa between 1727 and 1770, this church is most celebrated for its harmonious proportions – the unity of curves and straight lines on the facade, and the sense of space generated by what is in reality a modest nave and chancel. Manuel Francisco only added the finishing touches to the interior, and the other contributing sculptors remain largely unknown. After a nine-year restoration, the church reopened in late 2022.

④
Mina do Chico Rei

◨ Rua Dom Silvério 108 ☎ (31) 3551 1749 🕓 8am-5pm daily

This former gold mine offers guided tours, which take visitors on a journey through the lives of miners, many of whom were enslaved people from Africa. It gives an insight into their technical skills, resilience, and the impact of their presence during the gold rush in Ouro Preto.

Some local legends maintain that this is the mine that Chico Rei, widely known as Galanga, later purchased as a free man. Rei bought his freedom in the 1740s with mined gold that he had hidden in his hair.

Must See

EAT

O Passo Pizzajazz
This upmarket pizzeria has great views and live jazz at weekends.

◨ Rua São José 56 🌐 opassopizzajazz.com

$⑤$$⑤$$⑤$

Confeitaria Largo do Rosario
A pretty little café offering delicious home-made cakes and snacks.

◨ Largo do Rosario 91 ☎ (31) 3551 5685 🕓 Sun

$⑤$$⑤$$⑤$

Restaurante Olga Nur
Head to this elegant hotel dining room for modern Minas cuisine.

◨ Rua Getulio Vargas 270 🌐 hotelsolardo rosario.com

$⑤$$⑤$$⑤$

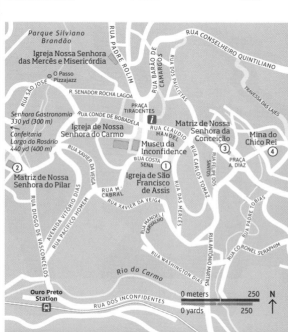

MULTICULTURAL SOUTHERN BRAZIL

More than anywhere else in the country, southern Brazil has been shaped culturally and economically by immigrants. Unlike tropical Brazil further north, the south was considered unsuitable for plantations, and immigrants were recruited by the government to occupy pieces of land and become small farmers. The south's isolation and distinction from the rest of Brazil is reflected in the languages and cultures of its population.

AZOREANS

In the beginning of the 1800s, settlers from the Portuguese island of the Azores arrived in Brazil to establish farming and fishing settlements. The Azoreans created villages along the coast of southern Brazil, in particular on the island of Santa Catarina, whose white-and-blue buildings resemble those seen on the Portuguese mid-Atlantic islands.

GERMAN HERITAGE

In the 1850s, Germans were the first to settle in southern Brazil after the Portuguese. They were drawn to Rio Grande do Sul's highlands and Santa Catarina's

↑ A band playing at the official Oktoberfest parade in Blumenau

Did You Know?

The Serra Gaúcha region is responsible for 80 per cent of Brazil's wine production.

northern valleys where German traditions and dialects are still strong. Cities like Blumenau, where South America's biggest Oktoberfest takes place, and Nova Hamburgo have some of Brazil's most well-preserved German architecture.

ITALIANS

The first Italian immigrants settled in Rio Grande do Sul in 1875, with tens of thousands arriving there, and in Santa Catarina and Paraná, over the next 50 years. The majority came from northern Italian provinces like Veneto and Trento, introducing rich culinary traditions and the skills and knowledge to cultivate lucrative grape vines on the steep hillsides. Vineyards in the Serra Gaúcha outside of Bento Gonçalves are as much a part of the landscape as they are in Italy.

SLAVS

Slavic immigrants from Central and Eastern Europe were drawn to Paraná, with Poles settling in and around Curitiba from 1869, Ukrainians in the southcentral part of the state from 1895, and Russians around Ponta

↑ The Ukrainian Memorial located in Park Tingüi in Curitiba, built in 1995

Grossa in the early 1960s. Today there are around 600,000 Brazilians of Ukranian descent, and 80 per cent live in Paraná. Prudentópolis, west of Curitiba, is the epicenter of Ukraine-Brazilian culture.

↑ Vineyards in the Serra Gaúcha outside of Bento Gonçalves, the center of Brazil's wine region

❷
DIAMANTINA

 E5 📮 Largo Dom João 134 🚆 Praça Antonio Eulálio 53; www.diamantina.mg.gov.br/turismo

Nestled in rugged hills and shrouded with *cerrado* forest, Diamantina is the prettiest and best preserved of all the colonial cities in the state, and also a UNESCO World Heritage Site. Diamonds were discovered here in 1728, when the city was a small settlement called Arraial do Tijuco. Within a few decades the encampment transformed into one of the wealthiest towns in Brazil.

①
Praça Guerra

The city is tiny and most of its historic buildings and churches lie within easy walking distance of the main square, Praça Guerra. This is an obvious point of orientation as it is dominated by the

Did You Know?

Vesperata is an annual tradition in the city, with musicians playing on balconies along Rua da Quitanda.

twin towers of the largest building in the city – the Catedral Metropolitana de Santo Antônio, which was built in the 1930s.

②
Casa de Chica da Silva

 Praça Lobo Mesquita 266 ☎ (38) 3531 2491 🕐 Noon-5pm Tue-Sat, 9am-noon Sun

The Casa de Chica da Silva, a smart townhouse one block south of the Nossa Senhora do Carmo, is best known for its former owner. Francisca (Chica) da Silva (1732–96) was an enslaved woman who became one of the few Black

people to be accepted by high colonial society through sheer force of personality.

③

Museu Casa do Diamante

 Rua Direita 14 ☎ (38) 3531 1382 🕐 10am-5pm Tue-Sat, 9am-1pm Sun

Just south of the Praça Guerra, in the adjacent Praça Juscelino Kubitschek, is the Museu Casa do Diamante. It houses stones, mining tools, and iron collars that were once fitted onto enslaved people.

④
Museu de Juscelino Kubitschek

🏠 Rua São Francisco 241 ☎ (38) 3531 3607 🕐 8am-5pm Tue-Sat, 8am-1pm Sun

South again is the Museu de Juscelino Kubitschek, the modest former home of the Brazilian president, Juscelino Kubitschek (1902–76), who built Brasília *(p232)*. Two blocks west is the city's most beautiful landmark, the Casa da Gloria, consisting of two houses

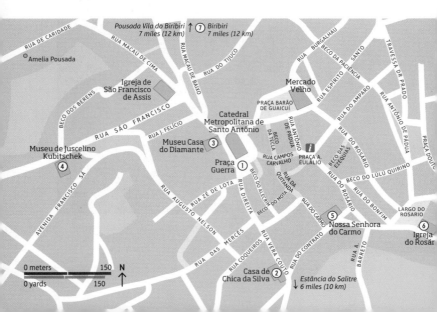

 A typical cobbled street lined with well-preserved buildings

on opposite sides connected by an enclosed, brilliant blue, second-story passageway.

Nossa Senhora do Carmo

🏠 Rua do Carmo 📞 (38) 3531 1188 🕐 2:30–5pm Tue, Thu & Fri, 9am–noon, 2–5pm Sat

Built between 1760 and 1784, the Nossa Senhora do Carmo was the town's richest church and attended by the elite white community. It is remarkable chiefly for the interior paintings by José Soares de Araujo. Araujo's works lie in many of the town's churches but those here are his finest – especially the ceiling paintings.

⑥
Igreja do Rosário

🏠 Largo do Rosário 📞 (38) 3531 1001 🕐 8am–6pm daily

This is the oldest of the city's several churches. It stands beside an 18th-century fountain in a square of the same name, to the northeast of the Praça Guerra. It was built and used by enslaved people and citizens deemed lower class.

Biribiri

Biribiri lies 9 miles (15 km) north of town. A historical village, Biribiri is home to many *fazendas* (ranches) and is surrounded by picturesque waterfalls and mountains. Next to Biribiri is a winding blackwater river and the Parque Rio Preto, a good location for bird-watching.

> Francisca (Chica) da Silva (1732-96) was an enslaved woman who became one of the few Black people to be accepted by high colonial society through sheer force of personality.

STAY

Some of the region's *fazendas* and *pousadas* have opened up to visitors, with comfortable accomodation, country-style cooking, and outdoor activities on offer.

Estância do Salitre
🏠 Rua Campos do Carvalho 15, Serra do Espinhaço
📞 (38) 99933 5413

$$$

Amelia Pousada
🏠 Rua da Caridade 199
🌐 ameliapousada.com.br

$$$

Pousada Vila do Biribiri
🏠 Praca Pedro Duarte 16, Biribiri 🌐 pousada viladobiribiri.com.br

$$$

3

BASÍLICA DO SENHOR BOM JESUS DE MATOSINHOS

⚠E5 ⬛Praça do Santuário, Congonhas 🚌Basílica from Av Júlia Kubitschek 1982 🕐Basílica: 6am–8:30pm Tue–Sun; Museu de Congonhas: 9am–5pm Tue–Sun (free adm Wed) 🛈FUMCULT, Alameda Cidade de Matosinhos de Portugal 153; (31) 3732 2526; www.congonhas.mg.gov.br

This twin-towered church is one of Latin America's greatest Baroque monuments and a UNESCO World Heritage Site. Perched on a hilltop, it is fronted by a dozen statues made by master sculptor Aleijadinho.

Completed in 1771, the Baroque church of Bom Jesus de Matosinhos was built by the diamond miner Feliciano Mendes, who, after recovering from the brink of death, vowed to build a church in homage to "Bom Jesus." At its entrance, 12 soapstone statues of prophets from the Old Testament overlook a garden, where six chapels with life-size figures commemorate the Passion of Christ. The church preserves the most impressive ensemble of statues in Latin America. Next door, the Museu de Congonhas is devoted to the church and Baroque art.

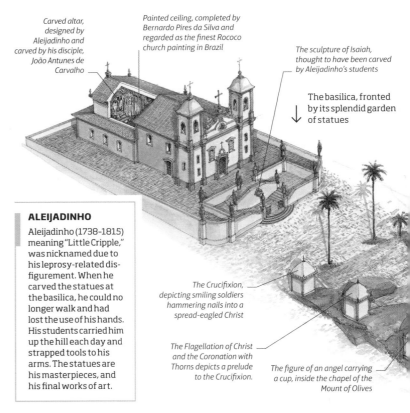

Carved altar, designed by Aleijadinho and carved by his disciple, João Antunes de Carvalho

Painted ceiling, completed by Bernardo Pires da Silva and regarded as the finest Rococo church painting in Brazil

The sculpture of Isaiah, thought to have been carved by Aleijadinho's students

↓ The basilica, fronted by its splendid garden of statues

ALEIJADINHO

Aleijadinho (1738–1815) meaning "Little Cripple," was nicknamed due to his leprosy-related disfigurement. When he carved the statues at the basilica, he could no longer walk and had lost the use of his hands. His students carried him up the hill each day and strapped tools to his arms. The statues are his masterpieces, and his final works of art.

The Crucifixion, depicting smiling soldiers hammering nails into a spread-eagled Christ

The Flagellation of Christ and the Coronation with Thorns depicts a prelude to the Crucifixion.

The figure of an angel carrying a cup, inside the chapel of the Mount of Olives

EXPERIENCE MORE

↑ Visitors lingering beneath the church's richly painted ceiling

Christ Carrying the Cross, a sculpture portraying one of the stations in the Passion of Christ

The Last Supper, with figures so life-like that some pilgrims are said to have greeted them

The Capture of Christ

④
Mariana

Ⓐ E5 🚍 🛈 Rua Direita 91; www.turismo.mariana. mg.gov.br

The oldest colonial town in Minas Gerais, Mariana, which was also a significant mining town, was the capital of the state in the first half of the 18th century.

The twin churches of **São Francisco de Assis** and **Nossa Senhora do Carmo** both date from the late 18th century. The church of São Francisco de Assis is decorated with ceiling paintings by Manuel da Costa Athayde; visitors should not miss the evocative scenes of the death of St. Francis. Although damaged by fire in 1999, Nossa Senhora do Carmo is still remarkable for its delicately balanced and very Portuguese exterior.

The city's other famous church is the **Basílica de Nossa Senhora da Assunção** (also known as the Catedral da Sé), which dates from 1760. Its exterior is modest, but the interior has some of the finest ceiling paintings by the 16th-century Portuguese artist, Manuel Rabello de Sousa.

> The interior has some of the finest ceiling paintings by the 16th-century Portuguese artist, Manuel Rabello de Sousa.

The **Museu Arquidiocesano de Arte Sacra** preserves paintings by Athayde, *objets d'art* by Aleijadinho, and antique liturgical objects.

Basílica de Nossa Senhora da Assunção
Ⓐ Rua Padre Gonçalves Lopes 📞 (31) 3557 1216 🕓 8am–5pm Tue–Sun

Museu Arquidiocesano de Arte Sacra
♿ Ⓐ Rua Frei Durão 📞 (31) 3557 2581 🕓 8:30am–noon, 1:30–5pm Tue–Fri, 9am–2pm Sat, Sun, & public hols

Nossa Senhora do Carmo
Ⓐ Praça Minas Gerais 🕓 9am–5pm Tue–Sun

São Francisco de Assis
Ⓐ Praça Minas Gerais 🕓 8am–noon & 1–5pm Tue–Sun

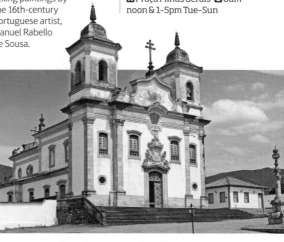

↑ The 18th-century Baroque church of São Francisco de Assis situated in Praça Minas Garais, Mariana

⑤
Parque Nacional Serra do Cipó

🅰E5 🚌From Belo Horizonte to Jaboticatubas, or Santana do Riacho ⏰8am-6pm daily (last adm 3pm) 🌐serradocipo.com

Just northeast of Belo Horizonte, the state capital, this 131-sq-mile (338-sq-km) national park lies in high rugged country in the Serra do Espinhaço mountains. Cipó protects some pristine areas of *cerrado* as well as the watersheds of many of the tributaries of the São Francisco and the Doce rivers. Waterfalls, plants, rare animals, and birds are abundant, making this one of the most beautiful national parks in Minas Gerais. Here you can spot pumas, giant anteaters, ocelots, maned wolves, and howling monkeys. It is particularly lovely in May and June when the skies are invariably blue, the rivers full, and many of the numerous wildflowers are in bloom.

⑥
Belo Horizonte

🅰E5 ✖🏛🚌 ℹRodovia Papa João Paulo II, Serra Verdel; www.secult.mg.gov.br

The capital city of Minas Gerais resembles a mini São Paulo, and is known worldwide for its visionary modern architecture. Its highlights are the buildings in the suburb of Pampulha, designed by the renowned architect Oscar Niemeyer, set in expansive gardens by Roberto Burle Marx (1909–94).

The most impressive is the **Igreja de São Francisco de Assis**. Built in 1943 as a series of parabolic arches in concrete, this church has a wonderful sense of light and space. On the outside walls are a series of *azulejos* (Portuguese blue tiles) painted by Brazil's foremost Modernist artist Cândido Portinari (1903–62). Other city highlights include the dance hall Casa do Baile, and the twin sports stadia.

In the inner city, the **Museu Mineiro** preserves some fine colonial-era religious art,

Did You Know?

The Curral del Rey mountains encircling Belo Horizonte gave the city its name - "beautiful horizon."

including a number of paintings attributed to artist Mestre Athayde (1762–1830).

Igreja de São Francisco de Assis

🚶 📍Av Otacilio Negrão de Lima 3000, Pampulha 📞(31) 3427 1644 ⏰8am-noon & 1-5pm daily

Museu Mineiro

🚶 📍Av João Pinheiro 342 📞(31) 3269 1103 ⏰Noon-7pm Tue-Sun

⑦
Tiradentes

🅰E5 🚌 ℹRua Belica 90; (32) 3355 1412; open 8am-5pm Mon-Fri

Like mining towns Ouro Preto and Mariana, Tiradentes became rich on gold, producing some of the most lavish Baroque church interiors and

Belo Horizonte's striking Igreja de São Francisco and *(inset)* its eye-catching *azulejos* ↓

facades in all of Brazil. The imposing **Matriz de Santo Antônio**, built between 1710 and 1752, is one of the finest Baroque churches in Brazil, with wonderful wood carvings and gilt interiors.

The town's multicolored Portuguese cottages and miniature Baroque churches flank the cobbled roads on the steep, low hills around the Rio Santo Antônio. Horse-drawn carriages gather in Largo das Forras, the town's main plaza, and a narrow gauge steam train, Maria Fumaça, puffs its way to and from neighboring São João del Rei. A cultural center, **Centro Cultural Yves Alves**, hosts concerts, theatrical performances, films, and exhibitions.

Matriz de Santo Antônio

🏠 Rua da Camara 🅲 (32) 3355 1238 🕒 9:30am–5pm Wed–Fri, 9am–4:30pm Sat, 9am–2pm Sun & Mon

↑ The imposing exterior of the Matriz de Santo Antônio in Tiradentes

---

EAT

Glouton

This fusion restaurant beautifully blends French and Brazilian cuisine. Try the *pirarucu* (amazon river fish) with peanut, banana, tucupi, and palm-heart crème.

🅰E5 🏠 Rua Bárbara Heliodora 59, Belo Horizonte 🌐glouton. com.br

$⑤$$⑤$⑤

Emporio Santo Antonio

A family-run restaurant dishing up rustic Minas Gerais food and an all-you-can-eat buffet at weekends.

🅰E5 🏠 Rua Belica 133, Tiradentes 🅲 (32) 3355 2433

$⑤$$⑤$⑤

Centro Cultural Yves Alves

🏠 Rua Direita 168 🅲 (32) 3355 1604 🕒 9am–6pm Sun–Wed (to 10pm Thu–Sat)

8

São João del Rei

🅰E5 Maria Fumaça from Tiradentes 🚌 From Tiradentes, Belo Horizonte, Rio de Janeiro, São Paulo ℹ️ Rua Padre José Maria Xavier 167, Centro; www. saojoaodelrei.mg.gov.br

The largest of the historic towns of Minas Gerais, Sao João del Rei is a bustling place with well-preserved colonial buildings. The principal reason for visiting is to see the **Igreja de São Francisco de Assis**, whose unusual curved facade, turtle-back roof, and intricately carved medal overlook a square lined with towering palms. The square is in the shape of a lyre and at sundown the shadows of the palms form the instrument's strings.

Inside a colonial-era mansion, the **Museu Regional de São João del Rei** has a range of antique furniture and sacred art.

Igreja de São Francisco de Assis

🏠 Praça Frei Orlando 🅲 (32) 3371 1127 🕒 7am–noon & 1–5pm Mon–Fri

---

Museu Regional de São João del Rei

⊗ 🏠 Rua Marechal Deodoro 12 🅲 (32) 3371 7663 🚫 For restoration

---

9

Parque Nacional Serra da Canastra

🅰E5 🚌 From Belo Horizonte to Piumhi, from Piumhi to São Roque de Minas 🕒 8am–6pm daily (last adm 4pm) ℹ️ Praça Alibenides da Costa Faria 10, São Roque de Minas; www.gov.br/icmbio

In the extensive Parque Nacional Serra da Canastra, bare granite peaks rise to almost 4,920 ft (1,500 m), and are surrounded by sparse *cerrado* forest sprinkled with boulders. Of the numerous waterfalls, set among stretches of lush, gallery forest, the most famed is the Cachoeira d'Anta. Here the river's ice-cold waters form a series of pools before plunging off an escarpment. The park's most famous trail, the Trilha Casca d'Anta, begins in front of the waterfall and offers a spectacular view out over the park.

RIO GRANDE DO SUL

Rio Grande do Sul once formed part of the Guaraní homelands, a vast area that also encompassed parts of modern-day Argentina and Paraguay. In 1494, the Treaty of Tordesillas divided South America between Portugal and Spain. Initially, the energies of Spain and Portugal were focused elsewhere, and this isolated area was virtually independent of both nations. The Jesuits arrived in 1626, eventually establishing seven missions – the Misiones Orientales – in what is now Brazilian territory and converting thousands of Guaraní. The region's autonomy was ended by the Guaraní War of 1756, during which a combined Spanish-Portuguese army destroyed the missions and killed most of the Guaraní.

On the coast, Azorean settlers founded Porto Alegre in the mid-18th century, and by the early 19th century the cattle ranching and *charqueada* (beef jerky) industries had transformed the region, with Porto Alegre booming as the primary port for beef exports. *Gaúchos* slowly began to dominate the state. The failed Farroupilha Revolution (1835–45) was essentially a *gaúcho* war of secession; they again fought for autonomy during the Federalist Riograndense Revolution (1893–95).

Meanwhile, the region was being transformed by further waves of immigrants – primarily the Germans, who came between 1824 and 1859, and the Italians, who arrived between 1875 and 1915, establishing Brazil's modern wine industry. The state remained rebellious: the popular revolution that led to Getúlio Vargas becoming dictator of Brazil began in 1930 in Rio Grande do Sul, where he was serving as governor. The state was also where impeached former president Dilma Rousseff rose to power in the 1970s.

RIO GRANDE DO SUL

Must See

1 Porto Alegre

Experience More

2 Nova Petrópolis
3 São Miguel das Missões
4 Gramado
5 Canela
6 Caxias do Sul
7 Bento Gonçalves
8 Flores da Cunha
9 Torres
10 Antônio Prado
11 Parque Nacional dos Aparados da Serra

SANTA CATARINA
AND PARANÁ
p212

RIO GRANDE
DO SUL

Erechim

153

324

386

153

Passo Fundo

285

Lagoa
Vermelha

470

Rio das Pelotas

285

Vacaria

ta Barbara
Sul

irubá

Tapera

Vila Maria

Casca

324

116

285

Bom Jesus

Araranguá

101

resa
o Real

Jacuizinho

Soledade

Nova
Prata

129

🔟 ANTÔNIO PRADO

Salto do Jacuí

Estrela Velha

Boqueueirão
do Leão

Pouso
Novo

386

Guaporé

BENTO
GONÇALVES ⑦

⑧ FLORES DA CUNHA

⑥ CAXIAS DO SUL

110

PARQUE NACIONAL DOS
APARADOS DA SERRA

⑪

Lajeado

153

Santa Cruz
do Sul

NOVA
PETRÓPOLIS ② ④ ⑤ CANELA

GRAMADO

Novo Hamburgo

São Leopoldo

São Francisco de
Paula

453

101

⑨ TORRES

Riozinho

O SUL

Jacui

achoeira
do Sul

Pantano
Grande

290

Salgado Filho
International Airport ✈ ①

Canoas

290

PORTO
ALEGRE

Osório

Tramandaí

Butiá

Guaíba

Viamão

Capivarita

Palmares do Sul

Quintão

Encruzilhada
do Sul

Cerro Grande
do Sul

Sentinela do Sul

ntana da
oa Vista

Dom
Feliciano

471

116

Tapes

Amaral
Ferrador

392

Camaquã

Cristal

Lagoa dos Patos

101

Canguçu

Boqueirão

São Lourenço
do Sul

Mostardas

Piratini

116

293

Pelotas

Bojuru

Atlantic

Ocean

Pedro
Osório

Piratini

Estreito

São José do Norte

116

Rio Grande

Cassino

Arroio
Grande

Taim

471

Lagoa Mirim

Lagoa
Mangueira

0 kilometers   75

0 miles   75

N
↑

Porto Alegre's downtown skyline, the tight-packed buildings lit up at night

displayed in this museum, as well as a section on 19th-century art. The museum also hosts traveling exhibitions.

 ③

Praça Marechal Deodoro

Better known as the Praça da Matriz, this square is home to a number of notable buildings, including the 1773 Catedral Metropolitana. Reconstructed in 1921, it features classical columns and a large hemi-spherical dome.

Nearby, on Rua Duque de Caxias 1205, is the Museu Júlio de Castilhos, with artifacts relating to the region's history. The Palácio Piratini, west of the cathedral, dates from 1909 and houses the state government and the governor's residence, while the grand Neo-Classical Teatro São Pedro is the city's prestigious concert hall.

 ④

Usina do Gasômetro

🏠 Av Presidente João Goulart 551 ☎ (51) 3289 8112 🔄 For renovation

Built in 1928 as a thermo-electrical power station, the Usina opened in 1991 as a cultural center hosting theater and art exhibitions. It also houses a wine museum and a cinema, and the west-facing terrace offers lake views.

 ⑤

Caminhos Rurais

🏠 Southern Porto Alegre 🌐 caminhosrurais.com.br

In Porto Alegre's large rural area, Caminhos Rurais, or Rural Paths, is a collection of small

 ①

PORTO ALEGRE

🅐 D7 ✈ 4 miles (6 km) N of city 🚌 ℹ Largo Glênio Péres, Mercado Público; open 9am-6pm Mon-Sat; www.prefeitura.poa.br

Founded in 1772 on the right bank of the Rio Guaiba, Porto Alegre served as a Portuguese military garrison that guarded against Spanish encroachment into southern Brazil. Today, it is Rio Grande do Sul's capital and an important hub for culture, business, and events. Most sights and the city's lively street life are located in the Centro Histórico, Cidade Baixa, Moinhos de Vento, and Rio Guaiba's waterfront.

①

Mercado Público

🏠 Praça Quinze de Novembro ⏰ 7:30am-7:30pm Mon-Fri, 7:30am-6:30pm Sat (Tourist office: 9am-6pm Sat)

Dating back to 1869, this Neo-Classical-influenced Public Market has a vast collection of stalls selling fresh produce and household goods. Character-istic of the region are the herb stalls selling *chá mate* (herbal tea) as well as *bombas* and *cuias* (silver straws and drinking gourds). Also of interest are stalls devoted to Afro-Brazilian religions, a reminder of those traditions in a part of the country associated primarily with European culture.

②

Museu de Arte do Rio Grande do Sul

🏠 Praça da Alfândega ⏰ 10am-7pm Tue-Sun 🌐 margs.rs.gov.br

Late 20th-century works by local artists are prominently

properties offering ecotourism experiences such as organic wine tasting and horseback rides on nature trails.

_____

 ⑥

Casa de Cultura Mário Quintana

 Rua dos Andrades 736 🕙 10am-8pm Tue-Sun 🌐 ccmq.rs.gov.br

This Neo-Classical building was designed as a hotel in 1923. For many years, it was also the home of Mário Quintana, one of the state's foremost poets. Today, it hosts a range of attractions including cinema, theater, and exhibitions relating to art and literature.

_____

⑦

Memorial do Rio Grande do Sul

 Praça da Alfândega 📞 (51) 3224 7210 🕙 10am-5pm Tue-Sun

This memorial houses exhibits relating to the state's political

and social history, the state archives, and an interesting oral history center reflecting its gaucho heritage.

_____

⑧

Farol da Santander

 Rua 7 de Setembro 1028 📞 (51) 3287 5500 🕙 9am-7pm Tue-Sun 🌐 farol santander.com.br

This vibrant arts complex features an impressive repertoire of music, cinema, and art exhibitions. The Neo-Classical building originally served as a bank in 1927–1932. Despite extensive renovations, it retains many of its original features including stained-glass windows.

_____

⑨

Brique da Redenção

🏛 Av Ipiranga 6681 📞 (51) 3320 3521 🕙 9am-5pm Sun

This weekly cultural fair has 300 stalls selling food, crafts, jewelry, and antiques, and features live arts performances.

Must See

↑ A sweeping staircase within the Santander Cultural arts complex

⑩

Museu de Ciência e Tecnologia

🏛 Av Ipiranga 6681 📞 (51) 3320 3521 🕙 9am-5pm Tue-Fri, 10am-6pm Sat & Sun

At one of Latin America's largest science museums visitors can interact with more than 800 experiments and observe marine life in 30 aquarium tanks.

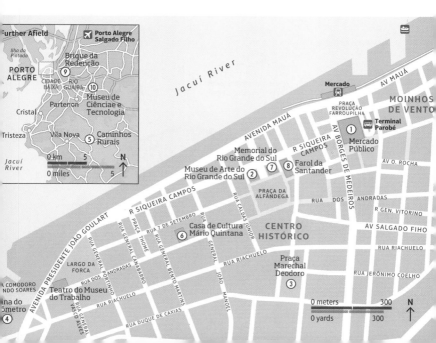

EXPERIENCE MORE

Nova Petrópolis

D7 **66 miles (106 km)
N of Porto Alegre** **Rua
Sete de Setembro 385, Praça
das Flores, Centro; www.
novapetropolis.rs.gov.br**

German immigrants arrived here in the 1820s and were the first to settle in the hills north of Porto Alegre. Nova Petrópolis, founded in 1858, remained relatively isolated until the mid-20th century and today, it retains a strong German character.

Stretching along Avenida 15 de Novembro, the town's commercial center features a number of German-style buildings. Midway along the avenue is the **Parque Aldeia do Imigrante**, which pays tribute to the region's early settlers. Set within an araucaria forest, the park houses beautifully

Illustration of the
Guaraní-Baroque style
São Miguel das Missões ↓

reconstructed, half-timbered buildings dating from 1870 and 1910, which re-create the atmosphere of a 19th-century German hamlet. The park also hosts festivals and concerts and features a large bandstand as well as a beer hall.

The hamlets and farmsteads surrounding Nova Petrópolis also have a German flavor, and German is still the dominant language here.

Parque Aldeia do Imigrante

 **Av 15 de Novembro
1966** **(54) 3281 1490**
9am–6pm daily

São Miguel das Missões

D7 **São Miguel**
**From Porto Alegre
to Santo, then bus**
saomiguel-rs.com.br

Surviving through several centuries of neglect, São Miguel Mission, a UNESCO World Heritage Site, presents a truly fine example of the Guaraní-Baroque style, a blend of Indigenous and Iberian architectural elements. These influences are visible in the carved stonework and in the wooden sculptures housed in the museum. Designed in 1937 by Lúcio Costa, the early Modernist building that houses **Museu das Missões** was inspired by Jesuit-Baroque architecture. It includes statues and other relics excavated locally.

Although the surrounding area has been given over to farmland, it retains an air of isolation. Little remains of the workshops, school rooms, cloisters, and living quarters of the Jesuit mission. However,

4,000

The number of people the original mission site housed at its height.

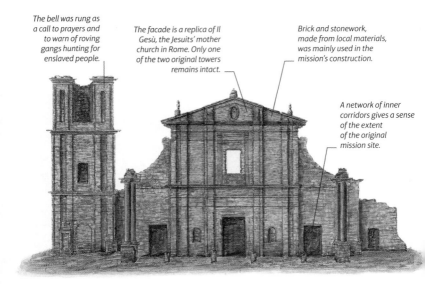

The bell was rung as a call to prayers and to warn of roving gangs hunting for enslaved people.

The facade is a replica of Il Gesù, the Jesuits' mother church in Rome. Only one of the two original towers remains intact.

Brick and stonework, made from local materials, was mainly used in the mission's construction.

A network of inner corridors gives a sense of the extent of the original mission site.

it is still possible to make out their distinct areas in the ruins.

Museu das Missões

 Rua São Luiz 1245
2–6pm Mon, 9am–noon & 2–6pm Tue–Sun

---

4 Gramado

D7 From Porto Alegre
Av Borges de Medeiros 1675; www.gramado.rs. gov.br

Brazil's best-known mountain resort, Gramado, mimics a central European village. The hilly landscape, reaching 2,706 ft (825 m), offers fantastic views.

"Swiss chalet" is the dominant architectural style and the profusion of geranium-filled window boxes, chocolate shops, and restaurants specializing in cheese fondues gives a feeling of being in Switzerland. However, only a tiny minority of the population is actually of Swiss origin.

The city's flower-filled Parque Knorr and the Lago Negro, an artificial lake bordered by pine trees from Germany's Black Forest, allow for pleasant strolls.

During mid-August, the city hosts the Festival de Gramado, one of Brazil's most prestigious film festivals.

↑ The twinkling lights of the mountain resort of Gramado, known for its Swiss-style architecture

Lying some 10 miles (16 km) east of Gramado's main avenue is the Vale do Quilombo. Approached by a steep dirt road, much of the valley's original dense Mata Atlântica (Atlantic rainforest) remains and the climate is warmer and more humid. The **Ecoparque Sperry** supports myriad fauna including coati, toucans, and howler and capuchin monkeys. Forest trails pass magnificent waterfalls that enhance the valley's scenic splendor.

Ecoparque Sperry

Vale do Quilombo
(54) 99629 8765 9am– 5pm Tue–Sun

---

5 Canela

D7 From Porto Alegre
Rua Fernando Ferrari 407, Vila Luiza; https:// canela.rs.gov.br

Chilly winters, refreshing summers, and unspoiled nature attract visitors to Canela, once a stop-off point for cattle being herded across Rio Grande do Sul's grasslands. The town is dominated by the Igreja Matriz Nossa Senhora de Lourdes, an imposing stone church built in 1953 in English Neo-Gothic style. Other buildings around town are an eclectic mix of local and European styles. The presence of students from local tourism colleges gives the town a vibrant feel.

Approximately 5 miles (8 km) north of Canela is the **Parque do Caracol**, a forest reserve with a 429-ft (131-m) waterfall. A highlight here is the 927-step stairway leading to the base of the cascade from where visitors can best appreciate its force and the surrounding forests. A farther 3 miles (5 km) north along the road from Caracol is the **Parque da Ferradura**, a forest reserve notable for the dramatic views of the horseshoe-shaped Rio Caí and of the Arroio Caçador canyon and waterfall. The area is a popular destination for adventure tourism, with rafting along the fast-flowing Rio Paranhana. Rappeling down the park's gorge allows for close-up views of the terrain.

Parque do Caracol

Estrada do Caracol, Rodovia RS 466 (54) 3282 5199 9am–5:30pm daily

Parque da Ferradura

Estrada do Caracol
(54) 3278 9000 9am– 5pm Tue–Sun

> **The profusion of geranium-filled window boxes, chocolate shops, and restaurants specializing in cheese fondues gives a feeling of being in Switzerland.**

GAÚCHO CULTURE

Gaúcho culture developed during colonial times when the Europeans arrived in Argentina, Uruguay, and southern Brazil. Since then the stern-faced cowboy (traditionally always referring to a man) has become the icon of Rio Grande do Sul, where the *gaúcho* traditions are still an integral part of daily life. Cattle drives, led by men and women on horseback, are also a common sight across southern Brazil.

THE ORIGINS OF THE GAÚCHO LIFESTYLE

Originally a nomadic lifestyle, *gaúchos*' were skilled horsemen and cowhands who wandered the pampas (large treeless plains) hunting wild cattle for their hides. When Europeans introduced border and land agreements, these cowboys began to work as ranch hands, traveling where work was needed.

← A Pantanal cowboy with a traditional cow horn

SEMANA FARROUPILHA

Every September, regional horsemen and women celebrate traditional *gaúcho* life at this week-long festival. The annual event pays homage to the leaders of the Farroupilha Revolution, the *gaúcho*-led civil uprising between 1835–45, which was an attempt to liberate Rio Grande do Sul from Brazil. Despite their defeat, modern-day *gaúchos* take to the streets of the capital Porto Alegre, as well in and around the state of Rio Grande do Sul, and celebrate with traditional music, folk dancing, and local fare.

A group of Pantanal *gaúchos* on horseback running a herd of Brazilian cattle ↑

GAÚCHO DRESS

Traditional *gaúcho* attire is worn daily by people on *fazendas* in rural Rio Grande do Sul and by city dwellers on special occasions. Traditional dress consists of a wide-brimmed felt-hat, *bombachas* (wide cotton pants), high leather boots, linen shirt, and a colorful kerchief. A true *gaúcho* also carries a knife, tucked in between his trousers and his *tirador* (sash). Women, called *gaúchas*, dress the same, sometimes with a long skirt or in a lace dress.

GAÚCHO CUISINE

Meat and *chimarrão* – a hot bitter herbal drink – is at the heart of the *gaúcho* diet. In the Rio Grande do Sul countryside, *gaúchos* sip chimarrão through a *bomba* (silver straw) from a *guia* (gourd). Ubiquitous in southern Brazilian farm life is *churrasco* (Brazilian barbecue), where beef on long metal skewers is grilled over charcoal or firewood flames. Rice with jerked beef and stews with pumpkin and squash are also part of the culinary tradition.

MUSIC AND DANCE

The accordion and the acoustic guitar are the most common folk instruments featured in traditional *gaúcho* music. Polkas and marches are the most traditional dances and the music is a mix of Portuguese, Spanish, Basque, African, German, and Italian tradition, with songs about local life.

↑ The Estátua do Laçador statue of a *gaúcho* wearing traditional dress

↑ Grape crushing at the biennial Festa da Uva in Caxias do Sul

6

Caxias do Sul

🅰D7 🚌🚐 *i* Rua Ludovíco Cavinato 1431, Nossa Sra. da Saúde; www.curta caxiasdosul.com.br

Founded in 1875, Caxias do Sul was one of the earliest Italian *colonias* to be established in the Serra. At first commercial activity revolved around wine production, but over the next century other agro-processing industries, as well as textiles and metalworking, developed. Today, Caxias is Rio Grande do Sul's second-largest city after Porto Alegre. Its wine-making heritage is celebrated at the biennial Festa da Uva.

Although concrete buildings have overtaken much of Caxias, some visible traces of the city's colonial and Italian heritage survive. The **Museu Municipal**, built in 1880 as a private residence, documents the history of Caxias, starting with the arrival of the first immigrants from Veneto. The **Museu Casa de Pedra**, housed in a carefully preserved stone farmhouse built in 1878, sheds light on the lives of the pioneer settlers, with displays of tools, furniture, and photographs.

Museu Municipal

 Rua Visconde de Pelotas, 586 📞 (54) 3221 2423 🕙 9am-5pm Tue-Fri, 11am-5pm Sat

Museu Casa de Pedra

 🏠 Rua Matteo Gianella 531, Bairro Santa Catarina 📞 (54) 3901 1463 🕙 10am-4pm Tue-Sat

---

7

Bento Gonçalves

🅰D7 🚌 *i* Rua Mal Deodoro 70; open 8am-5pm Mon-Fri; www.bento.tur.br

Examine a bottle of Brazilian wine and it is likely the label will indicate Bento Gonçalves as its place of origin. The city's economy relies mainly on grapes and wine production, as a result of which Bento's vintners dominate the Brazilian market.

Along with Caxias do Sol, Bento was one of the earliest Italian settlements in the Serra Gaúcha. However, the rapid growth of the city's urban center in the 20th century has left few traces of Italian influence during the early years of immigration. The **Museu do Imigrante** has artifacts relating to Bento's pioneer settlers, with rooms focusing on the arrival of the immigrants and the central role of the Catholic church in the community and farming.

→

Vineyards blanketing the Vale dos Vinhedos, near Bento Gonçalves

The **Cooperativa Vinícola Aurora** is an enterprise of 16 grape-growing families and is the most prominent wine producer in Brazil. Visitors are shown the entire production process and tours culminate with a tasting. Fine wines are also produced by some smaller wineries around the beautiful Vale dos Vinhedos *(p210)*.

Adventure lovers can try extreme sports such as bungee-jumping, climbing, and rapeling at the **Parque de Aventuras Gasper**, located 5.5 miles (9 km) outside town.

Garibaldi, a small town just 12 miles (20 km) south of Bento Gonçalves, is known for its surprisingly good champagne-style sparkling wines. Part of the attraction of getting to this little town is the 15-mile (23-km) ride on the steam engine known as Maria Fumaça, or "Smoking

33.7

million cases of wine are produced in Brazil every year.

"Mary," a name commonly given to tourist steam trains; the route takes an hour and a half.

Museu do Imigrante

🏠 Rua Erny Hugo Dreher 127, (Planalto) 📞 (54) 3451 1773
🕐 8am–5pm Tue–Fri, 8am–noon & 1–5pm Sat

Cooperativa Vinícola Aurora

🚫 🏠 Rua Olavo Bilac 500, Cidade Alta 📞 (54) 3455 2000 🕐 7:30am–5:30pm Mon–Thu (to 4:30pm Fri)

Parque de Aventuras Gasper

🏠 Linha Eulália Alta 📞 (54) 3454 1072 🕐 9am–6pm Wed–Sun

8

Flores da Cunha

🅐 D7 🚌 From Caxias do Sul 🌐 floresdacunha.rs.gov.br

The fact that Flores da Cunha claims the title of the largest wine-producing city in Brazil will come as no surprise. Just about every available patch of land in the municipality is given to grape vines and *cantinas* (bars), ranging from small artisan wine producers to large operators.

The town has a beautiful setting and friendly people, and the same can be said of the surrounding villages, which could be mistaken for Italian farming communities. The people maintain the Venetian dialect of their immigrant for-bears, making Flores da Cunha the most Italian of Brazilian towns. Visit **Museu Municipal** to learn more about its history.

Located in a picturesque valley, 8 miles (13 km) south-west of Flores da Cunha, Otávio Rocha is especially striking, with vines extending down to the main streets. The village has become a popular place to eat, with a range of restaurants specializing in tasty, northern Italian country fare.

Museu Municipal

🏠 Av Vinte e Cinco de Julho 1608 📞 (54) 3292 2777
🕐 9am–6pm Mon–Fri

❾ Torres

🅰 D7 🚌 From Porto Alegre or Santa Catarina
ℹ Rua José Antonio Picoral 79; https://torres.rs.gov.br/vivatorres

The main highlight of the long coastline of Rio Grande do Sul is Torres, located near the border with the neighboring state of Santa Catarina. Torres is named for three huge basalt rocks, or "towers," that jut into the ocean and break the otherwise seemingly unending beach. The towers are located in the **Parque da Guarita**, on the southern perimeter of the town. Between the sea-cliff towers are sandy coves offering protection from fierce Atlantic rollers. From a hill at the southern edge of

the park, visitors can enjoy tremendous views of the beautifully rugged coastline or trek through the dunes of 2-mile- (4-km-) long Praia de Itapeva. The water at Itapeva is tranquil and favorable for swim-ming. Off Torres's coast is Ilha dos Lobos, a small island and wildlife refuge.

❿ Antônio Prado

🅰 D7 🚌 From Caxias do Sul
ℹ Rua Luiza Bocchese 68; https://antonioprado.tur.br

Antônio Prado, the last of the major settlements in Brazil,was established in the Italian colonial zone in 1886. Located in the zone's northern extreme and, until fairly recently, with poor links to

other centers, it failed to make the transition from farming community to industrial town. The lack of development is one of the reasons why the town was declared a National Heritage Site in 1989.

The town is particularly well-known for the many wooden, stone-base buildings erected by Italian immigrants. Clustered around the town's leafy and expansive central square, the Praça Garibaldi, and the roads that extend off it, are some 48 historic buildings, all protected and perfectly maintained. Most of the brightly painted clapboard structures with their unchanged interiors have been turned either into shops or into small government offices. One of these buildings on Praça Garibaldi is now the town hall. Also situated on Praça Garibaldi is the **Museu de Antônio Prado**, which offers an interesting and useful historical overview of the development of the small town.

> **Torres is named for three huge basalt rocks, or "towers," that jut into the ocean and break the otherwise seemingly unending beach.**

Beautiful beaches lining the edge of the pretty seaside town of Torres

Museu de Antônio Prado

Rua Luisa Bochese 34
(54) 3293 5656 8:30–
11:30am & 1:15–5:30pm Mon–
Fri, 10am–4pm Sat & Sun

Parque Nacional dos Aparados da Serra

D7 From Canela to
Cambará do Sul, then taxi,
or from Caxias do Sul or
Criciúma RS-427, Km 18;
(54) 3251 1277

The highland plateau of
southern Brazil emerged from
the accumulation of layers of
ocean sediment, with the
resulting rock formations lifted
up to form the Brazilian Shield,
a part of the Earth's continen-
tal crust. Some 150 million
years ago, lava poured onto
the shield to create a thick
layer of basalt rock. Cracks
emerged at the edge of the
plateau, taking the form of
narrow, but deep, canyons. It is
around one of the largest of
these canyons – Canion do

Itaimbezinho – that the Parque
Nacional dos Aparados da
Serra was created in 1959.

Canion do Itaimbezinho is
a 2,360-ft- (720-m-) deep,
4-mile- (6-km-) long canyon
featuring several ecosystems
merging into one another. The
plateau around Itaimbezinho
is mainly cattle pasture, while
dense Mata Atlântica (p140)
covers Itaimbezinho's lower
reaches. The abundant flora
ranges from lichens and
mosses to orchids, as well as
other flowering plants and
giant araucaria pines. Trails
around the canyon's edge are
well marked, varying in length
between 1 mile (2 km) and
4 miles (6 km), with observa-
tories offering views of
the canyon.

The best season to visit the
park is in winter (May to August), when visibility stretches
to the base of the canyon and
toward the coast. September
is the worst time to come here,
with low cloud and heavy rainfall. During the rest of the year,
fog often obscures views,
though it can lift very quickly.

A DRIVING TOUR
VALE DOS VINHEDOS

Length 16 miles (25 km) **Stopping-off points** A good selection of restaurants can be found along the route; small chapels are also a peaceful place to stop

Some of the best wine in Brazil is produced in Vale dos Vinhedos. The majority of inhabitants here are descendants of immigrants from the Veneto in Italy, and life in the Vale dos Vinhedos follows a pattern very similar to that in the corner of northeast Italy. The production of wine is central to the year's activity, and the Catholic chapels are cornerstones for the maintenance of Italian traditions.

Among the oldest wineries in the valley, **Famiglia Tasca** *consists of typical stone and wood farm buildings.*

Famiglia Tasca

444

Vinícola Pizzato

Leopoldin

Vinícola Miola

Still small-scale producers, the Pizzato family, who run **Vinícola Pizzato***, offer tastings and sell an extensive range of wines.*

The largest vineyard in the valley, **Vinícola Miolo** *produces some of Brazil's best wine. The visitors' center tells the story of Miolo's development and also allows tastings.*

← Young vines on a sunny, hillside plantation in Vale dos Vinhedos

RIO GRANDE
DO SUL

Vale do
Vinhedos

Locator Map

↑ Rows of flourishing vineyards
in the Casa Valduga's estate

*Comfortable guest rooms
and excellent food is offered
at* **Casa Valduga**, *a pioneer
of the production of high-
quality Brazilian wines
and agritourism.*

Maria Goretti

Linha
Zemitt

470

Built in 1907, **Capela
das Neves** *is the
earliest surviving chapel
in Vale dos Vinhedos.*

FINISH
Cidade
Alta
Capela das
Neves

Bento
Gonçalves

Bento
Gonçalves

START

Casa Valduga

Vale dos Vinhedos

Vinosul

Merlot
444

Memorial   Capela das
do Vinho   Graças

470

Garibaldina

💬 INSIDER TIP
Wine and Dine

Wine country makes for
some excellent culinary
experiences; head to
remote Valle Rustic
*(www.vallerustico.com.
br)* and sample the eight-
course tasting menu
that can include lamb
with mint and yogurt
foam, and fish with
chayote pasta. Open
for dinner Tuesday to
Friday; Saturday and
Sunday lunch only.

Memorial do Vinho *is a
small, fascinating exhibition
charting the development
of the local wine production
from 1875 to present.*

Honoring Our Lady of Grace,
Capela das Graças *is one of
the many Catholic chapels
that are central to the valley's
Italian immigrants.*

0 kilometers   2
0 miles   2

N
↑

SANTA CATARINA AND PARANÁ

This region of southern Brazil was once inhabited by the Indigenous Carijó, Kaingang (Caingangues), and Tupí-Guaraní peoples. These groups were displaced during the 17th and 18th centuries by Portuguese settlers, who established military garrisons all along the southern coast to guard against possible Spanish incursions. Immigrants from the Portuguese Azores islands were brought in to establish farming and fishing settlements, which, over time, grew into important towns. Florianópolis became the capital of the new state of Santa Catarina in 1738, and Curitiba, set on the trade route between Rio Grande do Sul and Minas Gerais, became the capital of the new state of Paraná in 1853 – both were soon counted among Brazil's most dynamic cities.

From 1840 to the mid-1900s, the interiors of Paraná and Santa Catarina were opened to immigration, with waves of European and other settlers staking out small farms. The newcomers settled along ethnic lines, with Polish immigrants concentrated around Curitiba, Ukrainians in southern Paraná, Germans in Santa Catarina's Itajaí Valley, and Italians in the southern part of Santa Catarina, giving both states a distinctly multicultural identity they retain today.

The devastating Contestado War, a guerilla war for land, took place between settlers and land-owners from 1912 to 1916, but since the end of the conflict, the economy of both states has boomed, led by the farm sector (especially in soybeans, corn, sugarcane, and cattle), a diversified manu-facturing base, and growing tourism, especially to the spectacular Foz do Iguaçu waterfalls.

SANTA CATARINA AND PARANÁ

Must Sees
1 Foz do Iguaçu
2 Serra da Graciosa
3 Florianópolis and Ilha de Santa Catarina

Experience More
4 Curitiba
5 Paranaguá
6 Ilha do Mel
7 Ilha de Superagüi

SÃO PAULO STATE *p170*

Marília

Assis

ndeirantes

Jacárezinho

Botucatu

Piraju

Venceslau Bráz

Ibaiti

Represa de Jurumirim

Represa Chavantes

ntania

Capão Bonito

Jaguariaíva

Itararé

Piraí do Sul

Castro

Cerro Azul

Ribeira

Ponta Grossa

Palmeira

SERRA DA GRACIOSA

ILHA DE SUPERAGÜI

CURITIBA 4

2

7

Iguaçu

Afonso Pena International Airport

PARANAGUÁ 5

6

ILHA DO MEL

Lapa

Guaratuba

Baía de Guaratuba

Rio Negro

Serra do Mar

São Francisco do Sul

Joinville

Jaraguá do Sul

Bara Velha

Itaiópolis

Blumenaú

Itajaí

A t l a n t i c

O c e a n

Rio do Sul

Brusque

João Paulo

Porto Belo

Tijucas

Baía de Tijucas

Ituporanga

FLORIANÓPOLIS AND ILHA DE SANTA CATARINA

Lajes

São José, Santa Catarina

3

Serra Geral

Paihoça

Florianópolis

Bocaino do Sul

Hercílio Luz International Airport

São oaquim

Lagoa do Mirim

Imbituba

Orleaès

Laguna

Criciúma

Tubarão

Araranguá

Lagoa do Sombrio

Torres

0 kilometers   80

0 miles   80

N

❶ ⧉ ⧉

FOZ DO IGUAÇU

⬙D6 ⬙Paraná ⬙Aeroporto Internacional do Foz do Iguaçu
⬙Rodoviária Internacional ⬙CAT: Av das Cataratas 2330; Foz open 8am–8pm daily, (45) 2105 8128

Before these mighty waterfalls even come into view, their rumbling roar and great clouds of spray hint at the spectacle about to unfold. Drenching the surrounding tropical forest, the Iguaçu Falls cascade over blood-red rocks and hurtle down the wide river canyon in an awesome display of the power of nature.

The Iguaçu Falls rate as one of South America's great natural sights. The falls are formed by a succession of 275 interlinking cataracts up to 246 ft (75 m) in height cascading over a 1.8-mile- (3-km-) wide precipice. The falls owe their origins to several successive volcanic layers of rock built up over 110 million years. Shared between Brazil and Argentina, they are completely surrounded by nature preserves. The two preserves of Brazil's Parque Nacional do Iguaçu and Argentina's Parque Nacional Iguazú contain one of the largest surviving tracts of Atlantic forest in South America.

↑ The majestic pink facade of the five-star Hotel das Cataratas

THE ARGENTINA FALLS

Although the Brazilian side is best for panoramic views, the trails on the Argentinian side can get you closer to the main cataracts. The forest preserve here is larger than the Brazilian one, with good walkable trails, requiring time to explore. There is also a greater likelihood of spotting some of the area's wildlife on the Argentinian side. Local buses travel from Brazil to Argentina; get off at the immigration borders on both sides to get your passport stamped.

Both national parks are also abundant with wildlife (including jaguar and harpy eagle) and offer sweeping views of the falls, as well as options to go closer to the cascades by boat.

The falls are located near the Brazilian city of Foz do Iguaçu and the sleepy Argentinian town of Puerto Iguazú. This majestic area has excellent access roads and tourist facilities; the Brazilian national park is also home to the highly acclaimed Hotel das Cataratas. The Iguaçu region, meaning "Great Waters" in Tupí-Guaraní, was declared a UNESCO World Heritage Site in 1986.

↑ The tumbling falls, which draw *(inset)* visitors for their spectacular views

EXPLORING IGUAÇU

① ⊗ Ⓜ

Foz do Iguaçu

🅐D6 🚗400 miles (639 km) W of Curitiba 🚆🚌 🛈Av das Cataratas 2330, Km 2.5; (45) 2105 8128

Foz do Iguaçu, also referred to just as Foz, was a quiet little border town until the 1970s, when construction work began on the nearby Itaipu Binacional, the world's largest hydroelectricity plant. Today, Foz is an excellent base from which to visit the city's main attraction, the spectacular waterfalls located to the east *(p216)*. The pleasant border town also offers a wide range of accommodations, as well as reasonably good bars and restaurants.

② ⊗

Parque das Aves

🅐D6 🚗Rodovia das Cataratas Km 17 🕐8:30am–5:30pm daily 🌐parquedas aves.com.br

Located close to the main entrance of the Parque Nacional do Iguaçu, the Parque das Aves serves as an introduction to Brazilian birdlife. The park has large aviaries housing some 1,400 birds of 140 species from different ecosystems, which include macaws, toucans, red-winged tinamous, and flamingos. The park also has a butterfly habitat, reptile exhibit, and a successful breeding program that focuses on Brazilian endangered species.

③ ⊗ Ⓜ

Parque Nacional do Iguaçu

🅐D6 🕐9am–5pm daily (adv booking, online only) 🌐cataratasdoiguacu.com.br

Created in 1939, Brazil's second-oldest national park is today one of the most visited sights in the country. Public and tour buses leave visitors at the visitors' center near the park's entrance where they transfer onto electric-powered, open-topped buses for the falls, located 6 miles (10 km) into the park. The bus stops at the Estação Macuco Safari, where a smaller vehicle can (for an additional charge) take visitors along a forest trail to the Rio Iguaçu. There, inflatable powerboats carry visitors across rapids toward the Garganta do Diabo (Devil's Throat) and to virtually the foot of the falls. Along the way are various rest points with spectacular panoramic views of the main series of falls. At the trail's lowest point there is a secure walkway that leads to a platform where one can peer into the stunning Garganta do Diabo, a deep gorge into which the fierce, cascading waters of the falls plummet.

> ### WILDLIFE IN THE IGUAÇU REGION
>
> The extent of native flora and fauna that the parks offer is varied. Over 2,000 species of flora have been identified, and the region serves as a habitat for a similarly varied range of wildlife, lured by fruit, nesting spots, and dens. There are 450 varieties of bird amid this forested area, which can be best spotted early in the morning and at dusk, when toucans, parrots, and hummingbirds abound. Some 80 kinds of mammals, with five varieties of feline, also rove the forest. Early morning and evening are the best time to see animals, with monkeys sometimes seen swinging overhead through the forest's canopy. The most commonly sighted mammal is the coati.

↑ Visitors lining a bridge within the Parque Nacional do Iguaçu

Parque Nacional Iguazú

🅰 D6 🕐 8am-6pm daily (adv booking, online only) 🌐 iguazuargentina.com

Where the Brazilian park's great attractions are the spectacular panoramic views of the falls, the Argentinian park has an extensive network of forest and waterside trails, which offer visitors close-up views of the smaller falls. As well as the Garganta del Diablo trail, there are routes called the Paseo Inferior and the Paseo Superior. From the visitors' center, a miniature railroad leads to the Estación Central where the Paseo Inferior and Paseo Superior circuits begin. From the Paseo Superior, visitors can look down onto and across dozens of cataracts. This circuit has concrete catwalks going behind the falls, while the Paseo Inferior is shorter, offering even more breathtaking views of the falls from below. Especially remarkable are the parts of the trail across catwalks allowing amazing views over cascading water. At the lowest point, boats make the short crossing to the Isla San Martín, an island located in the heart of the falls. Walking here requires a high level of fitness, as it involves clambering up steep slopes and across some jagged rock formations.

⑤

Puerto Iguazú

🅰 D6 🚗 6 miles (10 km) S of Foz do Iguaçu ✈️ 🚌 ℹ️ Av Victoria Aguirre 66; https://visitiguazu.travel

Traveling between Foz and the Argentinian park by public transport involves changing buses in Puerto Iguazú, Argentina's most north-eastern city. Although Puerto Iguazú has few sights of note, its quiet, tree-lined streets make for attractive wandering, with wooden, rather than concrete, buildings predominating.

A short walk along Puerto Iguazú's main artery, Avenida Victoria Aguirre, leads to the Hito Tres Fronteras (Triple Borders Landmark). From here there are beautiful views of the Iguaçu and Paraná rivers and across the rivers to Brazil and Paraguay.

2

SERRA DA GRACIOSA

⚠E6 🏔Paraná 🚂Serra Verde Express 🚌Viaçao Graciosa 🛈Casa
Rocha Pombo: Largo José Pereira S. Andrade, s/n; (41) 3415 1104

This stretch of Atlantic rainforest offers breathtaking views over the treetops to the coast. Wander along the nature trails in the Serra da Graciosa's state park or board the Serra Verde Express as it winds its way along sheer mountainside for an unforgettable train journey.

The mountain range that separates Paraná state's coast from its interior is known as the Serra do Mar. Its southern extension, Serra da Graciosa, is one of the largest remaining areas of Mata Atlântica (Atlantic rainforest) in southern Brazil. The Serra is rich in flora and fauna, ranging from lowland subtropical to cloud forest varieties. The road and railroad linking Morretes and Curitiba are amazing feats of 19th-century engineering, zigzagging through some of the most spectacular terrain in the country. The area is often atmospherically shrouded in mist or fog, the result of cool air from the highlands colliding with the warm air of the subtropical coast. The forest thrives on such precipitation.

[1] The Serra Verda Express train route offers passengers gorgeous views.

[2] The region is home to an array of plantlife, such as this vibrant bromeliad.

[3] The nearby city of Morretes is a pleasant place to stay, with many restaurants and cafés.

THE SERRA VERDE EXPRESS

One of the world's greatest train rides, the remarkable Curitiba-Paranaguá railroad line passes through 13 tunnels, and across 30 bridges and viaducts. For much of the route, the line clings to the mountainside from which, on clear days, there are wonderful views across pristine forest toward the coast. There are three classes of service. Bookings are recommended in summer *(www.serra verdeexpress.com.br).*

↑ Passengers gazing out of the colorful Serra Verde Express as it threads through coastal jungle

Florianópolis, with the Hercilio Luz Bridge stretching away from the shore ↑

4

FLORIANÓPOLIS AND ILHA DE SANTA CATARINA

🅰E6 🏠Santa Catarina ✈7 miles (12 km) S of Florianópolis 🚌 ℹ Terminal Rodoviário Rita Maria: Av Paulo Fontes 1101; www.turismo.sc.gov.br

Santa Catarina's capital, Florianópolis, is one of South America's hippest destinations. The city's industrial zone occupies the mainland, while the colonial center sits across the bay on the island. The island's north shore has pretty beaches and warm, tranquil waters that are popular spots to relax. The Atlantic rollers of the east coast have made the island one of the world's great surfing centers. In the daytime, Praia Mole and Praia Joaquina are crowded, and the bars of Lagoa bustle until early morning.

①
Florianópolis

✈7 miles (12 km) S of Florianópolis ℹ Avenida Rio Branco 611, Centro; (048) 3324 0070; open 10am-noon, 1-7pm Mon-Fri

Linked to the mainland via the Hercilio Luz Bridge – the longest suspension bridge in Brazil – Florianópolis is the overland point of entry to the island. Though most visitors come to Ilha de Santa Catarina for its

beaches, this booming city has attractions of its own, not least a vibrant cultural scene as well as a few architectural gems.

The historic heart of downtown Florianópolis is **Praça XV de Novembro**, a peaceful square shaded with tall palms and giant fig trees. It is flanked on one side by the **Catedral Metropolitano**, a handsome church that was built in 1908 on the site where Francisco Dias Velho, a Portuguese explorer, consecrated the island's first chapel in 1678.

In the 18th century, many Portuguese Azoreans settled in Santa Catarina, developing cotton and linen industries. The city holds an annual festival around mid-September, in recognition of their contribution and that of the thriving oyster-farming community: Fenaostra – National Oyster and Azorean Culture Festival. Attractions include stalls selling food and Azorean crafts such as intricate bobbin lace, while live music and entertainment keep the

crowds amused. Adjacent to the cathedral is the state history museum, the **Museu Histórico de Santa Catarina**. Housed in the former governor's palace, this magnificent 18th-century building features an eclectic collection, with items such as antique musical instruments and the city's first electric light fitting.

Just a few blocks from Praça XV is the **Mercado Público**, the city's beautifully restored historic market. It is open daily, with more than 100 stalls selling fish, fresh produce, clothing, handicrafts, and souvenirs. The surrounding bars and restaurants stay open till late, buzzing with local life.

Besides its many chic nightclubs and cocktail bars, open year-round, Florianópolis also has a lively calendar of events. Held annually in February–March, Pop Gay Carnaval is a lively

parade that culminates in a contest to crown a Beauty Queen and Drag Queen. Crowds of more than 150,000 people cram into the city center, for what is one of Brazil's biggest LGBTQ+ events. A more traditional event, but equally popular, is the Festa do Divino, which can fall in May, June, or July. One of the most important dates in the Catholic calendar, it is dedicated to the Holy Spirit, with costumed parades, concerts, and parties in the city center.

Praça XV de Novembro
⌂ Praça XV de Novembro

Catedral Metropolitano
⌂ Rua Pe. Miguelinho 55
🕐 6:15am–8pm Mon–Fri, 8am–noon & 2–8pm Sat, 7am–noon & 4–9pm Sun
🌐 catedralflorianopolis. org.br

Museu Histórico de Santa Catarina
⌂ Rua Tenente Silveira 343
🕐 10am–6pm Tue–Fri (to 4pm Sat & Sun) 🌐 cultura.sc.gov.br

Mercado Público
⌂ Rua Jerônimo Coelho 60, Centro 🕐 7am–7pm Mon–Fri, 7am–2pm Sat, 7am–noon Sun
🌐 mercadopublicofloripa. com.br

←

Mercado Público at dawn, before the arrival of the stalls and shoppers

EAT

Restinga Recanto

With a terrace located right on the seafront, this acclaimed Azorean-Portuguese restaurant is famous for its excellent oysters.

 Rodovia Rafael da Rocha Pires 2759, Florianópolis (48) 3235 2093

$ $ $

Villa Maggioni

Widely considered one of the best restaurants on Santa Catarina, Villa Maggione is beautifully located beside a lagoon. The Italian menu is fused with delicious Mediterranean and Moroccan influences.

 Rua Canto do Amizade 273 (48) 3232 6859

$ $ $

---

②

Fortaleza de São José da Ponta Grossa

Servidão da Carioca, s/n, Praia do Forte 9am–noon & 1–5pm daily fortalezas.ufsc.br/fortaleza-ponta-grossa

Dating from the mid-18th century, this fortress looms large on a rocky hilltop overlooking the sandy Praia do Forte, on the northwest coast of Brazil. It was built by Santa Catarina's first governor, Brigadier Jose da Silva Pais, in order to ward off potential coastal invasion. The site was never effectively used, however, and by the mid-1970s the fortress had been abandoned and had fallen into ruin. Over the next couple of decades, a long-term restoration project recovered the site, which includes a chapel, barracks, and guardhouse. There is also the Commander's House, which now houses an exhibition with artifacts that were recovered during excavations here. Today the fortress is open to the public and protected as a historic site of national heritage.

---

③

Praia Mole

Jornalista Manoel de Menezes, 1164–1204

Surfers and hang-gliding enthusiasts favor the laid-back Praia Mole to showcase their talents. A number of relaxed beach bars and food spots line the sandy beach, which is also popular with the island's sizable LGBTQ+ community. A few simple hostels can be found in the village, but most visitors come on a day trip from Florianópolis, which lies some 8 miles (13 km) to the west.

---

④

Barra da Lagoa

Rue José Serafim dos Santos, 123

Around the headland to the north of Praia Mole, this pleasant fishing village and beach sits at the mouth of the Rio Barra. Lined with a choice of accommodations and restaurants, it is particularly lively in the summer season (December through February). The clear river water is perfect for swimmers, while the nearby Lagoa de Conceição has a range of facilities for watersports, including kayaks

and jet skis. Equipment for such activities can be rented, and there are also a number of surf schools in the area for those seeking a little tutition; the gentle waves in this part of the island make it a good spot for beginners. The white sandy beach runs into the adjoining Praia do Moçambique, which stretches for some 5 miles (8 km) northward.

↑ Interior of the 18th-century Nossa Senhora das Necessidades Church, in Santo Antônio de Lisboa

 ⑤

Santo Antônio de Lisboa

This charming little village is tucked away on a sheltered bay in the northwest of Santa Catarina. With Nossa Senhora das Necessidades Church as its focal point, it is the best preserved of the island's 18th-century Azorean set-tlements. Its streets are lined with simple, colonial-era cottages with terra-cotta tiled roofs, and cafés that serve up succulent locally caught oysters, fish, and seafood –fishing provides the community's basic livelihood, along with tourism. The calm seas and quiet streets here attract many families and other visitors looking for a peaceful alternative to the island's livelier resorts.

 ⑥

Campeche and Ilha do Campeche

🖈 Rua Tereza Lopes 065

Campeche is renowned for having one of the finest beaches on the island. Together with Praia Joaquina to the north, the two beaches comprise a long sweeping bay along the southeast of Santa Catarina. With some of its biggest waves and strongest winds, they are the island's most popular destination for watersports enthusiasts. Praia Joaquina, in particular, is one of Brazil's most famous surfing centers. It's not particularly novice-friendly, however, and the cold water and rough seas should be approached with caution. Boats take day trips to the offshore Ilha do Campeche, with its unspoiled beaches and clear seas providing excellent conditions for divers.

 HIDDEN GEM
Island Hike

At the southern tip of the island, Praia dos Naufragados is reached by a rugged trail from tiny Caieira da Barra do Sul. Hikers are rewarded with spec-tacular views of the islands that surround Ilha de Santa Catarina.

 ←

Colorful houses lining the edges of the crystal waters in Barra da Lagoa

EXPERIENCE MORE

④ Curitiba

 D6 🗺 Paraná ✈ 🚉 From Morretes ℹ Praça Garibaldi 7, Setor Histórico; www. turismo.curitiba.pr.br

Founded in 1693 as a gold-mining encampment, Curitiba developed to become the largest city in southern Brazil and has grown into one of Brazil's most dynamic cities. Since the early 1990s, it has rivalled São Paulo as a location for corporate investment, which is in large measure attracted by the city's quality of life and public services.

Dating from 1737, the Igreja da Ordem is the city's oldest church and the finest example of Portuguese ecclesiastical architecture in the state.

Alongside the church is the **Museu de Arte Sacra** with its small but well-presented collection of relics gathered from churches in Curitiba.

Up the hill from here are Praça Garibaldi and Praça João Cândido, surrounded by brightly painted houses. In the grand Palácio São Francisco built in 1929, is the **Museu Paranaense**, where the displays concentrate on Paraná's archaeology, anthropology, and history.

In the commercial center is the **Jardim Botânico**, a French-style botanic garden with greenhouses, fountains, waterfalls, and lakes.

Representing modern Curitiba, the **Museu Oscar Niemeyer** is popularly referred to as "The Eye" after the construction's central feature. The building is considered one of Oscar Niemeyer's greatest architectural achievements.

Museu de Arte Sacra
🏛 Largo da Ordem s/n 📞 (41) 3321 3265 🕐 9am-noon, 1-6pm Tue-Fri, 9am-3pm Sat & Sun

Museu Paranaense
🏛 Rua Kellers 289 📞 (41) 3304 3300 🕐 9am-6pm Tue-Fri, 10am-4pm Sat & Sun

Jardim Botânico
🏛 Rua Eng Ostoja Roguski 📞 (41) 3264 6994 🕐 6am-7:30pm daily

Museu Oscar Niemeyer
 🏛 Rua Marechal Hermes 999 (Centro Civico) 📞 (41) 3350 4400 🕐 10am-6pm Tue-Sun

---

> **BARREADO**
>
> In Paraná's coastal towns, *barreado* is listed on the menu of most restaurants. The dish is made of beef, bacon, tomatoes, onion, cumin, and other spices; traditionally these ingredients are placed in layers in a large clay urn before being cooked in a wood-fired oven for up to 15 hours. *Barreado* is served with *farinha* (manioc flour), which is spread on a plate; the meat and gravy is placed on top, and the dish is eaten with banana and orange slices.

⑤ Paranaguá

 E6 🗺 Paraná 🚌🚉 From Curitiba ℹ Av Arthur de Abreu 44; www. paranagua.pr.gov.br

Founded in 1585, Paranaguá is one of Brazil's most important ports.

Paranaguá's historic center is small enough to explore on foot. The oldest buildings are located in the compact

↑ One of the many beautiful untouched beaches found on the Ilha do Mel

historic core on the shore of Paranaguá Bay. Most of these dilapidated, but distinguished-looking, 19th-century merchants' houses now serve as shops or inexpensive hotels. Also set along the shore is the former Colégio dos Jesuítas, an imposing building that now houses the **Museu de Arqueologia e Etnologia**, whose rich collection relates to the region's Indigenous peoples and popular culture.

Two churches in the historic center are worth seeking out. The Igreja de Nossa Senhora do Rosário, built between 1571 and 1575, has suffered considerable changes over the centuries but the main structure retains a Portuguese colonial appearance. Built between 1600 and 1650, the Igreja de São Benedito remains an excellent example of popular colonial architecture. The simple, whitewashed building has undergone renovation and contains a small collection of sacred art.

Museu de Arqueologia e Etnologia

 ⌂ Rua 15 de Novembro 575 ☎ (41) 3721 1200
⊙ 8am–8pm Tue–Sun
ⓦ mae.ufpr.br

←

The city of Curitiba, seen from the verdant Jardim Botânico

6
Ilha do Mel

🅐 E6 ⌂ Paraná 🚢 From Paranaguá ⓦ ilhadomel online.com.br

The most beautiful of Paraná's islands, Ilha do Mel offers a combination of undeveloped beaches, isolated coves, and sandy trails. The island guards the entrance to Paranaguá Bay where there are well-preserved ruins of the mid-18th-century fort, Fortaleza de Nossa Senhora dos Prazeres, which was constructed to ward off English, French, and Spanish attacks. The Farol das Conchas (Conchas Lighthouse), imported from Glasgow and placed on the island's most easterly point in 1872, is the best place for a stunning panoramic view.

There can be few more peaceful spots on the southern Brazilian coast than this; visitor numbers to the Ilha do Mel are controlled, and there are no roads or motor vehicles on the island. The beaches, some with waves suitable for surfers, others with warm, calm water, are never overcrowded. Some of the best beaches, such as Praia Grande and Praia de Fora, are on the eastern part of the island.

In the summer, Ilha do Mel transforms into a party island, with beachside bars open through the night.

7
Ilha de Superagüi

🅐 E6 ⌂ Paraná 🚢 From Paranaguá

Just a few dozen people who make a living from fishing and tourism inhabit the island of Superagüi. The island is part of the **Parque Nacional de Superagüi**, a large stretch of intact Atlantic rainforest. The park is home to jaguars and parrots, and is known for its mangroves and salt marshes, where an amazing variety of orchids grow. The island is reached by boat, most easily from Paranaguá. Most of the low-lying island is covered with shrub forest and mangrove. Very basic accommodation is available at Barra de Superagüi, a village located on the southeast of the island. The only other part of the island that is accessible to visitors is Praia Deserta, a glorious 24-mile- (38-km-) long expanse of white sand. The island attracts various migrating birds, but the flocks of rare, red-faced parrot (Amazona brasiliensis) are endemic.

Parque Nacional de Superagüi

🕙 ⌂ Barra de Superagüi
🕐 24 hrs (book guided boat tours at the Superagüi Pousada Centauro hotel)
ⓦ pousadacentauro.com.br

BRASÍLIA, GOIÁS, AND TOCANTINS

The Indigenous peoples that once lived in this region have largely died out – today only the Karajá (Carajá) and Tapuia retain territory in Goiás, while the Apinayé, Krahô, and Xerente are the most populous in Tocantins. The Portuguese discovered gold in Goiás in the 1680s, but their first real settlement – Cidade de Goiás – was founded only in 1725. Pirenópolis began as a gold camp in 1727, and hydrothermal mega-resort Caldas Novas traces its roots to 1777, when Portuguese settlers found hot springs on the Rio Caldas. Cattle ranchers arrived in the 19th century, and agriculture and cattle farming remain key industries in the region today.

The central highlands of Brazil remained sparsely populated well into the 20th century. Only *bandeirantes* (fortune hunters) had ventured into the wilderness – a land of *cerrado* (savanna), *mesetas* (plateaus), and giant winding rivers – until Goiás was chosen as the site for a new national capital in 1956. Driven by Brazil's then president Juscelino Kubitschek and designed by storied architect Oscar Niemeyer, Brasília rose swiftly from the dust and scrub of the *cerrado*, and the federal government was officially transferred to the new city in 1960. Its growth since has been explosive, and it is now Brazil's third most populous city.

After accusing the federal government of decades of neglect, landowners in the northern part of Goiás pushed for autonomy, and the state of Tocantins was created in 1988. Its capital, Palmas, was only founded in 1990. Today, much of this young state's economy is based on cattle ranching and soybean farming.

BRASÍLIA, GOIÁS, AND TOCANTINS

Must Sees

1. Brasília
2. Pirenópolis
3. Parque Nacional Chapada dos Veadeiros

Experience More

4. Cidade de Goiás
5. Palmas
6. Jalapão
7. Ilha do Bananal
8. Parque Nacional das Emas

0 kilometers — 150

0 miles — 150

N

São Félix do Xingu

Fre

Liberdade

Cachimbo

Juruena

Peixoto de Azevedo

S. José do Xingu

322

Juína

Peixes

Sinop

Moniisaud Missu

Arraias

Cordillera Orienta

Porto dos Gaúchos Óbidos

158

Utiariti

Arinos

Jatobá

Culiene

MATO GROSSO

Juruena

174

Nobres

Pontes-e-Lacerda

Paranatinga

Cuiabá

70

MATO GROSSO AND MATO GROSSO DO SUL
p246

Aragarça

Piranhas

Araguaia

Caiapônia

Rondonópolis

364

Mineiros

158

Ja

50

BRASÍLIA, GOIÁS, AND TOCANTINS

984

Corrents

PARQUE NACIONAL DAS EMAS 8

163

184

Coxim

Itarum

MATO GROSSO DO SUL

Paraíso

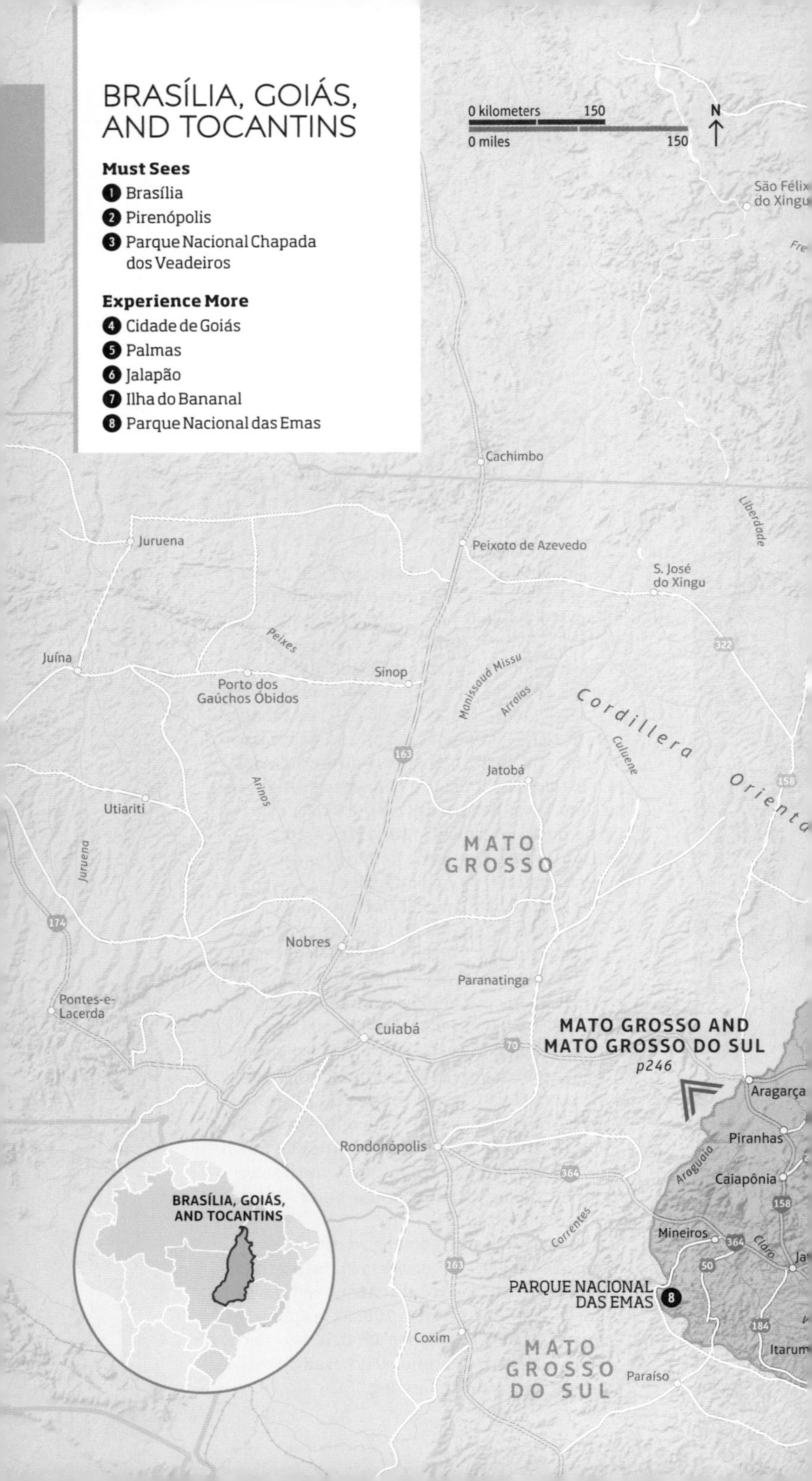

BRASÍLIA

A E4 **A** Brasília Distrito Federal ✈🚌🚇 *i* Presidente Juscelino Kubitschek International Airport; https://turismo.df.gov.br

Brasília is the embodiment of President Juscelino Kubitschek's promise of "fifty years of economic and social development in five." The city was built by vast teams of *candangos*, workers from the northeast, who carved it from the *cerrado* at breakneck speed. The capital of Brazil shifted here from Rio de Janeiro in 1960, and in 1987 Brasília was added to UNESCO's list of World Heritage Sites as an example of daring urban planning.

① Praça dos Três Poderes

A Eixo Monumental

This vast square is flanked by buildings that form the locus of the Brazilian government. The Congresso Nacional e Anexos is a harmonious fusion of lines and curves, creating the most monumental architecture in the city. On the other side of the square stand the Palácio do Planalto, the executive office of the presidency, and the headquarters of the Supreme Court.

Nearby are the Palácio Itamaraty and the Palácio da Justiça, two of Brasília's few buildings that are more aesthetic than monumental. Inside the latter is a vast hall decorated with fine sculpture and paintings. The highlight is 19th-century artist Pedro Américo's *O Grito de Ipiranga*, depicting the moment when Dom Pedro I proclaimed Brazilian Independence (*p66*).

② Santuário Dom Bosco

A Av W3 Sul, Quadra 702 **C** (61) 3223 6542 **O** 7am–8pm daily

The city's finest church honors the 19th-century Italian saint and founder of the Salesian order. His proclamation that a new civilization would arise in the third millennium between the 15th and 16th parallels of latitudes, inspired Kubitschek to build Brasília on the edge of an artificial lake. In the late afternoon, shafts of light penetrate the building, illuminating a vast cross whose vertical was carved from a single piece of tropical cedar. The church was blessed by Pope John Paul II on his 1980 visit.

③ Quartel General do Exército

A Setor Militar Urbano **C** (61) 3415 7882 **O** 10am–4pm Sat & Sun, Mon–Fri by appt only

This complex of imposing buildings is set in a sea of lawns and watched over by a towering obelisk. It was built during the military dictatorship and was intended to show the presence of military power in the government, something that was notably absent from the Praça dos Três Poderes. Brazilian architect Niemeyer (*p237*) was determined that the monumentalism of these generals should not be eclipsed by that of President Juscelino Kubitschek (*p67*).

④ Templo da Boa Vontade

A Setor Garagem Sul 915 **C** (61) 3114 1070 **O** 24 hrs daily

Many religions, some orthodox, some decidedly alternative, thrive in and around Brasília.

→
Os Candangos by Bruno Giorgi, which stands at Praça dos Três Poderes

↑ The unusual rounded architecture of the Congresso Nacional e Anexos

This marble pyramid with seven open sides was built to reflect the city's ecumenical attitude toward spirituality. The building's geometry is based on multiples of seven in accordance with sacred numerology. Spiral steps wind around the interior, and the central portion of the temple is illuminated by light that filters through an enormous and priceless rock crystal found at Cristalino in Goiás.

⑤
Catedral Militar de Nossa Senhora da Paz

🏛 Canteiro Central do Eixo Monumental O ☎ (61) 3323 3858 ⏰ 7am-10pm Mon-Fri

This triangular church echoes the French Notre Dame du Haut, designed by Niemeyer's mentor, Le Corbusier. It was built to house the altar used by John Paul II on his 1980 visit.

Must See

TOP 4 MODERNIST HIGHLIGHTS

Memorial Juscelino Kubitschek
Built in honor of the president responsible for the construction of Brasília, this monument holds his mausoleum.

Memorial dos Povos Indígenas
Fashioned like a maloca, a traditional longhouse, this is a tribute to the Indigenous peoples.

TV Tower
The best place to get a bird's-eye view of the city, with a 426-ft (75-m) observation deck.

Os Candangos
Standing in the Praça dos Três Poderes, artist Bruno Giorgi's *Os Candangos* honors the migrant workers from northeast Brazil who went by this nickname and helped build Brasília.

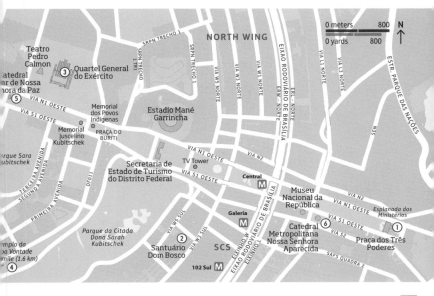

⑥

CATEDRAL METROPOLITANA NOSSA SENHORA APARECIDA

🏠 Esplanada dos Ministérios 🕐 8am-4:45pm Tue-Sat, 9am-4:45pm Sun
🕐 During masses: 12:15pm Tue-Fri, 5pm Sat, 8am, 10:30am & 6pm Sun
🌐 catedral.org.br

Dominating the open space of the Esplanada dos Ministérios, Brasília's cathedral is one of the city's most famous buildings and its most visited site. With Oscar Niemeyer's trademark curvaceous design, the ribbed exterior reaches skywards, while the glowing stained-glass windows and hovering angels inside create a suitably heavenly aura.

Designed by Oscar Niemeyer to resemble a crown of thorns, this cathedral features 16 soaring curved pillars, spread like an open hand and held together at their apex by a steel high-tensile ring. Between them, a filigree of glass windows is united by a fluid series of colors, creating a breathtaking spectacle inside the

church. The main altar and the altarpiece was given by Pope Paul VI in 1967, who also blessed the metal cross sitting atop the building. The statues of the four evangelists outside the cathedral are by the Mineiro sculptor Alfredo Ceschiatti, who also created the archangels suspended from the ceiling inside.

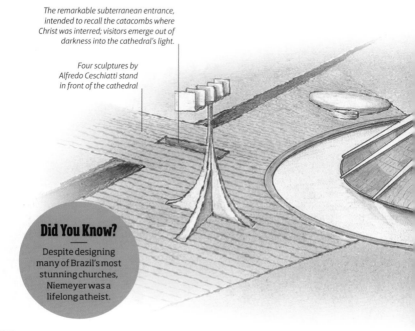

The remarkable subterranean entrance, intended to recall the catacombs where Christ was interred; visitors emerge out of darkness into the cathedral's light.

Four sculptures by Alfredo Ceschiatti stand in front of the cathedral

Did You Know?

Despite designing many of Brazil's most stunning churches, Niemeyer was a lifelong atheist.

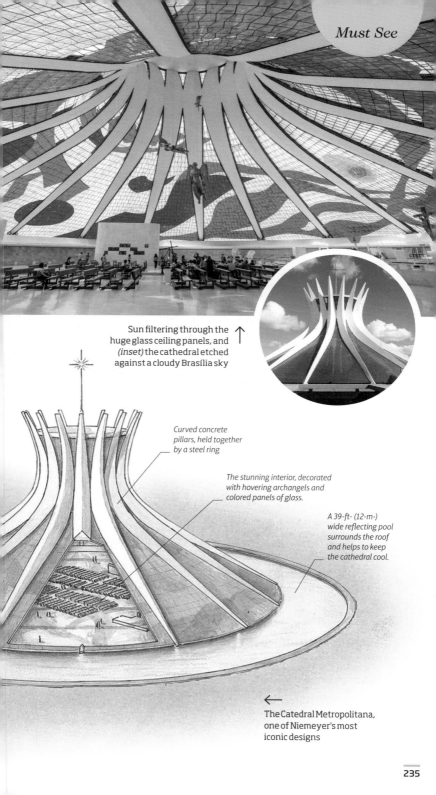

Sun filtering through the
huge glass ceiling panels, and
(inset) the cathedral etched
against a cloudy Brasília sky

Curved concrete
pillars, held together
by a steel ring

The stunning interior, decorated
with hovering archangels and
colored panels of glass.

A 39-ft- (12-m-)
wide reflecting pool
surrounds the roof
and helps to keep
the cathedral cool.

← The Catedral Metropolitana,
one of Niemeyer's most
iconic designs

CREATION OF A CAPITAL

Located at the heart of the country, Brazil's capital city is on UNESCO's list of World Heritage Sites, and is famous for its innovative urban planning and daring architecture. This purpose-built city, situated atop the Brazilian highlands, features a deliberate design of urban zones entwined around green, open spaces.

CITY OF DREAMS

In 1883, Italian priest Dom Bosco dreamt of a utopian city in central Brazil. His prophecy defined the exact location of the city, situated between the 15th and 20th latitude, the position of modern-day Brasília. Bosco's vision is believed to be the inspiration for transferring Brazil's capital from Rio de Janeiro to this new location. It took more than half a century for his prophecy to become a reality.

A GRAND DESIGN

Juscelino Kubitschek was the president of Brazil between 1956 and 1961 and was responsible for the creation of Brasília as the new, modern capital of the country. Acting on Bosco's vision, Kubitschek and his team of designers, planners, and architects, led by Oscar Niemeyer, envisaged Brasília not only as a city, but also as a monument to the

national motto: "Order and Progress." The team turned to European Modernism, following the doctrine of Charles-Edouard Jeanneret (1887–1965), for their inspiration.

↑ The striking arches of the landmark Juscelino Kubitscheck bridge

The Towers of Congress and the Chamber of Deputies, and *(inset)* a statue of Juscelino Kubitschek

Jeanneret's concept stated that modern cities should be zoned functionally with separate areas for housing (in high-rise blocks), recreation, and administration, broken by green belts and roads. Inspired by this, Lúcio Costa and Roberto Burle Marx, Brasília's urban planner and landscape designer, intended that every element, from the layout of the residential and administrative districts to the symmetry of the buildings, should be in harmony with the city's overall design. Today, Costa and Burle Marx's deliberate plan can be seen in Brasília's distinctive shape, which has been variously interpreted as an airplane, a bird in flight, and a bow and arrow.

> **Bosco's vision is believed to be the inspiration for transferring Brazil's capital from Rio de Janeiro to this new location.**

A NEW CAPITAL IS BORN

Construction of the new capital began in 1956. *Candangos* – northeastern workers – were brought to Brasília in vast numbers to build the city. By 1959, an estimated 30,000 *candangos* were here.

On April 21, 1960, Brasília was inaugurated by President Kubitschek. The main bodies of the federal government administration were transferred from Rio de Janeiro to Brasília, forming the new headquarters of the three branches of federal power: the judiciary, the legislative, and the executive.

Today, the former president is memorialized with the Juscelino Kubitscheck bridge, one of Brasília's famous landmarks. Opened in 2002, the striking construction, designed by architect Alexandre Chan, links the eastern shore of Lake Paranoá to the center of the city.

② PIRENÓPOLIS

 E4 🏠 Goiás 🚭 🚌 ℹ️ Central de Atendimentoão Turista: Rua do Bonfim s/n, Centro; www.pirenopolis.com.br

This picturesque town is gathered around the Rio das Almas, surrounded by verdant *cerrado* woodlands. It skillfully balances the old and the new, with cobble-stoned streets and tempting, chic little restaurants.

①
Igreja Matriz de Nossa Senhora do Rosário

🏠 Praça da Matriz
🕐 7am-5pm Thu-Mon

This parish church, founded in 1728, is the largest and the oldest ecclesiastical building in Goiás. Until 2002, when the entire edifice was gutted in a fire, it also had one of the

Did You Know?

Pirenópolis was founded in 1727 as a gold mining town, but it also had a thriving cotton industry.

finest Baroque interiors in the state. These included an altarpiece decorated with motifs taken from the surrounding *cerrado* and an impressive ceiling. The church was restored and reopened in 2006, but a shortage of funds has left it with a plain interior.

② 🎬
Cine Pireneus

🏠 Rua Direita 3, Centro
📞 (62) 3331 2657

Originally built as a theater in Neo-Classical style in 1919, the town's first cinema was created in 1936 with a striking Art Deco facade. Today, following several further renovations, Cine Pireneus serves as a multipurpose

FESTA DO DIVINO ESPÍRITO SANTO

This festival is based on Iberian lore dating from the Crusades and Catholic Whitsun celebrations. It begins 15 days before Pentecost Sunday, at the Matriz, where a gathering of riders proceed out of the town into the surrounding countryside. Parades, masked dancers, and many musical events follow. It all culminates on Pentecost Sunday in the stadium, the Cavalhodrómo.

arts center. Besides film screenings, it also hosts theater productions, art exhibitions, and live concerts.

③
Igreja Nosso Senhordo Bonfim

🏠 Praça do Bonfim
🕐 Noon-6pm Wed-Mon

This simple but elegant little church on Rua do Bonfim was built between 1750 and 1754. One of the best-preserved

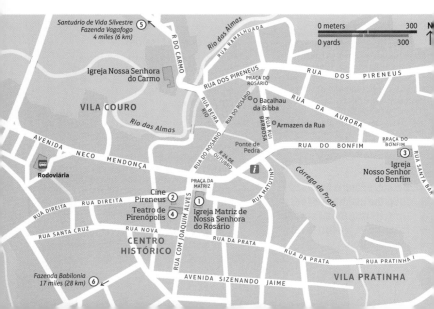

↑ Rustic 18th-century bungalows in the historic center of Pirenópolis

churches in Goiás, it is architecturally similar to the Matriz de Nossa Senhora do Rosário and has a plain white facade. The image of Nosso Senhor do Bonfim, in the main altarpiece, was brought here from Salvador by a convoy of 250 enslaved people.

---

④

Teatro de Pirenópolis

◩ Praça da Matriz s/n
☏ (62) 3331 2029 (box office) ◷ 8–11am & 1–5pm Mon–Fri, 9am–8pm Sat, 9am–3pm Sun

This delightful, restored miniature 19th-century theater is one of the town's hidden treasures. It is best visited during one of its regular plays, performances, and shows. The Goiás singer-songwriter Maria Eugenia and the Tocantins *forró* singer Dorivã regularly play here. Just around the corner, on the Rua do Direita, is the little Art Deco Cine Pireneus, whose eclectic program includes films, plays, concerts, and art exhibitions.

⑤

Santuário de Vida Silvestre Fazenda Vagafogo

◩ 4 miles (6 km) NW of Pirenópolis ☏ (62) 3335 8515 ◷ 9am–5pm daily

A beautifully preserved patch of forest lined with streams and exquisite trails, Santuário Vagafogo makes for a good excursion. This stunning nature preserve of *cerrado* and gallery forests is home to a number of bird and animal species. The sanctuary offers activities, such as tree climbing and rappeling.

---

⑥

Fazenda Babilonia

◩ GO 431, Km 3, Pirenópolis
☏ (62) 9294 1805 ◷ 9am–4pm Wed–Sun (by appt)
🌐 fazendababilonia.com.br

This late 18th-century *fazenda* used to be the largest sugar-cane refinery in Goiás. It was founded by Joaquim Alves de Oliveira, and also produced manioc flour and cotton.

EAT

O Bacalhau da Bibba
A romantic restaurant that specializes in Portuguese dishes.

◩ Rua do Rosario 42A
☏ (62) 3331 2103

$$$

Armazem da Rua
Located in the heart of old Pirenópolis, this atmospheric bar-deli serves great snacks.

◩ Rua Rui Barbosa 10
☏ (62) 33311714

$$$

Today, the well-preserved farm is still a working ranch. Visitors can take guided tours of the grounds. The tours include the Nossa Senhora da Conceição chapel, which retains its original interior. The restaurant serves food made from the *fazenda's* produce.

3

PARQUE NACIONAL CHAPADA DOS VEADEIROS

🅐 E4 🅐 Goiás 🚌 From Brasília to Alto Paraíso, then bus 🛈 Av Ari Valadão, Alto Paraíso, (62) 3446 1159; São Jorge: (62) 3455 1114, open 8am–5pm daily

The vast savannas of Brazil's interior are split by deep gorges and topped with high plateaux, home to thousands of endemic species of flora and fauna. This magnificent national park is one of the finest stretches of *cerrado* (tropical savanna) in the country, with great opportunities to discover some of Brazil's wildlife.

Named for the marsh deer that inhabit the area, the Chapada dos Veadeiros National Park sits on the edge of the *cerrado*, one of the largest areas of wild country in the interior of Brazil. Most easily accessed from the small town of Alto Paraíso, the park is set in a stunning landscape. The surrounding area features sprawling forests, broken by rushing waterfalls and meadows, and dotted with stands of buriti palms. This remarkably isolated destination offers truly spectacular walks and pretty trails for nature lovers, as well as more thrilling outdoor adventure activities such as rappeling and canyoning.

> 📷 PICTURE PERFECT
> **Vale da Lua**
>
> The light in this shallow but mesmerizing canyon is particularly beautiful at sunset. Over millions of years, the black rocks have been sculpted into strange, Dalí-esque shapes by the rushing Rio São Miguel.

① The pretty Chuveirinho meadow flower is indigenous to this region.

② The nearby town of Alto Paraíso de Goiás makes a good base for exploring the area's natural attractions.

③ Giant anteaters are one of the larger mammals found in the park.

↑ The undulating rocks of the Vale da Lua within the Parque Nacional Chapada dos Veadeiros

↑ The whitewashed exterior of the Museu de Arte Sacra, surrounded by palm trees

EXPERIENCE MORE

④
Cidade de Goiás

 D4 🏠 Goiás 🚌 ✈ ℹ Secretaría de Turismo: Praça da Bandeira, Centro; http://prefeituradegoias.go.gov.br/turismo

Also known as Goiás Velho, or just Goiás, Cidade de Goiás is a magical little city nestled at the foot of the rugged Serra Dourado hills. Like most colonial towns in Brazil's interior, Cidade de Goiás grew rich on gold. Until the middle of the 20th century, it was the capital of what was once the largest Brazilian state apart from Amazonas. Winding cobbled streets lined with 18th-century townhouses lead to hills capped with churches, leafy squares, and little markets. Life here seems to trot along as it has done for centuries. While historic, Goiás is far from being lost in a bygone age. The city's busy social calendar is a testament to its successful fusion of the old with the new, from thoroughly traditional processions of Semana Santa (Holy Week) to some of the best film festivals and classical music concerts in Brazil.

A variety of buildings and museums testify to the city's illustrious past, and Goiás is small enough to see them all leisurely on foot. The best place to begin a tour is at Praça Brasil Caiado, where there are a number of museums and monuments. These include the **Museu das Bandeiras**, the former seat of government, which preserves a forbidding dungeon and a set of rooms with period furniture, a magnificent

> **Winding cobbled streets lined with 18th-century townhouses lead to hills capped with churches, leafy squares, and little markets.**

 INSIDER TIP
Torchlit Parade

Visit Cidade de Goiás during Holy Week to spy the Procissão do Fogaréu (Procession of Fire). This eye-catching parade sees devotees wind their way through the town carrying flaming torches.

Baroque public fountain, and the Quartel do Vinte, an 18th-century barracks, which now houses the tourist office.

Immediately north of Praça Brasil Caiado is another square, Praça do Coreto. The most interesting of all the city's museums, **Museu de Arte Sacra** in the Igreja de Boa Morte, is located here, preserving a series of haunting, lifelike religious effigies by José Joaquim da Veiga Valle (1806–74). Opposite this museum is the **Palácio Conde dos Arcos**, complete with 18th-century furniture and still used by the governor on city visits.

Museu das Bandeiras

⊕ 🏛 Praça Brasil Caiado
📞 (62) 3371 1087 🕐 9am-7pm
Wed-Sat, 9am-1pm Tue & Sun

Museu de Arte Sacra

⊕ 🏛 Rua Moretti Foggia 14
📞 (62) 3371 1207 🕐 9am-
5pm Tue-Sat, 9am-1pm Sun

Palácio Conde dos Arcos

⊕ 🏛 Praça Dr Tasso de
Camargo 📞 (62) 3371
1200 🕐 9am-5pm Tue-
Sat, 9am-3pm Sun

⑤

Palmas

🅰 E3 🏛 Tocantins
➡️ 🚌 ℹ️ CATUR: Av 103
Norte (TO-080), Palmas;
(63) 2111 2773

Built in 1989, Brazil's newest
state capital sits beside the
Tocantins River, at the base
of a range of forested low
hills. Palmas is a pleasant,
but sprawling, modern city.

Most visitors come to
Palmas as it is a good
jumping-off point for the
numerous attractions that lie
within the interior of Tocantins
state, in particular the state
park of Jalapão and the vast
and wild Ilha do Bananal.

Aside from the immense
Palmas lake formed by the
dam on the Rio Tocantins,
Palmas' most interesting area
is its vast, grassy main square,
Praça Giróssois, which is lined
by grandiose public buildings
and various monuments
dedicated to its founder, José
Wilson Siqueira Campos, and
his legacy.

The tree-shaded
banks of Palmas'
vast lake, and
(inset) sky-
scrapers lining
the water's edge ↓

EAT

Rancho Baião
Set by the banks of the
Rio Tocantins, this
restaurant features a
beach and a water slide.

🅰 E3 🏛 Av LO15,
Cacara 35, Palmas
📞 (63) 99957 2006

💲💲💲

**Santo Cerrado
Risoteria e Café**
Savor delicious risotto at
this Italian restaurant
near the Chapada dos
Veadeiros National Park.

🅰 E4 🏛 Viela C, Sao Jorge
📞 (61) 9974 1150

💲💲💲

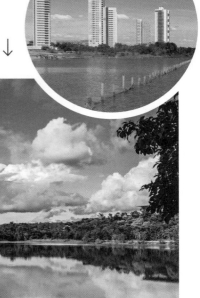

Jalapão

E4 **Tocantins**

A journey through Brazil's interior would be incomplete without a visit to Jalapão, which stretches across 13,130 sq miles (34,000 sq km). Located deep within eastern Tocantins, this breathtaking area is one of South America's great wilderness destinations. The best time to visit Jalapão is the dry season between June and September; guided tours can be organized through the safari camp operator, **Korubo**.

Beyond the inaccessible reaches of southern Piauí, the arid *cerrado* forests and incipient *caatinga* thornlands are more pristine here than anywhere else. Many fast-flowing rivers cut through spectacular canyons and thunder over waterfalls throughout Jalapão. A number of rivers are born in limpid glassy springs that bubble forth from the sands of Jalapão. Others wind their way through groves of buriti palms called *veredas*. These are visited by Spix's macaws and Brazilian Merganser ducks, two of the extremely rare birds lost to the rest of the continent but still found here.

Towering over Jalapão's seemingly interminable plains and striding out to the endless horizons are stands of monolithic tabletop mountains, winding yellow sand dunes, and craggy rock pinnacles. The air is so clear that even when these are far in the distance, they appear close enough to touch. Trails running across the mountain summits range from moderate to difficult. The views from the top of the mountains and dunes are mesmerizing.

Korubo
 jalapao.com

STAY

Jalapão Ecolodge
Bordering Jalapão State Park, this eco-lodge offers glamping, with bamboo chalets and straw-roofed cabins.

E4 **Serra da Catedral, Rodovia TO-0 30, Tocantins** **jalapao ecolodge.com.br**

$$$

Pousada Recanto do Sossego
Chalets and a hotel-boat by the Araguaia River, ideally located between Ilha do Bananal and Araguaia State Park.

D4 **Av Treze de Maio s/n, São Félix do Araguaia** **araguaiatur.com**

$$$

Pousada do Ipe
This lodge has comfortable chalets and a self-catered apartment with an outdoor pool.

E5 **Rua Coronel Luiz Guedes de Amorim 22, Goias Velho** **(62) 3371 2065** **pousadadoipe goias.com.br**

$$$

Ilha do Bananal

D4 **Tocantins**

The Rio Araguaia runs from southern Goiás across Tocantins state to join the Rio Tocantins before draining into the Amazon. In the middle of this

The fast-flowing waterfalls of New River State Park in Jalapão ↑

river sits the Ilha do Bananal, an island so vast that it has its own rivers running through it. Access to the island's wild interior is not easy. Visits here are only possible with a licensed tour operator such as **Ecoturismo CCTrekking**.

Three ecosystems converge on the island – rainforest, wetland, and *cerrado*. Bananal's southern extremes are mostly Terras Indígenas (Indigenous territories), where tourists are not welcome. Its center and north are impenetrable without a guide. Indigenous communities, including the Javaés and the Karajás, inhabit the island, some of whom produce carved wooden animals and pottery figurines.

The southern part of the island also comprises seasonally flooded forests, lakes, and swamps filled with wildlife. This is a wonderful area for bird-watching, particularly water birds.

Ecoturismo CCTrekking

77680000 Caseara, Tocantins (63) 8405 5011

8 (M3)
Parque Nacional das Emas

D5 Chapadão do Céu CAT: Av. Ema s/n, Quadra 52, Centro, Chapadão do Céu ; (64) 3634 1310

Tucked far away in the southwest corner of Goiás and surrounded by a sea of soya, Emas National Park is a 500-sq-mile (1,300-sq-km) island of grassland and sparse *cerrado*, dotted with termite hills and cut by blackwater rivers. The park is considered the best preserved *cerrado* in Brazil.

Populations of larger mammals, particularly the armadillo, maned wolf, and puma, are very healthy here – there is also a small jaguar community. The park is an important destination for bird-watchers, with the largest concentration of blue-and-yellow macaws outside Amazônia, and a population of the namesake emu.

Although there is no compulsion to go on a guided tour, it is a good idea to organize a

↑ A burrowing owl at Parque Nacional das Emas

trip through a tour operator in Pirenópolis, such as **Savanah EcoTurismo**, or through the tourist office in the nearby town of Chapadão do Céu, east of the park. Facilities at the park are minimal. A reasonable range of accommodation is available in Chapadão do Céu.

Savanah EcoTurismo

Rua Direita 57, Centro Histórico Pirenópolis (62) 99624 1207 savanah.tur.br

MATO GROSSO AND MATO GROSSO SUL

The Mato Grosso (literally "thick bushes") was considered wild, inhospitable territory by the Portuguese colonists well into the 18th century. The Paiaguá people of the Pantanal remained fiercely independent, as did the Bororo in the east and the Parecis in the northwest. Explorations were limited to nature expeditions and Jesuit missionaries – until the discovery of gold. The resultant gold rush led to fierce clashes between the Europeans and the Indigenous groups. Several gold mining camps were set up, and by the 1780s, most of the Parecis were enslaved to work the gold mines, the Bororo were pushed into the rainforest, and the Paiaguá were virtually wiped out after a series of violent campaigns.

Southern Mato Grosso was invaded by Paraguay in 1864 as part of its disastrous War of the Triple Alliance (1864–70). As a result, Brazil stepped up colonization in the region and, in the 1890s, began building telegraph lines across the state to improve communications.

The state was split into two halves in 1977, with the southern part becoming Mato Grosso do Sul. Around the same time, air travel and new highways began to spark real development in the region. Today, agriculture, especially soybean production, dominates the economies of both states, although tourism into the Pantanal – the world's largest tropical wetland – is also growing in importance.

Gradaús
Redenção
Araguaína
Santana do Araguaia
Villa Rica
Porto Alegre do Norte
rência
arana
Cocalinho
va antino
Araguapaz
Pirenópolis
Caiapônia
Cassilândia
ocência
arecida buado
s as

Miracema do Tocantins
Palmas

TOCANTINS

Dianópolis
Peixe
Barreiras
Santana
Campos Belos
São Domingos
Coribe

BRASÍLIA, GOIÁS, AND TOCANTINS
p228

Lago de Serro da Mesa

Barro Alto

International Aírport Brasília

Brasília

GOIÁS

Hidrolândia
Edéia
Quirinópolis
Itumbiara
Uberlândia

MINAS GERAIS
p182

Prata

São José do Rio Preto

Araçatuba

SÃO PAULO STATE
p170

Limeira
Bauru
Ourinhos
Campinas
Lorena
Cabo Frio
Rio de Janeiro
São Paulo
Represa de Jurumirim
Itapetininga
ringa

MASSO GROSSO AND MATO GROSSO DO SUL

Must See
❶ Pantanal

Experience More
❷ Chapada dos Guimarães
❸ Cuiabá
❹ Xingú
❺ Corumbá
❻ Miranda
❼ Alta Floresta
❽ Campo Grande
❾ Bonito

0 kilometers   200
0 miles   200

N

TOP 5 ANIMALS TO LOOK OUT FOR

Capybara
The world's largest rodents, these sheep-sized mammals can often be spotted grazing at the water's edge.

Anaconda
Though they prefer an aquatic habitat, these giant constrictors rest on land to digest.

Caiman
These iconic Pantanal creatures can be spotted in abundance at night.

Toucan
Keep your eyes peeled for these unmistakeably colorful birds.

Howler Monkeys
More often heard than seen, these large monkeys are most vocal at sunrise.

1

PANTANAL

🗺 D5 🏛 Mato Grosso and Mato Grosso do Sul ✈ Campo Grande and Corumbá 🚌 Caceres and Cuiabá 🛈 Av Afonso Pena 4909, Campo Grande; (67) 3314 3142

In these remarkable seasonal floodplains, an abundance of rare fauna co-exists alongside herds of ranch cattle, from irresistibly cute capybara to rare and elusive tapirs. Unlike the Amazon Basin, the Pantanal also has the visitor-friendly attraction of having vast open landscapes, making its wildlife that much easier to glimpse.

The world's largest wetland, the Pantanal provides a habitat for the greatest concentration of animals in the Western Hemisphere. Innumerable waterbirds gather toward the end of the dry season; there are five types of kingfisher in the region for example, including the green kingfisher that makes its nest in a tunnel. The region is also home to five species of macaw. There are plenty of reptiles and large mammals, including caimans, tapirs, giant anteaters, and all of Brazil's eight feline species, including the jaguar. The secret to the vast numbers of animals lies in the diversity of vegetation and the geography of the Pantanal, a gently sloping bowl which floods when nutrient-rich tributaries drain from the ancient sedimentary rocks of the Brazilian Shield and get trapped. Aquatic plants breed profusely and these provide ample food for fish and birds, who, in turn, feed the rest of the food chain. Wildlife viewing is consequently excellent, and visitors can travel around by car, or take an organized boat trip on the various Pantanal rivers.

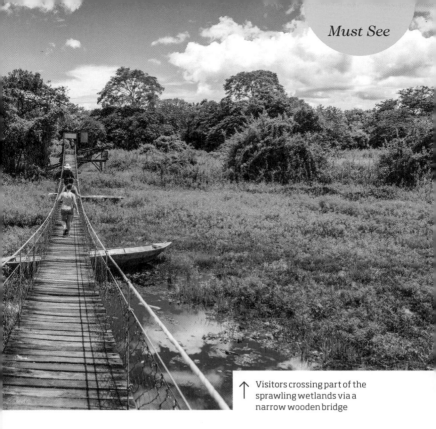

↑ Visitors crossing part of the sprawling wetlands via a narrow wooden bridge

A chestnut-eared Aracari, which is a relatively common sight in the region ↑

→ A magnificent jaguar lazing on the banks of a Pantanal river

STAY

These *fazendas* (cattle ranches) offer accommodation and an insight into local working life.

Hotel Fazenda Baia das Pedras
⌂ MS228, Aquidauana, MS 79200-000 ⊠ baia daspedras.com.br

⑤⑤⑤

Fazenda San Francisco
⌂ BR262, Km 586, Miranda ⊠ fazenda sanfrancisco.tur.br

⑤⑤⑤

EXPERIENCE MORE

2

Chapada dos Guimarães

🅐D4 🄼Mato Grosso 🚌From Eco Turismo Cultural, Rua Cipriano Curvo 655, Centro 🇧www.chapadados guimaraes.com.br

The town of Chapada dos Guimarães is set on a plateau of the same name. Said to be up to 500 million years old, the majestic tablelands and escarpments of the plateau are among the oldest rock formations in the world. As the continent's geodesic center, the tablelands of the Chapada dos Guimarães are reputedly imbued with energizing powers strong enough to reduce the speed of a car and said to attract UFOs. While local residents claim that this effect has been documented, skeptics believe otherwise.

The little town has numerous cafés, and a daily fair selling crafts. There are also several spiritual centers devoted to the New Age movement, which has been growing in popularity for the last 50 years or so in Brazil.

Nature lovers come here for the scenery. The edge of the Chapada offers sweeping vistas over the patchy, remnant *cerrado* forests of the Mato Grosso plains. There are several waterfalls in the area, the tallest of which is the Véu de Noiva, or the Bridal Veil Falls.

Although the Chapada has seen more aggressive agricultural development than its counterparts in Goiás and Tocantins, many upland bird species that are not found in the Pantanal *(p250)* or the Amazonian forests are seen here. The high *cerrado* pasturelands, forests and savannas of the Chapada are popular with bird-watchers, who come here to catalog the variety of birds,

---

 GREAT VIEW
A Veil of Water

Follow a short, marked trail to reach the impressive lookout of Véu de Noiva (Bridal Veil Falls), an 86-m- (282-ft-) tall waterfall crashing into the canyon below in Chapada dos Guimarães National Park.

---

and perhaps catch a lucky glimpse of mammals, such as maned wolves, ocelots, and black-tailed marmosets.

3

Cuiabá

🅐C4 🄼Mato Grosso 🛫🚌 🇧Sedtur, (65) 3613 9300

Mato Grosso's capital and the warmest city in Brazil sits on a low, languid plain at the foot of the Chapada dos Guimarães hills. Situated on the banks of the Rio Cuiabá, a tributary of the Rio Paraguai, the city has a variety of leafy squares and is known as the Cidade Verde (Green City). Cuiabá is also a good starting point for excursions into the vast wetland area of the Pantanal.

Like Cidade de Goiás *(p242)* and Ouro Preto *(p186)*, Cuiabá was originally a flourishing gold-mining town, full of decorative buildings and fine churches. Almost all of these buildings were demolished as the town modernized in the late 1960s. Consequently, the town has lost most of the splendid works of José Joaquim

da Veiga Valle (1806–74), one of the country's greatest Baroque artists. Fortunately, some of his craftsmanship can still be seen in the well-preserved interiors of the Catedral do Bom Jesus, which has an unusual Moorish facade.

The most interesting of the city's sights is the **Museu Rondon de Etnologia e Arqueologia (MUSEAR)**, in which some priceless pieces of Indigenous art are kept. These include exhibits of the Xavante, Bororo, and Karajá peoples. The museum houses some beautiful Bororo and Rikbaktsa headdresses and superb pieces of Kadiwéu ceramics.

Museu Rondon de Etnologia e Arqueologia (MUSEAR)

⊘ 🏠 Av Fernando Correia da Costa, Boa Esperança, Campus Universitário 📞 (65) 3615 8489 🕐 Until further notice

Xingú

🅰 D3 🅰 Mato Grosso 🚌 ℹ️ Fundação Nacional dos Povos Indígenas (Funai): Rua 8, Qd 15 Cuiabá; www. funai.gov.br

By the end of the 19th century the great Amazon tributaries

↑ Xingú people participating in a bow and arrow competition deep in the Amazon

had all been explored and colonized, and their Indigenous peoples had been enslaved or killed. The remote region of Xingú, in the extreme northeast of Mato Grosso, was the only Indigenous settlement to survive the onslaught and has since been established as an important preserve.

Home to one of the largest areas inhabited by Indigenous people in the country, Xingú is a large island of forest in a vast ocean of soya plantations. These tracts of land are concentrated around the beautiful clear-water Rio Xingú.

The Indigenous peoples flourishing in the Xingú region specialize in furniture-making

and basket-weaving, among a variety of other crafts and activities.

Tourism is extremely limited here and visits to Indigenous villages can only be undertaken with prior permission from Fundação Nacional dos Povos Indígenas (Funai).

EAT

Mahalo
Restaurant serving gourmet dishes such as fish with caramelized bananas, and duck with brie risotto and edamame beans.

🅰 C4 🏠 Presidente Castelo Branco 359, Cuiabá 🌐 mahalo restaurante.com.br

Choppão
Popular restaurant-bar where Cuibá locals enjoy ice cold beer and eat *escaldado* - a chicken soup with eggs.

🅰 C4 🏠 Praça 8 de Abril 44, Cuiabá, Mato Grosso 🌐 choppao.com.br

↑ The skyline of Cuiabá, dotted with green spaces and colorfully painted buildings

←
A 1930s British girder railway bridge over the river, close to Miranda

TERENA PEOPLE

There are around 26,000 Terena people living in Mato Grosso do Sul; the majority reside on Indigenous lands such as in the traditional villages clustered near Miranda. Many work in urban centers, and the group is considered by Funai *(p253)* to be one of the most successfully "integrated" peoples in Brazil.

5

Corumbá

C5 Mato Grosso do Sul Along Rio Paraguai Secretaría de Turismo: Rua Domingos Sahib 560, Porto Geral; (67) 3231 2886

Corumbá, on the banks of the Rio Paraguai, is a city enveloped by the Pantanal region's unspoiled beauty. Boat trips along the river and wetland excursions are Corumbá's major attractions. Sportfishing, one of the main highlights, is provided at the nature lodges, floating hotels, and charming *fazendas* in this area. Corumbá throws a party for Carnaval and is one of the most festive places to be for it, with big parades and samba schools.

Corumbá was explored by Portuguese and Spanish adventurers in search of gold and minerals. By the 18th century, the growing strategic importance of the Rio Paraguai led to the construction of forts here. The **Forte Junqueira**, built during the Paraguayan War of 1865 to 1870, is the only fort still standing intact.

Another place worth a visit is the **Casa do Artesão**, a former prison housing an interesting museum of Indigenous and local *objets d'art*. The **Museu de Historia do Pantanal** also has a small collection of Indigenous art.

Forte Junqueira
Rua Cáceres 425
(67) 3231 5828 9am-5pm Tue-Sun

Casa do Artesão
Rua Dom Aquino
8am-5pm Mon-Fri, 7:30-11:30am Sat

Museu de Historia do Pantanal
Rua Manoel Cavassa 275
(67) 3231 0303 1-6pm Tue-Sat

6

Miranda

C5 Mato Grosso do Sul Setur; (67) 3242 2471

The tiny town of Miranda, in the heart of the Pantanal, hosts the region's liveliest festival, the Festa do Homem Pantaneiro. This grand celebration of the ranching and cowboy way of life features lasso contests (in the mornings for women, at night for men), and rodeos. Live *sertanejo* bands and dancing carry on all night.

Miranda is an ideal base for visiting the southern Pantanal's various *fazenda* (ranches), many of which lie on the outskirts of town. The Fazenda San Francisco is one of the best locations in inland Brazil for wild cats, especially ocelot and jaguar. The Fazenda Baía Grande preserves a diverse range of Pantanal habitats, including a large caiman-filled lake and extensive forest. The Pantanal Ranch Meia Lua lies just on the edge of town and is an ideal soft adventure option.

Alta Floresta

🅰C3 🅼Mato Grosso
➕To Cuiabá, then bus
🛈Prefeitura de Alta Floresta: Travessa Álvaro Teixeira Costa 50; (66) 3512 3100

Situated in the extreme north of Mato Grosso, Alta Floresta sits on the edge of the southern Amazon rainforest, and is a rapidly growing frontier town.

This remote town is also a thriving agricultural settlement. Its surrounding areas are said to be some of the best in the Brazilian Amazon for spotting rare birds and varied mammals.

One of the many highlights of Alta Floresta is the four-star hotel, Floresta Amazônica, which serves as a base for the Cristalino Jungle Lodge. The lodge lies deep in the forest, north of Alta Floresta. The lodge is situated on the banks of the Rio Cristalino, which is the blackwater tributary of the Rio Tapajós, whose blue waters flow into the Amazon at Santarém *(p356)*.

The site is most famous for the profuse birdlife surrounding it, as well as a huge variety of butterflies and other insects, reptiles, and mammals. All the large neotropical rainforest mammals, including the endangered white-nosed bearded saki monkey, brown titi monkey, giant river otter, and three-toed sloth, as well as jaguar, puma, and tapir are present and can often be spotted here.

Clouds over the *cerrado* forest, and *(inset)* bird-watching at Cristalino Jungle Lodge ↓

⑧
Campo Grande

D5 Mato Grosso do Sul CAT: Av Noroeste 5140; (67) 3314 9968

Mato Grosso do Sul's capital Campo Grande is also known as Cidade Morena because of its red earth. It is a prosperous, modern city devoted far more to agro-business than tourism. Yet most visitors to the southern Pantanal arrive here because the tourist infrastructure is excellent. The city itself has few major attractions, though there are many good restaurants, hotels, and bars, particularly along and around Rua Barão do Rio Branco.

💬 INSIDER TIP
Exploring Bonito

Most sites are outside of town; there are no public buses and paying for taxis to every site can get very pricey. The best way to see Bonito's attractions is with a guided tour. Confirm that transportation is included when booking.

⑨
Bonito

C5 Mato Grosso do Sul Comtur Rua Coronel Pilád Rebuá 1780, Bonito; (67) 3255 2160

A one-street town, Bonito is lined with *pousadas*, restaurants, shops, and tour operators whose lifeline is tourism. It lies just beyond the Pantanal's southern extremities, in the Serra do Bodoquena, a low, cerrado-covered range of rugged hills busy with primates and birds, including the black-collared hawk. There are numerous sights around Bonito, all protected by regulations. Only Bonito-based tour agencies can organize trips and arrange permits.

One of the natural springs in the area, the **Aquário Natural Baía Bonita**, features an aquarium, which contains 30 different varieties of fish. The complex also features a swimming pool.

The glassy **Rio Sucuri** is broken by waterfalls and large pools filled with 3-ft-(1-m-) long *piraputanga* (ray-finned fish, typical of the Rio Paraguai basin) and silver dourado fish. Many pools are set in woodland cut with wildlife trails. The gentle flow of the Rio Sucuri and the excellent facilities draws a plethora of snorkelers and rafters. Particularly popular are the flotation points where visitors begin a pleasant 1-mile (1.6-km) float downstream.

↑ *Piraputanga* swimming in the Aquário Natural Baía Bonita

↑ The skyscrapers of Campo Grande reflecting the golden morning light

The azure underwater lake and rock formations of the Gruta do Lago Azul ↑

The Serra do Bodoquena is dotted with caves, the most spectacular of which is the **Gruta do Lago Azul**. The main highlight is a radiant underground lake that shines as blue as a sapphire in the morning light. From the cave's mouth, a narrow path leads deep down through striking stalactite formations. At the bottom lies the lake, illuminated by ambient light that streams through the cave's opening.

Some of the best hiking opportunities are offered in the **Estância Mimosa** trail, which features rivers, natural pools, and as many as ten waterfalls. The trail goes past the gorgeous riverside forest of the Rio Mimoso, with caves and a rich array of wildlife.

A pothole that descends 237-ft (72-m) deep leads to the **Abismo Anhumas**, a cavern filled with a large, clear, blue lake featuring vast stalagmites and stalactites, among other cave deposits. The entrance to the cave is by rappel. Once visitors have descended to the lake, they can float in it, snorkel, and take a boat tour. Book with the **Abismo Anhumas Training Center** in advance as preparation is required.

Aquário Natural Baía Bonita
⊛ 🅰 4 miles (7 km) SE of Bonito ⏰ 8am–3pm daily 🌐 aquarionatural.com.br

Rio Sucuri
🅰 12 miles (20 km) SW of Bonito 🛈 Rio Sucuri Ecoturismo: (67) 99831 3371

Gruta do Lago Azul
⊛ 🅰 12 miles (20 km) W of Bonito ⏰ 7am–5pm daily 🌐 grutadolagoazul.com.br

Estância Mimosa
⊛ 🅰 15 miles (24 km) NW of Bonito ⏰ 7:30am–5pm daily 🌐 estanciamimosa.com.br

Abismo Anhumas
⊛ 🅰 16 miles (25 km) W of Bonito ⏰ 8am & noon daily (pre-booked visits only) 🌐 abismoanhumas.com.br

Abismo Anhumas Training Center
🅰 Bonito 📞 (67) 3255 3313

EAT

Casa do João
Well-run family restaurant specializing in Pantanal cuisine.

🅰 D5 🅰 Rue Nelsom Felício dos Santos 664, Bonito 📞 (67) 3255 1212

💲💲💲

Juanita
Popular restaurant with an appealing outdoor deck serving a variety of local dishes.

🅰 C5 🅰 Rua Nossa Senhora da Penha 854, Bonito 📞 67 3255 1924 🌐 juanita.com.br

💲💲💲

Figueira Churrascaria
Steak house slightly outside of town serving skewers of perfectly cooked meat.

🅰 D5 🅰 Av Cônsul Assaf Trad 3514, Campo Grande 🌐 figueira churrascaria.com.br

💲💲💲

The glassy Rio Sucuri is broken by waterfalls and large pools filled with 3-ft- (1-m-) long *piraputanga* (ray-finned fish, typical of the Rio Paraguai basin).

SALVADOR

Salvador was once the political and economic heart of Brazil, serving as its capital from 1549 to 1763, and with its grand mansions and churches financed by the sugar trade of the 17th and 18th centuries. The city was officially founded in 1549 by Portuguese conquistador Tomé de Sousa, who displaced or enslaved the Indigenous Tupinambá peoples. Despite its brief capture by the Dutch in 1624, Salvador went on to become incredibly rich thanks to the vast sugarcane plantations in the surrounding Recôncavo region.

As a result of the growth of the plantations, the city also turned into Brazil's main port of entry for enslaved Africans. The Malê Revolt of 1835, led by enslaved African-born Muslims, was the most significant uprising in the city's history. Although the authorities reacted harshly, this rebellion is considered to be a turning point, with slavery finally being abolished throughout the country in 1888. The legacy of this transatlantic trade can still be seen in Salvador's cultural diversity. Today, the descendants of Africans transported from the Portuguese Gold Coast and Angola make up the bulk of the population, and the city is the primary center of Afro-Brazilian culture, with its cuisine, capoeira, Carnaval, percussion-based music, and the spiritualist Yoruban Candomblé religion all having roots in Africa.

In the 19th century the city was largely bypassed by industrialization, barely surviving the decline of the sugar trade by diversifying into tobacco, pepper, and cloves. Today, however, Salvador has rebounded to become Brazil's fourth-largest city, and is a major port and oil refining hub with a booming tourist industry.

SALVADOR

Must See

❶ Igreja e Convento de São Francisco

Experience More

❷ Fundação Casa de Jorge Amado
❸ Museu Tempostal
❹ Museu Afro-Brasileiro
❺ Nosso Senhor do Bonfim
❻ Praça da Sé
❼ Catedral Basílica
❽ Palácio Rio Branco
❾ Elevador Lacerda
❿ Mercado Modelo
⓫ Solar do Unhão
⓬ Museu de Arte da Bahia (MAB)
⓭ Casa do Carnaval
⓮ Forte de Santo Antônio
⓯ Museu de Arte Sacra

Eat

① Bar Zulu, Pelourinho
② Paraiso Tropical, Cabula
③ Donana, Brotas

Drink

④ Jam no MAM, Comercio
⑤ Portela Café, Rio Vermelho
⑥ Casa do Amarelindo Bar, Pelourinho

Shop

⑦ Katuka Africanidades, Centro
⑧ Apoena, Pelourinho

Baía de Todos os Santos

Terminal Marítimo Turístico

CIDADE ALTA

AVENIDA LAFAYETE COUT

AVENIDA LAFAYETE COUTINHO

RUA DA CONCEIÇÃO DA PRAIA

RUA M VITOR

SALVADOR

AVENIDA LAFAYETE COUTINHO

RUA VISCONDE DE MAUÁ

Museu de Arte Sacra
⓯

RUA DO SODRE

RUA SANTA THEREZA

AVENIDA CAB

CENTRO

Bahia Marina

0 meters   150
0 yards   150

N
↑

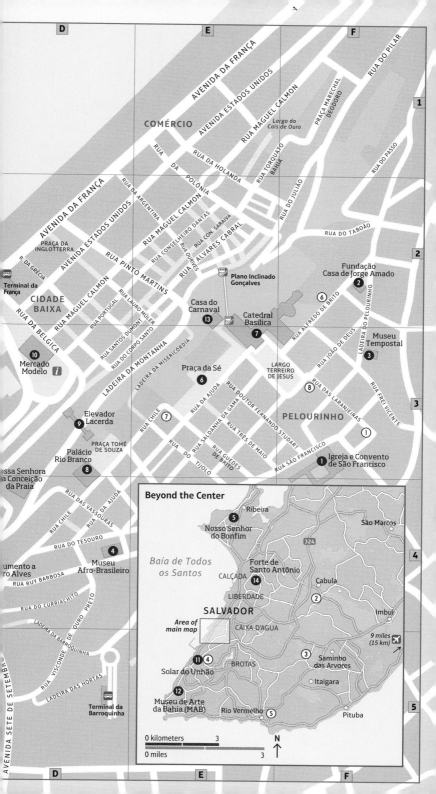

Map labels

D · **E** · **F**

1

RUA DO PILAR

AVENIDA DA FRANÇA

AVENIDA ESTADOS UNIDOS

RUA MAGUEL CALMON

PRAÇA MARECHAL DEODORO

COMÉRCIO

Largo do Cais de Ouro

RUA DA HOLANDA

RUA TORQUATO BAHIA

RUA DO PASSO

RUA DA POLÓNIA

RUA DA ARGENTINA

RUA DO JULIÃO

RUA DO TABOÃO

2

AVENIDA DA FRANÇA

RUA DA GRÉCIA

PRAÇA DA INGLOTTERRA

AVENIDA ESTADOS UNIDOS

AVENIDA MAGUEL CALMON

RUA PINTO MARTINS

RUA MAGUEL CALMON

RUA CONSELHEIRO DANTAS

RUA OUVIRES

RUA CON. SARAIVA

RUA ALVARES CABRAL

Plano Inclinado Gonçalves

Fundação Casa de Jorge Amado ②

⑥

LADEIRA DO PELOURINHO

Terminal da França

CIDADE BAIXA

RUA MAGUEL CALMON

RUA LAURO MÜLER

RUA PORTUGAL

RUA SANTOS DUMONT

RUA DO CORPO SANTO

Casa do Carnaval ⑬

Catedral Basílica ⑦

RUA ALFREDO DE BRITO

RUA JOÃO DE DEUS

Museu Tempostal ③

RUA DA BELGICA

LADEIRA DA MONTANHA

LADEIRA DA MISERICÓRDIA

Praça da Sé ⑥

LARGO TERREIRO DE JESUS

RUA FREI VICENTE

3

⑩ **Mercado Modelo** *i*

RUA CHILE

⑦

RUA DA AJUDA

RUA DOUTOR FERNANDO STUDART

RUA DAS LARANJEIRAS

⑧

PELOURINHO

①

⑨ **Elevador Lacerda**

PRAÇA TOMÉ DE SOUZA

Palácio Rio Branco ⑧

Nossa Senhora a Conceição da Praia

RUA CHILE

RUA DO TIJOLO

RUA SALDANHA DA GAMA

RUA TRÊS DE MAIO

RUA GUEDES DE BRITO

RUA SÃO FRANCISCO

Igreja e Convento de São Francisco ①

RUA DAS VASSOURAS

RUA DA AJUDA

Beyond the Center

RUA DO TESOURO

umento a ro Alves

RUA RUY BARBOSA

Museu Afro-Brasileiro ④

RUA DO CURRIACHITO

LADEIRA DA BARROQUINHA

RUA VISCONDE DE OURO PRETO

LADEIRA DAS HORTAS

AVENIDA SETE DE SETEMBRO

Terminal da Barroquinha

Ribeira

⑤ **Nosso Senhor do Bonfim**

Baía de Todos os Santos

CALÇADA

Forte de Santo Antônio ⑭

LIBERDADE

São Marcos

324

Cabula ②

Imbuí

SALVADOR

CAIXA D'AGUA

Area of main map

9 miles (15 km) ✈

BROTAS

③ Saminho das Árvores

⑪ ④ **Solar do Unhão**

Itaigara

⑫ **Museu de Arte da Bahia (MAB)**

Rio Vermelho ⑤

Pituba

0 kilometers 3

0 miles 3

N ↑

4

5

D · **E** · **F**

1 🤿 Ⓜ

IGREJA E CONVENTO DE SÃO FRANCISCO

📍 E4 🏛 Largo Cruzeiro de São Francisco: Praça Anchieta, Pelourinho; Igreja da Ordem Terceira de São Francisco: Rua da Ordem Terceira s/n 📞 (71) 3322 6430 🕐 9am–5pm Mon–Sat, 10am–4pm Sun; Igreja da Ordem Terceira: 8am–noon, 1–5pm daily

Located in the historical center of Pelourinho, this stunning 18th-century monument is one of Salvador's most precious architectural gems. Behind its worn facade the church interior glows with gold leaf, while the convent cloisters and inner courtyard provide visitors tranquil seclusion from the world outside.

The complex of the Igreja e Convento de São Francisco, which was constructed between 1708 and 1750, is one of Brazil's most impressive Baroque monuments. The convent's church stands out for its rich and opulent interior; the inner walls and the ceiling are highly decorative and dazzling in gold.

The main altar and the large side altars are magnificently carved out of wood and in typical Baroque style, ornately designed with angels, birds, mermaids, fruits, and leaves. An enormous silver chandelier hangs above intricate wooden carvings, and hand-painted blue-and-white Portuguese tiles.

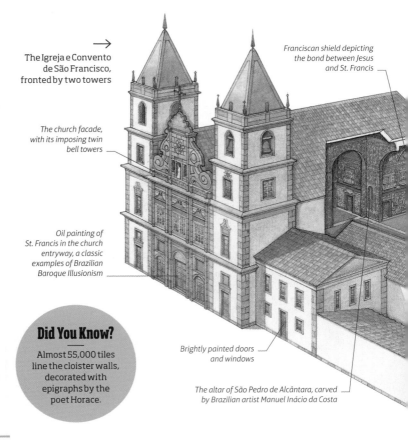

→ The Igreja e Convento de São Francisco, fronted by two towers

Franciscan shield depicting the bond between Jesus and St. Francis

The church facade, with its imposing twin bell towers

Oil painting of St. Francis in the church entryway, a classic examples of Brazilian Baroque Illusionism

Did You Know?

Almost 55,000 tiles line the cloister walls, decorated with epigraphs by the poet Horace.

Brightly painted doors and windows

The altar of São Pedro de Alcântara, carved by Brazilian artist Manuel Inácio da Costa

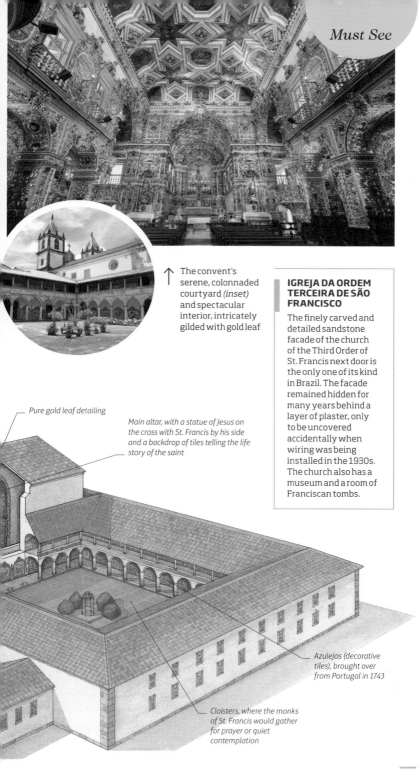

↑ The convent's serene, colonnaded courtyard *(inset)* and spectacular interior, intricately gilded with gold leaf

IGREJA DA ORDEM TERCEIRA DE SÃO FRANCISCO

The finely carved and detailed sandstone facade of the church of the Third Order of St. Francis next door is the only one of its kind in Brazil. The facade remained hidden for many years behind a layer of plaster, only to be uncovered accidentally when wiring was being installed in the 1930s. The church also has a museum and a room of Franciscan tombs.

Pure gold leaf detailing

Main altar, with a statue of Jesus on the cross with St. Francis by his side and a backdrop of tiles telling the life story of the saint

Azulejos (decorative tiles), brought over from Portugal in 1743

Cloisters, where the monks of St. Francis would gather for prayer or quiet contemplation

EXPERIENCE MORE

❷
Fundação Casa de Jorge Amado

📍F2 🏛Largo do Pelourinho s/n ⏰10am-6pm Mon-Fri, 10am-4pm Sat
🌐jorgeamado.org.br

Although Brazilian author Jorge Amado (p289) never lived in Pelourinho, many of his beloved novels were set in this part of Salvador. Opened in 1987, the Casa de Jorge Amado is a small museum housed in a pretty blue colonial building located at the top end of Largo do Pelourinho. It is one of the main monuments dedicated to Bahia's most famous author.

The museum's four floors comprise the entire archive of Amado's work and also include a small research center. The interesting collection on display consists mostly of covers of his books and a range of personal belongings that tell the story of his life. A mural on the ground floor depicts the languages into which his works have been translated.

The on-site café-theater regularly hosts theatrical, literary and musical events, with a focus on new talent.

49
The number of languages Jorge Amado's novels have been translated in.

❸
Museu Tempostal

📍F3 🏛Rua Gregorio de Matos 33, Pelourinho
📞(71) 3117 6383
⏰10am-4pm Tue-Fri, noon-4pm Sat

Housed in a beautiful building in the heart of the Pelourinho neighborhood, this museum displays only a fraction of founder Antônio Marcelino's collection of 33,000 postcards and photographs. Most date from the 19th and 20th centuries. Antique postcards comprising the main display tell the history of Salvador as it has developed. Some cards are enlarged to give visitors a better view of the photographic details. A smaller exhibit of belle époque postcards showcases elaborate samples of postcard "art," some adorned with embroidery, others painted like aquarelles.

❹
Museu Afro-Brasileiro

📍D4 🏛Largo do Terreiro de Jesus s/n 📞(71) 3283 5540 ⏰9am-5pm Mon-Fri
🌐mafro.ceao.ufba.br

This small museum in the former Faculty of Medicine building houses a collection of photographs, artwork, and artifacts all related to the African diaspora in Brazil. The main exhibit displays objects and crafts from the original African cultures of regions such as Angola and Nigeria where Brazil-bound enslaved people were captured. The highlights of the collection are the 27 life-sized wood carvings of the orixás (p284) by artist Carybé (1911–97), depicting their weapons and regalia along with the animals or domain over which they are thought to rule. Sea Goddess Yemanjá is shown with a fish, seashells, and the mirrors and trinkets offered to her by supplicants; the warrior Ogun is displayed with his sword and armor.

↑ The bright blue Fundação Casa de Jorge Amado looking over Largo do Pelourinho

 The colonial Portuguese Basílica Nosso Senhor do Bonfim, on Largo do Bonfim

5

Nosso Senhor do Bonfim

📍E4 🏠Largo do Bonfim
📞(71) 3316 2196 🕐7am-6pm Mon-Thu & Sat, 5:30am-6pm Fri & Sun

Nosso Senhor do Bonfim (Our Lord of Good Success) stands atop a small hill on the Bonfim Peninsula, a strip of land jutting out into the Baía de Todos os Santos about 6 miles (10 km) north of Pelourinho. The church was built between 1746 and 1754 by Captain Rodrigues de Faria in fulfilment of a pledge he made in the midst of a fierce Atlantic storm. While the hilltop setting is picturesque, what sets the church apart is not its architecture but the role it plays in Bahia's Afro-Brazilian religion. The church is dedicated to God the Father, but it also honors Oxalá, the supreme deity in the Candomblé religion *(p283)*.

On Fridays, worshippers dress in white and dedicate their prayers to Oxalá. On other days, in a small chapel just to the right of the main altar, visitors can explore the Sala dos Milagres (Chamber of Miracles). Believers come here to offer items made of wax, wood, and sometimes even gold. The item represents a miracle that has been bestowed upon them. The room is packed with tiny replicas of hearts, lungs, livers, and breasts, as well as babies, houses, and even cars.

⬆ The stunning gilded interior of Nosso Senhor do Bonfirm

EAT

Bar Zulu
Affordable spot serving Bahian specialties like *moqueca* (shrimp stew with coconut milk) and vegetarian dishes.

📍F3 🏠Rua das Laranjeiras 15, Salvador 📞(71) 98784 3172

$$$

───────

Paraíso Tropical
Expect experimental regional dishes from chef Beto Pimental at this off-the-beaten-path restaurant, a 20-minute taxi ride from Pelourinho.

📍F4 🏠Edgar Loureiro 98b, Cabula 📞(71) 3384 7464

$$$

───────

Donana
A family-run *boteco* serving delicious Bahian seafood dishes.

📍F5 🏠Centro Comercial do Conjunto dos Comerciários, Rua Teixeira Barros, Brotas, Salvador 📞(71) 3676 0473 🕐Mon

$$$

The impressive 16th-century **Forte de Nossa Senhora de Monte Serrat** is located not too far from the church, in the neighborhood of Boa Viagem. Just below the fort is the popular beach, Praia de Boa Viagem, which is usually bustling with locals and lined with busy stalls.

Forte de Nossa Senhora de Monte Serrat
🏠Rua da Boa Viagem 📞(71) 3313 7339 🕐9am-4:30pm Mon-Sat

6
Praça da Sé

E3

Pelourinho's Praça da Sé blends the modern with the historic. The square is a transition point between the Terreiro de Jesus and the Praça Tomé de Sousa.

A cathedral originally stood here but it was demolished in the 1930s. Extensive renovations have added fountains and benches, so people can linger and enjoy the capoeira presentations or other cultural events often held in the square.

The belvedere, a lookout point on the north side of the square, provides a beautiful

The hilly streets of Salvador's historic city center, where *(inset)* many locals live

view of the Lower City and the Baía de Todos os Santos (Bay of All Saints).

7
Catedral Basílica

E3 ⌂ Praça da Sé, Terreiro de Jesus ☎ (71) 3321 4573 ⏰ 9am–5pm daily

Salvador's main cathedral, built between 1657 and 1672, is considered to be one of the richest examples of Portuguese Baroque architecture in the country. The cathedral's facade is made of Portuguese *lioz*, a type of limestone. The interior walls and tall pillars are also covered with the pale-colored stone, which gives the church a bright and spacious feel.

The vaulted ceiling of the main nave is made from wood. The decorations are carved in relief and stand out from the ceiling with an almost three-dimensional

effect. The main altar and two smaller side altars are also carved out of wood and covered in gold leaf.

Dedicated to St. Francis, the altar contains a silver-plated statue of Nossa Senhora das Maravilhas (Our Lady of Miracles), which is said to have inspired Father Antônio Vieira, a 17th-century Jesuit priest who fought against the enslavement of Indigenous people. His fiery, anti-slavery sermons did not sit well with the Inquisition, who subsequently ordered his arrest.

The former Jesuit library now holds a small museum of religious art. The collection includes silver and gold

→

People mingling in front of the Palácio Rio Branco

> **The fine interior of the Palácio Rio Branco is a lively blend of beautiful Rococo plasterwork and intricate frescoes.**

religious artifacts such as ornate chalices and candleholders. The most modern piece in the cathedral is the German organ. This powerful instrument features more than 500 pipes, 18 registers, and two keyboards.

Palácio Rio Branco

D3 **Praça Tomé de Sousa** **(71) 3116 6928** **10am-noon, 1-5pm Tue-Fri**

The original Palácio Rio Branco has nothing in common with the building that currently goes by that name. The first palace was built on this site in 1549 to house Bahia's first governor, Tomé de Sousa. The Portuguese queen and later the prince regent resided in this palace temporarily in 1808, when the entire Portuguese court relocated to Rio de Janeiro

in order to escape Napoleon's invasion of Portugal. The building survived until 1900, when the whole structure was leveled and then rebuilt from scratch in Renaissance style. A fire in 1912 forced another major overhaul by the Italian architect Júlio Conti, giving the building the eclectic look it still has today.

Used as an official government building until 1979, the Palácio Rio Branco was rededicated in 1986 as a cultural foundation, the Centro Memoria da Bahia. The former reception hall on the ground floor now tells the history of Bahia's 40 governors through paintings, historic documents, and their personal belongings.

The fine interior of the Palácio Rio Branco is a lively blend of beautiful Rococo plasterwork and intricate frescoes. Of particular note are the grand dome and the magnificent views from the belvedere in the wing looking onto the sea, as well as the iron and crystal stairway and a sculpture representing Tomé de Souza.

Visitors can take guided tours, which explore some of the palace's rooms; make sure to call ahead for times and to book a place.

DRINK

Jam no MAM
Affiliated with Salvador's Museum of Modern Art, this popular jazz club puts on open-air sessions.

E5 **Av Lafayette Coutinho, Museu de Arte Moderna Solar do Unh** **jamnomam.com.br**

Boteco do Samba
This no-frills bar, which has a loyal local following, has live samba till late on weekends.

Ladeira da Água Brusca, 100, Santo Antônio Além do Carmo **(71) 99995 1020** **Mon-Thu**

Casa do Amarelindo Bar
Hotel rooftop bar offering a spectacular view of Baia dos Santos as well as caipirinhas with a regional twist.

F2 **Rua das Portas do Carmo 6, Hotel Casa do Amarelindo** **casa doamarelindo.com**

9

Elevador Lacerda

📍 D3 🏛 Praça Tomé de Sousa s/n (Upper City); Praça Visconde Cairu (Lower City) 🕐 7am-10pm Mon-Fri, 7am-7pm Sat & Sun

Built by merchant Antônio Francisco de Lacerda in 1873 from an original Jesuit-installed manual pulley, the Elevador Lacerda connects Salvador's Upper and Lower cities.

A popular site in Salvador, the elevator is used by more than 30,000 people daily. The building's current Art Deco look dates from a 1930s restoration. Four elevators make the 236-ft (72-m) trip up vertical shafts in just 30 seconds, where the view across the bay on a clear day is simply stunning.

10
Mercado Modelo

📍 D3 🏛 Praça Visconde de Cairu, Comércio 📞 (71) 3241 2893 🕐 9am-7pm Mon-Sat, 9am-2pm Sun

The Mercado Modelo was built in 1861 as a customs building. The square behind the market, now used by *capoeiristas*, was where boats would dock to unload their merchandise for inspection. The building was transformed into an indoor craft market in 1971, and renovated after a major fire in 1984. Nowadays, the market's two floors house 263 stalls that offer a variety of northeastern arts and crafts. Popular items include paintings of the Pelourinho neighborhood by local artists, *berimbaus* (a stringed instrument), embroidered lace tablecloths, and hammocks.

11
Solar do Unhão

📍 E5 🏛 Av do Contorno s/n 📞 (71) 3117 6144

A renovated colonial sugar mill, the Solar do Unhão beautifully blends old and new. The original design is typical of the 17th century – a chapel, a big house with quarters for enslaved people on the lower floor, and a large mill where cane was transformed into sugar.

In the 1940s it was chosen as the site for the **Museu de Arte Moderna**. The complex displays paintings, etchings, and sculptures by some of Brazil's best-known modern artists. In the evenings, it hosts a presentation of traditional Bahian dance and folklore.

Museu de Arte Moderna
🕐 1-6pm Tue-Sun
📞 (71) 3117 6132

SHOP

Katuka Africanidades
Shop celebrating Bahian African culture and selling jewelry, books, and clothing. Literature talks and workshops are also hosted here.

📍 E3 🏛 Praça da Sé, Centro, Salvador 📞 (71) 3322 1634

Apoena
The second floor of this shop and art gallery is dedicated to Indigenous crafts, with work from famous artists like José Garcia Pinto from the Kuripako community.

📍 F3 🏛 Largo Terreiro de Jesus 21-185, Pelourinho 📞 (71) 99884 4055

The Art Deco Elevador Lacerda looking out over the bay ↑

↑ A Brazilian drumming group performing on the streets of the Pelourinho neighborhood

CARNAVAL IN SALVADOR

Salvador's signature event, the Carnaval, is celebrated during February or March. The tradition was started in the 1950s with Dodó and Osmar, two local musicians who took their music to the street on top of a 1929 Ford.

TRIO ELÉTRICO

The centerpiece of Carnaval is the *trio elétrico*, a giant flatbed truck carrying a massive array of speakers, topped by a rectangular stage. Running out from behind the truck, a large roped-off area serves as a movable dance floor. Access to this area is restricted to those in an *abadá*, or uniform-style tank top. Revelers outside this area are called *pipoca*, or popcorn, as they pop up everywhere.

↑ Timbalada, an Afro-Brazilian *bloco*, perform in the Carnaval parade

BLOCOS AND PERFORMERS

Blocos (neighborhood groups) parade along one of three Carnaval routes – Pelourinho, Campo Grande, and Ondina. Performers include major Brazilian artists such as Daniela Mercury, Caetano Veloso, Gilberto Gil, and Carlinhos Brown, and popular groups such as Olodum, Ara Ketu, and Chiclete com Banana. In addition to these famous performers, there are Afro-Brazilian *blocos* such as Ilê Aye, which only allow people of Black heritage in their parade. As the six-day event comes to a close in the early hours of Ash Wednesday, the *blocos* make their way to Praça Castro Alves for the Encontro dos Trios, a last late-night jam that marks the Carnaval's grand finale.

↑ A performer wearing a colorful Carnaval mask

12

Museu de Arte da Bahia (MAB)

📍 E5 🏠 Av 7 de Setembro 2340, Corredor da Vitória 📞 (71) 3117 6903 🕐 1–6pm Tue–Fri, 1–5pm Sat & Sun

The Bahia Art Museum offers a glimpse of the opulent lifestyle of Salvador's colonial elite. The lavish collection includes paintings, azulejos (decorative painted ceramic tilework), furniture, silverware, glass, china, and crystal used by the local ruling families during the 18th, 19th, and early 20th centuries. The south wing features landscape paintings by Brazilian artists such as José Joaquim da Rocha.

Did You Know?

The MAB was one of the first ten museums founded in Brazil; it's also the oldest in Bahia.

↑ Vibrant sculptures of masked Carnaval figures located at the Casa do Carnaval

13 🖐 🎵 🛍

Casa do Carnaval

📍 E2 🏠 Praça Ramos de Queirós s/n, Pelourinho 📞 (71) 3324 6760 🕐 11am–7pm Tue–Sun

The Casa do Carnaval is a highly visual and interactive museum that tells the story of Salvador's lively Carnaval, capturing the sense and feel of the event through an explosion of color.

The displays include historic photos and a variety of videos of the jovial festivities, as well as a collection of elaborate costumes and musical instruments that are regularly used during Carnaval. This museum is particularly ideal for visitors who want to learn more about the context of traditional Bahian revelry.

Don't miss the excellent gift shop downstairs and the stunning terrace, which has sweeping views of the Baía de Todos os Santos (Bay of All Saints). A detailed guided audio tour in English is available on request.

The historic Forte Santo Antônio standing sentry on the edge of the coast ↑

Forte de Santo Antônio

E4 **Praça Almirante Tamandaré, Largo do Farol s/n, Barra** **9am-6pm daily** **museunautico dabahia.org.br**

One of Salvador's best-known landmarks, the Forte de Santo Antônio, known locally as Farol da Barra, was erected in 1535. The fort was strengthened in the early 17th century, in response to Dutch attacks on the coast, and upgraded to its present star shape at the beginning of the 18th century.

A lighthouse atop the fort, the Farol de Barra, was originally built in 1698, and is still used by boats navigating the entrance to the bay.

Inside the fort, the Nautico da Bahia (Bahia Nautical Museum) shows historic navigation instruments and a variety of charts. There is also a notable collection of coins and china from a Portuguese galleon that foundered in 1668, off Rio Vermelho beach. Household items give a sense of what life was like here

centuries ago, and of the importance of the sea in Brazilian life, both in Salvador and beyond.

The fort also includes a café with an outdoor area offering views of Salvador's skyline.

Museu de Arte Sacra

C5 **Rua do Sodré 276, Cidade Alta** **(71) 3283 5600** **10am-6pm Mon-Fri**

One of Brazil's best collections of religious art can be found in this museum, which is housed in a graceful former Carmelite convent. The building still features its original cloisters and confessionals.

The serene and beautiful structure was built between 1667 and 1697, and serves as the perfect backdrop for the varied exhibits. The collections include statues, icons, paintings, *oratorios* (portable altars), and numerous finely wrought silver crosses, candlesticks, chalices, censors, and other artifacts from the 16th to 19th centuries.

ATLANTIC COAST BEACHES

Porto da Barra
Close to Salvador's Pelourinho, this beach has a lovely lighthouse – a great place from which to watch the spectacular sunset.

Ondina Beach
Offering the ideal mix of urban convenience and sunny relaxation, Ondina is a great pick for a day by the sea.

Amaralina
Regular strong winds and large waves make this beach popular with surfers. Baianas *(p285)* selling traditional street food add to the spot's lively atmosphere.

Itapuã
This gorgeous stretch of sand with reefs and marine life, was immortalized by lyricist Vinicius de Moraes in "Tarde da Itapuã."

Praia Jardim de Ala
Framed by lofty palms, this beach features grassy slopes and inviting natural pools at low tide.

A SHORT WALK
PELOURINHO

Distance 0.5 miles (1 km) **Nearest metro**
Campo da Pólvora **Time** 15 minutes

Salvador's restored historic center, Pelourinho, which
means whipping post, originally described only the
small triangular plaza in the heart of the city where
enslaved people were publicly flogged. Located on a
high bluff overlooking the commercial city below,
Pelourinho was built by the Portuguese in the boom
years of the 18th and 19th centuries as a residential
and administrative center. Abandoned for a greater
part of the 20th century, Pelourinho was designated
a UNESCO World Heritage Site in 1985. Today,
visitors can explore its magnificent colonial houses,
Baroque churches, and museums.

*The large wood carvings
of the Candomblé deities
by renowned artist
Carybé are the highlights
of* **Museu Afro-
Brasileiro** *(p265).*

Built in 1657, the **Catedral
Basílica** *(p266) has a
cedar-wood altar, and two
smaller side altars, both
covered in thin layers of gold.*

Praça da Sé *(p266)
offers views across the
Baía de Todos os Santos*

LARGO DO CRUZEIRO DO SÃO FRANCISCO

START

RUA MONTE ALVERNE

0 meters 100 N ↑
0 yards 100

Terreiro de Jesus, *one of
the most beautiful squares in
Pelourinho, was laid out by
governor Tome de Souza.*

*A silver chandelier weighing 176 lb
(80 kg) hangs over the ornate
carvings of* **Igreja e Convento de
São Francisco** *(p262).*

←
Colorful buildings
lining the cobbled
streets of Pelourinho

Fundação Casa de Jorge Amado
(p264) *is a café decorated with hundreds of Jorge Amado's book jackets.*

FINISH

Locator Map
For more detail see p260

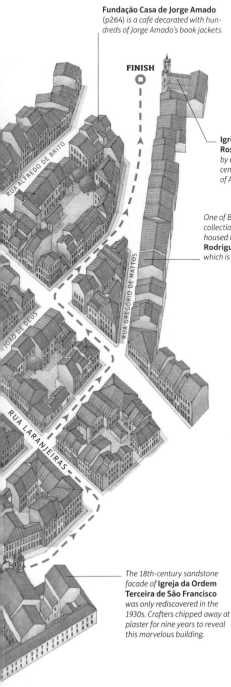

Igreja Nossa Senhora do Rosário dos Pretos *was built by enslaved people in the 18th century and remains a center of Afro-Brazilian traditions.*

One of Brazil's largest private collections of sacred art is housed in **Museu Abelardo Rodrigues Solar do Ferrão,** *which is temporarily closed.*

The 18th-century sandstone facade of **Igreja da Ordem Terceira de São Francisco** *was only rediscovered in the 1930s. Crafters chipped away at plaster for nine years to reveal this marvelous building.*

↑ The ornate, golden facade of Igreja da Ordem Terceira de São Francisco

Did You Know?

The Igreja da Ordem Terceira de São Francisco contains over 27,000 azulejos.

BAHIA

Heavily populated in pre-Columbian times, Bahia is home to only small Indigenous communities today – notably the Atikum and Pataxó – most having been wiped out by disease following European colonization in the 16th century. Bahia was where Portuguese explorer Pedro Álvares Cabral had his fateful first sighting of Brazil in 1500. His compatriots rapidly settled the coast thereafter: Porto Seguro was founded in 1526, Ilhéus in 1534, and Salvador in 1549. Southern Bahia became home to cocoa plantations – the state still produces two-thirds of Brazil's cocoa – while the Recôncavo region was dominated by sugarcane and tobacco plantations, worked by enslaved Africans.

The tragic story of the town of Canudos, founded in 1893 by Messianic religious leader Antônio Conselheiro, also unfolded in Bahia. Attracted by his enigmatic personality and message of equality, thousands of impoverished laborers and Indigenous people flocked to the town. Fearing a major insurrection, the central government sent in the army in 1897. The resulting annihilation of Canudos, with up to 30,000 possible deaths, was one of Brazil's bloodiest conflicts.

The first half of the 20th century saw cocoa plantation owners continuing to fight each other for dominance, a bloody struggle chronicled by Bahian novelist Jorge Amado in *The Violent Land*. Beginning in the 1950s, Bahia harnessed the mighty Rio São Francisco's hydroelectric potential, finally sparking industrial development in the state. As a result, although cocoa remains important, Bahia is today also home to major petrochemical plants and a car manufacturing industry.

PIAUÍ AND
MARANHÃO *p322*

BRASÍLIA,
GOIÁS, AND
TOCANTINS
p228

BAHIA

LENÇÓIS **15**

PARQUE NACIONAL DE
CHAPADA DIAMANTINA **1**

MINAS GERAIS
p182

Brejo da
Porta

Eliseu
Martins

Afrânio

Bom Jesus

São Raimundo
Nonato

Casa Nova

Alto
Parnaíba

Redenção

Paçarrão

Gilbués

Sento Sé

Barragem de
Sabradinho

Delfir

Formosa do
Rio Preto

Xique-Xique

Umburanas

Jacaré

Cariparé

Morpara

Central

Irecê

Morro do
Chapeu

Capixaba

Utinga

Ipupiara

Barreiras

Brotas de
Macaúbas

Wagner

Ibotirama

Diamantina

Paratinga

Iaetê

Santana

Macaúbas

Piatã

Correntina

Bom Jesus
da Lapa

Paramirim

Iramaia

Barra da
Estiva

Coribe

Riacho de
Santana

Ituaçu

São
Domingos

Caetité

Brumado

Cocos

Carinhanha

Guanambi

Aracatu

Anagé

Mambaí

Matias
Cardoso

Verde Pequeno

Caculé

Vitória da
Conquista

Serra
Bonita

Monte Azul

Urandi

Pandeiros

Januária

Unaí

São
Francisco

Salinas

Jequitinhonha

Santa Fé
de Minas

Montes
Claros

Araçuaí

Paracatu

Bocaiúva

João
Pinheiro

Poté

Teófilo
Otôni

Corinto

Diamantina

0 kilometers   150

0 miles   150

N

SERGIPE, ALAGOAS,
AND PERNAMBUCO
p292

Santa Cruz

116

122

Abáre

São Francisco

116 210

Curaçá

Macururé

Mata
Grande

etrolina

Paulo
Afonso

423

uázeiro

Vargem

Formosa

110

Massaroca

235

8 CANUDOS

Pão de
Açúcar

Uauá

Jeremoabo

407

Poço

Senhor do
Bonfim

Carira

Campo Formoso

Euclides
da Cunha

235

Itapicuru

Queimadas

Tucano

Cipó

bina

120

Itapicuru Mirim

Nova
Soure

101

cuípe

Conceição
do Coité

116

Serrinha

110

Mairi

324

Inhambupe

Esplanada

Mangue Seco

52

Alagoinhas

101

2 LINHA VERDE

Ipirá

Feira de
Santana

Pojuca

99

eraba

Capivari

Porto Sauípe

46

CACHOEIRA **5** **4** SANTO AMARO

laçu

SÃO FÉLIX **6**

Salvador-Deputado
Luís Eduardo Magalhães
International Airport

Amargosa

ILHA DE **3**
ITAPARICA

Salvador

racás

116

7 MORRO DE SÃO PAULO

30

Jequié

anuel
orino

Camamu

9 PENINSULA DE MARAÚ

Ipiaú

Marau

30

10 ITACARÉ

Poções

Itabuna

Gongogi

Ibicaraí

11 ILHÉUS

262

Buerarema

Itapetinga

101

Una

Pardo

lacarani

Potiraguá

Canavieiras

Itapebi

Belmonte

Santa Cruz Cabrália

12 PORTO SEGURO

Guaratinga

13 TRANCOSO

Jucuruçu

Monte Pascoal
1,758 ft (536 m)

Itamaraju

Itanhém

101

Prado

Itanhém

Alcobaça

419

biranhém

Caravelas

Helvécia

ucuricí

Mucuri

14 PARQUE NACIONAL
MARINHO DE ABROLHOS

A t l a n t i c

O c e a n

BAHIA

BAHIA

Must Sees

1 Parque Nacional da Chapada
   Diamantina

2 Linha Verde

Experience More

3 Ilha de Itaparica

4 Santo Amaro

5 Cachoeira

6 São Félix

7 Morro de São Paulo

8 Canudos

9 Peninsula de Maraú

10 Itacaré

11 Ilhéus

12 Porto Seguro

13 Trancoso

14 Parque Nacional Marinho
    de Abrolhos

15 Lençóis

1 ⑬

PARQUE NACIONAL DA CHAPADA DIAMANTINA

🗺 F4 🏠 Bahia 🚌🚐 ℹ SETUR: Av Sete de Setembro 35, Centro, Lençóis; www.nasalturas.net

The northern end of a mountain chain stretching from Minas Gerais to Bahia, this rugged region features mesas (flat-topped ridges and hills) that overlook rolling grasslands and deep ravines. With its array of natural wonders, the Chapada Diamantina is an outdoor playground for extreme adventure lovers, with expert-led trips running from Lençóis, the nearest town inside the national park.

Towering red rock formations, interspersed with lush vegetation, characterize this 587-sq-mile (1,520-sq-km) national park in the hinterland of Salvador, established in 1985. Numerous small rivers crisscross the highlands, cascading over waterfalls, carving through canyons, and tumbling down waterslides. Countless trails lead to caves and caverns. It is possible to camp in such spaces overnight and no permit is required, although these undefined paths are best navigated with a guide. For those who would prefer not to camp, guides are often able to arrange overnight stays in local homes.

A traveler surveying the vast landscape of the Parque Nacional da Chapada Diamantina ↑

ADVENTURE ACTIVITIES IN THE PARK

There is a huge range of activities available in the park for the adventurous traveler, with specialist companies based in Lençois. Rock climbing and bouldering are especially popular around Igatu, while the Gruta do Lapao is a huge cave most favored for rappeling. For water babies, Marimbus is a network of pools and rivers near Andarai where kayaking, canoeing, and paddle-boarding is practised. There are also many mountain-bike routes throughout the park, including one challenging trail that leads from Lençois to Barro Branco, a former diamond mine settlement.

Numerous small rivers crisscross the highlands, cascading over waterfalls, carving through canyons, and tumbling down waterslides.

Morro do Pai Inácio

▲ This striking cylindrical mesa is the park's signature mountain formation. The 3,675-ft (1,120-m) plateau offers breathtaking views of the northern half of the park.

Vale do Paty

The multiday hike up this scenic valley offers extraordinary views of the highlands from Morro do Castelo. Other attractions include abandoned miners' settlements and waterfalls with natural swimming pools at Cachoeira dos Funis, as well as the sound of Barbado monkeys that inhabit this vast wilderness.

Cachoeira da Fumaça

▶ Cachoeira da Fumaça, or the Waterfall of Smoke, wears a veil of mist as the water plunges down the 1,150-ft (340-m) precipice.

Cachoeira do Buracão

Near the park's southern edge, this waterfall plunges 394 ft (120 m) into a vast pool. The river then carves its way through a deep gorge of sedimentary rock. Strong swimmers can swim downstream toward the trailhead.

Poço Encantado

▼ At the bottom of a deep cavern, the cobalt-blue Enchanted Pool is one of the park's most popular spots, accessible via a steep trail and a narrow entrance. Between April and September, sunlight streaming through an aperture reaches the surface of the water, making both the cavern and pool glow.

The stunning coastline Praia do Forte beach, which hosts *(inset)* an effective turtle conservation program ↑

2

LINHA VERDE

⚄ F4 **⚄ Bahia** **⚄ From Salvador**

This palm-fringed coastline is dotted with many of the loveliest beaches in northeast Brazil, offering visitors an array of natural attractions and leisure activities. With its ecotourism projects, watersports, and luxury resorts, the Linha Verde (Green Line) is one of the most popular holiday destinations in Bahia.

The Linha Verde is the 152-mile (252-km) stretch of coast that runs north from Salvador all the way to Mangue Seco on the Sergipe border. It is often referred to as the Estrada do Côco, or Coconut Highway, because of the thick stands of palm trees that line the beaches. This part of the coast offers several popular holiday destinations and well-developed resorts. The most favored destinations are Praia do Forte and Costa do Sauípe. The custom-built village at Costa do Sauípe offers high-end recreation, including spas, sailing, and golf. Praia do Forte is less built up, with natural pools at its north end providing excellent snorkeling and swimming areas. As part of a conservation plan in the area, five turtle species are reared at Praia do Forte.

Farther north, the beaches are pristine and beautiful. Praia Sítio do Conde is a popular strand that is visited by locals at the weekends. Small reefs here form natural pools at low tide, so it is a good choice for gentle safe swimming. The neighboring beach of Barra do Itariri is a particularly pretty spot, with green palm trees, bleached white sands, and mangroves.

→

A simple blue-and-white church in the popular beach resort of Praia do Forte

---

CONSERVATION EFFORTS IN LINHA VERDE

With its coral reefs, beaches, sand dunes, mangroves, and Mata Atlântica (Atlantic rainforest), the Linha Verde has a rich biodiversity. Several conservation projects operate here, such as the Sapiranga Reserve, located close to Praia do Forte. This former *fazenda* comprises part of the Atlantic rainforest in recuperation, carrying out research supported by ecotourism. Nearby, Projeto TAMAR *(www. tamar.org.br)* is a marine conservation program, helping to protect the five turtle species found along the coast.

EXPERIENCE MORE

Ilha de Itaparica

▲F4 🚢 From Salvador

The largest island in the Baía de Todos os Santos (Bay of All Saints), with summerhouses lining its shore, Itaparica is a popular weekend refuge for the residents of Salvador.

On the northern tip of the island, the main city is guarded by the Forte de São Lourenço, built by the Dutch in 1711. The island's main attractions include the historic Nossa Senhora da Piedade (Chapel of Our Lady of Piety) and the 1610 Igreja de São Lourenço.

The island is connected to the mainland by a bridge at its narrow southern tip. The Praia da Penha, 10 miles (6 km) south, is a lovely beach with views of Salvador.

Santo Amaro

▲F4 🚢 From Salvador

The laid-back town of Santo Amaro lies in the Recôncavo, the fertile zone at the top end of the Baía de Todos os Santos, which formed the backbone of Salvador's colonial economy for almost 300 years. The region's high humidity, abundant rainfall, and rich soils were conducive to growing tobacco and, more significantly, sugarcane. Dilapidated mansions of the erstwhile plantation owners can still be seen along the old streets. Nowadays, the town is known for its paper industry. It is also famous as the hometown of two popular singers, Caetano Veloso and Maria Bethânia.

Many of the enslaved people, who were brought from Africa to work on plantations, remained in this area after slavery was abolished in 1888. The region still has a very high percentage of Afro-Brazilian residents, and Santo Amaro plays a key role in preserving their distinct traditions. Every year, the city commemorates the abolition of slavery with a five-day festival of the Bembé do Mercado (mid-May). During this time, offerings are made to Yemanjá, Goddess of the Sea, to celebrate freedom of religion. In the main square in

View of São Félix and *(inset)* the railway bridge that connects the town with Cachoeira ↓

front of the town market, local groups perform capoeira (a martial art that combines dance and acrobatics). Theater performances of pieces, such as *Nego Fugido* (Runaway Slave), recount stories of enslaved people escaping plantation owners to join *quilombos*, independent communities set up by runaways.

 ⑤

Cachoeira

F4 🚌 **⑦ Rua Ana Neri 27**

Historically more powerful than Santo Amaro and São

Félix, Cachoeira was also the most prominent town in the Recôncavo. Its strategic location, between the Baía de Todos os Santos and the inland roads, made it a key crossroads between Salvador and the rest of the state.

The city once had a busy river port on the Paraguaçu. Boats sailed upstream from Salvador to load up with sugar and tobacco produced in the Recôncavo region. The town's privileged position as a commercial center is reflected in its imposing colonial architecture. However, with the creation of road access to Salvador, Cachoeira lost its important position and its port gradually faded away.

In the old city center, many of the city's churches and wealthy merchants' houses are still standing, although in a dilapidated condition. Cachoeira has, however, begun to renovate and preserve its historic center. Today, the city is as much celebrated for its robust wood-sculpting tradition as for its production of the best tobacco in Brazil.

⑥

São Félix

F4 🚌 **From Cachoeira**
⑦ Av Luiz Eduardo Maga-lhães s/n; (77) 3491 2921

Regarded as the twin of Cachoeira, São Félix lies across the Rio Paraguaçu, on a hillside overlooking the river. The railway bridge connecting the two towns was commissioned

by Dom Pedro II, and built by British engineers in 1895; it's now shared by cars, trains, and foot traffic. Several times a day, São Félix comes to a standstill as freight trains roll right through the town center.

Larger in size, though not as impressive as Cachoeira, São Félix used to earn a living in its own right as a producer of fine *charutos* (cigars). The heart of this industry was the famous Dannemann cigar factory. Blessed by optimum conditions for growing and processing tobacco, the Dannemann factory quickly became one of the area's finest cigar producers. The region still makes Dannemann cigars, but the original factory has since been converted into a cultural center, known as the **Centro Cultural Dannemann**. A small exhibit of old machinery here tells the story of the early factory days. On weekdays, visitors are able to watch the factory workers rolling cigars.

Centro Cultural Dannemann
Av Salvador Pinto 29
📞 **(75) 3438 2500** 🕐 **Until further notice**

1872

The year in which Brazilian-German cigar label Dannemann was founded in São Felix.

AFRO-BRAZILIAN CULTURE

Brazil's African culture is a direct legacy of the 300 years of enslavement that occured during the colonial period. Over many years, enslaved Africans, Europeans, and their descendants created a blend of cultures and bloodlines with west African, Native American, Portuguese, and Dutch elements. This has uniquely resulted in what is now called Afro-Brazilian culture, visible in the community's people, clothing, food, religion, and music. The Afro-Brazilian culture is an integral part of the country's identity, particularly in Salvador, where 80 per cent of the population are of African heritage.

RELIGIOUS BELIEFS AND RITUALS

Enslaved people from the western and central parts of Africa, where the Bantu and Yoruba languages dominated, introduced many African religions to Brazil. Most of the country's early populations believed in different deities, or *orixás*; gods and goddesses endowed with their own personality and unique powers. *Orixás* like Yemanjá, the Goddess of the Sea, are spirits who intervene between humans and Olorun, the supreme creator. As the

CARLINHOS BROWN

Famed Brazilian pop star Carlinhos Brown is one of the country's traditional singers who has become world-famous with his percussion-heavy rhythms. This noted advocate of Afro-Brazilian culture hails from Bahia.

Portuguese tried to sway the enslaved to convert to Catholicism, Afro-Brazilian religions like Candomblé, Umbanda, and Batuque emerged, mixing European and African beliefs.

RHYTHM AND BEATS

Music and dance are an integral part of Afro-Brazilian culture and some of the country's most popular music styles derive from its African heritage. During the 20th century, African music and samba became part of the mainstream. Bahia's characteristic Afro-Brazilian music grew in many forms, with *axé* being the signature sound of Salvador's Carnaval. In Pernambuco, various rhythms developed, including Recife's signature beat, *frevó*.

DRESS

Baianas are Afro-Brazilian women from Bahia, who often wear white dresses, turbans, and colorful beaded necklaces. They are often seen selling *acarajés* (stuffed bean fritters). Baianas play an important role in keeping the Afro-Brazilian tradition alive. Their attire is believed to derive from the traditional garb of Nigerian women. While they may appear similarly dressed, Baianas wear unique jewelry paying homage to their *orixá*.

↑ An Afro-Brazilian drummer performing in the historic district of Pelourinho

↑ Afro-Brazilians carrying a statue of the *orixá* Yemanjá at the annual festival in Salvador

↑ The turquoise waters of Morro de São Paulo bay dotted with boats

❼ Morro de São Paulo

🅰F4 🚤From Salvador 🛥From Salvador 🅦morro desaopaulo.com.br

Although within easy reach of Salvador, the coast immediately south of the state capital does not have many large, developed tourist areas, apart from Morro de São Paulo. Now a picturesque beach destination, Morro de São Paulo, on the northern tip of Ilha da Tinharé, once played a key role in the coastal defenses of Bahia. In 1630, Governor General Diego Luiz de Oliveira ordered Fortaleza do Tapirando to be strategically built here where it could control the Itaparica channel, one of the main approaches to Salvador. The ruins of the fort have been designated a National Heritage Site. The view of the sunset from the fort's crumbling walls is spectacular, and dolphin sightings are quite common.

Still accessible only by boat or plane, Morro maintains much of its original charm. Lined with *pousadas*, boutiques, and friendly restaurants, the "streets" are primarily made of sand, and wheelbarrows are often used for transporting goods. In the evenings, the village square transforms into a craft market, the small stands often lit only by dim candlelight, making for a very cozy atmosphere. Morro's beaches are famous

Did You Know?

The sandy town of Morro de São Paulo is car-free; bicycles are the primary mode of transport.

in Brazil for their parties. During high season, there are parties every night and the beaches are packed. As you move away from the village, the beaches get wider and less developed. From Quarta beach onward, the coast remains blissfully unspoiled, offering long stretches of white sand, backed by waving groves of coconut palms.

Just south of Morro, **Ilha de Boipeba** offers a quiet, idyllic island getaway, with pristine, deserted beaches. One of the most picturesque is Ponta de Castelhanos, which is especially known for diving. Travelers can get here via boat or 4WD jeep from Morro de São Paulo. Visitors coming from Salvador can drive to Valença, then take a boat.

Ilha de Boipeba
🅰30 miles (50 km) S of Morro
🅦ilhaboipeba.org.br

↑ An abundance of colorful fruit on display at a cocktail vendor on Morro de São Paulo

CAPOEIRA

Bahia, the birthplace of capoeira, offers plenty of opportunities to see this dazzling mixture of dance, gymnastics, and martial arts. Capoeira was developed by enslaved people from Africa in Brazil as a form of self-defense against plantation owners. The music was added as a disguise.

THE HISTORY OF CAPOEIRA

Outlawed in 1890 and forced to go underground, the sport made a slow comeback over the next few decades as white Brazilians began to accept and celebrate the African aspects of Brazil's culture. Capoeira was fully rehabilitated in the 1930s, when President Vargas, calling it "the only true Brazilian sport," invited one of the most renowned *capoeiristas* of the day, Mestre Bimba, to perform in the presidential palace.

CAPOEIRA MOVES

Capoeiristas exhibit incredible muscle control, strength, and flexibility as they carry out acrobatic moves, while keeping their opponent at bay. The capoeira moves are performed at lightning speed, but with a dance-like fluidity, where each move is a combination of skill, balance, and beauty.

Escorpião, or the scorpion move, is a combination of back flips and cartwheels. *Au malandro* starts like a cartwheel, but only one hand goes down while the opposite leg kicks up in a swift, fluid move. The *esquiva* (escape), a low ducking move, is very common since *capoeiristas* primarily attack with kicks and sweeps.

↑ A dancer suspended in the air while performing a daring capoeira move

↑ *Capoeiristas* engaging in the sport at the Salvador carnaval in Bahia

---

Canudos

Ⓐ F3 🚌

Traveling through the sleepy town of Canudos, it is hard to imagine that this was once the staging ground for a brutal civil rebellion in 1897. Led by influencial preacher Antônio Conselheiro the year-long war cost more than 20,000 people their lives and almost destroyed the future of the Brazilian Republic.

The original settlement of Canudos now lies at the bottom of the Lagoa Cocorobó, which flooded the area in 1970. However, many of the original battlefields escaped the deluge and today form part of an open-air museum, within the **Parque Estadual de Canudos**. Access to the state park is via the **Memorial de Canudos**, on the outskirts of the town. The principal museum sites here include Morro do Conselheiro (Counsellor Hill), Vale da Morte (Valley of Death), the Estrada Sagrada (Holy Road), and the Vale da Degola (Valley of Beheadings).

In the Canudos region during the war, Republican soldiers were camped in the hills that were covered by *favela* trees, the small thorn-covered shrub very common in the dry interior in Bahia. Upon their return to Rio, the soldiers never received the land they had been promised. They ended up squatting on the hills and naming their community "favela" after the trees – hence the name favela (*p111*), traces its origins to the Canudos War.

Visitors to Canudos will be struck by the impressive surrounding *sertão* landscape where plants like *caatinga* bushes, cacti, bromeliads, *umbu* trees, and *favelas* thrive in the dry soils. After the April rains, the landscape briefly turns lush and animals such as deer, hyacinth macaws, and armadillos can be spotted frequently.

Parque Estadual de Canudos
🕙 **C** (75) 3494 2000

Memorial de Canudos
🕙 **C** (75) 3494 2194

9
Peninsula de Maraú

 F4 🚌 **From Itacaré or Camamu to Barra Grande** 🛈 **Barra Grande; www.barragrande.net**

The main destination at the northern tip of the Peninsula de Maraú is Barra Grande, a delightful, remote fishing village. Beautiful beaches are scattered along the entire length of the peninsula, but it is difficult to get around without a car. Four-wheel drives take passengers from *pousadas* to various beaches around the peninsula. Alternatively, the 31-mile (50-km) walk across various palm-fringed beaches along the coastline is spectacular.

Most of the peninsula is covered in native Mata Atlântica rainforest, which has been relatively well preserved. The Baía de Camamu, one of Brazil's largest bays, separates the peninsula from the mainland. The long dirt road heading down the peninsula (often impassable after rains) leads to some of the best beaches. Praia Taipús de Fora, 4 miles (7 km) south of Barra Grande, is considered one of Brazil's most stunning beaches. At low tide, the coral reefs form a clear, natural pool, perfect for snorkeling.

There are also a handful of small fishing villages scattered along the coast. Local fishers offer excursions to Lagoa Azul (Blue Lagoon) and down the Rio Maraú.

10
Itacaré

 F4 ✈ **Ilhéus** 🚌 🛈 **Rua Rui Barbosa, Centro; www.itacare.com**

The fishing town of Itacaré is part of Brazil's Discovery Coast. Portuguese explorer Pedro Álvares Cabral (*p64*), who was the first European to reach Brazil, landed in Porto Seguro, not far from Itacaré, in 1500.

Large areas of protected Atlantic rainforest, which were given World Heritage Site status by UNESCO in 1999, meet the sea along the coast of Itacaré. Relatively isolated, the town is favored by nature lovers. Itacaré is also known for its relaxed lifestyle and typical Afro-Brazilian culture.

The beaches here have towering waves, making it a popular surfing destination. Most are surrounded by fertile forest and can only be accessed on foot. Prainha, Itacaré's main attraction, is considered to be one of Brazil's most beautiful beaches, and is accessible only by a trail through the rainforest.

↑ A beautiful, palm-fringed beach on the Peninsula de Maraú

 HIDDEN GEM
Candlelit Caraíva

Near the mouth of Rio Caraíva, a 1.5-hour drive south of Trancoso, is this charming car-free village with sandy streets where the *forró* nights are the main event of the week. With its frequent power cuts, it's the perfect spot for enjoying relaxed, candlelit nights in true Brazilian beach style.

> **Prainha, Itacaré's main attraction, is considered to be one of Brazil's most beautiful beaches, and is accessible only by a trail through the rainforest.**

JORGE AMADO

Son of a cocoa plantation owner, Jorge Amado (1912–2001) was born near Ilhéus. He published his first novel, *O País do Carnaval* in 1931. His 1958 novel, *Gabriela, Clove and Cinnamon*, was based on the warring cocoa barons of his native city.

The 49-mile (80-km) drive to Ilhéus, on the **Estrada Parque** (the Park Drive), traverses a strand of Atlantic rainforest and allows access to a string of secluded beaches. Care has been taken not to disrupt the ecosystem and to protect animals crossing the highway. In places, nets have been strung from tree to tree to provide safe passage for monkeys crossing the road.

⓫
Ilhéus

🗺 F4 🚌 🛈 Setur: Praça JJ Seabra; https://turismo. ilheus.ba.gov.br

When farmers began growing cocoa trees in the early 20th century, Ilhéus, the largest city on Bahia's southern coast, established itself as a major cocoa-growing region. Disaster struck in 1989 when a parasite infected the plantations and destroyed the entire crop. The industry is yet to recover, but several old plantations have been converted into museums.

Ilhéus is best known as the setting for several novels by Bahia's most beloved author, Jorge Amado. One of his books, *Gabriela, Clove and Cinnamon*, takes place in the city's historic core. Today, visitors can see the Bar Vesúvio and Bataclã

Cabaret that feature in his novel. The author's childhood home, **Casa de Cultura Jorge Amado**, is open to visitors.

Among the city's other sights is the 16th-century **Igreja de São Jorge**, which houses a museum of sacred art, and the **Catedral São Sebastião**. The cathedral, a fine Neo-Classical structure, was erected in the 1930s. Its dome, however, took another 30 years to build and was completed only in 1967.

Casa de Cultura Jorge Amado
♿ 🏠 Rua Jorge Amado 21 📞 (73) 3231 7531 🕐 9am–noon, 2–5pm Mon–Fri & 9am–1pm Sat

Igreja de São Jorge
🏠 Praça Rui Barbosa 🔒 For renovation

Catedral São Sebastião
🏠 Praça R. Dom Eduardo 📞 (73) 3633 5236 🕐 Hours vary, call ahead

→ The elegant spires of Catedral São Sebastião, rising above Ilhéus's shore

⑫ Porto Seguro

🅰F5 🔁🚌 ℹ Av Portugal 350, Passarela do Descobrimento, Centro; http://conheca.portoseguro.ba.gov.br

Porto Seguro (Safe Port) is officially recognized as the site of the first Portuguese landing in 1500, where Pedro Cabral and his fleet arrived and said mass on Brazilian soil.

The city's small historic center (Cidade Histórica) has several stately old buildings, including the Matriz Nossa Senhora da Pena, built in 1535. Its altar has an image of Saint Francis of Assisi, the first religious statue to be brought to Brazil in 1503. On the same square is the former jail, built in 1772.

STAY

UXUA Casa Hotel and Spa

Boutique hotel with impeccably decorated *casas* (bungalows) and a relaxed beachside bar. The hotel's Seu Peudrinho *casa*, with its pink doors, is a favorite.

🅰F5 🅐Praça São João Batista, Trancoso 🆆uxua.com

$$$

Hotel Casa de Perainda

Intimate hotel that feels like a home away from home. Breakfast is enjoyed at a long table with other guests.

🅰F5 🅐Rua do Porto 103, Trancoso 🆆casadeperainda.com

$$$

Today, Porto Seguro is best known for its buzzing nightlife, beach parties, music festivals, and the notorious "Passarela do Alcool" (alcohol boardwalk), the nickname for the city's main street, Passarela do Descobrimento, where vendors set up kiosks selling fresh fruit cocktails with a heavy alcoholic kick. Visitors looking for a more tranquil holiday experience usually head farther south to the lovely neighboring villages of Arraial d'Ajuda and Trancoso, both of which are in easy reach of the city.

Immediately south of town are a few beaches that mainly attract backpackers. Less developed, but serene, these beaches can be accessed from Porto Seguro airport, which receives daily flights from all over Brazil. Road access to the town can often be challenging, as distances are long and the coastal highways are in a state of disrepair.

⑬ Trancoso

🅰F5 🔁Porto Seguro 🚌 🆆trancosobahia.com.br

Though just a short drive from Porto Seguro, Trancoso has a sense of tranquility that sets it apart from the nearby party town. Set on a high bluff overlooking the ocean, the town center, or *quadrado*, is a long, grassy space, anchored by a

↑ Attractive pink buildings in Arraial d'Ajuda, near Porto Seguro

small church and framed by houses, many of which have turned their gardens into tasteful little cafés.

Trancoso offers a variety of sophisicated services which focus on high-end travelers – upscale B&Bs, fine dining, and popular music events – unsurprisingly, the town is very popular with the jetsetter crowd. The beaches are backed by red sandstone cliffs, and remain largely secluded and unspoiled.

EXPERIENCE Bahia

❶❹

Parque Nacional Marinho de Abrolhos

F5 Ibama, Praia do Kitongo, Caravelas; (073) 297 1111; www.abrolhos.net

Remote and uninhabited, the archipelago of Abrolhos offers excellent opportunities for viewing wildlife. Its five islands are located just off the coast of southern Bahia. In 1983, the islands, together with 351 sq miles (909 sq km) of surrounding ocean, were declared a National Marine Park, the first such park in Brazil. Known for its rare formations of south Atlantic coral, the park teems with sea turtles, squid, and a rich assortment of fish. A variety of bird species come to feed and lay eggs on the islands, which are otherwise dry and covered in grasslands. Humpback whales can also be spotted here; the best time to see them is between June and November, when the archipelago becomes a calving ground for them.

Visitors can land on only one of the five islands, Siriba. However, it is possible to book day excursions or multinight onboard stays within the park's boundaries from the town of Caravelas on the mainland. For snorkeling and diving enthusiasts, underwater visibility is best between December and April. Guided tours to the national park should only be made with an operator accredited by Brazil's environmental agency, IBAMA.

Did You Know?

The music video to Beyoncé's "Blue" features the artist playing football on Trancoso's *quadrado*.

❶❺

Lençóis

F4 16 miles (25 km) E of town Sectur: Av Sete de Setembro 35, Centro, Lençóis; www.lencois.ba.gov.br/site

Located in the foothills of the striking Chapada Diamantina mountains in central Bahia, the town of Lençóis sprang up almost overnight, as diamond fever struck in these interior highlands at the end of the 19th century. The name of the town, meaning "sheets," derives from the camp that grew up here during the diamond strike. The miners, too poor to afford tents, made do with sheets draped over branches instead.

Unlike many other mining boomtowns, however, Lençóis has a colonial air, with small Baroque churches, and tiny houses and shops painted in pastel colors. The town's distinguished main square, Praça Horácio de Matos, consists of 19th-century houses, characterized by high, arched windows. Another town landmark, Praça Otaviano Alves, lined with gracious colonial homes, is farther south of the main square.

Lençóis has reinvented itself as the base camp for eco-tourists venturing out to explore the caves, waterfalls, and isolated mountaintops of the surrounding highlands. The town's colonial homes now house trekking equipment stores, cafés, and tasteful photo galleries.

Tropical Trancoso's beautiful Nativos beach, lined with palms and beach loungers

SERGIPE, ALAGOAS, AND PERNAMBUCO

Northeast Brazil was once the domain of the Caeté and Tabajara Indigenous peoples, but within a century of the arrival of the Europeans most had been enslaved, decimated by disease, or driven far inland. The Portuguese established Olinda in 1537, and it soon flourished thanks to Brazil's sugar boom and the trade of enslaved Africans that fueled it. Less than a century later, Portugal's dominance was challenged by the Dutch, who occupied Olinda in 1630 and controlled much of the northeast until 1654. In contrast, Palmares, the largest and most famous of all of Brazil's rebellious *quilombos* (communities of those freed from enslavement), was effectively independent between 1605 and 1694. Up to 11,000 fugitives may have lived there, led by a legendary figure known as Zumbi.

The region was rocked by a series of rebellions in the 19th century, including the Pernambucan Revolution of 1817, which led to Alagoas being carved out of the state's territory; Sergipe followed in 1820. Recife, founded by the Dutch, replaced Olinda as Pernambuco's capital in 1827. In 1839 Alagoas picked Maceió as a capital, prompting its transformation from sleepy village to major port, and in 1855, Sergipe established Aracaju as a purpose-built capital. Today, both Alagoas and Sergipe remain largely dependent on sugarcane and tourism, while Pernambuco has diversified into heavy industry and technology. Globally however, the northeast may perhaps be best known for being the home of Luiz Inácio da Silva, or Lula, twice president of Brazil from 2003 to 2010, and again since January 2023, and famed for being one of the most popular politicians in Brazilian history.

SERGIPE, ALAGOAS, AND PERNAMBUCO

Must Sees
1. Recife
2. Olinda
3. Ilha de Fernando de Noronha

Experience More
4. Aracaju
5. São Cristóvão
6. Penedo
7. Rio São Francisco
8. Cânion Xingó
9. Marechal Deodoro
10. Porto de Galinhas
11. Maceió
12. Ilha de Itamaracá
13. Caruaru

RECIFE

G3 Pernambuco Aeroporto dos Guararapes, 7 miles (11 km) S of city center 9 miles (14 km) SW of city center Recife CVB, Av Domingos Ferreira 4023, Boa Viagem; https://visit.recife.br/en

The Dutch took over Pernambuco in 1630, and Count Maurice of Nassau commanded the dyking of the flat islands at the mouth of the Rio Capibaribe. These islands, Santo Antônio, Boa Vista, and Recife Antigo (Old Recife), were then connected to each other and the mainland via a system of bridges to form the city of Recife.

↑ Vibrantly colored buildings lining a busy high street in Recife

① Around Marco Zero

In the heart of downtown Old Recife, the bronze plaque, known as Marco Zero (Ground Zero) and the surrounding square, mark the official point where the city was founded as well as the site of the original pier. Boats can be taken from here across to the Parque das Esculturas, which features an imposing collection of sculptures by one of Brazil's leading ceramic artists, Francisco Brennand (p299).

Though modern Recife stretches onto the mainland, its center comprises the islands of Santo Antônio, Boa Vista, and Recife Antigo. Skyscrapers exist alongside a handful of colonial buildings, lending the city a striking character. The area north of the center is dotted with museums and parks.

② Paço Alfândega

Rua da Alfândega 35 8am–6pm Mon–Fri, all day Sat, Sun & public hols pacoalfandega.com.br

At the edge of the historical quarter, this former customs building dates back to 1826, when Recife was one of Brazil's major ports. It now houses an art gallery, restaurants, and a shopping center.

③ Torre de Malakoff

Praça do Arsenal da Marinha, Rua do Bom Jesus (81) 3184 3180 Until further notice

A relative newcomer, the Malakoff Tower was built in 1845 as South America's first astronomical observatory, and is still functional today. Visitors can climb to the top terrace for a splendid view of the city courtesy of the LX 200 telescopes.

④ Forte do Brum

Praça Comunidade Luso-Brasileira (81) 3224 7559 9am–noon & 1–4:30pm Tue–Fri, 2–5pm Sat & Sun

One of few constructions to pre-date the Dutch, Forte Brum was built by the Portuguese in 1629, before being taken over by the Dutch in 1630, and strengthened and expanded. Today it is a military museum.

⑤

Museu Cais do Sertão

A Av Alfredo Lisboa **C** (81) 3182 8266 **O** 10am–4pm Thu & Fri, 11am–5pm Sat & Sun

This well-designed, interactive museum explores the history and culture of the *sertão* region and pays tribute to the Recife Carnaval, giving a taste of the lifestyle here.

⑥

Paço do Frevó

A Praça do Arsenal da Marinha s/n **O** 10am–4pm Thu & Fri, 11am–5pm Sat & Sun **W** pacodofrevo.org.br

This culture center focuses on Recife's unique musical rhythm. It includes a Music School, Documentation Center, School of Dance, and various other exhibitions.

⑦

Kahal Zur Israel Synagogue

A Rua do Bom Jesus 197 **C** (81) 3224 2128 **O** 9am–5pm Tue–Fri, 2–6pm Sun

Built in 1637, during the city's period of Dutch rule, this synagogue recounts the history of the Jewish community in Recife. It was the first synagogue anywhere in the Americas. At the height of Dutch rule, about half of Recife's white population was Jewish. Unfortunately, the period of religious tolerance was short-lived, and when the Dutch surrendered to the Portuguese in 1654 the Jews were given three months to leave. The synagogue was dismantled and the building torn down in the 20th century.

Archaeologists have confirmed the exact location of the original synagogue,

FREVÓ

Recife's signature beat is *frevó*. Fast and lively, the rhythm is particularly popular during Carnaval *(p58)*. One of the accessories of a *frevó* dancer is the colorful parasol that is used in the choreography. First recorded in the 1930s, the rhythm had entered the repertoire of mainstream Brazilian musicians by the 1950s and 1960s.

which was forgotten for many years, after digging up part of a *mikveh* (ritual bath). The current synagogue has been rebuilt from the ground up, and also now houses a museum that relates the history of Jewish people in Recife.

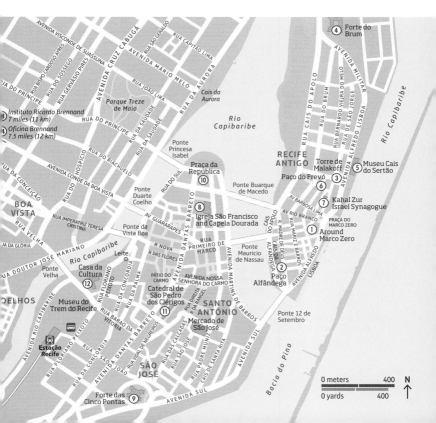

↑ Azulejos in the Igreja
São Francisco showing
the adoration of the maji

Igreja São Francisco and Capela Dourada

⌂ Rua do Imperador, Santo Antônio ☎ (81) 3224 0530 ⏰ 8-11:30am, 2-5pm Mon-Fri, 8-11:30am Sat

One of the major attractions in Recife, Igreja São Francisco served as the convent of the Third Franciscan Order. It was built in 1606, when the island of Santo Antônio only had 200 inhabitants. During the Dutch occupation of Recife the convent was used as army barracks. Renovations began after the return of the Franciscans, when a courtyard and decorative elements were added. The *pièce de résistance* is the Capela Dourada (Golden Chapel), added in 1695 in an annex of the main church. The chapel's intricately carved altars, arches, and beams showcase some outstanding Portuguese Baroque art. One of the walls in the church is adorned with a painting that depicts the Crucifixion of a group of Franciscan saints.

Forte das Cinco Pontas

⌂ Praça das Cinco Pontas ☎ (81) 3355 3107 ⏰ 10am-5pm Wed-Sat (to 4pm Sun)

Somewhat deceptively, the Forte das Cinco Pontas (Five-Pointed Fort) actually only has four points. The original Dutch fort, built in 1630 to protect the new Dutch-Brazilian capital of Mauritsstad, had five. When the Dutch withdrew in 1654, the Portuguese leveled the unique shape and put up a more traditional four-pointer. Wonderfully restored, the fort now houses the city museum and contains an impressive collection of maps, paintings, and artifacts that tell the history of Dutch rule.

Praça da República

☎ (81) 3425 2124 ⏰ Palácio do Campo das Princesas: 9-11am & 2-4pm Thu & Fri, 10am-noon Sun; Teatro Santa Isabel: call to check for performance timings

Modern Recife's main civic square, Praça da República, is located at the tip of Santo Antônio island. Some of the city's finest public buildings can be found here. The Palácio do Campo das Princesas (Governors' Palace) was built in the 1840s. Over the years, renovations and additions have altered the original Neo-Classical design and made the building more eclectic. The lovely interior garden was designed by Brazil's premier landscape artist, Roberto Burle Marx. Unfortunately, the only view available to the public is the one through the wrought-iron fence posts.

The Teatro Santa Isabel, a renovated pink theater, hosts many of Recife's prime cultural productions and is an elegant example of classic imperial architecture. The Palácio da Justiça, with its dome-shaped cupola, was constructed in 1930 to mark the presidency of Getúlio Vargas.

Catedral de São Pedro dos Clérigos

⌂ Rua São Pedro s/n, Santo Antônio ☎ (81) 3224 2954 ⏰ 8am-noon, 2-4pm Mon-Fri

Dating back to 1728, Catedral de São Pedro dos Clérigos is one of the most impressive churches in Pernambuco. Its striking facade is dominated by a statue of St. Peter, which was added in 1980. Although the church walls look perfectly square and straight from the outside, on the inside the church nave is octagonal. The main altar and most of the interior elements were renovated in the 19th century in the Rococo style. The only original pieces that remain are the two gold-painted pulpits.

The square in front of the church, Pátio de São Pedro, is one of Recife's most popular public squares and hosts a number of cultural events.

→

An impressive display of armor within the Instituto Ricardo Brennand

---

EAT

Leite

One of the oldest and most highly rated restaurants in Recife, Leite has been serving up traditional Brazilian cuisine since 1882. The *cartola* - baked banana - is to die for.

⌂ Praça Joaquim Nabuco ☎ (81) 3224 7977

$ $ $

> Brennand (b. 1927) is best known for his collection of phallic-shaped ceramic sculptures, nearly all of which are striking and larger than life.

Terça Negra (Black Tuesday), takes place every Tuesday night, and is widely known for showcasing regional Afro-Brazilian musical styles, such as *afoxé*, *maculelê*, and *coco*.

Casa da Cultura

🏠 Rua Floriano Peixoto s/n, São José 📞 (81) 3184 3152
🕐 9am–5pm Mon–Sat, 9am–2pm Sun

Used as a jail until 1973, this former penitentiary now houses the Casa da Cultura, the city's largest arts and craft market. Each of the old cells holds a shop showcasing some of the finest leather, lace, and ceramic crafts of this region. Built in 1850, the jail was modeled after US prisons and has four wings set in a cross shape. The center publishes the monthly *Agenda Cultural*, a listing of cultural events.

⑬
Instituto Ricardo Brennand

🏠 Av Antônio Brennand, Várzea 📞 (81) 2121 0352
🕐 1–5pm Fri–Sun

Founded by the cousin of ceramic artist Francisco Brennand, this institute includes a small castle, the Castelo São João, which houses a large collection of European art, a medieval weaponry collection, and an extensive archive of paintings and documents from the years of the Dutch conquest of Brazil.

Also worth seeing is the Pinacoteca gallery, which features a large collection of 17th-century paintings and drawings by landscape artists Frans Post and Albert Eckhout. The exhibit also includes antique maps and documents that recount the brief but eventful history of the Dutch in Brazil.

Oficina Brennand

🏠 Access via Av Caxangá, Várzea 📞 (81) 3271 2466
🕐 7am–5pm Mon–Thu, 8am–4pm Fri, 10am–4pm Sat & Sun

Acclaimed as the most unusual cultural attraction in Recife, the Oficina Brennand is the famed artist's personal gallery. Brennand (b.1927) is best known for his collection of phallic-shaped ceramic sculptures, nearly all of which are striking and larger than life. His collection is creatively displayed inside a brick factory and its surrounding gardens, beautifully landscaped by Burle Marx.

The collection also showcases thousands of playfully designed ceramic tiles, as well as some of his paintings and drawings. Around 90 of Brennand's sculptures are also on display in a park on an offshore reef. It's accessible via boat from Marca Zero or by road via Brasilia Teimosa neighborhood. Admission is free.

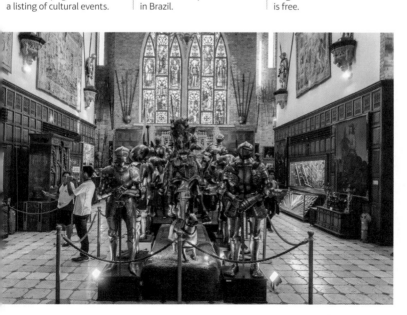

↑ Olinda Lighthouse rising before the turquoise ocean, with the cityscape in the distance

 2

OLINDA

🅰 G3 🏠 Pernambuco ✈ Recife International Airport 🚌
ℹ Av Liberdade 68, Carmo; www.olinda.pe.gov.br

One of the best-preserved colonial cities in Brazil, Olinda was founded in 1535 by the Portuguese – though the land was previously occupied by the Caetés and Tupinambá people. Much of the city was burned down during the Dutch occupation in 1631 but was later restored, and Olinda was designated a UNESCO World Heritage Site in 1982. Its narrow cobblestoned streets are perfect for exploring on foot.

① Igreja e Mosteiro de São Bento

🏠 Rua São Bento 📞 (81) 3316 3290 🕐 9–11:45am & 2–5pm daily

Built in 1582, this monastery was destroyed by the Dutch along with most of the city, and rebuilt in the late 18th century. It is acclaimed for its Baroque altar in the chapel and intricate wood carving, which features the image of São Bento (St. Benedict) himself. The original wood altar has been repainted with gold leaf, a process that took more than a year and 30 professionals during a period of restoration in 2001. The sacristy's three large paintings, by 18th-century artist José Eloy da Conceição, portray scenes from the life of the saint. On Sundays, Gregorian chanters add a special touch to the morning mass.

② Convento de São Francisco

🏠 Rua de São Francisco 280 📞 (81) 3429 0517 🕐 9am–12:30pm & 2–5:30pm Mon–Sat

The Convento de São Francisco was the first convent built by the Franciscan order in Brazil. When the Dutch invaded Olinda in 1630 the convent was abandoned, before being rebuilt in the 18th century. Today the complex includes a 1585 church, Nossa Senhora das Neves (Our Lady of the Snow), and the adjacent chapels of St. Anne and St. Roque, built in 1754 and 1811, respectively. The highlight of the convent is the beautiful arcade surrounding the cloister. The tiled walls, decorated with Portuguese *azulejos*, tell the story of St. Francis of Assisi. Inside the sacristy there are more tiles, along with religious paintings

↑ Interior of St. Roque chapel at the Convento de São Francisco

and beautiful Baroque furniture, carved from dark jacaranda wood, that are equally impressive.

Museu de Arte Contemporânea

📍 Rua 13 de Maio 149, Carmo 📞 (81) 3184 3153 🕐 9am–5pm Tue–Sun

Housed in a fine 18th-century building that originally served as an *ajube*, or jail, working in conjunction with the Catholic church, the Museum of Contemporary Art displays both permanent and temporary exhibits. During the Inquisition, religious prisoners were brought here to pray and confess their sins. Today, the place holds some interest for those with an interest in modern art. Works by contemporary Pernambucan artists are regularly displayed in front of the stairs.

Museu do Mamulengo

📍 Rua do Sao Bento 344 📞 (81) 3493 2753 🕐 10am–5pm Tue–Sat

One of the region's unique gifts to the cultural scene in Brazil, *mamulengo*, or puppetry, is showcased in this fascinating museum. Nearly 1,000 puppets are featured here, with a portion of the

> ### 🔺 GREAT VIEW
> #### Alto da Sé
>
> The Alto da Sé is one of the highest points in Olinda and offers a magnificent view of Recife *(p296)* in the distance. In the evenings, locals gather here to browse the crafts market and eat pancakes made from manioc (cassava-root flour).

THE OLINDA CARNAVAL

Every year during Carnaval, the cobblestoned streets of Olinda become the stage for a week-long party. The meeting place is the square, known as *quatro cantos* (four corners), on the corner of Rua do Amparo and Rua Prudente de Moraes. Here, *blocos* (neighborhood groups) begin their parades through the streets, playing music, singing, and dancing as they go. Dominating the festivities are enormous papier-mâché puppets that *bloco* members proudly carry along the parade route. The music varies from *frevó (p297)*, an upbeat, almost frenetic beat unique to Pernambuco, to *maracatu*, a much more African beat.

collection dating from the 1800s. Having performed before political figures, royalty, and luminaries through the ages, these puppets are today used as popular entertainment. During folk festivals, and especially during the city's lively Carnaval, the puppets can be seen enacting comedies, skits, and Pernambucan folk legends. For those particularly interested in the puppets' historical background, there is a curator who can explain it by asking the puppets themselves.

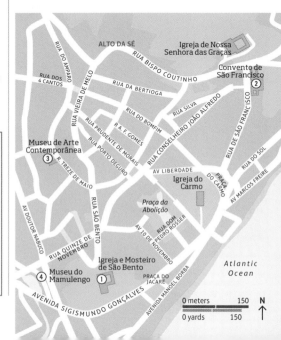

INSIDER TIP
Limited Access

A maximum limit of 450–500 visitors per day is enforced on the islands, to help protect their natural landscapes and fragile ecosystem. It is important to plan ahead and book flights in advance.

Crystal turquoise waters lapping against a secluded curve of sand in the Ilha de Fernando de Noronha ↑

3

ILHA DE FERNANDO DE NORONHA

🅰 G2 🏠 Pernambuco ➕ From Recife or Natal ℹ Divisão de Turismo, Palácio São Miguel, Vila dos Remédios; www.noronha.pe.gov.br/turismo

This cluster of rocky volcanic islands is Brazil's most important marine national park and a UNESCO World Heritage Site. Its rich marine life and translucent seas offer superb snorkeling and diving opportunities, as well as plush hotels and sandy beaches aplenty for those seeking a more relaxing trip.

Discovered in 1503 by Amerigo Vespucci, the 21-island archipelago of Fernando de Noronha was fought over for the next two centuries by the French, Dutch, and Portuguese, who built forts on strategic lookout points. The island, located 220 miles (354 km) off Brazil's northeastern coast, was used in a variety of ways, including as a political prison during World War II.

In 1988, the Parque Nacional Marinho de Fernando de Noronha was created in order to protect the fragile marine and island ecology of the archipelago. Today, a combination of crystal-clear water, fascinating wildlife, diverse marine life – which includes multicolored fish, rays, turtles, dolphins, sharks, and whales – and stunning, undeveloped beaches make Fernando de Noronha one of the most beautiful destinations in Brazil.

DIVING AND MARINE LIFE

Protected as a marine national park, Fernando de Noronha offers the best scuba diving in Brazil. Its water temperature ranges from 27–29° C (81–84° F), and the depth of underwater visibility is almost 98 ft (30 m). Underwater there is an astounding variety of marine life - rays of all types, green sea turtles and the rare hawksbill turtle, monk-fish, lemon sharks and reef sharks, clownfish hiding in anemones, and surgeon fish are just some varieties. Due to the island's volcanic heritage, there are also many swim-throughs.

↑ A surfer riding a wave off Praia do Boldró, one of the archipelago's many beaches

EXPERIENCE MORE

4

Aracaju

🅰F4 🏠Sergipe 🔁 𝒊Centro de Turismo Praça Olímpio Campos; www.aracaju.se.gov.br

In 1855, Sergipe's capital moved to Aracaju, situated at the mouth of the Rio Sergipe; by 1901, the quiet fishing village had become a stately capital.

Today, Aracaju is a large city with a commercial downtown area along the south river-bank. Sea-life enthusiasts should visit **Oceanário**, which has models of various marine habitats, plus sea turtles and a shark tank. Another of the city's top attractions is the **Museu da Gente Sergipana**, a museum exploring the history, culture, and traditions of the Sergipe region.

Aracaju's lively beach neighborhoods lie 6 to 12 miles (10 to 20 km) south of the city center. The most popular suburban beach is Atalaia, with its recreation facilities, cultural events, and seafood joints.

Oceanário

 🏠 Av Santos Dumont 1010 📞(79) 3214 3243 🕐10am–6pm Wed–Sun

Museu da Gente Sergipana

 🏠 Av Ivo do Prado 398 📞(79) 3218 1551 🕐10am–3pm Tue–Sun

5

São Cristóvão

🅰F4 🏠Sergipe 🚌From Aracaju 𝒊Largo da Praça do São Francisco; https://turismosao cristovao-se.com.br

A designated National Historic Heritage Site, São Cristóvão was founded in 1590, and is considered one of the oldest cities in Brazil. It served as the capital of Sergipe in the 17th and 18th centuries, but when the capital shifted to Aracaju it soon dwindled to the quiet interior town it is today.

The town's charming historic center is a panoply of colonial squares and buildings, and is also a hub of commerce. The most beautifully preserved square, Praça de São Francisco, is easily identified by the large Franciscan cross at its center. Here, the **Museu de Arte Sacra** (Museum of Sacred Art) has a fine collection of silver chalices, and a few beautifully sculpted statues of saints.

Museu de Arte Sacra

 🏠Praça de São Francisco 📞(79) 3261 1385 🕐9:30am–4pm Tue–Sat, 10am–1pm Sun

6

Penedo

🅰G4 🏠Alagoas 🚌From Maceió 𝒊Rua Damazo do Monte 2, Centro Historico; www.penedo.al.gov.br

The oldest settlement in Alagoas, Penedo was founded in 1565 on a strategic bluff overlooking the Rio São Francisco, about 19 miles (30 km) upstream of the delta. Today, Penedo's historic center has been designated a National Historic Monument. Particularly noteworthy is the complex housing the **Convento de São Francisco** and **Igreja de Santa Maria dos Anjos**, built over a period of 100 years.

The **Igreja Nossa Senhora da Corrente,** built in 1765, was used by enslaved people as a refuge.

Did You Know?

The name Aracaju comes from the Tupí-Guaraní words meaning "the cashew tree of the parrots".

↑ View over Aracaju, which sits at the mouth of the Rio Sergipe

↑ Igreja Nossa Senhora da Corrente overlooking the Rio São Francisco

Convento de São Francisco and Igreja de Santa Maria dos Anjos

🏛 Rua 7 de Setembro 218
🕐 8–11:30am, 2–5pm Tue–Fri, 8am–11pm Sat & Sun

Igreja Nossa Senhora da Corrente

⊛ 🏛 Praça 12 de Abril
🕐 8am–5pm Mon–Fri

Rio São Francisco

🗺 E4 🏛 Sergipe, Alagoas, Pernambuco & Minas Gerais

The largest and most vital river in the region, the Rio São Francisco has long served as the irrigation lifeline and main transport link for the people in the small towns of the arid northeastern interior to the bigger cities along the coast. Considered a symbol of national unity, Brazilians revere the São Francisco, and it is the subject of many myths and fables. The 1,760-mile (2,830-km) river meanders through five states. Originating in the Serra da Canastra mountains in Minas Gerais, it flows north through Bahia, and crosses briefly into Pernambuco before continuing east, marking the border between Sergipe and Alagoas in its final run to the sea.

Cânion Xingó

🗺 F3 🏛 Sergipe 🚌 From Aracaju ℹ Reservatório de Xingó; (81) 3229 2901

Standing on the Rio São Francisco, the Xingó Dam in Sergipe is one of the largest in Brazil. When it was completed in 1994, the dam blocked off the São Francisco canyon at a point about 155 miles (250 km) from the ocean, causing the river to rise and create the Xingó Reservoir (now a destination itself).

Catamarans and schooners depart from the dam and travel upstream, crossing the reservoir and re-entering the main part of the river.

Situated 2 miles (3 km) from the dam, the **Museu de Arqueológia de Xingó** displays numerous archaeological objects from nearby sites that were flooded when the dam was created. Objects from the earliest sites, dating from around 5000 BCE, include rock paintings, stone mortars, and fish-cleaning tools.

Museu de Arqueológia de Xingó

⊛⊛ 🏛 2 miles (3 km) from Xingó dam at Rodovia Canindé-Piranhas, Trevo da UHE Xingó 📞 (82) 98849 2622 🕐 8:30am–4:30pm Wed–Sun

---

LAMPIÃO AND MARIA BONITA

In the 1920s and 1930s, bandit leader Lampião and his wife Maria Bonita led a band of 40 outlaws, nicknamed *cangaceiros* (*cangaço* means badlands), on a 15-year spree of robberies, hold-ups, and shoot-outs across the northeast. As their raids continued, the Bonitas became notorious figures throughout Brazil. The police and militia searched for them endlessly but were unable to capture them. Finally, in 1938, Lampião, Maria Bonita, and nine *cangaceiros* were ambushed and killed by the police in Sergipe.

STATUES OF THE BONITAS

The stately Convento do São Francisco in Marechal Deodoro

9

Marechal Deodoro

G3 Alagoas From Maceió (82) 9157 1117

The capital of Alagoas until 1839, Marechal Deodoro was founded in 1611 as Vila Madalena. The city's name was changed in honor of its native son, Marshall Manuel Deodoro da Fonseca (1827–92), elected as Brazil's first president in 1891. Fonseca's childhood home is now a small museum, displaying original furniture.

The city's 18th-century colonial center features the Rococo **Igreja de Santa Maria Madalena**. Adjoining the church, the **Convento do São Francisco** houses an interesting museum.

Convento do São Francisco
Praça Pedro Paulinho
(82) 3263 1623 10am–4pm Wed–Sun

Igreja de Santa Maria Madalena
Rua Dr Melo Morães 1-117
10am–4pm Mon–Sun

10

Porto de Galinhas

G3 Pernambuco Recife Guararapes International Airport, 38 miles (60 km) N of town, then bus Rua Caraúna 260; (81) 98957 4263

Porto de Galinhas is one of the most popular tourist destinations in northeast Brazil, and deservedly so. There are no high-rises dwarfing the beach here, just low-scale *pousadas* and bungalows. The star attractions of the area, in addition to the beach, are the natural tide pools that form in the reefs just a short distance offshore. Colorful *jangada* rafts take swimmers and snorkelers out to the clear shallow waters that teem with tropical fish.

Porto de Galinhas also offers a lively atmosphere with excellent restaurants and shopping, and, better still, it does not take much effort to get away from the bustle. A short distance south along the beach leads to Ponta de Maracaípe, a beautiful spot with a large white sandbar, where the Rio Maracaípe runs into the ocean.

11

Maceió

G3 Alagoas (82) 3036 5200 Av João Davino 913, Centro; www.maceioconvention.com.br

The capital of Alagoas, Maceió is known for its many beautiful urban beaches. The best known, from north to south, are Jatiúca, Ponta Verde, Sete Coqueiros, and Pajuçara. Protected by reefs, the beaches have little or no surf, warm water, and a Caribbean turquoise-green color.

QUILOMBOS

In the African Yorubá language, *quilombo* means dwelling place. In Brazil, the term was used to describe a community of runaway enslaved people. Brazil's most famous *quilombo* was Quilombo dos Palmares in Alagoas. In the late 1600s, Zumbi, the *quilombo*'s second leader, successfully defended it from repeated Portuguese attacks. However, the Portuguese were relentless, and Palmares fell in 1694; Zumbi was beheaded and the community destroyed. Zumbi's legacy is remembered every year on November 20, on Zumbi dos Palmares Day.

A STATUE OF ZUMBI

About 1 mile (2 km) offshore from Pajuçara, a series of coral reefs are partially exposed at low tide, forming natural pools that can be explored with a mask and snorkel.

In addition to the beaches, Maceió has a small historic core. One of the loveliest mansions on the waterfront houses the **Museu Théo Brandão**. Named after a local writer who wrote about Alagoan folk art and anthropology, the small museum has a good collection of local art.

The southern end of the city borders the Lagoa Mundaú, which encompasses several mangrove islands teeming with marine life.

Museu Théo Brandão
 Av da Paz 1490, Centro **(82) 3214 1713** Until further notice

---

12

Ilha de Itamaracá

G3 Pernambuco From Recife

The island of Itamaracá played an important strategic role during the Dutch interregnum in Brazil. In 1631, the Dutch built the **Forte Orange** here to protect their new domain from invading forces. The Portuguese destroyed this in 1654 but created a new fort in stone on the site.

Just across from the fort is a small island, Coroa do Avião, which has natural reef pools.

Boats to the island leave from the beach in front of the fort. Itamaracá is also home to the Projeto Peixe Boi, a manatee research and rehabilitation center. Manatees live along the Brazilian coast from Alagoas to Amapá, but scientists estimate that there are only around 400 animals in the wild along this coast. The center works to rehabilitate injured manatees. Unfortunately, it is closed to visitors until further notice.

Forte Orange
 Estrada do Forte, Km 5, Praia do Forte **(81) 3544 1646** 9am–4pm Wed–Sun

---

13

Caruaru

G3 Pernambuco From Recife Praça Senador Teotônio Vilela caruaru.pe.gov.br

Located on the mainland, 100 miles (160 km) southwest of Itamaracá, Caruaru is a town whose fame rests on its ceramic *figurinhas* (figurines). Artist Vitalino Perreira dos Santos (1909–63) made many of these painted sculptures, and his hometown, Alto de Moura, a community of potters located 4 miles (6 km) west of Caruaru, still specializes in producing figurines. **Casa Museu Mestre Vitalino** in Alto do Moura is dedicated to this artist, and displays his tools.

Caruaru's open market is the largest in the northeast.

Besides figurines, leather bags, straw baskets, and ceramic pots are also sold at some of the best prices in Brazil. In addition, Caruaru, known as the capital of *forró* (p42), hosts Brazil's largest month-long *forró* festival. The **Museu do Forró Luiz Gonzaga** pays tribute to Luiz Gonzaga, the father of *forró* music.

Casa Museu Mestre Vitalino
Rua Mestre Vitalino 281 **(81) 3725 0805** 9am–6pm Wed–Sun

Museu do Forró Luiz Gonzaga
Praça José de Vasconcelos **(81) 3721 2545** Until further notice

Boats in the shimmering, tranquil waters off the coast of Maceió

PARAÍBA, RIO GRANDE DO NORTE, AND CEARÁ

Today this region is Brazil's holiday paradise, a land of sun, sand, and coconuts, but it wasn't always that way. As in much of Brazil, the original inhabitants, including the Kiriri, Tarairiu (Tapuya), and Tremembé, were enslaved and destroyed by disease after the arrival of the Portuguese in the 16th century.

The colonial economy was initially driven by sugar – João Pessoa, the capital of Paraíba, was founded in 1585 and boomed as a port for sugar; it also became a major entry point for enslaved Africans. Ranching also fueled the economy – Natal, the capital of Rio Grande do Norte, was established in 1599, and for centuries was mainly dependent on cattle; today salt is another big earner. In 1618, the Portuguese established a permanent presence in Ceará, a dependency of Pernambuco that became autonomous only in 1799. With transport to Europe becoming easier, its capital Fortaleza became a regional export hub.

In the 19th century the cotton industry came to dominate much of the region, but was impacted in 1884 when Ceará became the first Brazilian province to abolish slavery. Although agriculture – especially fruit and sugar – remains important in all three states, Ceará and Paraíba have also developed major footwear industries, while Rio Grande do Norte is a key exporter of seafood. Increasingly, however, tourism dominates all three economies today.

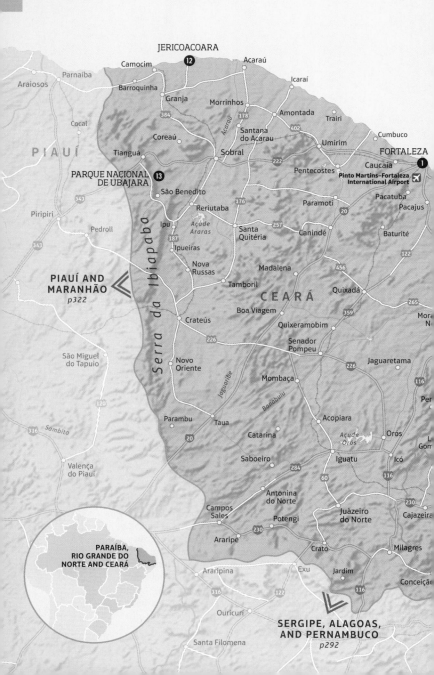

Atlantic
Ocean

JERICOACOARA

PIAUÍ AND
MARANHÃO
p322

SERGIPE, ALAGOAS,
AND PERNAMBUCO
p292

PARAÍBA,
RIO GRANDE DO
NORTE AND CEARÁ

PIAUÍ

CEARÁ

Araiosos
Parnaíba
Camocim
Acaraú
Icaraí
Barroquinha
Granja
Morrinhos
Amontada
Trairi
Cocal
Coreaú
Santana
do Acaraú
Umirim
Cumbuco
Tianguá
Sobral
Pentecostes
FORTALEZA
Caucaia
Pinto Martins–Fortaleza
International Airport
PARQUE NACIONAL
DE UBAJARA
São Benedito
Pacatuba
Pacajus
Piripiri
Reriutaba
Paramoti
Pedroll
Ipu
Açude
Araras
Santa
Quitéria
Canindé
Baturité
Ipueiras
Nova
Russas
Madalena
Quixadá
Tamboril
Boa Viagem
Crateús
Quixeramobim
Senador
Pompeu
Jaguaretama
São Miguel
do Tapuio
Novo
Oriente
Mombaça
Parambu
Taua
Acopiara
Orós
Catarina
Açude
Orós
Icó
Valença
do Piauí
Saboeiro
Iguatu
Sambito
Antonina
do Norte
Campos
Sales
Potengi
Juàzeiro
do Norte
Cajazeira
Araripe
Crato
Milagres
Araripina
Exu
Jardim
Conceiçã
Ouricuri
Santa Filomena

Serra da Ibiapaba

Acaraú
Jaguaribe
Banabuiú

12
13
1

384
178
402
222
143
176
20
343
187
257
122
456
265
226
359
226
116
120
316
284
60
116
230
230
316
122
116

PARAÍBA, RIO GRANDE DO NORTE, AND CEARÁ

Must See
1 Fortaleza

Experience More
2 João Pessoa
3 Cariri
4 Genipabu
5 Natal
6 Sousa

7 Maracajaú
8 Costa Branca
9 Mossoró
10 Campina Grande
11 Canoa Quebrada
12 Jericoacoara
13 Parque Nacional de Ubajara

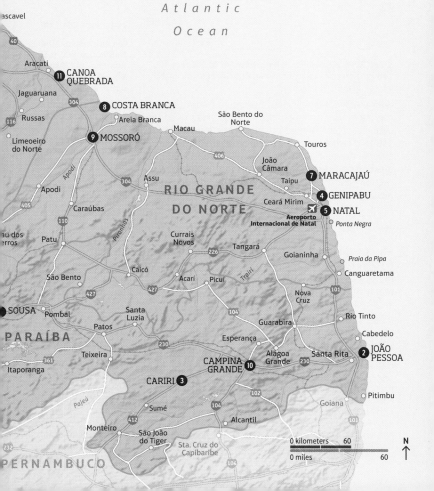

The dazzling skyscrapers of Fortaleza, sprawling right to the ocean's edge

❶
FORTALEZA

▲F2 **▲Ceará** **✈4 miles (6 km) S of town** **🚌** **ℹ Ceara Convention and Visitors Bureau, Rua Gilberto Studart 55, Cocó; www.visiteceara.com**

With pretty urban beaches, a pleasant climate, and a cooling breeze coming off the ocean, Fortaleza has an appealing resort-like atmosphere. Founded in the early 1500s, it remained a small town until after Brazilian independence in 1822, when it rapidly developed into one of Brazil's largest ports. There is a small historic section near the old port, but beyond that Fortaleza has a spacious, modern feel.

❶
Theatro José de Alencar

🏛 Rua Liberato Barroso 525 **📞(85) 3101 2583** **🕐 Hours vary, call to check**

Named after one of Brazil's famous novelists, the Theatro José de Alencar was built in 1908. The theater's high-Victorian cast-iron structure was imported from Glasgow. Additional decorative elements, such as the stained-glass windows and interior furnishings, were done in the Art Nouveau style.

❷
Museu do Ceará

🏛 Rua São Paulo 51 **📞(85) 3101 2609** **🕐 For renovation**

Inaugurated in 1932, this was the first major public museum to be opened in Fortaleza. Today it is housed in the former Legislative Assembly building and possesses a vast archive of things relating to the history of Ceará – coins, paintings, furniture, Indigenous artifacts, folk art, and more. Its most prized exhibit is the dagger belonging to notorious outlaw Lampião (p305).

❸
Mercado Central

🏛 Rua Maestro Alberto Nepomuceno 199 **🕐 9am-5pm Mon-Sat, 8am-1pm Sun** **🌐 mercadocentral defortaleza.com.br**

Fortaleza's huge indoor central market is the cheapest place in town for fine leatherwork, lace, or textiles, with more than 500 stalls across four stories. The market is also an excellent place to sample local ice cream made from regional fruits.

❹
Centro de Turismo

🏛 Rua Senador Pompeu 350 **📞(85) 3212 3014** **🕐 8am-5pm Mon-Fri, 8am-3pm Sat, 8am-noon Sun**

This former 19th-century prison has been transformed into a bustling market, with a different shop in each of the old jail cells. The market specializes in local artisan handicrafts, including fine lace, leather, and figurines. The market is a good place to stock up on top-quality cashew nuts, and there is also a tourist office here.

⑤
Centro Cultural Dragão do Mar

🏛 Rua Dragão do Mar 81, Iracema ⏰ 9am–9pm daily (museums closed Mon; hours for café, cinema, planetarium, and shops vary) 🌐 dragaodomar.org.br

Fortaleza's cultural center is a striking white building with a circular design. It houses the Museum of Contemporary Art, a history and anthropology museum, a planetarium, and a cinema and theater venue.

---

⑥
Praia de Cumbuco

🏛 21 miles (33 km) W of town

Cumbuco is the city's favorite beach playground, with the Lagoa da Banana offering a

Did You Know?

Slavery was abolished in Fortaleza in 1884, four years before the rest of Brazil.

THE STORY OF IRACEMA

Written by José de Alencar in 1865, this story tells of the love that a Tabajara princess bore for Martim, a white Portuguese settler. Iracema uses magic to make Martim fall in love with her, and is ostracized by her community. Away from her people, she loses her magical powers and her lover. A statue of Iracema on Meireles beach is sited where, according to legend, she stood awaiting the return of her beloved.

wide variety of watersports. Lagoa do Parnamirim, just south of Cumbuco, is ringed by tall dunes, making it perfect for "ski-bunda" (bum-skiing), where skiers slide down a dune into the lagoon.

---

⑦
Praia do Futuro

Praia do Futuro is one of the best beaches in the city for swimming and is also a nightlife destination, with many restaurants and several beach discos that are popular on weekends. On Thursday nights, Fortalezans head to open-air restaurants such as Chico do Caranguejo Praia for fresh crab and live *forró (p43)* music.

⑧
Praia de Iracema

Though called a beach, this is actually a former port, now transformed into the city's most popular nightlife and dining area. The focal point of the area is a long pier, built in 1920, and modeled on the piers of Brighton, in the UK.

---

⑨
Praia de Meireles

This pretty urban beach is lined with thick groves of coconut palms and waterside cafés. Although the water is not good for swimming, this is a great spot for strolling, sunbathing, or people-watching.

EXPERIENCE MORE

2
João Pessoa

🅐G3 🄰Paraíba 🛧7 miles (11 km) W of city center 🚌Rodoviária at Rua Francisco Londres, Varadouro 🄘Centro Turístico Tambaú, Av Almirante Tamandaré 100; www.joaopessoa.pb.gov.br

Brazil's third-oldest city, João Pessoa maintains an air of old-world charm, with a host of well-restored colonial churches, convents, and monasteries. Local visitors, however, flock here mainly for the easy atmosphere of its great white sandy beaches. The dense tropical forest that once covered the coastal strip of Paraíba now thrives only in patches, one of which lies within João Pessoa, forming one of the largest areas of natural wilderness in any city in the world.

One of the less developed cities in Brazil, João Pessoa has a small historic core, which remains little changed. Modern João Pessoa gravitates toward the beaches.

↑ Colorful houses in the old center of João Pessoa

One of the city's most striking churches, **Igreja de São Francisco** sits majestically atop a hill. This 18th-century church has an impressive altar, which contains a statue of St. Benedict, one of the church's few Black saints. The church is part of the Centro Cultural de Sao Francisco complex, which also includes the Convento de Santo Antônio, the Fonte de Santo Antônio, an 18th-century stone fountain, and a museum of popular and sacred art.

Praia do Cabo Branco is a beach area looking out over the easternmost point in the Americas, Ponta do Seixas (Seixas Point). The point is topped by a lighthouse, with a monument marking the spot.

Praia de Tambaú,
one of João Pessoa's
scenic beaches

Actually a large coral reef, Ilha
de Picãozinho is a popular spot
north of the center. At low tide,
boats take visitors over to swim
and snorkel in the natural
tide pools.

Another low-tide attraction
is Ilha de Areia Vermelha (Island
of Red Sand), 12 miles (20 km)
north of town. For approximately 25 days every month, low
tide exposes a beautiful beach
of striking red-orange sand.
It makes a perfect spot for
swimming, snorkeling, or
sunbathing. It is accessible
from Praia da Camboinhas.

Igreja de São Francisco

🏛 Praça São Francisco,
Centro Histórico 📞 (83) 3221
0779 🕐 9am-4:30pm Mon-
Fri, 9am-2:30pm Sat

Cariri

🗺 G3 🏛 Paraíba 🚌 From
Campina Grande

Situated in the Cariri Paraíbano,
a large plateau in the Serra da
Borborema, Cariri is the point
at which the *sertão* region
begins. Tours in this area of

FESTAS JUNINAS

One of the most popular folklore traditions of the
northeast, the Festas Juninas began as a peasant
celebration of the corn harvest and the June solstice, the
longest night of the year in the Southern Hemisphere.
June also coincided with the feasts of St. Anthony, St.
John, and St. Peter. Over the years, the pagan rituals and
Catholic events were melded together. The atmosphere
is burlesque, as partygoers dress up in peasant outfits
and perform square dances to the sounds of *forró (p43)*.

Indigenous rock carvings and
huge rock formations can be
organized by **Cariri Ecotours**.

One of the formations, the
Lajedo do Pai Mateus, sits
on the private grounds of a
fazenda. A vast slab of bare
granite, it is littered with
boulders bigger than houses,
as if a giant had scattered
their collection of pebbles –
unsurprisingly, it's known as
the "Devil's Marbles" locally.

From the plateau, there are
breathtaking views of the
Borborema valley. The diverse
landscape consists of small
trees, bushes, cacti, and
bromeliads. Sightings of
emus, an ostrich-like avian
(though considerably smaller),
are common in this area.

Cariri Ecotours

🕐 🏛 Natal 🌐 caririecotours.
com.br

↑ Cyclists approaching the
Lajedo do Pai Mateus, or
"Devil's Marbles"

④

Genipabu

🅰 G3 🄰 Rio Grande do
Norte ✈ Natal Airport 🚌
ℹ ACPBA, Rua Cruzeiro 405;
www.extremoz.rn.gov.br

The main reason to visit
Genipabu is to view the
magnificent dunes. This
small town is located north
of Natal, close to the edge
of an impressive landscape of
moving sands that pile up into
high dunes and plunge down
to the edge of the Atlantic
Ocean. Visitors can rent sand-
boards or dune buggies to
ride up and down the dunes.
Note that the Parque Dunas
de Genipabu, an area of
164-ft- (50-m-) tall shifting
dunes, is off-limits to all but
licensed buggy drivers.

Although buggy rides
are very popular in this area,
these motorized vehicles
have been known to have a
negative effect on the formation of dunes and growth of
local vegatation. For a more
gentle and environmentally
friendly experience, hike up
the ridges for spectacular
views of the coast. The best
time of day to visit the Parque
das Dunas is in the afternoon,
in order to enjoy the lovely
golden sunset over the dunes.

> Visitors have the full run of the Fort of
> the Magi, from the garrisons and the
> mess hall to the high ramparts, which
> offer terrific views of the city's skyline.

⑤

Natal

🅰 G3 🄰 Rio Grande do Norte
✈ 🚌 ℹ Centro de Turismo,
Rua Aderbal de Figueiredo
980; (84) 3211 6149

Natal is a pleasant, modern,
and safe city, increasingly
sought out as a sunshine
destination by winter-weary
Europeans. It has several
attractions, including beautiful beaches, sand hills, lagoons,
unusual sand art, and an
incredible nightlife.

The city and its most
famous landmark, **Forte dos
Reis Magos** (Fort of the Magi),
date back to December 25,
1598, when the Portuguese
established a fort and settlement at the mouth of the
Rio Potengi. In honor of the
season, the city was named
Natal, the Portuguese word
for Christmas. The fort was
named after the three wise
kings of the east who had
traveled to Bethlehem
bearing gifts. The Dutch
occupied the fort in 1633,
upgrading it into its current
five-pointed formation before
turning it back over to the

Portuguese in 1654. Access
to the fort is via a narrow
pedestrian walkway. At high
tide, the fort is cut off from
land by the waves. Visitors
have the full run of the Fort of
the Magi, from the garrisons
and the mess hall to the high
ramparts, which offer terrific
views of the city skyline.

Natal was never a large
trading center, and there are
few historic buildings. The
city's 19th-century peni-
tentiary has been converted
into the **Centro de Turismo**,
a showcase for regional arts
and crafts. All of the dozens
of prison cells along four corridors have been transformed
into shops selling leatherwork,
lace, ceramics, hammocks,
and figurines from north-
eastern folk festivals.
A restaurant and a cafeteria
offer some regional dishes.
On Thursday evenings, the
courtyard of the old prison
becomes an outdoor dance
hall, as the center plays host
to *forró com o turista*, an evening of *forró* dancing, with
live music and instructors
on hand to help shy and left-
footed foreigners with the
dance steps.

← Watching the sunset
from the dunes
at Genipabu

↑ The Forte dos Reis Magos, looking toward the city of Natal

Most visitors to Natal stay in Ponta Negra, a pleasant waterfront neighborhood in a modern part of the city featuring a lovely long beach with good waves for surfing. At the far end of the beach, the Morro do Careca, a towering 390-ft (120-m) sand dune, is now off-limits to climbers because of the danger of erosion.

On the coast between the old downtown and the modern parts of Natal there stands the beautiful **Parque das Dunas**, a 12-sq-mile (6-sq-km) reserve of coastal dunes and native vegetation, which can only be visited with a guide.

Did You Know?

The Vale dos Dinossauros contains fossilized footprints of over 80 dinosaur species.

Forte dos Reis Magos

⊘ ⌂ Praia do Forte
☎ (84) 3211 3820 ⏱ 8am–4pm Tue–Sun

Centro de Turismo

⌂ Rua Aderbal de Figueiredo 980 ☎ (84) 3211 6149
⏱ 8am–6pm daily

Parque das Dunas

⊛ ⊘ ⌂ Rua Themistocles Duarte ☎ (84) 3201 3985
⏱ 8am–5:30pm Tue–Sun

Sousa

⌂ F3 ⌂ Paraíba 🚌 From Campina

Brazil's most important prehistoric site, Sousa is located deep in the Paraíba interior, almost on the border with Ceará. It was a large shallow lake where hundreds of dinosaur species roamed, 130 million years ago. Prehistoric tracks can still be seen on the dry riverbed of the Rio de Peixe, also known as the Vale dos Dinossauros. The largest track forms a perfect 164-ft- (50-m-) long trail across the riverbed.

Scattered throughout the valley are numerous other tracks, most of which have not yet been catalogued or protected. Some, indeed, have yet to be discovered. **Grande Cariri Ecotours** can combine trips in this area with visits to Cariri.

Grande Cariri Ecotours

⌂ Rua Joaquim Fagundes, Natal 🌐 caririecotours. com.br

⑦ Maracajaú

🗺G3 🏛Rio Grande do Norte
🚌 ℹ️Rua Jundiaí 644, Natal;
(84) 3232 9065

Maracajaú's coral reefs offer one of the best spots for snorkeling along Brazil's north coast. The reefs lie approximately 4 miles (7 km) offshore. At low tide, the receding ocean leaves the reefs from just 3 to 9 ft (1 to 3 m) underwater, and forms natural pools, called *parrachos*, which combine the water with an array of marine life. They are shallow enough for snorkelers and swimmers to observe dozens of species of colorful, tropical fish. The water is crystal clear and warm year-round, making it a popular destination for swimmers. Tour operators offer scuba-diving trips, but the water is so shallow, it is hardly worth the expense.

The best way to reach Maracajaú is by a dune buggy, departing from Natal (or Genipabu) and traveling north along the coastline. Check the tide tables to time the journey in order to arrive in Maracajaú at, or a few hours before, low tide. The large **Ma-Noa Park**, replete with slides and swimming pools, en route to the coral reefs in Maracajaú, is an enjoyable stop for children.

Ma-Noa Park
⊘ 🕐10am-4pm daily
🌐parkmanoa.com

---

⑩ Campina Grande

🗺G3 🏛Paraíba 🚌🚌From
João Pessoa ℹ️Rua 13 de
Maio 329; (83) 3310 6100

Ideal for experiencing the unique *sertão* (backcountry) culture, Campina Grande is a large market town with some degree of industrial growth. The autumn harvest festival, Festas Juninas, although

REPENTISTAS

Repentista is a popular form of entertainment in areas such as Campina Grande, in the interior of the northeast. Singers engage in a musical duel, making their rhymes up on the spot, trying to score points off their opponent. Musicians sometimes accompany themselves with a tambourine or the viola *nordestina*, developed from the Portuguese seven-string guitar. The singing duelists take turns singing out a stanza, trying to win the favor of the audience by making fun of their opponent.

celebrated everywhere in the northeast, is biggest in Campina Grande. The vast, fairground, **Parque do Povo**, includes several smaller theme parks such as the Sítio São João, a reproduction of a traditional ranch where visitors can observe the rural *nordeste* lifestyle.
The fascinating **Museu de**

Arte Assis Chateaubriand has a striking collection of modern works, with a focus on the work of artists from the northeast.

Parque do Povo
⊘ 🏛Rua Sebastião Donato, Centro 🕐 (83) 3310 6100
🕐During Festas Juninas and other local events

Museu de Arte Assis Chateaubriand

🏛 Av Floriano Peixoto 718, Centro 📞 (83) 3341 1947
🕐 8am-5pm Tue-Fri

Costa Branca

📍 G3 🏛 Rio Grande do Norte 🚍 ℹ️ Centro de Convenções Ponta Negra, Via Costeira Sen. Dinarte Medeiros Mariz, Ponta Negra; www.setur.rn.gov.br

The Costa Branca lies in the far northwest of Rio Grande do Norte. Starting at **Porto do Mangue**, it stretches across the villages of **Areia Branca** and **Grossos** and ends at **Tibaú**. The name "Costa Branca" refers to both the white dunes and the salt works found along this coast. The region has not yet been impacted by mass tourism, and its beaches, mangroves, dunes, and lagoons are blissfully devoid of crowds. **Praia do Rosado**, just west of Porto do Mangue, is famous for its pinkish sand dunes. The red soil underneath the shifting network of dunes mixes with the white sand of the beach giving them an unusual and distinctly soft, pink hue. The coast's largest village, Areia Branca, offers the best tourist facilities for a few days exploring the region. Tibaú is the last village in Rio Grande do Norte, bordering Ceará. Its beach is mostly used by residents of Mossoró. Local artisans use the colored sand to make artistic designs inside small glass bottles.

Mossoró

📍 G3 🏛 Rio Grande do Norte ➡️🚍 ℹ️ SEDINT, Rua Rui Barbosa 282; (84) 3315 4812

Located 34 miles (55 km) inland from the coast, Mossoró is the archetypal *sertão* town of the northeastern interior.

The main places of interest in Mossoró are connected to a dramatic moment in history in 1924, when the towns-people fought off an attack by the legendary bandit leader Lampião *(p305)* and his gang of outlaws. The event is still commemorated every June 13 with great ceremony.

Mossoró is an ideal jumping-off point for visiting the **Lajedo de Soledade**, an archaeological site. Its lime-stone rocks were formed more than 90 million years ago. Tours begin at the visitors' center, at the Museu de Soledade. From here, visitors can depart on a guided walk featuring 10,000-year-old rock paintings, and impressive fossils containing the remains of a range of extinct animals, including saber-toothed tigers.

Lajedo de Soledade

🕐♿ 📞 (84) 3333 1017
🕐 8am-5pm Tue-Sun
🌐 lajedodesoledade. org.br

The cityscape of Campina Grande, and *(inset)* dancers at the city's lively Festas Juninas ↓

Gliding over the striking red cliffs at Canoa Quebrada's beach ↑

11 Canoa Quebrada

 F3 Ceará From Fortaleza Secretaría de Turismo, Rua Dragão do Mar 132, Centro, Aracati; www.aracati.ce.gov.br

In the 1970s, Canoa Quebrada transformed from a quiet fishing village into a popular hippie hangout; it is now a mainstream beach resort.

According to a legend, the name, meaning "Broken Canoe," originated with a Portuguese skipper who wrecked his ship close to shore and donated the useless craft to local fishers. Never having seen such a craft before, locals named the site after it.

The beaches of Canoa Quebrada, featuring red cliffs, fine sand, and offshore reefs, attract many visitors today. The bustling village is known for its cafés and restaurants, and for the bars and clubs lining the main cobblestoned street. Even at the busiest times, however, it is not difficult to get away from the crowds and find a spot on one of the more deserted beaches. Buggy tours are a popular way to get out of town. The tour to Ponta Grossa, 18 miles (30 km) southeast, travels along miles of empty beaches framed by red sandstone cliffs. Other activities include kitesurfing, and sailing on a *jangada* (traditional fishing boat).

About 6 miles (10 km) southwest is the small town of Aracati. It is one of the few historic towns in this part of northeast Brazil. An important center for the 18th-century cattle industry, Aracati has several buildings dating back to this time. Most noteworthy is the Mercado Central (Central Market), still used today.

EAT

Samba Rock
Vibrant central bar and restaurant with live music.

 F2 Praca Principal, Jericoacara

$ $ $

Naturalmente
Eco-conscious beachfront café serving salads, crepes, and açaí bowls.

 F2 Rua da Praia s/n, Jericoacara

$ $ $

Kaze Izakaya
Intimate sushi spot with a dimly lit outside deck.

 F2 Rua São Francisco s/n, Jericoacara

$ $ $

Ello Restaurante
Top-end restaurant offering a six-course tasting menu.

 F2 Rua s/n, Jericoacara

$ $ $

12 Jericoacoara

F2 Ceará From Fortaleza jijocade jericoacara.ce.gov.br

The isolated village of Jericoacoara is a beach lover's

paradise. The village consists of five streets made of sand; in 2002, the entire region was declared a national park, putting a complete halt to the construction of new buildings.

Surrounded by dunes and lagoons, Jeri (as locals call it) is a place for those who like water, waves, and wind. Windsurfers and sailors from around the world flock here from June to January.

Dune buggies are used to explore the surrounding beaches and dunes, and visit the various lagoons, the most beautiful of which are **Lagoa Azul** and **Lagoa do Paraíso**, located about 12 miles (20 km) east of the village. Jeri's postcard view is that of Pedra Furada, a basalt outcrop on the edge of the sea, about a 15-minute walk from the village. The red rock glows in the late afternoon light.

INSIDER TIP

Dunes by Horse

Pay for an afternoon guided horse ride to get some of the sand dunes to yourself. You'll ride away from the crowds and can take beautiful shots on the sand as the sun sets, with nobody else around.

13 Parque Nacional de Ubajara

F2 Ceará From Fortaleza Park: 8am-5pm Tue-Sun; Cable Car: 9am-3pm Wed-Sun icmbio.gov.br/parnaubajara

Located almost exactly halfway between Fortaleza and Teresina, the Parque Nacional de Ubajara is the smallest national park in Brazil. Situated close to the small town of Ubajara, the park features the Ubajara Cave. The entrance to the cave can be reached either by cable car or via a steep, marked trail through the forest. The 3,937-ft- (1,200-m-) long cave is filled with stalactites and stalagmites, the work of several centuries of erosion and calcium deposition.

Fifteen chambers totaling 3,674 ft (1,120 m) have been mapped, of which 1,377 ft (420 m) are open to visitors. Eight galleries are lit up to display some of the amazing formations that have taken shape inside the cave.

The elevation gain is just over 1,640 ft (500 m), and the trail leading up to the cave, though rather strenuous, offers some spectacular views of the Serra da Ipiapaba, as well as several waterfalls and beautiful natural pools. The hike takes about two hours, one-way.

Ubajara Cave, Parque Nacional de Ubajara, and *(inset)* the cable car to the cave ↓

PIAUÍ AND MARANHÃO

The sweltering, tropical state of Maranhão, with its lagoons, giant dunes, and deserted beaches, was originally the homeland of the Tupinambá peoples. Taking advantage of the Portuguese neglect of this area, the French founded the colony of France Équinoxiale in 1612, with coastal São Luís as its capital, by allying with the Tabajara against the Tupinambá (both Indigenous groups were decimated by disease in the 18th century). The French held on to their settlement for only three years before being driven out by the Portuguese. Soon after, the region saw a boom in the cotton and sugar industries, with thousands of enslaved Africans brought in to work the plantations. This boom funded the development of São Luís, now considered one of the most beautiful cities on the continent. After the abolition of slavery in 1888 these industries collapsed, leading to an economic slump that lasted well into the 20th century.

In contrast, the interior of Piauí was colonized before its coast. Portuguese cattle farmers migrated from the southeast in the 1670s, pushing out the Indigenous peoples. Oeiras was founded as a church settlement in 1695, becoming the capital of Piauí in 1759. The port city of Parnaíba was established in 1761, booming as a major exporter of dried meat. In 1852, the capital was transferred to Teresina, Brazil's first planned city, built on the banks of Rio Parnaíba in the searing hinterlands. Cattle ranching dominated the Piauí economy well into the 20th century, while Maranhão managed to exploit its aluminium reserves and palm oil products; however, both remain among the poorest states in the country today.

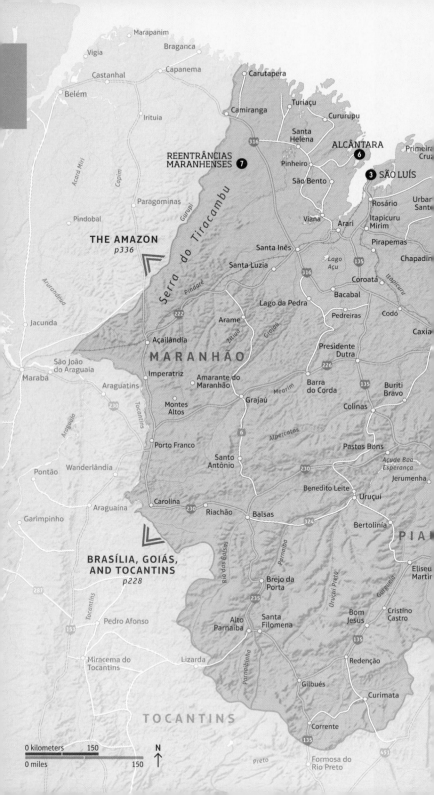

PIAUÍ AND
MARANHÃO

Atlantic

Ocean

PARQUE NACIONAL DOS
LENÇÓIS MARANHENSES
2

rreirinhas
Araiosos
Parnaíba
Camocim
Acaraú
São
Bernardo
Parnaíba
Cocal
Umirim
Fortaleza
Luzilândia
222
Piracuruca
Pinto Martins–Fortaleza
International Airport
guel
ves
Batalha
PARQUE NACIONAL
5 DE SETE CIDADES
Piripiri
Pedroll
coelho
eto
343
Santa
Quitéria
CEARÁ
José de
Freitas
Campo Maior
4 TERESINA
115
Castelo
do Piauí
Russas
on
narama
São Miguel
do Tapuio
PARAÍBA,
RIO GRANDE
DO NORTE,
AND CEARÁ
p308
almeirais
343
316
Sâmbito
120
20
RIO GRANDE
DO NORTE
Amarante
Taua
116
arão de
rajaú
Caninde
Valença
do Piauí
Orós
loriano
230
20
Picos
Fronteiras
Oeiras
Itaim
São José
do Peixe
Jaicós
Araripina
Flores
Fidalgo
Simplício
Mendes
407
316
Costa
Canto do
Buriti
Paulistana
SERGIPE,
ALAGOAS, AND
PERNAMBUCO
p292
São João
do Piauí
1 PARQUE NACIONAL DE
SERRA DA CAPIVARA
ão Raimundo
Nonato
Juàzeiro
BAHIA
p274
Sento Sé
Paçarrão
São Francisco
BAHIA
Canudos
Carira
Jeremoabo
ALAGOAS
Barragem de
Sobradinho
Jacaré
Xique-Xique
Jacobina
SERGIPE

PIAUÍ AND
MARANHÃO

Must Sees

1 Parque Nacional de Serra
da Capivara

2 Parque Nacional dos
Lençóis Maranhenses

3 São Luís

Experience More

4 Teresina

5 Parque Nacional de Sete Cidades

6 Alcântara

7 Reentrâncias Maranhenses

❶

PARQUE NACIONAL DE SERRA DA CAPIVARA

🗺F3 🏠 Coronel José Dias, Piauí 🚌 🕓 6am-6pm daily 🛈 Museu de Homem Americano, Bairro Campestre, São Raimundo Nonato; www.fumdham.org.br

Like a Surrealist's sculpture park, the unique rock formations that cluster this Caatinga scrubland form the heritage site of South America's first settlers.

> 💬 INSIDER TIP
> **Take a Hike**
>
> Well-marked trails provide a wide range of hikes. A trail guide (who can take groups of up to eight people) is required, and details are available from the park administration office in São Raimundo Nonato. A few English-speaking guides can be found, but for a slightly higher fee.

Piauí's most compelling park is the sprawling Serra da Capivara, which was inaugurated in 1979 and is located in the far south of the state. The park's impressive canyons, plateaus, and rock formations also form one of Brazil's most important prehistoric sites, one that was designated a UNESCO World Heritage Site in 1991.

Over 30,000 rock paintings have been discovered within the park, with scientists estimating that many of these were created

↑ The burnished colors of the park, as seen from the top of Pedra Furada

between 6,000 and 12,000 years ago. The oldest drawings may date as far back as 29,000 years. The paintings portray aspects of prehistoric life such as the hunt, dances, and other rituals.

The eroded massifs here are made of sandstone dating back some 430 million years. It is beneath such monumental rocks as Pedra Furada (Pierced Rock) that many of the paintings can be found. A series of trails through the park connect the many other rock shelters and overhangs that are decorated with paintings, which include signposted routes for mountain-biking and rappeling.

The park is best explored between January and July, when the lush vegetation provides more shade from the intense heat of the day. Entry is free, but a guide is required. An impressive museum of the site can be visited in the nearby town of São Raimundo Nonato.

> **The park's impressive canyons, plateaus, and rock formations also form one of Brazil's most important prehistoric sites, one that was designated a UNESCO World Heritage Site in 1991.**

CAPIVARA ROCK ART

Recognized by UNESCO as one of the world's most important archaeological sites, the rock art of Capivara provides a unique pictorial archive of the earliest peoples in the Americas. The paintings, which mostly form linear panels in the rock face, were made with natural pigments of red, yellow, and gray. They depicted aspects of everyday life, including sex, dancing and fighting, supernatural spiritual beings, and hunting scenes, featuring many animals such as deer, armadillo, jaguar, tapir, and the now-extinct giant rhea.

EXPERIENCE Piauí and Maranhão

PARQUE NACIONAL DOS LENÇÓIS MARANHENSES

⊞E2 ⊡Piauí/Maranhão ✈🚌From Teresina 🚌From Lençóis Maranhenses to Barreirinhas, then to Atins 🛈Rua Itaúna 1434, Parnaíba; (98) 3349 1267

This isolated expanse in the far north of Brazil comprises glowing lagoons, sun-bleached dunes, and endless empty beaches. The Parque Nacional dos Lençóis Maranhenses – and the nearby Parnaiba Delta – is a rich haven of birdlife, attracting the most adventurous ecotourists and others in search of the ultimate oasis.

Straddling Piauí and Maranhão, the Parque Nacional dos Lençóis Maranhenses offers miles of spectacular sand dunes created by strong coastal winds. From May to August, rain collects in the basins between dunes, forming countless crystal-clear freshwater lagoons. In June, when the water levels are at their highest, the Lençóis dunes look like an array of white stripes, interspersed with sparkling ribbons of blue, turquoise, and green. On foot, visitors can only access a small portion of the park; for the full impact, take a sightseeing flight from São Luís.

The undulating dunes of the park, broken up by dazzling pockets of turquoise ↑

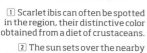

① Scarlet ibis can often be spotted in the region, their distinctive color obtained from a diet of crustaceans.

② The sun sets over the nearby Delta do Parnaíba, where the river meanders through some 83 islands.

③ Two swimmers take a dip in one of the park's turquoise lagoons.

THE VERSATILE BURITI PALM TREE

The delta area's dense vegetation is dominated by the multi-purpose buriti palm tree, known as the "Tree of Life" due to its versatility. The fruit is edible and used to make wine, juice, jam, and ice cream. The palm's trunk can be used for house poles, and its bark can be spun into twine. The plant's fronds can be made into thatch roofs and baskets, its twigs into placemats, and the seeds can be fashioned into jewelry.

3
SÃO LUÍS

 E2 Maranhão *i* Setur, Rua da Palma 53;
www.saoluis.ma.gov.br/setur

Home to Brazil's best examples of Portuguese colonial
architecture, São Luís was, ironically, founded by the
French in 1612. The city was settled under Portuguese
rule in 1644. By the late 1800s, as slavery ended and
the city's cotton industry began to struggle, São Luís
went into decline. In the 1970s, the government
invested in preservation, and in 1997, the core of São
Luís was designated a UNESCO World Heritage Site.

1
Palácio dos Leões

Avenida Dom Pedro II
9am-5pm Tue-Sun
sectur.ma.gov.br/
palacio-dos-leoes

Dominating the UNESCO-
recognized World Heritage
center of São Luís, this distinguished historic building is
now home to Maranhão
state's government. Fronted
by two bronze lions and
featuring an immaculately
symmetrical white facade,
the palace holds a strategic
shoreside position, built on
the former site of the French
Fort St. Louis, and flanked by
the Anil and Bacanga rivers.
One wing remains open to
the public today, housing a
fine collection dating from
the 16th century, including
period furniture, tapestries,
sculptures, and ornaments.

2
Centro de Cultura Popular Vieira Filho

Rua do Giz 221 (98)
3218 9926 9am-6pm
Tue-Sat, 9am-1pm Sun

The Center of Popular Culture
(also known as the Casa da
Festa) showcases the traditions and customs of the Festa
do Divino Espírito Santo. The
highlights of the museum are
the poster-size photographs
of the actual celebrations,
including some compelling
black-and-white images of
the elderly women who once
served as festival queens.

3
Centro de Criatividade Odylo Costa Filho

Rampa do Comércio 200,
Praia Grande (98) 3218
9932

This small but impressive arts
complex in the historic center
includes a theater, cinema,
and library. It also has extensive exhibition space, with
community activities including
dance workshops and craft
shows. Its exhibitions are free

↑ A steep, cobblestoned street in the historical center of São Luís, a UNESCO World Heritage Site

A unique folklore event endemic to northeast Brazil, the Festa do Bumba Meu Boi revolves around a legendary folktale about the life, death, and resurrection of a magical Brazilian bull. Over the centuries, the celebration has grown into a huge festival, with neighborhood groups competing to put on the best re-enactment of the story. A papier-mâché bull is created and displayed in raucous parades, where participants take on the roles of healers, peasants, and cowboys.

to the public, and cover a wide range, from photography to modern Afro-Brazilian art.

Casa do Maranhão

🏛 Rua do Trapiche s/n
🕐 9am–5pm Mon–Thu (until 5:30pm Fri)
🌐 saoluis.ma.gov.br/setur

The Casa do Maranhão is one of the city's most interesting museums, offering two floors of colorful exhibits that explain the Festa do Bumba Meu Boi, one of the most popular festivals in Brazil. Besides this, the collection focuses on the rich folklore and traditions from across Maranhão. Exhibits include musical instruments, costumed figures, and religious artifacts. Although the explanations are in Portuguese only, it's a richly rewarding site.

Igreja da Sé

🏛 Praça Dom Pedro II
🕐 8:30am–6:30pm

The city's twin-towered cathedral is built on the site of an original 1615 church named Nossa Senhora da Vitoria (Our Lady of Victory), in tribute to a battle won by the Portuguese over the French in the same year. Since then another church has been built, with renovations over the centuries. A Neo-Classical facade was added in 1922, lending the cathedral an imposing appearance.

São Luís Beaches

São Luís is blessed with a string of excellent beaches, all of which can be easily accessed by bus from the city center. Farther north, popular beaches include Ponta d'Areia, São Marcos, Praia do Calhau, Calhau, and Olho d'Agua. Calhau, located 6 miles (10 km) from São Luís, is widely considered to be one of the nicest beaches around the city. Many busy kiosks and restaurants line the beachside boulevard. Adjacent to this beach is the quieter Praia do Caolho, where the water is calm and the restaurants are fewer.

↑ Colorful flags hanging throughout the city in preparation for the Festa do Bumba Meu Boi

A SHORT WALK
SÃO LUÍS

Distance 1.3 km (0.8 miles) **Nearest bus**
Integration Praia Grande **Time** 16 minutes

The rich and diverse historical center of São
Luís makes it ideal for touring on foot. It is the
oldest part of the city, known interchangeably
as the Praia Grande, the Reviver, and the
Centro Histórico. All of the city's museums and
beautifully preserved historic sites are located
here. The center's cobbled streets are marked
by colonial mansions and brightly colored
buildings featuring distinctive Portuguese
tiles and cast-iron balconies.

Did You Know?

São Luís is known as
the "Island of Love" or
the "Brazilian Athens"
due to its many famous
poets and writers.

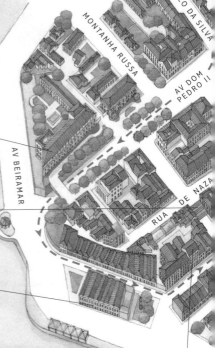

Palácio dos Leões (p330)
*was built in 1766 on the site of the
original French Fort St. Louis,
and is now home to the
Maranhão state government.*

Beco Catarina Mina *is a picturesque
18th-century alley connecting the
lower-lying streets of the historic center
with Avenida Dom Pedro II.*

*The former 19th-century customs
building,* **Casa do Maranhão** (p331),
*now houses a fine collection of Bumba
Meu Boi folklore. Guides walk visitors
through the colorful exhibits.*

**Museu de Arte
Visuais** *is covered
in elaborate, colored
Portuguese tiles.*

← A colonial building
decorated with colorful
Portugese tiles

Locator Map
For more detail see p330

↑ Vista of the Praça Benedito Leite in the historical center of São Luís

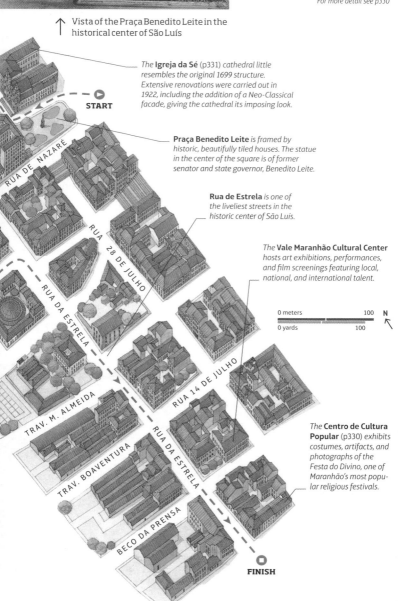

The **Igreja da Sé** (p331) *cathedral little resembles the original 1699 structure. Extensive renovations were carried out in 1922, including the addition of a Neo-Classical facade, giving the cathedral its imposing look.*

START

Praça Benedito Leite *is framed by historic, beautifully tiled houses. The statue in the center of the square is of former senator and state governor, Benedito Leite.*

Rua de Estrela *is one of the liveliest streets in the historic center of São Luís.*

The **Vale Maranhão Cultural Center** *hosts art exhibitions, performances, and film screenings featuring local, national, and international talent.*

RUA DE NAZARÉ

RUA 28 DE JULHO

RUA DA ESTRELA

TRAV. M. ALMEIDA

TRAV. BOAVENTURA

RUA 14 DE JULHO

RUA DA ESTRELA

BECO DA PRENSA

0 meters 100
0 yards 100

N

The **Centro de Cultura Popular** (p330) *exhibits costumes, artifacts, and photographs of the Festa do Divino, one of Maranhão's most popular religious festivals.*

FINISH

EXPERIENCE MORE

EXPERIENCE Piauí and Maranhão

④

Teresina

🅰F3 🏠Piauí ✈🚌 ℹ️Setur, Av Universitária, Edifício Diamond Center 750; www.pmt.pi.gov.br

Founded in 1852, Teresina was named in honor of the Empress Teresa Cristina, wife of Brazilian Emperor Dom Pedro II. Teresina has the dubious honor of being one of Brazil's hottest cities, although Rio Parnaíba and Rio Poti, as well as several large, tree-shaded squares scattered throughout Teresina, moderate the worst of the city's scorching heat.

Most historic buildings date back only to the end of the 19th century. One of the oldest buildings is the cathedral, **Nossa Senhora do Amparo**. Construction was started in 1851 but completed only in 1952. More modern, but also interesting, is the Palácio Karnak, Piauí's new state legislature. Built in 1926, the palace's facade was modeled on an ancient Egyptian temple. The former state legislature is now home to the **Museu do Piauí**. Its small collection provides a good overview of regional history, including both pre-historic artifacts and folk art.

Nossa Senhora do Amparo
🏠Rua Rui Barbosa 270, Centro 🕑7:15am-3pm daily

Museu do Piauí
🏠Rua Areolino de Abreu 900, Centro 📞(86) 3221 6027 🕑8am-5pm Tue-Fri

⑤

Parque Nacional de Sete Cidades

🅰F2 🏠Rodovia BR-222, Km 64, Piracuruca 🚌From Teresina ℹ️Ibama Office, Centro de Visitantes; (86) 3343 1342 🕑8am-5pm daily

The name Sete Cidades (Seven Cities) refers to seven distinct and unusual rock formations, spread out in the park along 7 miles (12 km) of trails. Only the first six are accessible to the public.

> ## CRISPIM, THE BOWL HEAD
>
> A Piauí legend (Cabeça de Cuia) tells the story of Crispim, a fisher who lived by the banks of the Rio Parnaíba. Frustrated after not catching any fish, he beat his mother with a bone. As she lay dying, she cursed him, condemning him to live as a bowl-headed monster in the river. Locals still tell of spotting Crispim there.

Sculpted by rain, wind, heat, and erosion, the rocks are said to resemble animals, people, mythological beings, and even human-made structures.

Among the shapes are Mapa do Brasil, a backward-facing map of Brazil, and Biblioteca (Library), both in Quarta Cidade (Fourth City). Segundo Cidade, the second of the seven "cities," has a 147-ft- (45-m-) tall lookout with views out over five of the cities of stone. There are also more than 2,000 prehistoric rock paintings, some 6,000 years old. The most impressive painting, Pedra de Inscrição (Inscribed Rock), said to be marked with cryptic historic runes, can be seen at Quinta Cidade (Fifth City).

Alcântara

A E2 **⌂** Maranhão **🚌** From São Luís **ℹ** Casa Municipal de Turismo; (98) 3485 1100

Just across from São Luís, Alcântara lies on the other side of the Baía de São Marcos. The city was colonized by the Portuguese in the 1640s, and used as a temporary capital and base during the campaign to drive the Dutch away from São Luís. Alcântara reached its zenith in the 19th century as the regional center for the surrounding sugar and cotton plantations. When slavery was abolished in 1888, the local economy crashed, the white upper class departed, and many of the fine mansions stood abandoned.

Restoration has been slow and quite a few of the city's churches, such as the striking São Matias church, and mansions remain as ruins, giving the city its own charm. These ruins are now the town's main tourist attractions. The Brazilian Heritage Institute, Iphan, has restored several of the old mansions as

← Unusual rock formations in the Parque Nacional de Sete Cidades

↑ The ruins of the 17th century São Matias church in Matriz Plaza, Alcântara

museums. The best is the **Museu Casa Histórica de Alcântara**, featuring period furniture and glassware. Informative wall plaques and well-trained guides make getting around in the museum easy.

Museu Casa Histórica de Alcântara

 ⌂ Praça de Matriz **🕐** 9:30am–4:30pm Tue–Sun

Reentrâncias Maranhenses

A E2 **⌂** Maranhão **🚌** From São Luís to Cururupu **🚤** From Cururupu **ℹ** Setur, Rua da Palma 53, São Luís; (98) 3212 6210/11

One of the world's largest wetlands, the Reentrâncias Maranhenses is also one of Maranhão's more off-the-beaten-track natural attractions. The small town of Cururupu to the north of São Luís offers the best access to the Reentrâncias Maranhenses, with boats departing regularly.

Spread over an area of 10,350 sq miles (26,800 sq km), the park forms an important habitat for shorebirds such as scarlet ibis, spoonbills, and black-bellied plovers, as well as an array of marine life, including sea turtles and manatees. The region is geographically diverse and consists of a complex riverine system of extensive bays, coves, and rugged coastline covered mainly by mangrove forest.

One of the more popular destinations here is the Ilha dos Lençóis, northeast of Cururupu. Its geography somewhat resembles the Lençóis Maranhenses (p328), with its endless landscapes of dunes and lagoons.

> **One of the world's largest wetlands, the Reentrâncias Maranhenses is also one of Maranhão's more off-the-beaten-track natural attractions.**

THE AMAZON

Humans have inhabited the Amazon for millenia: remarkably, the earliest ceramics known in the Americas were found near Santarém – not the Andes – and date back some 10,000 years. Spanish conquistador Francisco de Orellana, who claimed to have seen hundreds of inhabited towns and villages on his expedition here in 1542, named the region the Amazon when he saw Indigenous female warriors that reminded him of the Greek myth. In subsequent years, although only a handful of Portuguese settlers and Catholic missions penetrated the rainforest, the spread of diseases from Europe – such as smallpox – proved devastating, reducing an estimated five million Indigenous peoples to 200,000 by the 1980s.

Ravaged in 1835 by the Cabanagem – a bloody struggle for regional independence – the Amazon rebounded in the 1870s thanks to the rubber boom. Some of the world's wealthiest people made their fortunes on the backs of enslaved Indigenous *seringueiros* (rubber tappers). By 1900 Manaus and Belém were two of the richest cities in Brazil, but the boom ended by 1914 and the region once again became a backwater.

Gold mining and large-scale exploitation – and destruction – of the rainforest started in the 1960s and 70s, impacting the Indigenous population that still made their home in the region. Of particular note is the plight of the Yanomami, whose Roraima homelands have been invaded by illegal gold prospectors since the early 1970s. Deforestation has also continued, mainly due to slash-and-burn farming; in the first half of 2022, nearly 1,540 sq miles (4,000 sq km) of Brazilian Amazon rainforest was lost to fires, the worst figure since 2015.

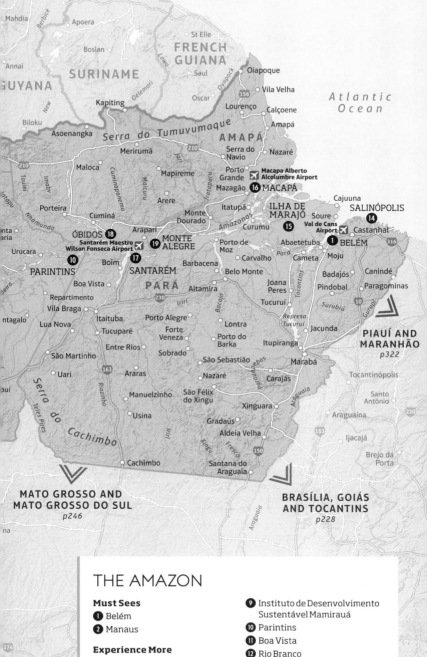

THE AMAZON

Must Sees
1. Belém
2. Manaus

Experience More
3. Presidente Figueiredo
4. Rio Negro and Ilhas de Anavilhanas
5. Novo Airão
6. Encontro das Aguas
7. Lago Manaquiri
8. Lago Mamori
9. Instituto de Desenvolvimento Sustentável Mamirauá
10. Parintins
11. Boa Vista
12. Rio Branco
13. Porto Velho
14. Salinópolis
15. Ilha de Marajó
16. Macapá
17. Santarém
18. Óbidos
19. Monte Alegre

①

BELÉM

▲E2 **🏛Pará** **✈7 miles (12 km) N of town** **🚌Praça da Leitura** **⛴From Macapá, Manaus & Santarém** **ℹ Belémtur, Av Presidente Vargas 158, (91) 3073 9802; Paratur, Rua General Gurjão 347, Campina, (91) 3110 8700**

Belém was founded in 1616 by the Portuguese to guard the mouth of the Amazon river against other European powers, and the city soon became a major trading port. It was ravaged during the Cabanagem Rebellion, a popular revolt in 1835, but had more than recovered its economic position by the late 19th century, largely due to the rubber boom. It is still the most important port in northern Brazil, and a fascinating place to explore.

Did You Know?

During Círio de Nazaré, locals drag an enormous rope through the streets in order to purge their sins.

①

Estação das Docas

🏛Blvd Castilho França, Campina **🕐10am-midnight daily (from 9am Sun; until 1am Wed & 2am Thu-Sat)** **🌐estacaodasdocas.com.br**

Three former warehouses overlooking the river have been turned into a stylish, air-conditioned shopping, dining, and entertainment space. Visitors can enjoy the lively atmosphere until late at night.

②

Forte do Presepio

🏛Praça Frei Caetano Brandão 117 **📞(91) 4009 8828** **🕐9am-5pm Tue-Sun**

This fort was first built of wood and mud plaster by the Portuguese colonists in 1616. It now houses the Museu do Encontro, a small historical museum presenting the city's history and the early conquest of the Amazon.

③

Ver o Peso

🏛Av Castilhos França **📞(91) 3241 2022** **🕐5am-6:30pm Mon-Sat (fish market to 2pm)**

Incredibly hectic early in the morning, Ver o Peso, or "See the Weight," was originally a colonial customs point (Posto Fiscal), where goods were assessed for taxation purposes. These days, its most obvious feature is the iron-built fish market, the Mercado de Ferro, which was designed and made in England and assembled here in the late 19th century. The variety of seafood inside is staggering. Outside, the main market expands into stalls that sell everything from jungle fruits and *farinha* (manioc, or cassava-root, flour) to medicinal herbs and aromatic oils.

↑ The city of Belém, sited on the Amazon

Prefeitura, but much of it can now be visited. It is home to the Museu de Arte de Belém and its fine collection of Brazilian 20th-century artworks.

---

⑤

Theatro da Paz

🏛 Praça da República 📞 (91) 4009 8750 🕐 Guided visits hourly: 9am–5pm Tue–Fri (until noon Sat & 11am Sun)

This Neo-Classical opera house was built in 1878, and its furnishings are still largely original. Legendary Russian ballerina Anna Pavlova is one of the great artists who performed here.

---

⑥

Basilica de Nossa Senhora de Nazare

🏛 Praça Justo Chermont (museum: Rua Padre Champagnat) 📞 (91) 4009 8400 🕐 7am–7pm Mon–Fri (to 6pm Sat), 7am–noon & 3–8pm Sun; museum: 10am–5pm Tue–Fri (until 2pm Sat & Sun)

The basilica's spectacular interior makes it one of the

most stunning churches in Brazil. Partially modeled on St. Peter's in Rome, it was completed in 1909 and stands on 16 major arches. It houses the miraculous Virgin image of Nossa Senhora de Nazaré, which attracts over a million visitors to the Círio de Nazaré, or the Festival of Candles, every October. Near the Forte do Presepio is the Museu do Círio, which is devoted to the cult of the Círio and exhibits some 2,000 pieces relating to the religious festival.

④

Palacio Antonio Lemos

🏛 Praça Dom Pedro II 📞 (91) 3114 1028 🔒 Until further notice

This palace housed municipal authorities between 1868 and 1883. It still has offices for the

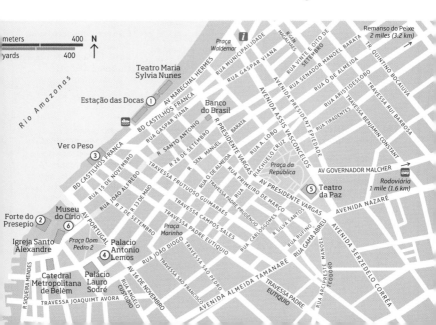

↑ A pleasant downtown square in the port city of Manaus

MANAUS

 **C2** Amazonas Av Djalma Batista 40, Manaus Porto Flutuante AmazonasTur, Manaus Airport; www.manausonline.com

Manaus is a legendary city, located at the heart of the Amazon forest on the banks of the Rio Negro, close to where this great river blends with the even larger Amazon river. Manaus is a busy city, combining the hectic pace of a modern port with the laid-back feel of a jungle town. Its brief economic boom between 1888 and 1912 – due to the export of rubber – catapulted Manaus into wealthy city status, but the only remaining signs of this are the port's European buildings and the splendid Teatro Amazonas (p344).

① Mercado Municipal Adolpho Lisboa

Rua dos Barés 46 (92) 3234 8441 For renovation

This municipal market was built in 1883, very close to the port. Looking up to its elegant ceiling and stunning Art Nouveau ironwork structure, it is not difficult to see that the design was inspired by Gustave Eiffel's work. The cultural evening held here on the last Friday of every month offers a chance to experience regional music, food, and entertainment.

② Alfândega

Rua Marquês de Santa Cruz (92) 3622 3025 8am-noon Mon-Sat

Constructed in 1906 at the height of the rubber boom, the Alfândega (Customs House), like many of the well-engineered features of Manaus from this period, was entirely pre-fabricated in England, with the stone used brought from Scotland. Much of this refined building's glory can be seen from the Praça Adalberto Valle opposite.

③ Palacete Provincial

Praça Heliodoro Balbi, s/n, Centro (92) 3631 6047 9am-7pm Tue-Thu (to 8pm Fri & Sat)

Built in 1874 originally to house the police headquarters, the

 GREAT VIEW Waterfront City

From the floating docks (Porto Flutuante) to the Mercado Municipal, the Manaus waterfront offers great scenes of the city's working life. There's a steady bustle of boats, from traditional Amazonian ferries to fishing trawlers and great cruise ships.

> A fascinating anthropology and ethnology museum, the Museum of Northern Man has exhibits on the way of life of the people of northern Brazil.

Palacete Provincial is now a cultural center, which is home to several interesting museums and collections. These include the Museum of Image and Sound, the Military Police Museum, and the Numismatic Museum. The Palacete's highlight is the art gallery, which features modern and contemporary art by regional painters, photographers, and installation artists. The exuberant paintings of local flora and fauna by Manaus local Rita Loureiro are especially noteworthy.

④
Palácio Rio Negro

⌂ Av 7 de Setembro 1546
☎ (92) 3232 4450 🕒 9am–3pm Mon–Fri (to 2pm Sun)

A remarkably well-preserved colonial-period mansion, the almost garish Palácio Rio Negro was built in 1903 during the rubber boom. It was originally home to an eccentric German rubber baron, Waldemar Scholz, and in later years housed the local government. These days, much of it has been opened to the public as a cultural center. The palace hosts art exhibitions, events, and film screenings.

⑤
Museu do Homem do Norte

⌂ Centro Cultural dos Povos da Amazônia, Praça Francisco Pereira da Silva
☎ (92) 2125 5300 🕒 9am–5pm Mon–Fri

A fascinating anthropology and ethnology museum, the Museum of Northern Man has exhibits on the way of life of the people of northern Brazil. It mainly focuses on people of mixed Indigenous Brazilian and European ancestry; this community, who live along the riverbanks, are known locally as the *caboclos* (copper-colored). Cultural, social, and economic aspects of life in northern Brazil are detailed with photographs, artifacts, and everyday objects, such as historic cooking utensils, costumes, and an interesting collection of Indigenous weapons, including the infamous *furador de olhos* (eye piercer). There are also displays on *guaraná* (a native plant) and rubber production.

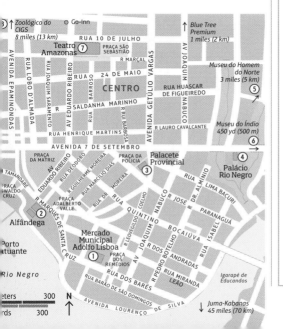

Museu do Índio

📍 Rua Duque de Caxias 296
📞 (92) 3635 1922 🕐 8:30–11:30am & 1–4:30pm Mon–Fri, 8:30am–noon Sat

An excellent ethnographic museum, the Indian Museum was established by Salesian nuns and is based on their work as missionaries in the Rio Negro area. There are many feather-work exhibits and some weapons and tools, as well as artworks, household and sacred objects on display. Explanations of the displays are in Portuguese, English, and German.

Teatro Amazonas

📍 Av Eduardo Ribeira 659
📞 (92) 3232 1768 🕐 9am–5pm Mon–Sat

Built at the end of the 19th century during the belle époque, when fortunes were made from the extraction of rubber in Manaus, the Teatro Amazonas remains one of the jewels of the Amazon region. This grand Renaissance-style opera house was designed by the Gabinete Português de Engenharia de Lisbon

(Portuguese Engineering Academy of Lisbon). Inaugurated on December 31, 1896, it was two more years before construction was completed and the prominent landmark with its glistening dome appeared above the port. The impressive

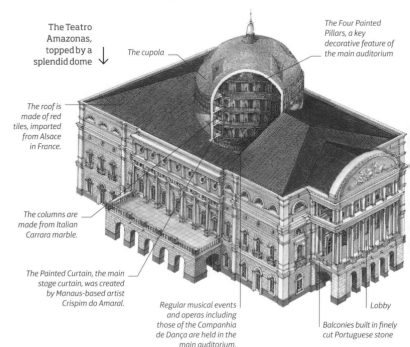

The Teatro Amazonas, topped by a splendid dome ↓

The cupola

The Four Painted Pillars, a key decorative feature of the main auditorium

The roof is made of red tiles, imported from Alsace in France.

The columns are made from Italian Carrara marble.

The Painted Curtain, the main stage curtain, was created by Manaus-based artist Crispim do Amaral.

Regular musical events and operas including those of the Companhia de Dança are held in the main auditorium.

Lobby

Balconies built in finely cut Portuguese stone

↑ The stage and curved balconies of the Teatro Amazonas's auditorium

Did You Know?

The four pillars in Teatro Amazonas's main auditorium were painted in Paris then built in Manaus.

cupola was created using 36,000 colorful ceramic tiles, imported from Alsace on the Franco-German border. Restoration work carried out in 2018 included renovation of the stage curtain, which is more than 100 years old.

Zoológico do CIGS

🏠 Av São Jorge   📞 (92) 2125 6402   🕐 9am–5pm Tue–Sun

One of the few places around Manaus where you might see a jaguar at close quarters is the fascinating Zoológico do CIGS. Located toward Ponta Negra in the army jungle training center, this small zoo is home to over 200 animals including many caimans, monkeys, birds, and an unforgettable large pit full of anacondas.

EXPERIENCE MORE

③

Presidente Figueiredo

🅰C2   🏠80 miles (128 km) N of Manaus   🚌   ℹ️ Centro Turistico, Km 107 (BR 174); (92) 9912 9174

Presidente Figueiredo is a small town linked to Manaus by a relatively good road. More than 100 waterfalls are dotted around the town, as well as some caves. Tours can be booked from Manaus or with local guides through the tourist information office located at the bus stop.

One of the best waterfalls is the Pedra Furada, where the water gushes out of a hole in the rocks. The waterfalls Cachoeira Iracema, Pedra da Lua Branca, and Natal are on the Rio Urubuí and only accessible by boat.

Located east of Presidente Figueiredo, off the AM-240, is Caverna Refúgio do Maroaga, and nearby, another attractive cave is Caverna Maruaga, which has shallow river running over its floor. Permission to visit the caves has to be obtained from the tourist information office in Manaus.

↑ A light waterfall creating a shallow stream at Caverna Maruaga

④

Rio Negro and Ilhas de Anavilhanas

🅰C2   🏠60 miles (90 km) NW of Manaus   🚌   ℹ️ Amazonastur, Av Ajuricaba s/n, Novo Airão; (92) 3365 1391

One of South America's least visited regions, the Rio Negro area possesses distinctive flora created by its acidic waters and soil type. There is a lower density of wildlife here than any other area along the Rio Negro. There are few towns and even fewer tourist facilities along the river, which stretches right up to the Colombian and Venezuelan borders.

Ilhas de Anavilhanas is a biological reserve and the largest group of freshwater islands in the world. Tours here are offered from Manaus or from Novo Airão. There are over 250 uninhabited islands stretching for more than 187 miles (300 km). Depending on the season and time of day, it is possible to see caimans, sloths, snakes, and a range of bird species. Sprawled across 1,350 sq miles (3,500 sq km) of protected rainforest on the left bank of the Rio Negro, the Estação Ecológica de Anavilhanas (Ecological Station of Anavilhanas) is part of the Anavilhanas islands. Created in 1998 and named after the Archipelago dos Anavilhanas, it has several species in great danger of extinction, including jaguars and night monkeys.

A day-and-a-half's journey from Ilhas de Anavilhanas, Barcelos, the only town of any size along the river, is an interesting place to start a jungle expedition. Another two days upriver is the town of São Gabriel Da Cachoeira, a beautiful place deep in the Amazon with stunning jungle scenery and wildlife.

Novo Airão

C2 71 miles (115 km) W of Manaus From Manaus From Manaus

The small town of Novo Airão is located on the western side of the Rio Negro, opposite the Archipelago dos Anavilhanas. Pleasant, yet laid-back, with only a handful of attractions, the town draws tourists mainly for the pink dolphins that come to a floating platform at Novo Airão's small port. They are fed fish every hour and visitors can see these friendly creatures up-close as they venture to the surface. Some visitors, however, may prefer to see the dolphins out in the wild by taking a boat tour.

The area neighboring Novo Airão is home to a number of interesting sights, such as Airão Velho, the overgrown ruins of the old town center, with prehistoric spiral and figure-like petroglyphs. The beautiful and peaceful Igarapé do Mato Grosso, a forested section of a tributary river nearby, makes a great place for a walk or a swim in fresh water. The **Parque Nacional Jaú** is a two-day trip from Novo Airão, and is a wonderful opportunity to visit virgin Amazon rainforest. A permit, from the **Ibama** office in Manaus, is required to visit here, and the trip is best done with a registered tour operator.

Parque Nacional Jaú
 (92) 3365 1345

Ibama
Rua Ministro João Gonçalves de Souza s/n, Manaus (92) 3878 7150

Did You Know?

Male Amazonian pink river dolphins can weigh up to 350 pounds (160 kg).

Encontro das Aguas

C2 From Manaus

One of the main tours offered from Manaus, the Encontro das Aguas (Meeting of the Waters) is where the Rio Solimões joins the Rio Negro. The relatively creamy and alkaline light-brown water of the Solimões (Amazon) river takes several miles to absorb the dark, acid water coming in from the Rio Negro. The Solimões is light because it starts mainly in the Andes and brings plenty of silt with it. The Rio Negro wells up primarily in the swamplands and smaller hills of the north-eastern Amazon and contains much more decomposed plant life than it does soil or silt.

Small boats go out from Manaus allowing people to take photographs and to see the clear line between light brown and black running down the middle of the river. The best time to visit is between 7am and 10am.

←

The reflective waters of the Rio Negro at Novo Airão

Local people traveling on a boat across the Amazon river ↑

 7

Lago Manaquiri

▲C2 ⏹40 miles (64 km) SW of Manaus 🆆amazon astur.am.gov.br

A five-hour boat ride from Manaus, the backwater lake of Manaquiri is best entered first via the Rio Solimões, then upstream to a tributary that leads to the lake. Its waters rise and fall with the seasons. Relatively isolated, the Lago Manaquiri is usually a good spot for seeing waterbirds, including the great egret (Casmerodius albus) and fish eagles. It is not unusual to see caimans and large Amazonian alligators on the sandy shore.

The lake provides sustenance to the small fishing town of Manaquiri, and the local economy depends more on this sector than on tourism. In 2005, however, both were hit by the worst drought in many years, when the lagoons evaporated, and thousands of dead fish lay on the bed of the dried-up lake.

The changed climatic conditions continue to deplete fish in the area. Nonetheless, fishing remains the main activity, and there are many tour operators based in Manaus offering budget fishing packages. It is always best to book your trip through

a travel company registered with the Brazilian Tourism Bureau. Some of the tour agencies provide typical Amazon riverboats, which may come fully equipped with kitchen, dining area, bathroom, shower, and canopied sundeck.

Fishing is best in the dry season, which usually lasts from August to December or January.

 8

Lago Mamori

▲C2 ⏹60 miles (96 km) SE of Manaus

Easily accessible by road and boat from Manaus, the elongated and breathtaking Lago Mamori is located in a lush rainforest setting. Much of it is surrounded by narrow creeks, hidden among forests full of sloths, monkeys, and colorful, noisy tropical birds. The river and lake offer the opportunity to see both pink and gray river dolphins, as well as to go piranha fishing. Nearby, the Lago Arara is great for fishing, and home to a pink dolphin feeding ground.

The local caboclo people, have been here for generations and live in scattered riverside communities,

occasionally coming together for celebrations. They earn their living by producing farinha (manioc flour), rearing cattle, and fishing.

Visits to the caboclo homes can be organized by **Amazon Gero Tours**. Run independently by English-speaking Gero Mesquita, the company can book hotels, arrange transport, and meticulously plan tours.

Farther upstream and deeper into the forest from here, the Rio Juma region offers better access to wildlife, but requires expedition-type preparation and several days.

Amazon Green Tours, a tour company based in Manaus, can arrange expeditions in Amazônia, offering short package tours, as well as longer safaris.

It is possible to stay either in a floating lodge, or in one of the many jungle lodges along the Rio Juma. Most of them offer jungle hikes, piranha fishing, and caiman spotting at night.

Amazon Gero Tours
🕙 ▣Rua Tapajós 27, Centro, Manaus 🆆amazon gero.com

Amazon Green Tours
🕙 ▣Rua 10 de Julho 718, Manaus 🆆amazongreen tours.com.br

On the water in the
Mamirauá Sustainable
Development Reserve ↑

Instituto de Desenvolvimento Sustentável Mamirauá

🅐 B2 🅐 280 miles (450 km)
W of Manaus 🆆 mamiraua.
org.br

Located at the confluence of
two rivers, the Rio Solimões
and Rio Japurá, the Mamirauá
Sustainable Development
Reserve covers an area of
5703 sq miles (14,770 sq km).
Since 1990, when it was
declared an ecological station,
the Mamirauá Reserve has
been one of Brazil's most
prized ecotourism spots.
Splendid and luxuriant, its
várzea (seasonally flooded)
vegetation offers plenty of
opportunity for spotting
abundant wildlife, including
endemic species such as the
white uakari monkey and
the black-headed squirrel
monkey. The annual flood
transforms the life of the
whole region. During the high-
water season (May–July), fish
invade the flooded forest and
disperse seeds as they move
about. More than 300 species
of fish have already been
catalogued in the reserve.
Mamirauá is also home to pink
river dolphin, great egret, and
the rare scarlet macaw. The
neotropic cormorant, whose
diet consists mainly of fish,

can be spotted swimming and
feeding in large, noisy flocks.
During the dry season
(September–November)
people can walk on trails, but
when the rainy season comes,
canoes must be used to travel
through the watery terrain.
The preserve's ecotourism
program features a range
of activities, which includes
nature expeditions in the
lakes and trails in the forest.
The preserve also offers
comfortable and ecologically
sound accommodation at
the floating Uakari Lodge –
which is close to forest trails,
jungle lakes, and *caboclo*
communities. Book through
a Manaus tour company, or
directly with the Instituto de
Desenvolvimento Sustentável
Mamirauá in Tefé, 16 miles
(25 km) to the south.

STAY

Uakari Lodge
Set deep in the jungle,
Uakari Lodge floats
within Brazil's largest
protected area, the lush
Mamirauá Sustainable
Development Reserve.
The complex is designed
to have a minimal
impact on the environ-
ment and the lodge
champions conserva-
tion projects. Uakari can
host 24 guests at a time.

🅐 B2 🅐 Mamiraua
Reserve 🆆 uakarilodge.
com.br
$$$

Exploring the waters ↑
of the Mamirauá
Reserve by boat

Parintins

C2 **Amazonas**
From Manaus

A large jungle town, Parintins was originally the refuge of a *caboclos* community, who were escaping Portuguese slave traders.

Today, Parintins is best known for its popular Festa do Boi Bumbá. The festival is celebrated across three days in late June, when the town gets so packed that visitors often stay on boats.

Though there is little else to see in the town, besides the well-preserved colonial architecture, Parintins is known for

FESTA DO BUMBA MEU BOI

The Festa do Bumba Meu Boi involves two teams of performers competing to deliver the most impressive dance recounting the death and rebirth of a legendary *boi* (ox). Originating on the 18th-century northeast plantations, the festival arrived in Parintins almost 100 years ago with the Cid brothers (who moved here in search of work). They brought with them the Bumba Meu Boi musical influence, steeped in the rhythms of the northeast.

Did You Know?

Two teams compete to retell a local tale about a resurrected ox via song and dance at the Festa do Bumba Meu.

its rich Indigenous culture, and the array of local handicrafts make particularly unique souvenirs.

The flea markets, which include one conveniently located near the port, sell a wide range of items including trinkets, intricate lace, beadwork, masks, and fine mahogany carvings.

During the dry season, boat trips can be arranged from the town to explore the nearby lakes and river beaches.

Did You Know?

Two thousand Indigenous women took part in Brazil's first Indigenous Women's March in 2019.

THE INDIGENOUS PEOPLES OF THE AMAZON

Today, around 900,000 Indigenous people from 305 ethnic groups live in Brazil, each with its own dialect and language, mythology, arts, and culture. The majority are seminomadic and live by hunting, gathering, fishing, and migratory farming. Many of the Amazon's Indigenous people live in close harmony with the rhythms of the rainforest, and their exposure to Western society varies greatly.

YANOMAMI PEOPLE

The Yanomami people live in the rainforests of southern Venezuela and northern Brazil. One of the most recently contacted groups in Amazônia (from a Western perspective; the Yanomamis have had continuous contact with neighboring communities throughout history), they number around 26,000 today. The Yanomami people live off agriculture and are known for being fierce warriors. The group consists of four subdivisions, each with its own language, including Yamomae and Sanima.

↑ Indigenous leaders at the first Great Assembly of the Alliance of Mother Nature in 2019

TUKANO PEOPLE

The name Tukano is used for a number of ethnic groups, including Arapaso Tariana, living in northwestern Brazil along the Rio Uaupés. Individual groups live in communal houses, which are spaced out along the river at a distance of several hours by canoe. Together with their neighbors, Tukano members are a part of a socially and politically open-minded society toward

Aerial view of Moikarako village, and *(inset)* its chief, Raoni Metuktire, delivering a speech

other groups where visitors, trade, intermarriage, and ritual feasts are common. In the Barasana and Desana subgroups, members need to marry people from other groups and who speak a different language.

KAYAPÓ PEOPLE

Around 7,000 Kayapós – also known as Mebêngôkres – live in the Amazon river basin with villages along the banks of Rio Xingú. One of the group's main symbols is the circle; traditional Kayapó villages are formed by a circle of houses built around a clearing. The shape represents the course of the sun and moon, and the villages are considered the center of the universe. One of the Kayapó people's most prominent political figures is Chief Raoni Metuktire, an environmental activist who has been fighting to preserve Kayapó territory against dam projects and deforestation for over 40 years. Metuktire can be recognized in Western media wearing the distinct lip disc, symbolizing a group member's warrior status and right to speak.

UNCONTACTED COMMUNITIES

In the depths of the Amazon there are communities uncontacted by Western society. The dense Amazonian forest and the Vale do Javari Reserve bordering Peru to the west are thought to be home to the largest concentration of Indigenous groups with no contact this is known of with modern society. In 2011, aerial footage, taken by FUNAI (Brazil's National Indian Foundation), was released to the world media, of an isolated community living in the rainforest near the Brazilian-Peruvian border. In 2014, seven members of an isolated group in Peru made contact with an Indigenous Brazilian village in Acre, the first official contact by such a group since 1996.

⑪
Boa Vista

🅰B1 🗺Roraima 🚗✈🚌
🛈Centro de Turismo, Rua
Coronel Pinto 267, Centro;
www.turismo.rr.gov.br

Created in 1991, Roraima is one of Brazil's newest states, and Boa Vista is its capital city. The surrounding savannas are important cattle-ranching territory, but the area also profited from the gold rush of the 1980s.

The Praça Cívica forms the heart of the town's arch-shaped street layout. The modern Palácio Municipal is here, beside the Monumento ao Garimpeiro, a local monument honoring the gold miners who brought wealth to the state.

There are good swimming beaches on the Rio Branco, 15 minutes by bus from Boa Vista. The sandy beaches in the town center offer excellent swimming when the river is low.

Boa Vista is blessed with lush tropical rainforest, endless stretches of savanna plains, and beautiful river beaches. Ecotourism has become quite popular over the years, with organized camping tours run by a number of companies such as **Roraima Adventures**.

Boa Vista is easily connected by bus to the Venezuelan town of Santa Elena de Uairén, located 147 miles (237 km) north. The route from Boa Vista to Santa Elena is dotted with interesting sights, including the ecological island preserve of Ilha do Maracá, known for its species preservation and biodiversity, and the enchanting Lago Caracaranã, fringed with groves of cashew trees.

Roraima Adventures
🕙 🌐roraimaadventures.com.br

---

⑫
Rio Branco

🅰B3 🗺Acre 🚗✈🚌 🛈Via
Chico Mendes s/n, Arena da
Floresta, (68) 3901 3019

Another relatively new state, Acre was annexed from Bolivia in the early 20th century by a pioneering army of Brazilian rubber-tappers.

Acre's capital, Rio Branco has shaken off much of its brash image. The Parque de Maternidade has transformed from a small-town water canal into a long, green city walk. In the town center stands the **Palácio Rio Branco**. Though restored, the building maintains its original Neo-Classical facade, with four columns at the entrance. It was built in the 1930s as a headquarters for the state government and houses the largest painting in Brazil, which depicts a scene in homage to the revolutionary fighters who liberated Acre from Bolivia. The palace also contains several large rooms dedicated to the prehistory and history of the region. The main focus of these rooms is on Acre's 20th-century history, and there is a superb room dedicated to Indigenous culture, displaying some finely crafted feather headdresses.

A few blocks north, the **Museu da Borracha** (Rubber Museum) focuses on the fascinating local culture, as well as rubber-tappers and *ayahuasca* churches – known for their ceremonial use of hallucinogenic herbs. The river's south bank, the Rio Acre,

---

> ### 🏔 GREAT VIEW
> ### Monte Roraima
>
> This mystical tabletop mountain is 9 miles (14 km) wide and 9,094 ft high (2,772 m), and is where Brazil borders Guyana and Venezuela. The peak inspired Sir Arthur Conan Doyle's *The Lost World*. The 6- to 8-day trek to the top is worth the breathtaking views.

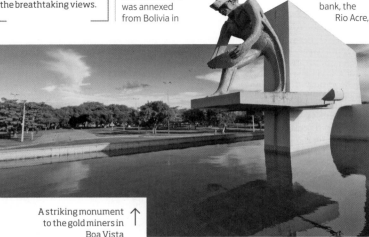

A striking monument ↑
to the gold miners in
Boa Vista

↑ The graceful Neo-Classical Palácio Rio Branco in Rio Branco

was a focal point during the rubber boom but has now been modernized with hotels, bars, movie theaters, and merchants' stores, along with the new north-based commercial center, which emerged in the mid-20th century, all of which makes for a lively atmosphere. The promenade, La Gameleira, hosts the perfect location for a riverside walk.

The **Parque Ambiental Chico Mendes** (Chico Mendes Environmental Park) is located in the former rubber plantation at Itucumã near Vila Acre, 6 miles (10 km) south of Rio Branco. It contains virgin forest areas, some replica malocas (Indigenous longhouses), rubber-tapper dwellings, a zoo, and a memorial to Chico Mendes.

Palácio Rio Branco

🏠 Praça dos Seringueiros ☎ (68) 3223 9241 🕐 8am–6pm Mon–Fri

Museu da Borracha

🏠 Av Ceará 1441 ☎ (68) 3223 1202 🕐 8am–5pm Mon–Fri, 4–9pm Sat & Sun

Parque Ambiental Chico Mendes

🏠 Rodovia AC-40 Km 7, Vila Acre ☎ (68) 3221 1933 🕐 7am–5pm Tue–Sun

---

⑬

Porto Velho

🅰 B3 🏠 Rondônia ✈🚌⛴ 🛈 Setur, Av Farquar 2986, Centro; (69) 3216 1028

A very fast-growing jungle city, Porto Velho, has rapidly developed in the last 100 years from a few streets near Rio Madeira into Rondônia's capital. River trips to the nearby beach of Santo Antônio are popular for freshly cooked fish at a waterside restaurant.

The star attraction, here is the **Madeira-Mamoré Museu Ferroviário**, where several steam locomotives, some under cover, still symbolize a rusting industrial vision in the middle of the Amazon jungle. In the main museum shed, there are interesting exhibits from the turn of the 19th century, when the railway was being built. Unfortunately, its

inauguration in 1912 was just in time to witness the collapse of Brazil's rubber industry.

Guajará-Mirim is located on the Bolivian border, some 187 miles (302 km) from Porto Velho. From here, it is possible to visit the lonely jungle fort, the ruins of the **Forte Príncipe da Beira**, which was built by the Portuguese in 1773.

The **Reserva Biologica do Guaporé** near Costa Marques, which is 282 miles (454 km) south of Porto Velho, is known for its diverse bird species.

Madeira-Mamoré Museu Ferroviário

♿ 🏠 Praça Madeira-Mamoré ☎ (69) 3901 3651 🕐 For refurbishment

Reserva Biologica do Guaporé

🏠 Av Cabixi com Limoeiro 1942 ☎ (69) 3651 3782

CHICO MENDES (1944–1988)

A rubber-tapper union leader and environmental activist, Chico Mendes helped establish the National Council of Rubber Tappers. He fought to preserve rubber reserves and won recognition from the UN in 1987, with a Global 500 award. He received another award from the Better World Society, before his assassination in December 1988.

The Parque Ambiental Chico Mendes is located in the former rubber plantation at Itucumã near Vila Acre, 6 miles (10 km) south of Rio Branco.

↑ Boating past the Amazon's mangrove forests near Souré

⑭ Salinópolis

🅐 E2 🏛️ Pará ✈️ Belém Val de Caes Airport, 110 miles (180 km) SE of town, then bus 🚌 Av Miguel Santa Brigada 🛈 Paratur; (91) 3423 2203

The town of Salinópolis, locally known as Salinas, is just about as far east as the Amazon river delta reaches. Very much the traditional summer resort for city folk, Salinas has plenty of beaches fringed with beach huts and second homes. The busiest beach is the central Praia do Maçarico, which has several bars and restaurants. More pleasant still, there is the

700,000

The population of water buffaloes in Ilha de Marajó, the largest in Brazil.

Praia do Atalaia, not far from the center of town, backed by sand dunes and well provided with *barracas* (palm-roofed stalls) for food and drink. A continuation of this beach, the Praia do Farol Velho, is thickly lined with beach houses, and is popular during July.

About 19 miles (30 km) west of Salinópolis is the relatively quiet fishing settlement and beach resort of Algodoal. The resort lies on the western edge of Ilha de Maiandeua, just a 40-minute boat ride away. There are no motorized vehicles in the village nor on Maiandeua island, adding to the remote and idyllic feel.

The main beach for the village is the Praia da Vila do Algodoal. More popular, however, is the palm-fringed Praia da Princesa do Farol, a stretch of sand secluded from the main beach by a short walk at low tide or a canoe ride. There are trails on the island, offering the opportunity to spot wildlife and explore the area around an inland lake. It is advisable to carry cash to visit the island, as there are no banks or ATMs.

 INSIDER TIP
Time Your Trip

Ilha de Marajó's rainy season is a great time to go boating down scenic waterways and spotting river-dwelling wildlife. Plan your trip during the dry season if jungle hiking or sunbathing is more to your liking.

⑮ Ilha de Marajó

🅐 E2 🏛️ Pará 🚢 From Belém to Porto Camará 🛈 Praça Municipal, Rua Primeira, Souré; (91) 98336 7919

The world's largest river island, Ilha de Marajó covers over 18,533 sq miles (48,000 sq km) and is mostly home to cattle ranches, or *fazendas*. The island is famous for having the biggest and finest buffaloes in Brazil. Their meat, leather, and dairy products are widely available to purchase. Ilha de Marajó was also the ancient home to the Indigenous culture of the

POTTERY ON ILHA DE MARAJÓ

The ancient inhabitants of Ilha de Marajó, the Marajoaras, left behind not only burial mounds, but also some very fine ceramics, leading archaeologists to believe that between the 5th and 13th centuries there were sophisticated societies living along the banks of the Amazon river. Excavations reveal the dead were buried in line according to their social ranking, with larger urns indicating higher status. Most of these ceramics, representing abstract feminine figures, demonstrate the matrilineal nature of this early Amazonian society. Some excellent examples of the urns can be found in the Museu Goeldi in Belém.

MARAJOARAS CERAMIC URN

Marajoaras, notable for their exquisite ceramic burial and ceremonial urns.

The unofficial capital of the island is Souré, which has the most shops and restaurants, but the ferry port is Porto Camará, some 16 miles (27 km) south of Souré. Located between Porto Camará and Souré, the best and most secluded beach is at the small town of Joanes, some 3 miles (5 km) off the main road. There are good beaches at the other town on the island, Salvaterra, where there are also several hotels and *pousadas*.

During the peak rainy season (February–May) many of the roads are inaccessible for long periods; this includes the road to Joanes and Salvaterra at times. Boats for moving around the island can be found easily at Souré, Salvaterra, and Porto Camará.

Macapá

🅰D2 🏳Amapá ✈⛴From Belém 🚌Bairro São Lázaro, (96) 3251 2009 🛈Rua Binga Uchôa 29, Centro; (96) 3212 5335

Split in two by the equator, Macapá is hot and humid all year round. The city, Amapá's

capital, is located on the northern bank of the Amazon river, very close to the giant river's mouth. It is rather isolated, with mostly air and boat transportation.

The city's history is rich and varied. Several European countries, including England and France, attempted to take it over from the Portuguese, but the Portuguese established their hold here by completing the grand **Fortaleza de São José de Macapá** in 1782, after almost 20 years of construction by slave labor.

The bricks used were brought over from Portugal as ballast on the ships.

These days, Macapá is the capital of a progressive state. Following the election of the environmentalist João Capiberibe as state governor in 1995, successive governors have kept the spirit of environmentalism alive. One such project is to connect the state's protected areas with wildlife or biodiversity corridors. Macapá is also home to the **Museu SACACA**, or Museum of Sustainable Development, a short distance south of the town center, which offers tours of replica *ribeirinho* (river-dweller) houses.

The Marco Zero monument, a large obelisk-cum-sundial, 4 miles (6 km) southwest of the city center, marks the equatorial line.

Fortaleza de São José de Macapá
🚹 🏠Rua Cândido Mendes 1611 📞(96) 3212 5118 🕐8am–5pm Tue–Fri, 9am–6pm Sat, 10am–5pm Sun

Museu SACACA
🚹 🏠Av Feliciano Coelho, 1509 📞(96) 3212 5361 🕐9am–5pm Tue–Sun

↑ The well-preserved Fortaleza de São José de Macapá, illuminated at dusk

17

Santarém

🅰D2 🅾Pará ✈🚗🚢From Docas do Pará (W of center) ℹSEMTUR, Av Curua-Una 42; (93) 2101 5100

Amazônia's fourth-largest city, Santarém sits at the mouth of the Rio Tapajós, surrounded by brilliant white sandy beaches. Modern Santarém began in 1661 as a Jesuit mission to an Indigenous Tapuiçu settlement originally located here. Later, in 1867, there was an influx of ex-Confederates from the USA, a handful of whose descendants still survive.

Santarém's rubber boom and strategic position as a pit stop en route along the Amazon river turned the town into a buzzing commercial center during the 19th century. In the latter part of this century, Henry Wickam, an English settler in Santarém, smuggled rubber tree seeds out to establish rubber plantations in Asia. Within 40 years, Asian rubber plantations were rapidly outproducing the Brazilian Amazon.

The local economy is still based on rubber, as well as logging, soya, Brazil nuts, and new influx of tourism. Colorful boats and the frantic movement of produce at the port and along the attractive riverfront are typical today.

One of the highlights of this vibrant city is the **Museu de Arte Sacra de Santarém**, which has a noteworthy collection of religious art. The **Museu de Santarém** is also worth a visit; it showcases the city's distinct Santarém Phase Pottery. The exhibits here prominently feature burial urns, reputed to be among the oldest in South America. Also known as Centro Cultural João Fona, the museum has a particularly striking interior which was painted by João Fona, an artist from Pará.

> One of the highlights of this vibrant city is the Museu de Arte Sacra de Santarém, which has a noteworthy collection of religious art.

Museu de Arte Sacra de Santarém
🅰Rua Siqueira Campos 439, Centro ☎(93) 3523 0658
🕐Until further notice

Santarém's striking blue church, viewed from the river ↑

 The rock paintings of Serra Paytuna are easily visited from Monte Alegre

Museu de Santarém

◈ ⌂ Rua do Imperador
☏ (93) 3523 0658 ⏲ 8am–5pm Mon–Fri

18

Óbidos

Ⓐ D2 ⌂ Pará 🚢 From Santarém ℹ Rua Dep. Raimundo Chaves 338; (93) 3547 2021

The real gateway to the deeper Amazon, Óbidos marks the narrowest section of the Amazon river valley. It was created 40 million years ago, when a massive inland lake burst through to the Atlantic here, where the Guyanan Shield meets the Brazilian Shield.

The pretty waterfront has some beautifully tiled buildings and the 17th-century Forte Pauxias. You can also visit the **Museu Integrado de Óbidos**, which features archaeological and historical exhibits.

Museu Integrado de Óbidos

⌂ Rua Justo Chermont 1826, Centro ⏲ Until further notice

19

Monte Alegre

Ⓐ D2 ⌂ Pará 🚢 Rua do Jaquara 320 ℹ Rua 15 de Março 125; (93) 3533 1010

Located impressively on top of a small hill beside the Amazon river, the town of Monte Alegre was one of the first places on the river to be colonized by Europeans. A band of English and Irish sailors were the earliest to settle here, in the 1570s, though they were soon to be expelled by the Portuguese. Over the last 200 years, Monte Alegre has benefited from ranching and the rubber industry. It is best known for the rock paintings of Serra Paytuna and Serra Ererê, located 19 miles (30 km)

POROROCA WAVE

Revered by surfers, the Pororoca is a legendary wave, over 16 ft (5 m) tall, that regularly rolls up the Amazon river. The name Pororoca comes from a local Tupí phrase meaning "great destructive noise." Predicted to occur twice daily during full moons between January and April every year, the wave comes in from the Atlantic causing some devastation along the riverbanks. Following a low tide in the rainy season, the force of the mighty river against the turning tide creates the large and powerful wave that rolls, unstoppable, up the Amazon. The surfing record so far is 37 minutes in time and 7 miles (12 km) in distance; the tidal waves are known to travel over 12 miles (20 km) per hour at times.

out of town. Estimated to be 10,000 years old, the paintings feature abstract patterns, mostly geometric in form, and some stylized representations of human and animal figures. It is obligatory to hire a guide and a vehicle to visit them.

In addition, Monte Alegre is renowned for scenic waterfalls and its wealth of birdlife, for which a local guide and a canoe will also be required.

NEED TO KNOW

BEFORE
YOU GO

Things change, so plan ahead to make the most of your trip. Be prepared for all eventualities by considering the following points before you travel.

AT A GLANCE

CURRENCY
Brazilian Real
(BRL)

AVERAGE DAILY SPEND

SAVE	SPEND	SPLURGE
$150	**$400**	**$1000+**

BOTTLED WATER	COFFEE	BEER	DINNER FOR TWO
$3	**$3**	**$9**	**$150**

ESSENTIAL PHRASES

Hello	Bom dia
Goodbye	Adeus
Please	Por favor
Thank you	Obrigado/Obrigada
Do you speak English	Fala inglês?
I don't understand	Não entendo

ELECTRICITY SUPPLY

Power sockets are type N for three-pin plugs, or type C for two-pronged plugs. Standard voltage is 127 or 220 volts.

Passports and Visas

For entry requirements, including visas, consult your nearest Brazilian embassy or check the **Polícia Federal** website. Brazil operates a reciprocal visa policy; as such, citizens of the UK, EU, Australia, New Zealand, US, Canada, Japan, Mexico, and South Africa do not need a visa, provided they have a return ticket and their stay in Brazil does not exceed 90 days.
Polícia Federal
🔲 pf.gov.br

Government Advice

Now more than ever, it is important to consult both your and the **Brazilian Government's** advice before traveling. The **UK Foreign, Commonwealth & Development Office**, the **US State Department** and the **Australian Department of Foreign Affairs and Trade** offer the latest information on security, health, and local regulations.
Australia Department of Foreign Affairs and Trade
🔲 smartraveller.gov.au
Brazilian Government
🔲 gov.br/mre/en
UK Foreign, Commonwealth & Development Office
🔲 gov.uk/foreign-travel-advice
US State Department
🔲 travel.state.gov

Customs Information

You can find information on the laws relating to goods and currency taken in or out of Brazil by checking the information available on the Brazilian government's website.

Insurance

We recommend taking out a comprehensive insurance policy with cover that includes theft, loss of belongings, medical care, cancellations and delays, and read the small print carefully.

Vaccinations

For information regarding COVID-19 vaccination requirements, consult government advice. Yellow fever vaccination is highly recommended, especially if you are planning to visit rural areas; be aware that visitors can be asked to provide a yellow fever vaccination certificate upon entering the country.

Ask your doctor or a travel clinic for an International Certificate of Vaccinations, an up-to-date list of the required vaccinations. The most commonly recommended are a DTP (diptheria, tetanus, and polio) booster, as well as vaccinations for typhoid and hepatitis A.

Booking Accommodations

Brazil has a range of places to stay, from luxury beach resorts to hostels. It is essential to book in advance for the peak seasons: from Christmas to Carnaval (held in February or early March), as well as for July and August. Booking through agencies can offer good deals, but cheaper rates may be available from hotel websites.

Money

The official currency is the Brazilian real (plural reais), denoted throughout this guide by the $ symbol. The only foreign currencies commonly accepted in Brazil are the US dollar and euro.

Exchange rates for cash transactions are usually not very good, and the highest rates can be obtained on credit card or *caixa automática* (ATM) transactions. Credit cards (especially MasterCard and Visa) are the best option; they are widely accepted and can also be used to withdraw reais. Contactless payments are gradually becoming more common, particularly in the larger cities. Tipping is not expected unless added in advance to the bill.

Travelers with Specific Requirements

Although it is relatively easy to find accessible hotels and restaurants, very few public places are wheelchair-friendly. Older buildings may lack elevators or ramps, and streets and sidewalks are often uneven or broken. The Rio de Janeiro and São Paulo metros have accessible elevators and ramps at many stations. For short distances, taxis are the best option. In Rio, **Especial Coop** have specially adapted taxis and English-speaking drivers. For long distances, buses are generally comfortable, with fully reclining seats. All main airports have wheelchairs. The **SATH** website is a useful planning resource.

Especial Coop
W especialcoop.com.br
SATH
W sath.org

Language

Portuguese is the official language, but several Indigenous languages are also spoken *(p53)*. Social niceties are important, so starting a conversation with *"bom dia"* will go a long way. Locals may speak some English in tourist areas, but in general, English is not widely spoken.

Opening Hours

> The COVID-19 pandemic proved that situations can change suddenly. Always check before visiting attractions and hospitality venues for up-to-date hours and booking requirements. .

Monday Several museums are closed on Mondays, so always check before visiting.
Sunday Most shops are closed, although some stores and malls are open until 4pm.

PUBLIC HOLIDAYS	
1 Jan	New Year's Day
Late Feb	Carnaval
10 Apr	Good Friday
21 Apr	Tiradentes Day
25 Apr	Liberation Day
1 May	Labor Day
11 Jun	Corpus Christi
7 Sep	National Independence Day
12 Oct	Our Lady of Aparecida
1 Nov	All Saints Day
2 Nov	All Souls Day
25 Dec	Christmas

GETTING AROUND

Whether you are visiting for a short city break or to explore the country, discover how best to reach your destination and travel like a pro.

AT A GLANCE

PUBLIC TRANSPORT COSTS

RIO DE JANEIRO

$4.70

Single Ticket
Metro, bus, tram

SÃO PAULO

$4.50

Single Ticket
Metro, bus, tram

BRASÍLIA

$5.50

Single Ticket
Metro, bus, tram

TOP TIP
Use Bilhetê Único contactless smart cards to pay on the Rio and São Paulo metros.

SPEED LIMITS

HIGHWAY (AUTOPISTA)
68 mph
(110 km/h)

RURAL ROAD
50 mph
(80 km/h)

URBAN AREA
37 mph
(60 km/h)

Arriving by Air

São Paulo's **Guarulhos International Airport** and Rio de Janeiro's **Tom Jobim International Airport** are the main entry points for visitors flying direct to Brazil. There are also international airports in other cities, including Brasília, Belo Horizonte, Manaus, Recife, and Salvador. Convenient connections are available on an extensive network of domestic flights, the preferred mode of transportation for a country as large as Brazil.
Guarulhos International Airport
W gru.com.br
Tom Jobim International Airport
W riogaleao.com

Long-Distance Coaches

Efficient and reliable long-distance coaches serve the whole country, with luxury express options available on major routes. Traveling by coach is an easy, comfortable, and economical way to see the country. Intercity bus stations, called *rodoviárias*, are usually located on city outskirts. Buses are operated by numerous private companies, but prices are standardized, and very reasonable. **Busca Ônibus** is a good source for checking routes, as is **Buses in Brazil**.

Several categories of buses operate on longer routes; most have onboard toilets. Regular buses (*ônibus comum*) sometimes do not have air-conditioning, so check beforehand. *Comum com ar* are regular buses with air-conditioning. The *executivo* bus is more comfortable – its seats are wider, recline further, and are equipped with footrests. The best buses for overnight trips are known as *semi-leito* or *leito*. *Semi-leito* have seats that recline almost horizontally and have large footrests. *Leito* buses offer a fully horizontal seat. Both normally offer onboard refreshments, blankets, and pillows. Buy your tickets online or direct from the *rodoviária* ahead of time, especially on public holidays.
Busca Ônibus
W buscaonibus.com.br
Buses in Brazil
W busbrazil.com

GETTING TO AND FROM THE AIRPORT

Airport	Distance to City	Taxi Fare	Journey Time
Guarulhos International Airport (São Paulo)	17 miles (28 km)	$210	40–120 mins (in rush hour)
Tom Jobim International Airport (Rio de Janeiro)	12 miles (20 km)	$170	40–90 mins (in rush hour)
Magalhães International Airport (Salvador)	17 miles (28 km)	$230	40 mins
Guararapes International Airport (Recife)	11 miles (18 km)	$125	20 mins
Eduardo Gomes International Airport (Manaus)	10 miles (16 km)	$170	25 mins
Salgado Filho International Airport (Porto Alegre)	4 miles (6 km)	$60	15 mins

ROAD JOURNEY PLANNER

This map is a handy reference for travel on Brazil's main roads. The table below shows distances from Rio de Janeiro. Journey times include refilling gasoline, as well as comfort stops, which coaches typically make every two to three hours.

Belo Horizonte	5.5 hrs
Brasília	14.5 hrs
Cuiabá (Pantanal)	26.5 hrs
Florianópolis	14.5 hrs
Fortaleza	46 hrs
Foz do Iguaçu	25 hrs
Manaus (via Cuiabá and Porto Velho)	69.5 hrs
Natal	38.5 hrs
Porto Alegre	18.5 hrs
Recife	33.5 hrs
Salvador da Bahia	24 hrs
São Paulo	5.5 hrs

••• Direct coach/ car routes

Boats and Ferries

In many parts of Brazil, boats are a vital form of transport. In the Amazon, rivers are still the major highways, and old-style wooden river-boats are an important part of the transportation system. The most common and popular route runs between Manaus and Belém. The journey takes four days downstream and five days upstream. On this route, there are also several larger and more modern boats, with air-conditioned cabins and enclosed hammock spaces. Continuing right up to Tefé, **AJATO** runs a twice-weekly speedboat service.

On most other routes, the boats are the older, smaller, traditional type, with small wooden cabins and two open decks where passengers sling their hammocks. Meals and water are included in the fare. The most common routes run between Manaus and Porto Velho; Manaus, Tabatinga, and São Gabriel de Cachoeira, near the borders of Peru and Columbia, respectively; and Manaus and Santarém, halfway to Belém. The Manaus–Santarém route also has a high-speed catamaran, which makes the journey in a single day.

AJATO
📞 (92) 3622 6047

Cruises

Several companies offer three- to five-day cruises, most typically between Santos, Rio de Janeiro as far as Salvador, or other northeastern cities. Another route starts in Recife and travels to Fernando de Noronha. There is also a regular cruise ship, the **Iberostar Grand Amazon**, that departs from Manaus on three- and four-day cruises on the Amazon. The old-style **Amazon Clipper Cruises** can be excellent for a tour of the Rio Negro.

Amazon Clipper Cruises
🌐 amazonclipper.com.br
Iberostar Grand Amazon
🌐 grandiberostar.com

Public Transport

In most Brazilian cities and towns, the main mode of transportation is the bus. Tickets are generally cheap and services run from early morning until late at night. São Paulo and Rio de Janeiro also have modern metro systems that offer quick access to the city and plentiful taxis.

Agencia Nacional de Transportes Terrestres is Brazil's main public transport authority. Safety and hygiene measures, timetables, ticket information, transport maps, and more can be obtained from the government website.

Agencia Nacional de Transportes Terrestres
🌐 gov.br/antt/pt-br/assuntos/passageiros

Metro

The metro is the safest form of public transport in Brasília, Rio, and São Paulo. These cities have very convenient metro systems, offering reliable transportation to a number of tourist attractions. It is often easier and faster to take the metro closest to a destination, particularly if far away, and then take a taxi, rather than figure out a complicated and traffic-clogged bus journey.

The **Brasília Metro** has two lines, which run from 6am to 11:30pm from Monday to Saturday and from 7am to 7pm on Sundays and public holidays. Both lines connect with the main bus station, but there is no metro line to the airport.

In Rio de Janeiro, **MetrôRio** has three main lines, which run from 5am to midnight Monday through Saturday, and from 7am to 11pm on Sundays and public holidays. The metro runs non-stop throughout the five days of Carnaval.

Metrô São Paulo is the largest metro system in Latin America, with six lines covering a large part of the city. Line 1 runs through the city centre, connecting with the Tiete main bus station. Trains run from 4:40am to midnight every day.

Rechargeable smart cards can be used on the metro systems. Sold at stations for about $4, they can be topped up with cash or bank card, online or via phone apps, saving time and money. A range of combined metro-bus-train tickets can also be bought; passengers must ask for a special integrated ticket (*integração*) at the time of purchase. In Rio, these tickets offer useful connections on air-conditioned buses to many of the city's attractions that are off the metro system, such as Sugar Loaf and Ipanema. Free metro maps are available via phone apps and at most ticket booths.

MetrôRio
🌐 metrorio.com.br
Metrô São Paulo
🌐 metro.sp.gov.br
Metrô DF - Brasília
🌐 metro.df.gov.br

Buses

Buses are plentiful in bigger towns and cities. Most lines in Rio and São Paulo run 24 hours a day, but with fewer circulating in the middle of the night. In Rio, most buses going from the south to the center will go to Copacabana. Tickets are sold on the bus by a ticket seller or by the driver. Keep small change handy, or use the Bilhete Único card, which is integrated with the metro network. Brazilian bus drivers can drive fast, so hold on at all times. Buses are often crowded, have long routes and are the target of thieves, particularly during rush hours. Taking buses is safest in the day; in the evenings, it is advisable to take taxis, especially if travelling with luggage. In São Paulo, a couple of the main

bus transfer points are at Praça da Republica and **Terminal Bandeira**, where it is also possible to catch buses to destinations within the city.
Terminal Bandeira
w sptrans.com.br

Taxis

Taxis are a plentiful and speedy mode of transportation. Most taxis work on the meter: "tarifa 1" all day except from 11pm to 6am, Sundays, and in December when "tarifa 2" is used. The only taxis allowed to charge a flat rate are radio taxis or cooperatives at airports, bus stations, or other specific locations. Another option is the motorcycle taxi (moto-taxi), a cheap and fast one-person ride more common in smaller towns. The driver carries an extra helmet, and the passenger just hops on the back and rides pillion after fixing a price.

Driving

Brazil has a total of 1.1 million miles (1.7 million km) of federal, state, and local roads but, of these, only around 138,000 miles (222,000 km) are paved and in decent condition. Driving around the country can be a challenge due to the long distances and the poor quality of many public roads. Traveling by night is best avoided – with few exceptions, highways are poorly lit and lacking in reflective paint, reflective signage, and reflectors showing the edge of the road.

Driving can be a convenient way to visit attractions close to the cities, though, and car rentals are widely available. However, in larger cities such as São Paulo, Salvador, and Rio, traffic is very chaotic, with long tailbacks during peak hours. Parking, expecially in cities, can be tricky due to security and space constraints. It is worth paying extra for a hotel with a lock-up garage facility. Do not leave valuables in the car.

Car Rental

All cities and most smaller towns offer car rental services. These include both the main international companies, as well as Brazilian firms such as **Localiza**, **Movida**, and **Unidas**. Rental offices, known as *locadoras*, can be found at every airport.

Foreigners will need to show a valid driver's license from their home country, province, or state; a valid passport; and a major credit card. It is also a good idea to carry an International Driver's Permit (IDP).
Localiza
w localizahertz.com
Movida
w movida.com.br
Unidas
w unidas.com.br

Planning

Rotas Brasil is a good tool for planning your journey, and gives detailed routes, distances, tolls and traffic information. Vehicles in Brazil run on either gasoline or hydrous alcohol. Service stations selling gasoline are more common, especially in remote areas. On long-distance trips, service stations may be few and far between, so ensure that you have enough fuel and that the car is in good condition.
Rotas Brasil
w rotasbrasil.com.br

Rules of the Road

Brazilians drive on the right side of the road. Right turns on red lights are not allowed and roundabouts are common only in Brasília. The right of way is always with the car already on the roundabout, or to the left. On highways, keep headlights and seatbelts on or risk being fined. All drivers are also legally obliged to carry an emergency triangle and fire extinguisher.

Brazilians can be aggressive drivers: they tend to drive fast, switch lanes constantly (normally without signaling), and overtake often. In case of an emergency, it is best to call the **Polícia Rodoviária** (Highway Police).
Polícia Rodoviária
c 191

Cycling

With its vast size, tropical climate and high-speed road network, Brazil is not ideal for cycling. However, some cities have hire bikes from **Bike Sampa**, available by the hour, day or longer. These can be picked up from access points, with suggested routes available. There are also organized bike tour companies like **Baja Bikes** in Rio or **Urban Bike SP** in São Paulo.
Baja Bikes
w bajabikes.eu/en/cycling-in-brazil
Bike Sampa
w bikeitau.com.br
Urban Bike SP
w urbanbikesp.com

Walking

Walking around Brazilian cities can be a good way to explore. In Rio de Janeiro, Lapa, Santa Teresa, and the beach neighborhoods are ideal for getting around on foot. Likewise, historic towns and cities, such as Ouro Preto, Paraty, and the Pelourinho district of Salvador, are best visited on foot. Bear in mind that many Brazilian cities have busy roads that are not always pedestrian-friendly, so use public transport to get to areas of interest and walk from there. Avoid quieter back streets after dark and, if traveling alone, consider joining a walking tour.

PRACTICAL
INFORMATION

A little local know-how goes a long way in Brazil. Here you will find all the essential information you will need during your stay.

AT A GLANCE

EMERGENCY NUMBERS

TRAFFIC POLICE
191

AMBULANCE
192

FIRE DEPARTMENT
193

POLICE
197

TIME ZONE
Brasilia Standard Time (most of the country). Daylight saving runs from third Sun in Oct to third Sun in Feb.

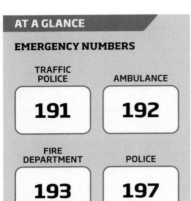

TAP WATER
The water is often highly chlorinated and its purity is unreliable, so to be safe drink bottled or filtered water.

WEBSITES

BRASIL
visitbrasil.com is the official Brazilian Tourism website.

Rio Times
Rio's English-language news site, riotimesonline.com, is a guide to what's on in Rio, São Paulo, and the country.

Personal Security

Although much of Brazil is safe for visitors, there are some safety considerations. When sightseeing, keep valuables in a money belt, and avoid carrying large amounts of cash. Public transport is safe in the day but taxis are a better option in the evening. It is recommended that travelers visit favelas only with a local guide. If you are victim of a crime, contact the police within 24 hours. Ask for a *boletim de ocorrência* (incident report form), which you will need in order to make a claim. The Polícia de Turismo (tourism police) have branches in most major tourist areas, including **Rio de Janeiro**, **São Paulo**, and **Salvador**.

Rio is probably the most LGBTQ+ friendly city in Brazil, with bars and nightclubs along the Copacabana and Ipanema beaches – particularly along Rua Farme Amoeda – popular meeting places for the local gay community. Elsewhere there is a mixed attitude, with macho culture and hostile behavior still common. Protections are, however, in place: same-sex couples have had the right to adopt since 2010; same-sex marriage was legalized in 2013; and trans people have been able to change their legal gender without restrictions since 2018.

Rio de Janeiro
⌂ Ave Afrânio de Melo Franco 159, Leblon
📞 (21) 2332 2924

Salvador
⌂ Rua Gregório de Matos 16, Pelourinho
📞 (71) 3116 6817

São Paulo
⌂ Rua Cantareira 390, Centro
📞 (11) 3257 4475

Health

By and large no special health precautions are needed. Food and drink hygiene is good in major tourist areas. Tap water is generally best avoided, but bottled water is sold everywhere. However, dengue fever and zika are both still present in the country, most abundant in and around towns and cities. Both viral diseases are transmitted mainly by mosquitoes, and there

are no vaccines to prevent them. Symptoms include high fever, joint pain, and headaches; zika symptoms also include a rash. Zika may be more serious for pregnant women, as there's evidence it causes birth defects. Use mosquito repellent, especially between dusk and dawn.

Farmácias, or pharmacies, can be found everywhere, are always well supplied, and are often open late. Every city will have at least one that is open 24 hours. Many medications available only by prescription in other countries can be bought over the counter.

Smoking, Alcohol, and Drugs

Smoking is more widely tolerated here than in the US and in Europe, although it is prohibited on public transport. Drink driving is strictly banned, with regular police checks. Be aware that even a small amount of alcohol in the blood may lead to a prison sentence. It is always best to exercise caution when someone unknown offers you a drink or even cigarettes. Instances of drugging or spiked drinks are not uncommon in Brazil. Severe penalties, including prison, are always enforced for anyone found in possession of illegal drugs.

ID

It is mandatory in Brazil to carry some form of photo identification. You may be asked to show some form of ID when entering an office building or government agency, or sometimes even a museum or library. To avoid carrying around a passport, keep a photocopy, and carry some other form of less valuable ID that has your picture, name, and date of birth.

Local Customs

Brazilians tend to be friendly and open. When introduced, men will greet each other with a handshake and a friendly slap on the shoulder. Good friends usually embrace. When introduced to a woman, it is customary to greet her with a handshake and a kiss on the cheek. Casual dress is the norm, even in smart hotels and restaurants; business suits are only needed for work and formal meetings. Nudity or going topless on the beach, however, is not accepted, except on designated naturist beaches.

Visiting Churches and Cathedrals

Most churches and cathedrals permit visitors during Sunday mass; some historic monuments charge entry. Although Brazil has a traditionally strong Catholic identity, Afro-Brazilian religions such as Candomblé are widely practised, particularly in the northeast.

When visiting religious buildings ensure that you are dressed modestly, with both your knees and shoulders well covered.

Cell Phones and Wi-Fi

Cell phones are common all over the country. Most tri-band GSM phones will work in Brazil. Coverage for 4G is available in most of the country, though it's faster in major cities. 5G is also being introduced. You can buy a local SIM card upon arrival to obtain a local number. Most local operators offer a very straightforward package for visitors, including data.

Post

The Brazilian postal service is quite efficient for registered mail. **Correios** (post offices) are mostly open from 8am to 5pm Monday to Friday, although some have longer opening hours. For guaranteed or registered delivery, the *correios* offer the excellent SEDEX (domestic express mail) and SEDEX Mundi (international).
Correios
🆆 correios.com.br

Taxes and Refunds

There are no VAT refunds included in the price of purchases. Departure taxes are usually included in international airfares, but it is advisable to check with your airline or travel agent.

Responsible Tourism

Before booking any organized tours, it is advisable to find out whether they are locally run, contribute to the local community, and encourage responsible waste collection. Protect local wildlife by not removing any plants or rocks, and only ever observing animals from a distance.

INDEX

PHRASE BOOK

The Portuguese spoken in Brazil differs in various ways from the Portuguese spoken in Portugal. In general, Brazilian pronunciation tends to omit far fewer sounds, especially the sounds at the end of words, and rarely runs two words together, both of which are common practice in Portugal. One feature of Brazilian Portuguese, particularly in the Rio de Janeiro area, is that an "r" sound can be spoken like an "h." So *carro* (car) may sound like "ka-hoo." Another difference lies in the ways of saying "you." The Portuguese form of placing the definite article in front of a person's name (*o* João, *a* Cristina), as a way of saying "you," does not exist in Brazil, where *você* and *vocês* are the most common words for "you." The Portuguese *tu* is not used much in Brazil. A huge number of other vocabulary differences exist, many at the level of everyday speech: train is *trem* in Brazil, *comboio* in Portugal; breakfast is *café da manhã* in Brazil, *pequeno almoço* in Portugal; bathroom is *banheiro* in Brazil, *casa de banho* in Portugal; goalkeeper is *goleiro* in Brazil, *guarda-redes* in Portugal; to drive is *dirigir* in Brazil, *conduzir* in Portugal. The sound indicated by "í" in the phrase book is like the "i" in English word "hi." "J" sounds like the "s" in the word "pleasure."

IN AN EMERGENCY

Help!	Socorro!	sookorroo
Stop!	Pare!	pahree
Call a doctor!	Chame um médico!	shamih oong mehjikoo
Call an ambulance!	Chame uma ambulância!	shamih ooma amboolans-ya
Where is the hospital?	Onde é o hospital?	ohnd-yeh oo oshpital
Police!	Polícia!	poolees-ya
Fire!	Fogo!	fohgoo
I've been robbed	Fui assaltado	fwee asaltadoo

COMMUNICATION ESSENTIALS

Yes	Sim	seeng
No	Não	nowng
Hello	Olá	ohla
How are you?	Como vai?	kohmooví
How is it going?	Tudo bem/ tudo bom?	toodoo bayng/ tooda bong
Goodbye	Tchau	tshow
See you later	Até logo	ateh logoo
Excuse me	Com licença	kong lisaynsa
I'm sorry	Desculpe	dishkoolp
Thank you	Obrigado *(if a man is speaking)*/ obrigada *(if a woman is speaking)*	obrigadoo/obrigada
Good morning	Bom dia	bong jeea
Good afternoon	Boa tarde	boh-a tarj
Good evening/ night	Boa noite	boh-a noh-itsh
Pleased to meet you	Muito prazer	mweengtoo prazayr
I'm fine	Estou bem/ tudo bem	shtoh bayng/ toodoo bayng
Today	Hoje	ohj
Yesterday	Ontem	ohntayng
Tomorrow	Amanhã	aman-yang
What?	O que?	oo kay
When?	Quando?	kwandoo
How?	Como?	kohmoo
Why?	Por que?	poorkay

USEFUL PHRASES

On the left/right	À esquerda/direita	a-shkayrda/jirayta
I don't understand	Não entendo	nowng ayntayndoo
Please speak slowly	Fale devagar por favor	falee jivagar poor favohr
What's your name?	Qual é seu nome?	kwal eh say-oo nohm
My name is...	Meu nome é...	may-oo nohm eh
Go away!	Vá embora!	va aymbora
That's fine	Está bem	shtah bayng
Where is...?	Onde está/fica...?	ohnj shtah/feeka
When does the bus leave/arrive?	A que horas sai/ chega o ônibus?	a kih orash sí/ shayga oo ohniboosh
Is this the way to the...?	Este é o caminho para...?	aysht-yeh oo kameen-yoo pra

USEFUL WORDS

big	grande	granj
small	pequeno	pikaynoo
hot	quente	kayntsh
cold	frio	free-oo
bad	mau	mow
good	bom	bong
enough	suficiente	soofis-yayntsh
open	aberto	abehrtoo
closed	fechado	fishadoo
dangerous	perigoso	pirigohzoo
safe	seguro	sigooroo
full	cheio	shay-oo
empty	vazio	vazee-oo
straight on	reto	rehtoo
under	debaixo	dibíshoo
over	em cima	ayng seema
in front of	em frente de	ayng frayntsh ji
behind	atrás de	atraj jih
first floor	primeiro andar	primayroo andar
ground floor	térreo	tehrryoo
lift	elevador	elevadohr
toilet	banheiro	ban-yayroo
men's	dos homens	dooz ohmaynsh
women's	das mulheres	dash mool-yehrish
quick	rápido	rapidoo
soon	cedo	saydoo
late	tarde	tarj
now	agora	agora
more	mais	mísh
less	menos	maynoosh
a little	um pouco	oong pohkoo
a lot	muito	mweengtoo
too much	demais	dimísh
entrance	entrada	ayntrada
exit	saída	sa-eeda
passport	passaporte	pasaportsh

POST OFFICES AND BANKS

bank	banco	bankoo
bureau de change	(casa de) câmbio	(kaza jih) kamb-yoo
exchange rate	taxa de câmbio	tasha jih kamb-yoo
post office	correio	koorray-oo
postcard	cartão postal	kartowng pooshtal
postbox	caixa de correio	kísha jih koorray-oo
ATM	caixa automática	kísha owtoomatshika
stamp	selo	sayloo
cash	dinheiro	jeen-yayroo
withdraw money	tirar dinheiro	tshirar jeen-yayroo

SHOPPING

How much is it?	Quanto é?	kwantweh
I would like...	Eu quero...	ay-oo kehroo
clothes	roupa	rohpa
This one	Esta	ehshta
That one	Essa	ehsa
market	mercado	merkadoo
supermarket	Supermercado	soopermerkadoo
Do you accept credit cards?	Aceitam cartão de crédito?	asaytowng kartowng jih krehditoo
expensive	caro	karoo
baker's	padaria	padaree-a
butcher's	açougue	asohgee
chemist's	farmácia	farmas-ya

SIGHTSEEING

museum	museu	moozay-oo
art gallery	galeria de arte	galiree-a jih artsh
national park	parque nacional	parkee nas-yoonal
beach	praia	prí-a
park	parque	parkee
river	rio	ree-oo
church	igreja	igray-Ja
cathedral	catedral	katidrow
district	bairro	bírroo
garden	jardim	Jardeeng
tourist office	informações turísticas	infoormasoyngsh tooreeshtsheekash
guide	guia	gee-a
guided tour	excursão com guia	shkoorsowng kong gee-a
ticket	bilhete/ingresso	bil-yaytsh/ ingrehsoo
map	mapa	mapa

TRANSPORT

bus	ônibus	ohniboosh
boat	barco	barkoo
train	trem	trayng
airport	aeroporto	a-ayroopohrtoo
airplane	avião	av-yowng

flight	vôo	voh-oo
bus station	rodoviária	roodohvyar-ya
bus stop	ponto de ônibus	pohntoo j-yohniboosh
train station	estação de trem	stasowng jih trayng
ticket	passagem	pasajayng
taxi	táxi	taxee
subway	metrô	metroh

HEALTH

I feel bad/ill	Sinto-me mal/doente	seentoomih mow/dwayntsh
I need to rest	Preciso descansar	priseezoo jishkansar
diarrhoea	diarréia	j-yarreh-ya
pharmacy	farmácia	farmas-ya
headache	dor de cabeça	dohr jih kabaysa
medicine	remédio	rimehd-yoo
sanitary towels/tampons	absorventes/tampões	absoorvayntsh/tampoyngsh
mosquito repellent	repelente de mosquito	ripelayntsh dih mooshkeetoo
doctor	médico	mehjikoo
condom	camisinha	kamizeen-ya

STAYING IN A HOTEL

hotel	hotel	ohteh-oo
boutique hotel	pousada	pohzada
guesthouse	pensão	paynsowng
hostel	albergue	owbehrgee
Do you have a room?	Tem um quarto?	tayng oong kwartoo
I have a reservation	Tenho uma reserva	tayn-yoo ooma risehrva
single/double (room)	(quarto de) solteiro/casal	(kwartoo jih) sooltayroo/kazow
shower	chuveiro	shoovayroo
sheet	lençol	laynsoh
bed	cama	kama
pillow	travesseiro	travisayroo
towel	toalha	twal-ya
toilet paper	papel higiênico	papeh-oo ij-yehnikoo

EATING OUT

I want to reserve...	Quero reservar...	kehroo rizirvar
Do you have...?	Tem...?	tayng
The bill, please	A conta, por favor	a kohnta, poor favohr
menu	cardápio/menu	kardap-yoo/maynoo
wine list	lista de vinhos	leeshta de veen-yoosh
glass	copo	kopoo
bottle	garrafa	garrafa
fork	garfo	garfoo
knife	faca	faka
spoon	colher	kool-yehr
restaurant	restaurante	rishtowrantsh
breakfast	café da manhã	kafeh da man-yang
lunch	almoço	owmohsoo
dinner/supper	jantar	jantar
(mineral) water	água (mineral)	agwa (minerow)
vegetarian	vegetariano	vigitar-yanoo
Is service included?	O serviço está incluído?	oo sirveesoo shtah inklweedoo

MENU DECODER

açúcar	asookar	sugar
alho	al-yoo	garlic
arroz	arrohsh	rice
azeite	azaytsh	olive oil
batatas fritas	batatash freetash	chips
bebida	bibeeda	drink
bem passado	bayng pasadoo	well done
bife	beefee	steak
café	kafeh	coffee
carne	karnee	beef
cerveja	sirvayja	beer
chá	sha	tea
churrasco	shoorrashkoo	barbecue
feijão (preto)	fayjowng (praytoo)	(black) beans
feijoada	fayjwada	bean and meat stew
farofa	farofa	dish based on manioc/cassava meal
frango	frangoo	chicken
fruta	froota	fruit
grelhado	gril-yadoo	grilled
lanche	lanshee	snack
leite	laytsh	milk

manteiga	mantayga	butter
muqueca de peixe	mookehka jih payshee	fish stew with coconut milk
ovo cozido	ohvoo koozeedoo	hard-boiled egg
pão	powng	bread
pão de queijo	powng jih kay-Joo	cheese cookie
pastel de carne	pashteh-oo jih karnee	puff-pastry patty filled with mince
pastel de queijo	pashteh-oo jih kay-Joo	puff-pastry patty filled with cheese
peixe	payshee	fish
pimenta	pimaynta	pepper
mal passado	mow pasadoo	rare
ao ponto	ow pohntoo	medium
quindim	keenjeeng	coconut and egg sweet
refrigerante	rifrigirantsh	soft drink
sal	sow	salt
sorvete	sohrvaytsh	ice cream
suco	sookoo	fruit juice
vinho	veen-yoo	wine

TIME

minute	minuto	minootoo
hour	hora	ora
half an hour	meia hora	may-a ora
next week	na próxima semana	na prosima simana
last month	no mês passado	noo maysh pasadoo
Monday	segunda-feira	sigoonda fayra
Tuesday	terça-feira	tayrsa fayra
Wednesday	quarta-feira	kwarta fayra
Thursday	quinta-feira	keenta fayra
Friday	sexta-feira	sayshta fayra
Saturday	sábado	sabadoo
Sunday	domingo	doomeengoo
January	janeiro	Janayroo
February	fevereiro	feverayroo
March	março	marsoo
April	abril	abree-oo
May	maio	mī-oo
June	junho	joon-yoo
July	julho	Jool-yoo
August	agosto	agohshtoo
September	setembro	sitaymbroo
October	outubro	ohtoobroo
November	novembro	noovaymbroo
December	dezembro	dizaymbroo

NUMBERS

1	um/uma	oong/ooma
2	dois/duas	doh-ish/doo-ash
3	três	traysh
4	quatro	kwatroo
5	cinco	seenkoo
6	seis	saysh
7	sete	seht
8	oito	oh-itoo
9	nove	novee
10	dez	dehsh
11	onze	ohnzee
12	doze	dohzee
13	treze	trayzee
14	catorze	katohrzee
15	quinze	keenzee
16	dezesseis	dizesaysh
17	dezessete	dizesehtee
18	dezoito	dizoh-itoo
19	dezenove	dizenovee
20	vinte	veentee
21	vinte e um	veentih-oong
30	trinta	treenta
40	quarenta	kwaraynta
50	cinqüenta	sinkwaynta
60	sessenta	sesaynta
70	setenta	setaynta
80	oitenta	oh-itaynta
90	noventa	nohvaynta
100	cem, cento	sayng/sayntoo
1000	mil	mee-oo

ACKNOWLEDGMENTS

DK would like to thank the following for their contribution to the previous editions:
Stephen Keeling, Madelaine Triebe, Alex Bellos, Shawn Blore, Susanne Hillen, Dilwyn Jenkins, Oliver Marshall, Helen Peters, Christopher Pickard, Alex Robinson, Neiva Augusta Silva

The publisher would like to thank the following for their kind permission to reproduce their photographs:

Key: a-above; b-below/bottom; c-center; f-far; l-left; r-right; t-top

123RF.com: marchello74 118-9t.

4Corners: Antonino Bartuccio 22t, 72c, 76-7, 106bl, 292-3; Giordano Cipriani 20cb, 246-7.

Alamy Stock Photo: A.F. Archive / The Film Company 44tl, / Film Company United Artists 117tr; Action Plus Sports Images 180bc; age fotostock / John Banagan 193br, / Berndt Fischer 50-1b, 240bl, / Alvaro Leiva 347tr; Arco Images GmbH / Therin-Weise 4; Art Kowalsky 96-7t; ArteSub 37cla, 256tr; Avalon / Photoshot License / Oceans Image 50tl; Vilmar Bannach 46-7t; Tibor Bognar 193tl; BrazilPhotos / Ricardo Siqueira 63tl, 355br, / Flavio Varricchio 37crb, 146t, / Flavio Veloso 86t; BT_World 19tl, 196-7; Cavan / Scott Hardesty 106-7t, / Vitor Marigo 35tl, 286t, 288t; Chris Schmid Photography 227tl; Chronicle 65br; Classic Image 64-5t; Gary Cook 321crb; André Costa 279tr; Cro Magnon 200tl, 232br; Cultura RM / Aziz Ary Neto 116-7b; Pedro Luz Cunha 240clb; Danita Delimont / Cindy Miller Hopkins 306bc; DanitaDelimont.com / Alida Latham 221tl; David Davis Photoproduction 74, 112-3; dbimages / dbtravel 263cla, 270-1b, / Marcia Chambers 265tl, 282cl, 282-3b; dpa picture alliance 46clb, / ZB / dpa-Zentralbild / Tino Plunert 348t; Redmond Durrell 10ca; EduardoMSNeves 148bl, 148-9t, 279cr; EyeEm / Rodrigo Soares 188-9b; Michele Falzone 36bl; Silvio Figueiredo 81tl; Foto Arena LTDA 147tr, 166cra, 210bl, 345tc, 346bl, 349tr, / Miriam Cardoso de Souza 206tl, / Bruno Fernandes 157tr, / T. Fernandes 334tr, 334b, / André Horta 144-5b, / Mauro Akiin Nassor 284tr, / Celso Pupo 120bc, / Jose Tauari de Medeiros Formiga 333tl; Leo Francini 32cr, 179tr; Fernando Ghelfi 48-9t; Granger Historical Picture Archive / NYC 63cla, 64tl; The Granger Collection 66tl; hemis.fr / Marc Dozier 350crb, / Jean Heintz 220-1b; Hiroshi Higuchi 28tr; Cindy Hopkins 57bl; imageBROKER / Guenter Fischer 329cr, / Matthias Graben 235t, Florian Kopp 44-5b, / Karol Kozlowski 24br, / Karsten Kramer 289b, / Harald von Radebrecht 348-9; Ingolf Pompe 57 318tr; Christopher Ison 342t; ITPhoto 147br; John Warburton-Lee Photography / Mark Hannaford 204cl; Jon Arnold Images Ltd 35tr, 108tl, / Peter Adams 81cra, 268b; Bjanka Kadic 145tl, 278-9b, 296c, 299b; Karol Kozlowski Premium RM Collection 32bl, 161cra, 164-5b, 175tl; Keystone Pictures USA 289tl; ton koene 253tr; Christophe Launay 118br; Lazyllama 21t, 53cl, 73t, 87b, 92-3, 96bl, 105tr, 107cr, 109b, 111t, 111crb, 111br, 119tc, 258-9, 267b, 269br, 272bl, 285tr; Yadid Levy 178-9b;

Pascal Mannaerts 266cra; MBV 26cr; Mechika 166t; John Michaels 124bl, 216cra, 255cc, 301cra, 329tr; MJ Photography 88bl; Carlos Mora 357tl; Walter Motta 290-1b; Graham Mulrooney 356-7b; National Geographic Image Collection / Edson Vandeira 254-5b, 328-9b; R.M. Nunes 232-3t; Odyssey-Images 63clb; Fernando Quevedo de Oliveira 40cra, 240cb; Sylvain Oliveira 329tl; Pacific Press Agency / Jonathan Raa 351cr, / Thenews2 / Adriano Mendes 55cr; Andrew Palmer 270tr; Stefano Paterna 31tr; Paul Taylor / *Portrait of Oscar Niemeyer* by Eduardo Kobra : © Kobra / © DACS 2019 150-1; Photo Arena LTDA 242-3t; PhotoLouis 313cra; Fred Pinheiro 162; Ben Pipe 110bl; Pulsar Imagens 26cl, 41tr, 52-3t, 62bc, 161b, 181b, 194b, 201tr, 244-5b, 279bc, 315cra, 315b, 319cr, 321b, 350-1t, 352b, 353tl; Francesco Puntiroli 51br; Marcel Rabelo 302-3; Kseniya Ragozina 51clb; Frederic Reglain 38-9t, 237cr, / *We Are One (Ethnicities)* 2016 by Eduardo Kobra © Kobra / © DACS 2019 45br; Ricardo Ribas 8bl, 188cra, 223bl, 225tr; robertharding / Godong 287cr, / Gavin Hellier 73bl, 100-1, / Alex Robinson 88-9t, / Michael Runkel 191t, / Marco Simoni 303br, / James Strachan 75, 122-3; Marco Rodrigues / *Smiling Child Mural* by Eduardo Kobra © Kobra / © DACS 2019 161cr; Rolf Nussbaumer Photography / Thomas Marent 13br; Andrzej Rostek 204-5b; Roussel Images 85br; Gustavo Rezende Santos 180tl; Thiago Santos 29tl, 205tr; Camila Se 175cra; Iryna Shpulak 290tr; Maria Adelaide Silva 105cra; Jan Sochor 59cla; Alexandre Sousa 46-7b; richard sowersby 85tl; Sue Cunningham Photographic 269crb; Eckhard Supp 211tr; Paul Taylor / *Portrait of Oscar Niemeyer* by Eduardo Kobra © Kobra © DACS 2019 17bl; Nicholas Tinelli 137br; João Paulo Tinoco 120-1t; Travel Pix 26bl; travelbild.com 266t; Genevieve Vallee 245tr; Chester Voyage 286bl; WENN Rights Ltd / Oscar Gonzalez 42clb; Westend61 GmbH / Florian Kopp 98b, 287cra; Oliver Wintzen 31tl; Xinhua 67crb; Y.Levy 87tc, 163br; Maarten Zeehandelaar 45clb; ZUMA Press, Inc. 155.

AWL Images: Peter Adams 30tl; Ken Archer 251clb; Jon Arnold 10-1b, 28tl; Christian Heeb 34-5ca; Gavin Hellier 19cb, 212-3; Hemis 32cl, 34tr; Karol Kozlowski 24cl, 81tr, 124-5t, 126-7b, 158-9b; Nigel Pavitt 251bc; Alex Robinson 12clb, 17t, 18bl, 24t, 24cr, 30tr, 99t, 130-1, 182-3, 298tl, 354t; Ian Trower 20tl, 26t, 228-9.

Bridgeman Images: Archives Charmet 65clb; The Stapleton Collection 63tr.

Courtesy by Pinacoteca of São Paulo: 45tr, 154ca, 154bl; Levi Fanan 154clb.

Depositphotos Inc: vitormarigo 139.

Dreamstime.com: Alejandro27 29tr; Vinicius Bacarin 160tl, 164cl, 165tl, 221ca; Bonandbon DW 281crb; Brasilnut 40-1b, 194clb; Dabldy 134t; Alexandre Durão 43tr; Ekaterinabelova 84b; Stefano Ember 281ca, 284-5b, 320-1t; Marina Endermar 264b; Espiegle 216-7b; Pedro Ferreira 243crb; Filipe Frazao 156t; Eric Gevaert 140cra;

This edition updated by
Contributor Huw Hennessy
Senior Editors Dipika Dasgupta, Alison McGill
Senior Art Editors Laura O'Brien,
Vinita Venugopal
Project Editors Anuroop Sanwaiia,
Tijana Todorinovic
Editor Mark Silas
Assistant Editor Utkarsh Bansal
Picture Research Administrator Vagisha Pushp
Picture Research Manager Taiyaba Khatoon
Publishing Assistant Simona Velikova
Jacket Designer Jordan Lambley
Cartographer Ashif
Cartography Manager Suresh Kumar
Senior DTP Designer Tanveer Zaidi
Senior Production Editor Jason Little
Production Controller Kariss Ainsworth
Managing Editors Shikha Kulkarni,
Beverly Smart, Hollie Teague
Managing Art Editor Sarah Snelling
Senior Managing Art Editor Priyanka Thakur
Art Director Maxine Pedliham
Publishing Director Georgina Dee

First edition 2007

Published in Great Britain by Dorling Kindersley Limited,
DK, One Embassy Gardens, 8 Viaduct Gardens,
London SW11 7BW, UK

The authorised representative in the EEA is
Dorling Kindersley Verlag GmbH. Arnulfstr.
124, 80636 Munich, Germany

Published in the United States by DK Publishing,
1745 Broadway, 20th Floor, New York, NY 10019, USA

Copyright © 2007, 2023 Dorling Kindersley Limited
A Penguin Random House Company

23 24 25 26 10 9 8 7 6 5 4 3 2 1

A CIP catalog record for this book
is available from the British Library.

A catalog record for this book is available
from the Library of Congress.

ISSN: 1542 1554
ISBN: 978 0 2416 2449 4

Printed and bound in China.

www.dk.com

MIX
Paper | Supporting
responsible forestry
FSC™ C018179

This book was made with
Forest Stewardship Council™
certified paper – one small
step in DK's commitment
to a sustainable future.
For more information go to
www.dk.com/our-green-pledge

A NOTE FROM DK EYEWITNESS
The rapid rate at which the world is changing is
constantly keeping the DK Eyewitness team on our toes.
While we've worked hard to ensure that this edition of
Brazil is accurate and up-to-date, we know that opening
hours alter, standards shift, prices fluctuate, places close
and new ones pop up in their stead. So, if you notice
we've got something wrong or left something out, we
want to hear about it.